Intercultural Commu

Intercultural Communication

An Interdisciplinary Approach: When Neurons, Genes, and Evolution Joined the Discourse

Mai Nguyen-Phuong-Mai

Amsterdam University Press

Cover illustration: Photo by Mai Nguyen-Phuong-Mai, taken in 2012 in La Habana, Cuba.

Cover design: Coördesign, Leiden
Typesetting: Crius Group, Hulshout

Amsterdam University Press English-language titles are distributed in the US and Canada by
the University of Chicago Press.

ISBN	978 94 6298 541 4
e-ISBN	978 90 4853 6511 (pdf)
NUR	612 / 757
DOI	10.5117/9789462985414

To Chị Lan

Table of Contents

Preface

It was a beautiful Sunday afternoon. We were twenty journalists from all over the world who had gone through a selection process in order to win a place for an intensive training with Reuters in London. On that day, as we were about to work on a news coverage, the door was suddenly thrust open. A dozen militants armed with machine guns violently rushed in. They shouted in a language we didn't understand and forced us to lie down. We were all shaken to the core when they pulled out blind folds and covered our eyes with them. In the darkness, we were led outside and into a truck that smelled like it had come straight from an abattoir.

It was the scariest training simulation I've ever had in my career. The coaches – very experienced war correspondents – put us through it so that we could experience what it would be like to be kidnapped. We kept analyzing the situation during the training, and through these discussions, I learned a few more lessons that had nothing to do with reporting in a war zone.

The first lesson came from a discussion in which an editor emotionally told me that the experience was very similar to living in Johannesburg. There, armed guards walked among pedestrians, and many houses look like fortresses. He then tried his hardest to kill my plan to go there. At that point, a British news anchor joined us and said: "We are journalists, not judges. Why do we have to *jump right into sensational differences?* Let's start with something we all share. Like, we all agree that French is not a real language." Everyone laughed.

While I didn't always understand the mocking, teasing, and mildly xenophobic jokes in Europe, I immediately got the message when another reporter expressed her surprise when I revealed that I had never watched the classic kidnapping masterpiece *Fargo*. She looked at me with half a smile: "*Where have you been?*" The micro-aggression was so subtle I didn't realize it at first and felt ashamed. This was the second lesson I learned: The world clearly revolved around the US. A known movie in this part of the globe is supposed to be a universal phenomenon. A country on the other side of the water is a distant, faraway land. The eurocentrism was also deafening. My name was praised for being "normal" because it was written with the Latin alphabet.

On the last training day, we interviewed a series of people on ethnic conflicts. In the simulation, we had to go through a checkpoint where the guards asked people to identify her/his racial background. An Italian colleague said: "White" and got into a row, because the guards blamed him for having dishonored his own race: "You look Arab. You are Arab. Point!" The message was clear: *Your biology defines your identity.* When it was my turn, I jokingly declared: "I'm Asian, but people call me 'banana' – yellow outside, white inside." Not missing a beat, the woman behind me whispered in my ear: "I'm a reversed coconut! No worries."

Soon after the training with Reuters, personal circumstances drove me away from journalism and onto the road of academia. I kept the nomad lifestyle, carrying with me the cultural baggage that revealed itself in the training as I moved across various borders. But the lessons I learned only took their shape during the time I taught intercultural management at the Amsterdam School of International Business (AMSIB).

As I delved deeper into the literature and conventional practices of the field, these lessons constantly popped up. They reminded me that even in a study that is meant to bring people together, differences are used as a warning, rather than a benefit. People are cautious of consequential conflicts, rather than seeing them as a promising synergy. Business students are told that if they don't learn about culture, they will fail in the future because the others are so different from us. This cultural gap is "a nuisance at best and often a disaster."[1] "The world is a more dangerously divided place today than it was at the end of the Cold War."[2] Every time a book or a lesson was opened with a cultural blunder or mismatch, the words of my colleague in the training flashed on: "Why do we have to *jump right into sensational differences?* Let's start with something we all share!"

This book is my attempt to put that remark into action. The journey to find similarities has taken me back to the subject of evolution, down to the biological level of genes and neurons, and opened me up to the newly emerging discipline of cultural neuroscience. The insight from neuroscience labs has excited many interculturalists with just two words: "brain plasticity." It means our brain is like a muscle, as it can grow and adjust, and it enables us to represent multiple cultures. I can't change my skin color, but with regard to the inside, to use the words of my dear friend Ida, I can be as white as a banana, or turn orange if I have to. Country of origin and biology need not to be the foundation of my identity. And thus, I've learned to introduce myself without carrying the cultural baggage that instantly invites stereotypes. Different contexts call for different values and practices. *Context is a dynamic force* that allows each one of us to be an active agent and problem solver, rather than a cultural dope. This is the spirit I want to share in this book.

In the writing process, I created a list of all the countries, main continents and gender pronouns. I carefully marked each time a place was mentioned and each time a "he" or a "she" was used. The result was a colorful coded sheet that shows my failure to give equal weight to all countries and cultures, despite my deliberate attention. Nevertheless, I now understand the reason why literature in our field as well as in others is so US-centric. American narratives dominate the media and the academy. Take a look at the curriculum you are using and start coding the cases, arguments and theories. Even though you already have an idea, the result may still surprise you.

In sum, while this book is meant as an introduction to intercultural communication, it is also a novel attempt to incorporate the much-neglected dynamic paradigm of culture in the literature, the insight from other disciplines, and the representation of non-mainstream cultures.

To all of those who helped me finish this book, I extend my thanks. I am grateful to all the people I had the honor to befriend and meet on my journeys from the early days of my journalistic career, whose stories inspired me and became part and parcel of this book. To my colleagues and students who reviewed the manuscript, I owe you my thanks. I would like to thank my program manager John Sterk for giving me the much needed support to arrange my work so that this book could be finished on time. Finally, I thank the staff at AUP for their professionalism, and my research assistant Blerta Kola for her dedication.

1. The Survival of the Most Cultured

Objective

At the end of this chapter, you should be able to:

- Explain the nature of culture and its roles in the evolution of human species.
- Identify the role of cultural diversity.
- Discuss and illustrate with examples the dynamic interaction between culture and other factors: environment, genes, brain, and behaviors.
- Describe the process of globalization from evolutionary biology's perspective.
- Distinguish the unique characteristics of globalization in the modern era.

Chapter outline

We are often amazed at the incredible tapestry of our cultures on this planet. They are not only rich, but also incredibly transferable, to the extent that humans from one corner of the world can benefit from inventions and traditions that originated from another, distant land.

While the flow of cultural exchange is incredible and beneficial, similarities and differences have dynamically pulled and pushed the interaction, acting as anything from opportunities to obstacles, relentlessly shaping and reshaping our lives throughout the history. This raises questions, such as why are these cultural boundaries in language, values, religions, and practices so persistent, yet also malleable? Why do they even exist in the first place? Why are we so different from each other, yet, so similar? And why are we so eager to learn from each other, yet so aggressive towards each other that we sometimes want to destroy those who don't think in the same way as us?

If we look at human beings from a biological point of view, we are genetically similar. Human beings are such a young species that, in fact, race does not exist. We may have different skin color or body structure, but genetically, we are not different enough to justify more than one distinct race among us. In terms of DNA sequence, we are up to 99.5% similar to any of our fellow humans.[1]

Race is a social construct with no genetic or scientific meaning, and it is also a new concept of the modern era. Ancient and classical civilizations tended to see differences in tribal affiliation, rather than skin color and physical appearance. Indeed, many African officers and soldiers patrolled Hadrian's Wall 2000 years ago.[2] Roman emperor Septimius Severus was born in Libya, and thus, he was the first black man to rule England. "Race" only entered our vocabulary during the 16th century,[3] as an attempt to classify human groups at a time when knowledge about genes did not exist.

UNESCO, supported by scholars such as Lévi-Strauss – a founder of ethnology – insisted that the term "race" should be replaced by "culture," and "racism" by "ethnocentrism." The diversity we see in human beings comes from geographical, historical, political, economic and social factors.[4] There is no inherent superior or inferior implication for advancement in our biological make-up, because all human beings belong to a single species.

While the above-mentioned statements are correct, genes are not mere onlookers in the dynamic evolution of culture. In this chapter, we will explore the role of biology and culture, and the many ways they have joined forces to shape the incredible state of our existence and advancement on this planet. We will discuss why diversity continues to divide us and why globalization seems so unstoppable. Only by understanding these core issues from such an interdisciplinary point of view, can we comprehend the immense dynamics represented in cross-cultural communication without risking oversimplification, or assuming the static nature of its components in order to make sense of everything.

1.1   The nature of culture

We must begin the reading of this book with an understanding of what "culture" actually is. However, "culture" is a complex word. There are as many definitions of culture as there are authors who have ever studied the subject. Rather than limit our investigations by selecting one definition of "culture" at this stage, we will first look for insight from a different angle, a discipline that forms part of our discourse in this book: evolutionary biology. In our search for an explanation for why culture exists, this approach will provide us with a better understanding of the nature of culture and its definition in our study's context.

1.1.1   A Power Transition from Gene to Culture

In the 18th and 19th centuries, the study of human diversity was accelerated by the emergence of two disciplines: evolutionary biology and anthropology. However, the development in these two fields has been highly divergent. Recently, some of the most impressive studies on culture have been conducted by natural scientists, who point out that culture is an integral part of biology.[5] As commentator McGrew admits, it is "a wee bit of irony"[6] that it takes colleagues from the natural sciences to convince us that nothing about culture actually makes sense, unless it is put under the interdisciplinary spotlight with biology. So how are culture and genes related to each other?

1.1.1.1   *Genes or Culture?*
Let's start with an example.

In 2006, Ms. Sandra Piovesan, 50, was found bleeding to death after being mauled by a pack of nine hybrid wolves, which she had raised as pets. The pups grew up in her backyard, were treated like her children, and, according to Ms. Piovesan, had given her "unqualified love."[7]

Unfortunately, such cases are not uncommon. No matter how close the human-animal relationship is, a wolf is a wolf and its genes tell it to hunt and attack, possibly even the human who raised it. Information stocked in its genes determines what it eats, how it moves, and what sound it makes. In short, a wolf does not behave like a human even if it lives with humans. Its genes overrule the social environment.

Now consider the reverse. In 1920, two little girls were found living with a pack of wolves in Northern India. They showed no trace of humanness and seemed to have the minds of wolves. According to the diary of the man who found them,[8] the feral girls "were more ferocious than the cubs, making faces, showing teeth." They "would run very fast, just like squirrels." Their eyes were "wide open at night," with "a peculiar blue gaze, like that of a cat or dog in the dark." They could "smell meat from a great distance like animals." It was clear that the girls were more like wolves in a human body. Their human genes somehow failed to tell them that they were human, that they should stand on two legs, speak a certain language, and behave in a human way. In sum, while a wolf living with humans does not behave like a human, a human living with wolves tends to behave like a wolf. For the wolves, their *genes overrule the social environment*. For humans, the reverse is true, their *genes give way to the social environment*.

1.1.1.2   *Culture as a Survival Strategy*

What does this tell us about the crucial role of social environment? The answer is, it tells us nearly everything that separates humans from other animals. In 2013, Mark Pagel published a ground-breaking book titled *Wired for Culture*,[9] praised by the prominent journal *Nature* as "the best popular science book on culture so far."[10] Approached from evolutionary biology, Pagel argues that social interaction, or culture, is the last stage of replacing genes in order to enable humans to deal with survival issues. Unlike other animals, we are much less dependent on our genes to tell us what to do. Instead of taking information from the pool of DNA that we inherit from our parents, we gain most of our survival information from culture: the food we eat, the clothes we wear, the tools we make and use, the language we speak, the Gods we believe in, the people we consider as friends and the enemies we should fight and kill in a war. Basically, all human beings are born with a receptive mind that absorbs the first culture seen; consequently, humans become actors in that culture. This is why the aforementioned feral children behave according to the wolves' culture, and not according to their human genes. A wolf brought up by sheep (or humans, for that matter) will remain a wolf and inevitably turn on its benefactors, because, for the wolf, it is the rules of the genes that count. But for a newborn human, it is the rules of the culture that count. It must be ready to join any cultural group on Earth, and behave according to that culture – cold Iceland, hot dry Central Africa, tropical Guyana, nomadic Arabia, or even a wolves' den, deep in the Indian forest – and to speak the language of that culture. Why? Because that is the only way this human can survive.

In animals, genes evolve to guide their behaviors and their survival. In human be-ings, genes have been largely replaced by culture. Culture evolves and guides our behaviors and teaches us how to survive.

1.1.2   How Did This Power Transition Happen?

According to Pagel,[11] our world is 4.5 billion years old, but culture appeared only around 200,000 years ago, with the *ability to learn from others*. It started with symbolic thinking in the form of art and adornment, which allowed us to communicate ideas to others through the meanings attached to each object or symbol. The ability to observe, copy, pick the best practices, and transfer them to others created an entirely new sphere of evolution. Of course, animals can observe and imitate others, but humans differ in the way that we are *conscious* of what we are copying and why we are doing so. We do not just mindlessly imitate others, but rather pick the best bits and teach them to someone else.

Culture was initially formed this way as its elements (i.e. ideas, languages, music, art, innovation, etc.) could act like genes, albeit much faster than genes. For example, genes can only make changes and improve when we reproduce the next generation in a different body. This takes a long time. Unlike genes, cultural elements can jump directly from one mind to another, circumventing the normal genetic routes of transmission. We must wait many generations to see some "good" genes become dominant in a population. However, culture allows us to acquire knowledge, belief, ideas and practices by watching, imitating and learning from others in a split second. While genes are rather fixed, i.e. from birth, we cannot really change a lot the sets of genes given to us by our parents, culture is a vast store of continuous and rich information, improved technologies, broadened knowledge and wisdom. Throughout your lifetime, you can sample from this sea of evolving ideas, adopting, considering, changing, rejecting, improving, accumulating, etc.

Clearly, culture is a superior guide of behaviors than genes. Not sur-prisingly, then, for the sake of our species, culture has gradually evolved to become a survival strategy. It has gradually taken over the running of our day-to-day affairs from genes, and has been providing us with many solutions to the problems of our existence. With our capacity for social learning, we no longer wholly rely on genetic improvement, such as better wings, feathers, shells, claws, toxins, etc. to ensure our survival. We have cultures with accumulated ideas and knowledge that are shared and passed down through generations. This makes us a powerful species. We may not have a genetic physicality suitable for living under water, but we have created submarines. We may not have the genes to fly, but we have flown to the moon and beyond. Humans have not only migrated from Africa to populate the whole world and radically alter the earth's biota, but we are also on the way to conquering outer space. We are no longer confined to one environment, but are able to transform the environment to suit our needs. As Pagel observes, if we fast-forwards a million years, our close genetic relatives the chimpanzees will still be sitting in the forest, using the same old stone cracking the same old nut. This is because their genes tell them to do so. They may be able to learn and imitate a certain act, but they cannot understand why; they cannot pick the best practices, cannot learn from mistakes, cannot improve an idea, and cannot teach it to others. Meanwhile, thanks to culture, which is essentially the ability to learn from others, humans have built skyscrapers and spaceships.

At this point, it is clear that, for our purpose, the definition of culture should contain the recurring theme of survival strategies through social learning. We have therefore chosen a definition from Triandis,[12] because it is the closest to what we are looking for, and adapted it as follows: "Culture is a set of evolving man-made elements that have increased the probability of survival, and thus become shared among those who could communicate with each other."

Culture is initially formed by the ability to imitate, to select the best practices, and to transfer them to others. Instead of waiting for a change in genes so humans can evolve wings to fly (which may never happen), culture allows us to pull ideas together and build air planes.

1.2   Cultural diversity

Language is one of the defining traits of being humans, but it also means that we are probably the only animal that can find itself in a situation where two individuals might not be able to communicate with each other, as if they were two different biological species. Even when we seem to speak the same language, different accents can make mutual understanding challenging. Hence, we make the mistake of, for example, assuming that people in the Middle East naturally understand each other because most of them speak Arabic. By comparison, an elephant would have little trouble knowing what to do if it is placed amongst another herd of elephants. In sum, we may be one species physically, but language seems to tell us that we are not. If, as we have suggested, that culture is a survival strategy, why, then, do all humans on this planet not share the same culture? Why do we need such vast diversity in language and many other aspects of culture? In this section, we will briefly explore the answers to these questions.

1.2.1   The Interaction of Environment – Culture

The biodiversity on our planet is impressive, and humans have used the capacity of culture to be able to live in all kinds of environment. Our species lives deep in the jungles, floats on the water, survives extreme cold, and conquers the desert.[13] This is why "biodiversity" is often used as a hypothesis to explain the "cultural diversity" among humans. But is this hypothesis correct?

1.2.1.1   Environmental Determinism
The natural environment has long been used to explain people's characters since the time of Greek, Roman and later Arab scholars. Aristotle, for example, argued that Europe's cold climate produced brave but unintelligent people who could not rule, while Asia's warm climate made the people there intelligent but demotivated, and therefore subject to slavery. He believed that his homeland Greece, the middle place, combined the best of both worlds and would be the center of power and knowledge.[14]

In the 19th century, Darwin and his monumental work on natural selection[15] laid the foundation for a theory called *environmental determinism*. It posits that living environment is the major reason why our societies developed in different ways. However, this theory was also used to justify imperialism and racism.[16] For example, African colonization was legitimized by the logic that tropical climates made people lazy and uncivilized, while the frequent variability of cold climates triggered hard work and thus led to more developed societies.[17] Environmental determinism also underlines Hitler's idea of race and superiority.[18]

Later, the theory of *neo*-environmental determinism steered away from issues of race and ethnicities and focused on the impact of environment on economic and political development. Jared Diamond, for example, argues that the number of wild plants and animals suitable for domestication in each continent was the initial deciding factor that led to surplus food production and, consequently, to a growth in human populations and other economic developments.[19] Domesticated animals and plants were most abundant in the Fertile Crescent (modern Egypt, Iraq, Israel, Palestine, Syria, and Turkey) followed by China, Mexico, and the Andes (modern Venezuela, Colombia, Ecuador, Peru, Bolivia, Argentina and Chili), while the least numerous and least productive suites arose in the eastern United States, New Guinea, and Ethiopia.

According to Jared Diamond, Europe became a power base because its nations grew out of the first farming societies, with the world's most easily domesticable animals. This gave them a head start to later conquer the rest of the world. The West is simply geographically privileged. However, Papua New Guinea is an exception. The crop here was not as productive as wheat crops in other early farming regions. They rot quickly and have to be eaten in a short time. The only big domestic animal was the pig, but it is not as productive as oxen or horses: no milk, wool, leather, hides, or the ability to pull ploughs. That is why despite being a cradle of agriculture, Papua New Guinea did not develop as far as other farming societies. To this day, pigs have a strong social significance and convey social status of a person.[20] A fully grown swine can cost over USD $2000, and it is not unusual to see people taking their pigs for a walk, or women breastfeeding young piglets. The Kuma people believe that their ancestors used to be half-human half-beast living in the mud under the ground. One day, they followed their pig outside, saw the sun for the first time, cut of their tails, developed to full human and escaped the dark age/ "A man with his piglet in the market at Tari, (Papua New Guinea)," MAI NGUYEN-PHUONG-MAI.

1.2.1.2 *Environmental Possibilism*

Environmental determinism theory clearly cannot explain phenomena such as the Kikuyu and Maasai tribes of Kenya, who live side by side but differ profoundly in terms of their physical measurements and culture. The Kikuyu are farmers and the Maasai are cattle raisers. Another puzzling example is Papua New Guinea, a small country in the western Pacific where more than 800 different languages are spoken. Within just a few miles, you can find tribes that have a language and culture of their own. In fact, cultural diversity is actively pursued here. The anthropologist Don Kulick gave one example of the Buian tribe, which purposely fostered linguistic diversity by switching all its masculine and feminine gender agreements, so that their language would be *different* from their neighbors' dialects.[21]

The San Bushmen are hunter-gatherers whose territories span Botswana, Namibia, Angola, Zambia, Lesotho and Zimbabwe. Their harsh and dry home ranges have significantly influenced their social, economic and spiritual relationships/ "Drinking water from the bi bulb plant found deep under the sand," DVL2.[22]

Environment undoubtedly influences human societies, likewise, humans have dramatically changed the environment as well. Humans have flattened forests, dried up rivers, reclaimed land from the ocean, and, for the first time since the dinosaur disappeared, humans are driving animals and plants to extinction faster than new species can evolve.[23] The interaction between the environment and humans is so intricate and dynamic that it has triggered the development of the *environmental possibilism* theory. This posits that human beings are active rather than passive agents, who see numerous possibilities in nature and actively shape it to suit our need for survival. This theory clearly goes in the opposite direction to environmental determinism, so much so that it has been criticized for underestimating the influence of nature. In short, environmental determinism goes too far, but environmental possibilism gives up too much.[24] This has, in turn, triggered the concept of *probabilism* – a mid-way view that sees physical environment not as deterministic, but as the most influential factor.[25]

1.2.1.3   Cultural Ecology

For many, Julian Steward's book *Theory of Cultural Change*[26] was the first synthesis of the discoveries of human diversity and uniqueness using ecological and evolutionary ideas. It combined different approaches and, while not without critics, it gave a simple, workable model with which to understand the dynamic interaction between environment and culture.[27] The most important tenet of cultural ecology is that humans are part of the environment, intrinsically embedded in earth surface processes, neither "victims" of its force (which is determinism), nor an outside force making an impact on it (possibilism). In this interdependent relationship, culture is not a "consequence" of nature or a tool to "control" nature, but rather a *strategy to interact* with nature.

An example of cultural ecology can be found in the worship of cows in India. The important role of cows in agriculture and transportation led to the development of a belief that cows were sacred and should not be eaten.[28] This belief was a good cultural strategy to ensure that people in India did not kill the animals that were crucial to their survival. In short, humans are expected to develop a sustainable and harmonious cultural relationship with the environment in which they live. This dynamic interaction leads to diversity in culture.

All parts of the cow are sacred, including cow dung and urine, which are often used in religious rituals and commercial products. All deities are believed to reside in "The mother of cows" Kamadhenu/ "Traffic gives way to a cow in Mumbai, (India)," MAI NGUYEN-PHUONG-MAI.

1.2.2   Cultural Diversity as a Tool for Resource Management

While it is clear how the world can be seen as a bio-culturally collabora-tive product, the question of why humans have formed so many different cultures to interact with an identical environment remains open.

The fact that we tend to diverge into sub-groups in densely populated areas can be puzzling, but, as Pagel argues, becomes understandable if we add the element of resources to the big picture. Bearing in mind that since culture is a survival strategy, the capacity of having a culture (i.e. learning from others) also means ideas, knowledge and resources can be stolen by one group at the expense of the other. If you see that my tool is catching more fish than yours, you can steal my innovation just by studying my tool carefully, and then making the same one, even better. That is not very fair to me, it seems. So what can I do to protect my cultural ideas? Basically, I have two choices: (1) to retreat into my small family group and only share knowledge with my relatives; (2) to develop a system that I can communicate with you and convince you that cooperation is actually better than stealing.[29]

Fortunately, our ancestors did not choose the first option, since that would have been the end of culture – the very mechanism that advances humans as a species. Culture is possible only by learning continuously from others, and small groups only offer a few ideas. Small groups can also completely disappear as a result of attacks, accidents or diseases, which means that any ideas and innovations are wasted.

We took the second option and, consequently, language evolved as a crucial mechanism for dealing with the possibilities of ideas being stolen.[30] I now have the ability to convince you to exchange my fish-catching tool for your technique for making clothes. If you agree, we can then start a good business relationship. If you don't, I will sell my innovation to someone else.

Language facilitates deal making, negotiation and agreement. And because its purpose is also to safeguard knowledge and information in competition with other groups, many languages were formed. When we don't know each other and I am not sure of your intentions, my distinctive language helps to keep any innovations within my own group and my own culture. It would be very difficult for you to steal my ideas if you don't know my language and the complex code of behavior that it governs. But once you have shown your intentions to be good and fair, we will somehow overcome the language barrier in order to cooperate. Trading across the globe has operated in more or less this way, with linguistic and cultural diversity as an inherent *regulator*, used by one group to safeguard and negotiate cultural resources with another. In fact, you don't need to look far to see the similarity of language evolution with what we still do every day: kids creating a secret language to write their diary or communicate with friends, codes and cyphers used by military and diplomatic forces to exchange confidential information, and businesses who send data that has been encoded to protect trade secrets.

The desire to manage cultural resources not only enables diverse languages to evolve, but also channels people into different sub-groups. As we band together to exert our authority over certain resources in competition with another group, *cultural diversity becomes an element for us to recognize an ingroup we can trust.* It rests on the notion that because this person has the same cultural traits (the way [s]he dresses and communicates or the values [s]he holds dear), it is highly likely that we share the same survival strategies, live in the same group and therefore this person is more trustworthy than others. This tendency to have a bias towards one's own group is crucial in understanding human behaviors across cultures. It can be uncomfortable to know that our cultural nepotism or *ingroup bias* (favoritism for those in the same group) is evolutionary.[31] However, we need to keep in mind that this is rooted in the notion that our culture is our survival strategy, and, for our own sake, we evolved to love it, to protect it, even to see our culture as superior than that of others (ethnocentrism). This will be a recurrent theme, which you will see from other points of view in this chapter and throughout the book.

Cultural diversity can be explained by:
· · The impact of environment, with theories ranging from a deciding factor (de-terminism), an influential factor (probabilism), a source of possibilities (possibi-lism), to an entity inseparable from the human species (ecology).
· The role of linguistic and cultural diversity, which are regulators for (1) safe-guarding cultural resources, recognizing who we can trust; and (2) negotiating cultural resources with other human groups for mutual interests.

1.3   Diversity pathways

The interaction between environment and culture is dynamic, but it is far from sufficient in terms of explaining human diversity. The complexity of our culture must be seen from a bigger angle, one that involves the physical and genetic make-up of our body. In this section, we will gradually add genes and neurons to the big picture. Each new interaction will reveal different pathways that contribute to the incredible diversity we see in our cultures today. To aid your understanding, a *Diversity Pathways* diagram will be constructed in steps and then patched together at the end of the section.

1.3.1   The Interaction of Environment – Culture – Genes

In the first section of this chapter, we discussed the transition of power from genes to culture. From this point of view, it may not be a strange idea to question the role of genes: What do they do now? If culture is so important, is it not handy for everyone to have the same genes? With regard to the role of the environment, if it is not a deciding factor, as environmental determinism insists, to what extent does it affect culture and genes after all?

Genes are the fundamental physical and functional unit of heredity. Therefore, the power transition from genes to culture is not mutually exclu-sive. In fact, genes are crucial mechanisms for *turning useful cultural values into genetic traits,* and vice versa. The *gene–culture co-evolution theory* is crucial in understanding human diversity. It posits that while culture shapes the expression and selection of genes, genes also influence the adoption and formation of certain cultural values.[32] Nature and nurture are both active in shaping the diversity of human cultures and behaviors. To gain a better understanding of how dynamic genes, culture and environment can interact simultaneously, let's have a look at the following case study.

CASE STUDY

Serotonin – a chemical found in the human body – is responsible for maintaining mood balance. Genes that carry serotonin have a shorter variant (s5-HTTL-PR), and this short allele is connected with depression.[33] In East Asia, people have almost twice the rate (70-80%) of a short allele or "depression gene" that white Westerners do (40-45%). However, they suffer less than half the rates of anxiety and depression.[34] Try to tackle this paradox with the following information:

1. Genes–Culture: Those who carry the short allele need more social support to maintain their well-being, without which they would have a 4.5 times greater risk of depression. Hence, they need to be surrounded by a close-knit network of friends and families. The short allele not only causes depression, but also makes people more sensitive. Hence, they are also more group-oriented, capable of recognizing and reacting to others' emotional states. In other words, short allele people both need and fit well in societies with richly interconnected networks. According to hypothesis 1: The depression gene was there first. Group-mindset culture became an established and strategic cultural value to cope with the depression gene.

2. Environment–Culture: Pathogens – infectious agents such as bacteria and fungus that cause disease – are historically high in warm and moist climates. In order to cope with the constant risk of infection, our ancestors who first migrated to these regions didn't wait for genes to evolve an immune system to battle diseases, as is the case in animals. Instead, they slowly developed a cultural strategy to deal with high pathogen loads: a group-oriented mindset that conforms to collective rules regarding sanitation, food preparation, etc. Over a period of time, those who followed the cultural rules of group conformity had a higher chance of survival. This gives us hypothesis 2: Group-mindset culture became an established and strategic cultural value to cope with pathogens.

3. Culture–Genes or Genes–Culture: The end result is that both "group-mindset" and "depression gene" still prevail in East Asia. Which came first, and which caused which?

a. People with depression genes need and fit better into the group-mindset culture, so their gene became dominant to support this value. Thus, a culture with a group-mindset was the consequence of the depression gene. In other words, the depression gene came first and culture became the strategy to cope with this gene.

b. A group-mindset culture was needed to cope with pathogens and hence it favors those with the depression gene because this gene helped people conform to the group's rules. In other words, culture came first and the depression gene prevailed as a consequence.

c. Both group-mindset culture and the depression gene gained ground together as a dual solution to high pathogen loads in the environment. Group-mindset and short allele were compatible as they reproduced each other to eventually develop a collectivistic culture that (i) is effective at coping with pathogens, and (ii) outweighs the negative impact of increased numbers of depression gene by providing more social support.

The Happy Planet Index measures elements that contribute towards a happy life in 140 countries and looked at factors such as life expectancy, well-being, inequality and ecological footprint. In 2016, Costa Rica topped this list, followed by Mexico, Columbia, Vanuatu and Vietnam[35] – all of them have a "group mindset culture." However, this index is different from several other studies in which the same countries score much lower. For example, a major discontent in Mexico is the bad reputation of the police. 63 per cent of Mexicans have little or no trust in their police force while 66 per cent view them as corrupt.[36] The complexity of this issue shows that we should interpret a phenomenon by taking into account the dynamic interaction of many factors, as we will continue to explore in this chapter/ "Riot police ready for action in Mexico City, (Mexico)," MAI NGUYEN-PHUONG-MAI.

The dynamic of the culture–genes coevolution shows us that it can be problematic to structure our understanding along the traditional binary spectrum of nature–nurtured opposites. As the case study shows, the interaction culture and gene is very dynamic, and is better understood as a vicious circle of cause and effect. What has been culturally "nurtured" for long enough (group mindset) will slowly become "nature" with genetic traits (depression gene). In turn, nature with genetic traits (depression gene) reinforces those behaviors that are part of the culture (group mindset). This dynamic interaction aims at the ultimate goal of evolving a culture that provides a survival strategy that allows humans to advance.

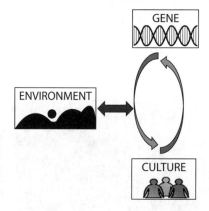

Figure 1.1. The interaction of Environment – Culture – Genes

The selection of genes depends on the coevolution with culture: a specific cultural value may prefer a certain gene, and a certain gene may slowly reinforce a certain cultural value.

1.3.2   The Interaction of Environment – Culture – Genes – Brain

Now that we have gained understanding of how environment, culture and genes dynamically interact with one another, it is time to add the brain to the picture. The brain is the central hub where these interactions converge and translate into behaviors that we see in our fellow humans every day. How do behaviors affect the neuro-mechanism of the brain? Is the brain wired differently across cultures, professions and genders? What role does the brain play in creating different diversity pathways? These are the questions we will discuss in this section.

1.3.2.1   Culture's Influences on the Brain

A brain consists of about 100 billion neurons connecting with each other to form complex circuits that carry electrical and chemical messages to make memories and govern behaviors.[37] However, brains across different cultures and contexts do not work in the same way, as the neural functions are shaped by culture and social experience. For example, experiments show that when solving simple arithmetic problems, despite ending up with similar result, English-speaking people relied on language processing, while Chinese-speaking people engaged a visuo-premotor association network,[38] which may be related to the logograms used in Chinese characters.[39] Religious beliefs also modulate neural mechanisms that underlie the perception of self. Buddhists, for instance, showed *reduced* neural processing of self-relatedness, arguably due to the doctrine of *"anatta"* (no-self) in Buddhism.[40] Although the study of cultural neuroscience is in its infancy, there is a plethora of evidence for similar cultural influence on brain function with regard to cognition,[41] emotion,[42] interpersonal perception,[43] self-awareness,[44] and empathy,[45] etc.

From a practical point of view, the culturally patterned brain enables us to voluntarily take actions that are appropriate in a specific culture.[46] Newly arrived or visiting people, whose brains are not (yet) equipped with the necessary neural basis, may find it challenging to conform to the behavioral scripts and social rules in the new social environment.

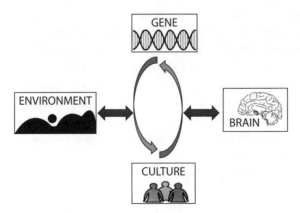

Figure 1.2. The interaction of Environment – Culture – Genes – Brain

1.3.2.2   *The Brain's Plasticity*

The neurons in our brain are separated by empty spaces called *synapse* clefts. When two neurons communicate, they do not physically touch each other but shoot neurotransmitters across the synapse cleft, from the axon (sender) of neuron A to the dendrites (receiver) of neuron B. Each neuron usually has only one axon, but, as the picture shows, many dendrites.

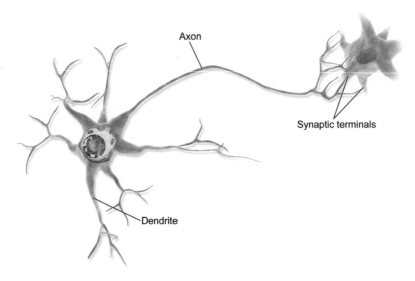

Figure 1.3. Thought is conducted by electrical impulses, sent from the axon (sender) of one neuron to the dendrites (receiver) of another neuron/ "Anatomy of a multipolar neuron," BRUCEBLAUS.[47]

Now look at figure 1.4. This is what happens when we have a repetition of a thought or when we practice something over and over again: the more neurotransmitters are shot through the synapse, the more receptors are created to receive the signals; eventually, the neuron will grow additional dendrite branches to make our thoughts easier. Around the axon (sender), glia cells will create a supportive layer to speed up the electrical impulses. The two neurons will also physically move closer together in order to decrease the distance the neurotransmitters have to travel. Thoughts that dominate your mind are those that have the shortest distance to cover and the easiest way to travel, a "cell assembly" of neurons that fire together rapidly without much effort.

This means repeated thoughts will be experienced more easily each time you have them. Conversely, thoughts that are triggered less frequently will disappear. How does this happen? Synapse connections that get used less are marked by a protein. When we sleep, our brain cells shrink by up to 60 per cent to create space for supporting glia cells. Glia cells are not only responsible for speeding up signals between neurons, but also for detecting the protein mark and destroying the "forgotten" synapses. This is why we often wake up from a sleep or a power nap feeling fresh, ready to take in new information. Our brain physically rewires itself so we can forge new pathways, create new habits and respond to the various demands of the cultural environment.

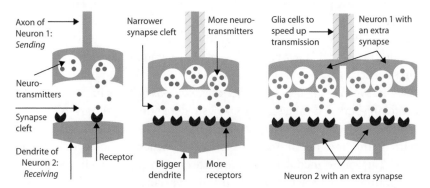

Figure 1.4. This is how learning changes the structure of our brain. Neurotransmitters are shot through the synapse cleft (stage 1). With many repetitions, neurons grow bigger dendrites and increase the number of neurotransmitters and receptors (stage 2). Finally, there are additional dendrites to make thinking easier, and electrical impulses are sped up along the axon by the support of glia cells (stage 3). The more connections there are, the easier it is for a group of neurons to fire together, then wire together, and move closer together. When such a change happens, our actions become automatic because there is a long-lasting effect between two neurons/ "Long-term potentiation," MAI NGUYEN-PHUONG-MAI.

The constant morphing and shifting of the brain tells us that our neural machinery system is intrinsically malleable or has "plasticity" – a term coined in 1894 by pioneering Spanish neuroanatomist Santiago Ramon y Cajal. Just like a muscle can change with exercises, we can develop our brain and induce changes in both its functions and structures. For example, when a person is blind, occipital regions can be recruited to process *sound* instead of *vision*, enabling people with impaired vision to have enhanced hearing ability.[48] Hence, historically, the image of blind musicians and poets is an important touchstone in many cultures: the travelling *biwa hoshi* in 20th century Japan, the *kobzars* of Ukraine, Homer of Greece, and many piano tuners in France and England during the 19th century.

Beyond recovering from impairment, our neural mechanism has an astounding capacity to rewire and adjust to high-level cultural experiences. London cab drivers,[49] who receive intensive training for between two to four years, learn to memorize and navigate 25,000 streets in order to obtain a license. As a consequence, the volume of their grey matter in the posterior hippocampus is enlarged. The longer they drive, the bigger this volume became. Similar changes in both neural structure and function of the brain has been found in people who juggle,[50] meditate,[51] or dance[52] as a profession or regular practice.

In fact, we don't need intensive training to see how malleable the brain is. Even very simple or subtle cues, such as an iconic building or the difference between using plural pronouns (e.g. "we" and "our") or singular pronouns (e.g. "I" and "me") can activate relevant cultural mindsets and their associate networks. People who are primed by these cultural cues, even just by looking at them briefly, will have responsive neural reactions that correspond with those cues, regardless of their original backgrounds.[53] Our brain is so flex-ible that we are capable of representing *multiple cultures* in our mind and switching between values simultaneously, depending on the given priming culture.[54-55-56] Consequently, people can be very self-centered when primed with "I" and "me," and think more collectively when primed with "we" and "our." The ventro-medial prefrontal cortex (vMPFC) – our selfhood loci in the brain[57] – can be active in both priming variances.

The plasticity of the brain shows us that our neural mechanism is able to adapt to a new environment that is as subtle as some cultural cues. Repeated behaviors can significantly rewire the brain and change both its physical form and functional features. The idea that the brain recreates itself and that there is no fundamental core of identity in the brain means that we can train the brain and learn new tricks, adapt to new environments, adopt new cultures, reshape and discover many different aspects of our identities and personalities.[58-59]

Neurons that fire together, wire together. Our thoughts change our brain physically. The brain's plasticity means that we are capable of adapting to new environments and representing multiple cultures in our mind, depending on the context.

1.3.2.3   The Sexist Brain?

Although studies have shown that the brains of men and women work slightly differently,[60] researchers have also argued that this difference is not as distinct as many want to believe,[61] and may be due to a difference in *size* rather than a difference in *gender*.[62-63] In any case, unlike genitalia, brains do not come in male or female forms.[64-65] Up to 53 per cent of brains cover both male-end and female-end features.[66] This means you can be highly masculine when undertaking one task, but highly feminine undertaking another. One can seriously challenge the assumption of "left brain for men" and "right brain for women" by pointing out that removing even half of the brain will *not* significantly affect how one mentally develops.[67] At the very least, men and women are no different than two men with unique emotional styles.[68]

If neural differences between men and women exist, regardless of the degree, they should always be seen in specific cultural contexts.[69-70] A woman's brain may show high levels of connectivity between two hemispheres, which allows her to be better at multi-tasking. But she was *not* born that way. Her brain is structured that way simply because her culture expects that of her, so she uses that part of her brain more often. The same is true for other stereotypical beliefs, i.e. that men are "hard-wired" to do better at jobs related to maths, cars and engineering. An array of brain studies have been criticized for *neurosexism* and failing to recognize the plasticity of gender differences[71] and thus contributing to inaccurate and harmful misunderstanding about the sexes.[72-73]

As early as the 1990s, a neuroscientist famously remarked: "If the neural systems used for a given task can change with 15 min[utes] of practice [...] how can we any longer separate organic structures from their experience in the organism's history?"[74] The field of cultural neuroscience has given a resounding response: "We cannot!" The plasticity of our brain means that anything that is said to be "hard-wired" should be treated with great caution. A brain is neither software, nor hardware, but a very versatile mechanism that tunes so finely with the cultural environment, a "cultural sponge"[75] of sorts, that it can constantly evolve, change and reorganize both its function and structure in response to internal and external environmental factors.

1.3.3   The Interaction of Environment – Culture – Genes – Brain – Behavior

While billions of neurons in the brain coordinate thoughts and behaviors, we now know that behaviors shape the brain as well. However, behavior is not the absolute end of the whole interaction cycle with environment, culture, genes and brain. The figure below, (inspired by a study of Chiao and colleague[76]), shows us many different pathways that diversity can create as a result of this dynamic interaction: environment can influence the coevolution of culture–genes, the brain takes guidance from genes and responds to demand from culture by sending signals to instruct behavior. This dynamic cycle is completed with the impact of behaviors on all the aforementioned factors. As we already know, repeated behaviors not only change the very structure and function of the brain, but have a significant impact on culture, genes and environment.

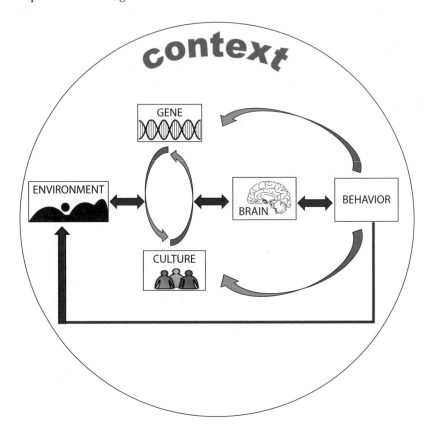

Figure 1.5. The Diagram of Diversity Pathways

1.3.3.1   *The Impact of Behavior on Genes*

Our genes determine a lot about who we are and how we interact with others, but this is not unidirectional, since behaviors can change our DNA as well. Identical twins have the same genes, yet they can have very different personalities, even physical traits. Behavioral epigenetics is a discipline that tries to address this question, i.e. how nurture shapes nature.

Since researchers cracked the code of the human genome in 2003, great strides have been made in understanding how our genes can be modified by the choices we make every day. In a period of only three months, changes in behaviors can turn on or off 500 good and bad genes.[77] A study of 30,000 people from all six continents tells us that 90 per cent of heart disease is entirely preventable by changing diet and taking exercise.[78] Pregnant women who witnessed the attack on the World Trade Center had "scars" on their DNA and passed on higher levels of stress hormone to their babies. Social environment such as economic status can also seriously influence the genes that control cognitive performance. Genetic influences on changes in cognitive ability were close to zero for children from poorer homes, compared to half of the variation for those from wealthier homes. In other words, rich children are not genetically superior, their genes simply have more opportunities to reach their full potential.[79]

The impact of behaviors on genes has important implications for the health industry. On the whole, healthcare budgets focus heavily on treating diseases in progress, and very little, no more than 5 per cent, is spent on precautions and active prevention.[80] Insurance companies and organizations have been advised to adopt a mental shift from medicine reimbursement to prevention policies, from treating the symptoms to seeking the root causes. Many diseases are preventable and reversible by adopting a pathway that would slowly influence the expression of "bad" genes and promote the impact of "good" ones. Researchers have argued that this approach will result in significant savings of up to 75 per cent of health costs in the long term.[81]

Our potential is not completely hard-wired in DNA. Genes are not totally fixed from birth, and can be modified by behaviors.

1.3.3.2   *The Impact of Behavior on Culture*

In the first section of this chapter, we learned that culture has almost replaced genes in guiding our behaviors, but this interaction is a two-way street. Societies with a strong group-mindset may prompt individuals to act with collective interests at heart, but it does not mean all behaviors are the consequences of this value, and behaviors cannot influence or change this value. Social learning allows behavior to be a dynamic force that both *reflects* and *reshapes* cultural values simultaneously.[82] The impact of repeated behaviors, a single policy, a single individual, or a single act can leave an enormous legacy and turn seemingly entrenched systems upside down.

CASE STUDIES

Cultural Reform

In 1922, Ataturk abolished the caliphate and conducted swift and sweeping reform in Turkey. New policies even banned religious dressing in public institutions, including the traditional fez and turban. The national legislation was constructed using business legal codes inspired by those from Germany, judicial codes from Italy, and civil codes from Switzerland. By replacing the Arabic alphabet with the Latin one, within two years, the literacy rate increased from 10 to 70 per cent. Women were granted suffrage in 1935, well ahead of many European countries, including those whose laws Turkey borrowed from. Ataturk famously said that "everything we see in the world is the creative work of women." In the space of 15 years, Ataturk transformed a conservative and feudal Turkey into a famously liberal, progressive and secular country from the ashes of the Ottoman Empire.

In 2010, the 26-year-old Tunisian street vendor Bouzizi set himself alight and triggered a revolutionary wave throughout the Islamic world. His act of defiance against injustice was the beginning of the so-called Arab Spring, which has been dramatically changing the political and religious landscape of three continents that make up the Middle East ever since/ "Visitors at the tomb of Bouzizi in Sidi Bouzid, (Tunisia)," MAI NGUYEN-PHUONG-MAI.

Enforced Behavior

The public greeting "Heil Hitler" was believed to be a powerful conditioning device.[83] It probably started as an outward token of conformity. For those who didn't support Hitler, but had to follow him, this greeting created a profound inconsistency between "behavior" and "belief" called cognitive dissonance. In order to solve this schizophrenic discomfort, people tried to establish their psychic equilibrium by consciously making themselves believe what they said and did,[84] mutating their conscience. Regardless of the nature of the government, many other acts of public conformity, political rituals and legal regulations employ repeated behaviors with the aim of changing culture.[85]

Sale Tactic

The "foot-in-the-door" compliance or the "lowball technique" is popular among sales people. It capitalizes on our tendency to align behavior and belief. First, customers are made to agree to a small request (e.g. agree to have a look a car with a very cheap price), and once some behaviors have been shown (e.g. about to sign the paper), a greater request will be revealed (e.g. extra charge for parts). Since the customers have already committed, either verbally or through an action, they experience an inner need to make their attitude consistent with their words and deeds by following through and developing the belief that the car is actually still a good buy. This tactic is especially effective when combined with the tactic of "but you are free," giving the customers the feeling they have been coaxed, not coerced into the sale.[86]

Corporate Culture Change

Within the realm of organizational culture, the conventional wisdom is that it takes years to change "the way we do things around here." But an $8 billion company in the US proved that by focusing on the guiding behavioral principles, the corporate culture can change quickly and effectively.

When a desired behavior was identified by the company, for example, people should talk directly to each other, it would be formally labelled "Direct with Respect." In combination with trainings, leaders would consciously mentor employees and demonstrate their "Direct with Respect." They would reward employees with a "thank you" when the targeted behavior was shown. After six months, a cultural pulse survey was conducted to assessment this behavior-focused strategy. This revealed a significant reduction in the number of employees leaving the company (from 12 to 6 per cent). Customers clearly noticed a change in service and the company's market share on certain products grew by two points without the addition of new features.[87]

Match the above cases with the following statements, each case can have more than one match:
1. People fight for what they believe, but also believe what they are fighting for.
2. Non-typical, random, radical or deviated behaviors are more than just exceptions and can gradually grow into new norms.
3. Even when the act is against the belief, repeated behavior can change attitudes and eventually deep-seated values.

4. "Thought is the child of action" (Disraeli). We forge the definition of the "self" by our deeds. Once given a role, it does not take long for us to act the role and become the role.

1.3.3.3   The Impact of Behavior on Environment

We previously discussed the role of environment in human diversity, with theories ranging from seeing environment as an absolute deciding factor, to a very influential force, or an "archive" of possibilities for human beings to take advantage of. It should be clear now, however, that similar to other interactions examined, this impact is not one-dimensional.

Natural environment has played an important role in diversifying human cultures and, in return, human cultures and behaviors have been reshaping and changing the environment significantly. For example, during the course of thousands of years, the Aboriginals in Australia burned forests to promote grasslands for hunting – a practice that affected the timing and intensity of the summer monsoon.[88] Early farming caused an anomalous reversal in natural declines of atmospheric carbon dioxide 7,000 years ago and these climatic changes set the Earth on an unnatural climate path.[89] Modernity and technology have sped up the pace that mankind is shaping the environment, with dramatic changes in landscapes, ecology and, of course, global warming.

Behaviors are not the end point of the interaction. They are both the consequence and the driving force of culture and environment. At the same time, behaviors are directed by genes, but can also modify genes.

At this point, we have completed the cycle of interaction between five factors that underline the immense diversity we see in our cultures, down to the level of gene and neuron. All factors dynamically and simultaneously relate to each other in such an intricate way that it is impossible to decide where the interaction starts or ends. Each factor is both a driving force and is impacted by other factors at the same time. None of the factors is static, all of them are dynamic. In other words, the term "plasticity" can be applied to all of them. The environment is powerful in shaping our diversity; at the same time, it is being reshaped by our culture and behaviors. Our genes control many of our behaviors, but they also coevolve with culture and can be modified by our behaviors. The plasticity of our brain means that it is capable of growing and developing just like a muscle, depending on the demand of the cultural and natural environment. Our behavior is guided by culture and genes, but behavior also wields incredible power in changing culture and genes. Culture is both a dynamic and stable survival strategy. Human beings are not only the product of culture and its interaction with genes and environment, but also active agents in producing culture, changing our own genetic make-up, while relentlessly shaping and reshaping our environment. Due to this complexity, any cultural analysis should take into account a particular context in which an event occurs. The force of environment, genes, brain, culture and behaviors varies in each circumstance. Hence, in our Diagram of Diversity Pathways, context is represented by a circle that envelops all varieties of interaction.

ACTIVITY

Look at Figure 1.5 – The Diagram of Diversity Pathways, and give each arrow of interaction a number. For each number, do some quick research and find an example to illustrate the dynamic relationship between these factors. You can use search phrases such as "influence of X on Y" or "interaction between X and Y."

1.4   Globalization

At this point, some healthy skepticism raises the question: "If our diversity is so immense, why do we have a seemingly unavoidable globalization that is apparently blurring cultural boundaries more than ever?"

Taking a look around, it is noticeable that societies are increasingly converging towards similar patterns. When Marshall McLuhan coined the concept of the "global village,"[90] he was referring to Plato's definition of a city's proper population, i.e. the ideal number of people who live within the range of a public speaker. Plato believed that the magic number was 5040 citizens. Nowadays, technology has replaced the public speaker and connects billions of people via networks of media, commerce, and migration. However, is globalization a new phenomenon? How is it possible for diversity and globalization, conflict and cooperation to coexist?

1.4.1   Effective Resource Management

As we learned from the previous section, resource management is a driving force for linguistic and cultural diversity. The differences between us are a regulator to either safeguard resources against outsiders, or negotiate resources with those we can trust. When the environment is rich, this tendency to form sub-groups is even greater, since it is possible for a small group to "safeguard" knowledge more frequently than "negotiate" knowledge and still survive with little sharing. In a nutshell, abundant nature can prompt the possibility of splitting off and forming sub-groups, thus creating vast cultural diversity.[91]

However, a rich environment is not a deciding factor that makes humans destined to live in small tribal groups and have tribal cultures. The main purpose here is about interacting with the environment and managing cultural resources effectively for survival. At one point, humans realized that large groupings work as well. The level of production increased but with more or less the same costs. This is the advantage of "economies of scale,"[92] which arise due to an inverse relationship between the quantity produced and per-unit fixed cost. Large groupings of people enable economies of scale, and the need to sub-divide into small cultures was removed by a system that provides for us sufficiently.[93] Examples can be found in many big and successful empires throughout history.

To conclude, regardless of rich or poor environments, resource management can lead to both the *dividing* and the *merging* of cultures. Looking at globalization, the next question we need to ask is: "Why does the tendency to merge seem to be the winner of the race?"

1.4.2   The Cooperative Nature of Humans

Theorists have long battled with the question of whether human nature is good or bad. Earlier theorists and theologians emphasized the warlike essence of the human mind with phrases such as "law of the jungle," "every man for himself," "dog eat dog," and "survival of the fittest." [94-95-96-97] This view is still supported by some modern thinkers, including the 21st century-Nobel Laureate Oliver Williamson.[98]

However, recent studies have consistently proved that human nature is not at all naturally evil.[99-100-101-102-103] In their book *A Cooperative Species: Human Reciprocity and its Evolution*, the economists Sam Bowles and Herbert Gintis argued that humans genuinely want to cooperate and sincerely care about the well-being of their own group.[104] This psychology helps to bond individuals in building a prosperous and united community for surviving and competing with other groups. Evolution hence favors cooperative traits, but there's a twist: this cooperation goes hand in hand with aggression towards outsiders. Groups that have a disproportionate number of selfish and warlike, or peaceful and altruistic people will die out. Interestingly, and also uncomfortably, the authors assert that war is a necessary tool for this cooperative trait to evolve in humans. However, wars and conflicts are not inevitable. According to the authors, humans are cultural animals, capable of making sure that our legacy need not to be our destiny.[105]

"Warfare is ultimately not a denial of the human capacity for cooperation, but merely the most destructive expression of it." – Lawrence H. Keeley / "The legacy of war in Sarajevo, (Bosnia and Herzegovina)," MAI NGUYEN-PHUONG-MAI.

Biologists have a generally sunnier view of humankind. For example, experiments show that infants of 18 months old would immediately open the door or pick up a dropped clothes peg when they see an *unrelated* adult whose hands are full, an altruistic act that is not enhanced by rewards, and not influenced by training.[107]

Although the argument that cooperation is totally innate may not receive a full consensus, it is hard to deny the fact that humans are the only animal who can extend care beyond kinship to large numbers of unrelated individuals. We can cooperate with members of a different blood line, beating the family-bound sociality that is typical of the animal kingdom.

With a capacity for culture, we are able to bring down the genetic fence and welcome strangers into our circle of trust. This psychology is so important that it has become our subconscious, intuitive response, or "first instinct."[108] Neuro-economic evidence has shown that this instinct makes us cooperative, even when we have nothing to gain and even at our own expense.[109] Think about the time when you rushed to give back a forgotten wallet to a stranger or helped a lost child find her/his parents.

Latest research in the interdisciplinary fields of neurosciences, biology and psychology has convinced many that the mainstream neo-classical economic theory of "homo economicus" is problematic. In 2015, the World Economic Forum published an article that dismissed the idea that we act rationally to maximize our own utility. This assumption of human nature underpins our current economic model, which allows Adam Smith's "invisible hand" to function freely for a better world.[110] As the author argues, we are not only motivated by power and wanting, but also by care and systems of affiliation,[111] which help us to form relationships and build trust even with strangers of a different group. This article is part of an emerging ideology featuring the *caring economy*[112-113] – a new paradigm that fully reflects what it is to be human as we shift from the industrial to the post-industrial knowledge era in an attempt to build a more equitable and sustainable world.

Norway is a good example of a caring economy. Norway and other Scandinavian countries (Finland, Sweden, Denmark and Iceland) follow the Nordic economic model that prioritizes a progressive welfare system. Norwegian parents are entitled to 46 weeks at full salary for childcare – one of many policies that helps women to fully contribute to the workforce and top the Global Gender Index/ "A child with the Tiger Statue in Oslo, (Norway)," MAI NGUYEN-PHUONG-MAI.

1.4.3   Reaching Out to Strangers

With the capacity of culture and, hence, the ability to go beyond kinship, during the last 10,000 years, the tension between "cooperation within in-group" and "aggression towards outgroups" has tended to give more weight to cooperation and softened group boundaries. Despite numerous wars, over a long period of time, reaching out to cooperate with strangers has steadily proved to be a successful cultural strategy that returns better outcomes than endless conflicts and revenge.

The consequence of this process is that human beings have evolved into larger and larger groups and communities. The history of mankind has witnessed a constant growth of the cooperation process that transformed small tribes into chiefdoms, chiefdoms to nascent city-states, city-states to nation states, and nation states to collections of nations such as ancient Rome or the European Union (EU). The next logical step is, of course, the "global village," or, in another word, "globalization."

In short, globalization is not completely new. It is the ultimate stage of a cultural adaption process that endows with the psychological capacity to cope with effective resource management, diversity, and other problems in the course of existence. A timely example EU countries' willingness to bail out Greece.[114] The money they gave away was worth less than the cost to their own economies if Greece defaults. In the end, richer Eurozone countries keep more of their wealth by giving quite a lot of it away. The very psychology that enables us to form groups larger than family also enables us to create an increasingly interconnected world.

Despite the immense diversity, humans are the only species who can extend cooperation beyond kinship and form larger communities of unrelated individuals, thanks to the capacity of culture. This insight questions the mainstream economic model of "homo economicus" – the notion that humans are rational, selfish, and will attempt to maximize their utility for gains.

1.4.4   The Driving Forces for Cross-Cultural Communication

At this point, it should be clear that the capacity for culture allows us to juggle two contrasting incentives: (1) the tendency to diversify in order to recognize those we can trust and to safeguard cultural resources and; (2)

the tendency to seek cooperation beyond kinship and ingroups in order to manage resources more effectively. We see this situation every day. For any cultural community, along with its endless calls to honor and preserve cultural heritage, there is always an effort to open up and seek allies. For example, Flemish-speaking people are very proud of their specific culture and language, but, at the same time, they are willing to maintain the status quo of being an integral part of three completely different countries: The Netherlands, Belgium, and France.

Globalization is not new, but today we are confronted with issues of international development that our ancestors did not have to deal with. *Technology and information* systems have reduced the distance between people. In a matter of decades, traditional methods of information exchange, which we have known for thousands of years, have been swept away. What once took us weeks or months to receive (a letter, for example) can now be achieved with the click of a mouse. It is not the change, but the *speed of change* that is so mind-blowing and led Toffler, back in 1970, to coin the term "future shock," a psychological state of having to cope with too much change in too short a period of time.[115] Going abroad, meeting people from different communities, or coping with a cultural clash are no longer a once-in-a-lifetime event. With technology flattening any distance obstacles, millions of people experience new cultures, customs and beliefs, etc. on a daily basis, something that our parents and (great-)grandparents only went through a few times in their life, and something that only the most adventurous of our ancestors got a chance to experience.

Next, the impetus for international contact is heavily attributed to an unprecedented and rapid increase in and redistribution of the world's *demographics*. Around 360,000 new babies are born each day, 133 million each year, and more than 230,000 million people live outside the country of their birth, and that is not counting immigrants and their descendants and massive global diasporas. This unprecedented increase in size and large-scale redistribution is a burden on resources, the planet's ecosystem, and heightens the likelihood of conflicts. Distance no longer matters. We all share vital natural resources such as oil and water; African dust storms from Chad and Mali can cause health alerts in Puerto Rico in the Caribbean and a decline in sea coral in the Bahamas and Barbados.[116] The refugee crisis that engulfed Europe in 2015-2016 as a result of wars and uprisings in Syria, Iraq and Afghanistan is just another example that illustrates how no geographically isolated country is immune to conflict. We have become so interconnected that nobody is untouchable.

Finally, we are witnessing the growth of an unprecedented *global economy*. Historically, international trade took place along the Silk Road, the Spice Route, the Incense Route, the Amber Road, etc. But the modern process of globalization distinguishes itself significantly from its predecessors. From a corporation's perspective, four critical elements stand out: (1) a globalized capital base, e.g. money is transferred across the globe in a matter of seconds; (2) a global corporate mindset, e.g. cultural diversity is viewed as a series of opportunities to exploit; (3) a global market presence, e.g. targeting customers in all major markets throughout the world; and (4) a global supply chain, e.g. accessing the most optimal locations for the performance of various activities in its supply chain.[117]

The aforementioned characteristics of our global economy have made individual economies around the world incredibly interconnected. While the advantages are undeniable, this interwoven network of international trading is prone to the "domino effect." The 1997 Asian crisis, for instance, originated in Thailand, but, as a consequence, Indonesia lost 13.5 per cent of its GDP that year, South Korea's national debt-to-GDP ratio more than doubled and Malaysia's GDP plunged 6.2 per cent. Mongolia's public revenues and exports collapsed and suffered a further loss of income as a result of the Russian crisis in 1999. Western markets were spared from collapse but severely hit. Ten years after this "Asian flu," a flood of irresponsible mortgage lending in the US eventually led to a global financial crisis that brought the entire system crashing down. In the global economy, one person sneezes and everyone catches a cold.

We are living in a world where diverse people are brought together at speeds that exceed those at which they can be successfully culturally integrated. Consequently, no nations, groups or culture can remain aloof or autonomous. As individual citizens of this globalized world, the good news is that as a result of *exposure to different cultures* and purposely *changing our behaviors*, our brains can become culturally tuned with new neural activities, forge new neural pathways, build new cells, etc. This enables us to adapt to any culture on demand, be it the society of Nauru – an island surrounded by the Pacific Ocean, or the international working environment of the financial business hub in Zurich, where all cultures simultaneously interact. We take guidance from culture to fit in, and use it in the most effective way to advance. But we are not hopeless products, since we can also be active agents in contributing new elements and changing the culture around us. If culture is a strategy, then it will be the survival of the most cultured.

The changes we are witnessing with globalization are fast, complex and on an international scale. More than ever in the history of mankind, a capacity for cultural adaption is vital, because intercultural contacts are pervasive and unavoidable.

- *Globalization is not new, but in the modern era, this process is driven by different factors: (a) speed of technology and information development; (b) rapid changes in global demography; and (c) the emergence of a global economy.*
- *By being exposed to different cultures and purposely changing our behaviors, our brains can become culturally tuned, allowing us to adapt to any culture on demand.*

ACTIVITY

Conduct research and discuss the following issues:

1. Is "country" a new concept? What has been the typical grouping form of humans throughout history? What are the advantages and disadvantages of viewing "country" as a default and independent variable when analyzing the impact of culture?

2. What is "nationalism"? What fuels nationalism? In terms of resource management, what are the advantages and disadvantages of nationalism? Give specific examples in both cases.

3. Nationalism and globalization are opposed to each other, but both are increasing. Discuss this paradox.

Summary

1. It is mostly our culture, not our genes that supplies the majority of solutions and guidance we use to survive and prosper in the society of our birth. Hence, culture is the survival strategy of our species. Instead of waiting for genes to evolve, we use ideas (culture) to advance.

2. The capacity for culture began with social learning, or the ability to learn and imitate others, to select the best practices, improve them, and teach them to others.

3. Cultural diversity is crucial because it is a regulator for (a) safeguarding cultural resources, recognizing who we can trust; and (b) negotiating cultural resources with other human groups for mutual interests. Effective resource management can lead to both the dividing and merging of cultures.

4. The diversity in human's many cultures is driven by many factors that dynamically interact with one another: environment, genes, brain and behavior. None

of them is static. Each one is simultaneously a driving force and impacted by the others (plasticity).

- The impact of environment on cultural diversity is influential, with theories ranging from a deciding factor (determinism), an influential factor (probabilism), a source of possibilities (possibilism), to an entity that is inseparable from the human species (ecology). According to the Diagram of Diversity Pathways, environment can take a dynamic role, both influencing and being subjected to the impact of cultural and human behaviors, depending on a particular context.
- Genes carry the codes of human development and behavior. However, genes are not totally fixed from birth and can be modified by behaviors. The selection of genes also depends on the coevolution with culture: a specific cultural value may prefer a certain gene, and a certain gene may slowly create a certain cultural value.
- The brain is a dynamic device that can grow, develop and rewire itself in response to new behaviors and adapt to a culture on demand. The brain's plasticity means that traits are unlikely to be "hard-wired" from birth, rather they are the consequence of repeated behaviors.
- Behaviors are both the consequence and the driving force of culture and environment. At the same time, behaviors are directed by genes and brains, but can also modify genes and the brain.

5. Despite the immense diversity, thanks to the capacity of culture, humans are the only species that can extend cooperation beyond kinship and form larger communities of unrelated individuals. This insight questions the mainstream economic model of "homo economicus" – the notion that humans are rational, selfish, and will attempt to maximize their utility for gains.

6. Globalization is not new, but in the modern era, this process is driven by different factors: (a) the speed of technology and information development; (b) rapid changes in global demography; and (c) the emergence of a global economy.

2.   The Evolving Culture

Objective

At the end of this chapter, you should be able to:

· Explain the "tree of culture" and position diverse cultural elements in accordance with this metaphor.
· Explain the dynamics and stability of the different elements in the tree metaphor with appropriate examples.
· Describe the Inverted Pyramid model and position a cultural case in the correct layer and unit of analysis.
· Prove the significance of intercultural competence in doing business internationally.

Chapter outline

In the previous chapter, we discussed how culture has largely replaced genes to guide humans in the survival game. We also explored how the notion of plasticity (i.e. adaptiveness) can be applied to culture, genes, environment, the brain and behaviors. The dynamic interaction of these factors creates an intricate web of possibilities to change, and that explains the immense level of diversity as well as globalization that we see today.

Since culture is such a dynamic force, in order to analyze different cultures effectively, we first need to agree on some generic frameworks. We want to know the generic components of a culture, the "size" of a culture, and the different levels of analysis. While culture evolves as a survival strategy, we nevertheless want to know some principles that, to a certain extent, can help us predict that process of evolution and change. Finally, from a practical point of view, what can we do to deal with this complexity and dynamics effectively? These will be the topics of discussion in this chapter.

2.1   The metaphorical tree of culture

If you were asked to name everything that belongs to "culture," the list would be unlimited. However, three major components of culture can be identified: fundamental concerns, values and outward expressions. We will use the metaphor of a *tree* to help us understand this complexity. Imagine that these three groups of cultural elements are represented by three layers of a tree: its trunk and roots, its branches, and its massive canopy of twigs and leaves (Figure 2.1).

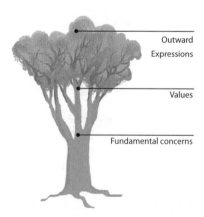

Figure 2.1. The Metaphorical Tree of Culture

2.1.1 Fundamental Concern

Fundamental concerns are the building blocks of our culture – the very foundation of the human social learning environment, which, as we discussed in the previous chapter, makes us different from other animals. This is the evolutionary root of culture as survival strategy. They are universal, generic and fundamental elements such as politics, arts, religion, and languages, etc. None of them can produce a product that directly affects our reproduction and survival, but they have been evolved to *enhance* our performance. For example, language developed because we need to negotiate cultural resources, while religion, art, and politics developed because they give us courage and hope, "coordinating our action, uniting us against common foes" and promoting "norms that glue society together."[1] Any human group that failed to acquire these building blocks could find themselves in competition with those who had. Imagine a tribe who goes to war with music, songs and poems that motivate their willingness to sacrifice, with a social system that promises them valuable rewards after a victory, or with a belief that God(s) is/are on their side. A culture that is sophisticated and supportive of the need to survive is more likely to help the tribe win the battle if their enemy is not equipped with an equally effective culture. These building blocks have become essential parts of culture because they promote survival and reproduction, regardless of whether they are true or false, moral or immoral, peaceful or violent. They are *fundamental concerns* of human beings, shared by all societies, because they are needed to advance the human species through the form of culture. They help us to reproduce, to survive and to dominate any given environment.

At a deeper level, fundamental concerns also extend to what we normally think of as values, such as loyalty, freedom or hierarchy. These cultural notions are universally seen as unavoidable concerns in any culture. Loyalty, freedom and hierarchy are essential since they are drivers in the forming of cultural groups, regardless of their size: a band, a tribe, a chiefdom, a city-state, a nation state, an empire, or a league of nations. Thus, in principle, all the values we can think of are also fundamental concerns.

In our metaphorical tree of culture, fundamental concerns are represented by the trunk and the roots of the tree. They indicate our commonality and sameness as human beings, without which we will be disadvantaged in the survival game. The trunk and the roots of the tree are grounded firmly in the earth, which symbolically reminds us of the ultimate biological reason why culture ever came to exist in the first place: to replace genes, helping us to survive and advance as a species.

2.1.2   Value

In essence, values project our attitudinal positions on the fundamental concerns. For example, while religion is a fundamental concern, values indicate *how important* religion is in a society, in a particular context: high, average or low. Religion may be a private matter as in secular France, where its government bars employees from displaying their religious by wearing, for example, the Islamic veil (*hijab/niqab*) or Jewish skullcap (*kippah*), but religion can also be seen as the ultimate source of power, as in the theocratic Vatican, Mauritania or Afghanistan, where God is recognized as the supreme civil ruler. In short, to indicate values, we can simply ask "how important XYZ is in a society?" Thus, religion is a fundamental concern, but one society, an individual, or a context can differ from another in terms of how important religion is. The same is true for almost every cultural notion we can think of: integrity, competition, altruism, freedom, democracy, bravery, wealth, power, etc. These are fundamental concerns, and values are the *degree of importance* each society, individual or context places on them.

2.1.3   Outward Expression

The third component of culture are the myriad of *objects, symbols* and *behaviors* that are outward expressions of the fundamental concerns and values. Outward expressions are visible, tangible, and include things such as specific kinds of clothes, specific styles of houses and technology, specific words and documents, specific policies, specific actions and practices, etc.

In short, our "tree of culture" consists of: (1) the roots and the trunk that represent the evolutionary purpose of culture, which, in turn, has become a fundamental concern of the human species; (2) the branches, which are the values that represent various degrees of importance each society, individual or context places on fundamental concerns; and (3) the leaves, which represent visible outward expressions of all the specific objects, symbols and behaviors that are the physical manifestation of our values and fundamental concerns.

The "tree of culture" has three components:
- *Fundamental concerns: e.g. hierarchy.*
- *Values: e.g. "Low," "average," or "high" degree of importance placed on "hierarchy."*
- *Outward expressions: e.g. respectful behaviors towards authority, seeking instruction from seniority, practicing inequality between subordinates and superiors, using honorific titles, etc.*

2.2   The change in culture

Technically, no scholars have ever stated that culture does not change. What diverts them, however, is the speed and nature of the change. In this section, we will review these schools of thought using insights from evolutionary biology and cultural neuroscience.

2.2.1   Static vs. Dynamic Cultural Paradigm

Theories of intercultural communication split into two main paradigms: static culture and dynamic culture.

2.2.1.1   *Static Paradigm*
The static paradigm of culture posits that culture is very stable. A conservative society will remain conservative in comparison with others, and it would be very difficult for this cultural value of "conservatism" to change. With regard to national cultures, they are "as hard as a country's geographic position."[2] If changes happen, they occur at a very slow rate, and since *the whole world changes together* at more or less the same speed, the gaps between national cultures remain more or less the same.

The advantage of seeing culture as stable is that it gives us the idea that culture can be predicted and controlled through expected behavioral outcomes,[3-4] hence, reducing ambiguity and variability.[5] For example, if we assume that this community is collectivistic (i.e. having a strong attachment to groups), we can then predict that families and friends in this community will have a strong bond, and any marketing campaigns will need to connect products with this value if customers are to relate to them.

2.2.1.2   *Dynamic Paradigm*
By contrast, the dynamic paradigm argues that culture is not stable, but rather dynamic in the process of responding to the external environment.[6-7-8-9-10] Depending on circumstances, culture is able to adapt to meet eco-socio-politico demands.[11] Thus, culture evolves in response to the impacts of influential individuals, historical events, environmental changes, and innovation development, etc.

This notion of culture as dynamic resonates strongly with the role of culture as a survival strategy. As a mechanism that has largely replaced genes to help human beings advance, culture should not be an "entity" that limits itself to a deterministic framework regardless of context. Any culture is a living organism with a life of its own and different upheavals, sentiments, dramas and contradictions. It is anything but a time-free "fossil."[12] In fact, culture can be seen as a series of dynamic responses to internal and external factors.

Changes can be so sudden, so fundamental and so fast that it is almost impossible for the average differences between cultures to remain the same throughout history. Think about the life of the many aboriginal communities and native tribes in Australia and the Amazon who came into contact with modernity within a very short period of time. A change of government can have a significant impact on a society such as Tunisia, where, in 1956, the president transformed the country into the most secular nation in the Arab world and *banned* the Islamic *hijab*.[13] Now compare this with Iran, where the revolution in 1979 turned the country into a theocracy with the *enforced* wearing of the Islamic *hijab* for every woman, including foreigners.[14] One needs to look no further than North and South Korea to see how the political context has divided one country, and each part has evolved a very different culture, despite sharing the same roots. In China, to cope with a growing population, the government followed a strict state-mandated one-child policy. Enforcement of this radical law has transformed the cultural perception of gender equality, filial piety, patrilineality and the notion of the male bread winner, since daughters are expected to take on as many responsibilities as sons.[15] Globalization and the interconnectedness of multicultural societies also act as powerful drivers for cultural change, as in the case of Canada, Japan and Morocco, where collectivistic values have become very dynamic over time.[16] These examples question the notion of static culture (i.e. that cultures only change very slowly, and the gaps between them remain more or less the same). As survival strategies, cultures around the world are more dynamic processes than entities that change together in unison. In fact, the word "culture" should be seen as a *verb*, not a noun.[17]

ACTIVITY

"Culture" is derived from the Latin word "colere" – to "till" the soil for farming. The concept signals growth and development rather than stability. In the Indonesian language, "budi" – understood as culture – has a deeply philosophical and religious meaning. Similarly, the Chinese word for culture "wen-hua," is the combination of two components: "literature" and "change." Carry out research and find out the meaning of "culture" in five other non-Latin languages.

2.2.1.3   *The Role of Context*

From the viewpoint of culture as a survival strategy that responds dynamically to internal and external factors, *context* becomes the ultimate power in terms of predicting the "change" within and between cultures. In our metaphor, it is represented by a circle around the tree. It implies that particular situations and circumstances will influence how fundamental concerns, values and outward expressions evolve, develop and adapt to fulfil the mission of helping human beings advance. This context is dynamic, as implied by the Diagram of Diversity Pathways (Chapter 1). In a given context at any particular time, depending on the circumstances (the age of the tree, the soil, the water, the surrounding environment, the seasons, the sun, the wind, other trees in the area, etc.), the tree grows and changes over time gaining different attributes. Similarly, branches and leaves come and go, grow and fall. The tree can expand, producing seeds to create new trees, be transplanted, or die. As a living ecology, this metaphor signals life, hence, change, development and even disintegration. The first president of Senegal – Leopold Sedar Senghor – is believed to have said: "True culture is getting rooted and uprooted. Getting rooted into the depths of one's native land and its spiritual heritage, but also getting uprooted, that is opening up to the rain, the sun, the fertile contributions of foreign civilizations." In other words, we are not only interested in understanding what culture "is," but we also need to know how culture "responds."

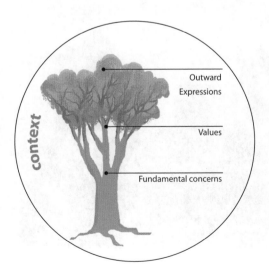

Figure 2.2. The Metaphorical Tree of Culture in Context

2.2.2   The Dynamics of Values

When scholars discuss "change" in culture, most of the time the focus is meant to be a change in values. But since we cannot *see* a value, we can only evaluate a change of value through the changes in outward expressions. This leads to many questions: "If conflicting outward expressions co-exist, does that mean conflicting values also co-exist?" "Will a change in outward expressions correlate with a change in values?" "Do outward expressions drive values, or do values dictate outward expressions?" Let's discuss each of these questions in turn.

2.2.2.1   *Cultural Paradox*

A paradox is defined as "the simultaneous presence of contradictory, even mutually exclusive elements."[18] Observing a culture, we will see that it intrinsically embraces paradoxes. If one chooses to see culture as static, one would be baffled by how often a culture can be both conservative *and* liberal, or both collectivistic *and* individualistic.[19] Global managers, for example, are frustrated by cultural contradictions that do not accord with the famous cross-cultural manual,[20] that Japanese negotiators don't "act Japanese,"[21] or Chinese negotiators are both very deceptive and very sincere.[22]

Contrasting values and outward expressions co-exist in Tunisia/ "Women in bikini and hijab on Tunis beach, (Tunisia)," MAI NGUYEN-PHUONG-MAI.

Travelers scratch their heads on learning that aggressive Thai boxing (*Muay Thai*) is traditionally taught in harmonious Thai Buddhist temples, and bar-goers may wonder why British hooligans are so infamous[23-24] given that the British character is regularly portrayed as very reserved.[25] While abundant in generally homogeneous cultures, paradoxes are a *normality* in multicultural societies such as Israel, Malaysia and South Africa, where opposing values and outward expressions co-exist.

If culture is viewed as dynamic, paradoxes should be understood as an inherent part of culture. Opposites co-exist simultaneously and can reverse their positions at a given point in history, depending on the context. The yin-yang philosophy, which intrinsically embraces paradoxes for a healthy existence and development, is a good way of understanding paradox.[26] Yin and yang produce each other, too much yin will provoke yang and vice versa. Each can be the cause or the effect of the other, and the effect of one can only be understood by considering the role played by the other.[27] Let's look again at the apparently contradictory example of Thai boxing in the Buddhist temple. A fundamental Buddhist teaching is that we cannot control what fate brings our way, but we can control our *attitude* to it. This notion is interwoven into martial arts across Asia, where practitioners are trained to purify their minds, to put themselves under the duress of attack and not show or respond with anger.[28] The calmness of the mind and the physical action seem to be opposing, but they are mutually complementary, and a balance of the two will lead to a desirable result, in this case, fighting that embraces equanimity, mutual respect, humility, honor and aesthetics.

The more we pay attention, the more we will be amazed at how often paradoxes exist, no matter how strong the dominant or stereotypical values are. A political party, a policy, a movement, a school curriculum, or even a movie can show a completely contradictory side to the collective assumption. Many people must struggle to understand why a TV series that features only pathetic losers, such as "The Big Bang Theory," gains so much popularity in a country like the US that is known for its competitive spirit and "rags to riches" mentality. Similarly, in the masculine culture of Japan, the *bishōnen* trend (beautiful [male] youth) praises the kind of male beauty that has distinctly feminine features: slender, clear and fair skin, stylish hair, high cheekbones and pouty lips.

The bishōnen *social phenomenon provides an outlet for the conventionally strict gender relations in conservative and masculine Japan/* "Example of a *bishōnen*," KISHI SHIOTANI.[29]

Thus, we are intrinsically both yin and yang, conservative and liberal, collectivistic and individualistic, depending on a particular circumstance. Again, the role of context is crucial in understanding not only cultural change, but also cultural paradox. Researchers have also suggested "indexing" context[30] (e.g. culture will change in *this* direction if facing *this* situation of, for example, "financial crisis"), or seeing culture as a "tool box"[31] or "card game"[32] in which we can respond to each particular situation in life by playing a different value (e.g. I choose to deal with this business partner assertively because it seems like a good strategy to work with her/him). This notion of "culture-as-situated cognition"[33] suggests that what matters is not whether collectivistic and individualistic values exist, but *when* they are activated and influence our concept of self and behaviors.

Neuroscience weighs in,[34-35-36-37] confirming what behavioral studies have proved,[38-39] i.e. that context drives different activations of neurons and prompts a person to have either collectivistic or individualistic thoughts, regardless of how (s)he normally behaves or identifies her/himself. The plasticity of our brain (see Chapter 1) enables simple cues such as "I" and "we" to trigger us to think in a self-oriented or group-oriented way. Neuroscientists have proved that we are capable of representing *multiple cultures* and opposing values in our mind, and switching between them simultaneously.[40] In other words, we can develop a *multicultural mind*.[41] You may describe yourself as typically competitive, but you can subconsciously or deliberately act extremely cooperatively if the context activates that element in you. Such a pragmatic approach to culture embraces people as active and creative problem solvers, rather than as passive "cultural dopes."[42]

2.2.2.2   *The Non-Binary Structure of Values*

Accepting the paradox of culture is a good start in terms of gaining a deeper understanding of how dynamic culture can be. With regards to the tree metaphor, we can now begin to explore the way context and paradoxes shape our view of values. Let's first take another look at neuroscience.

We often think about values in binary terms, i.e. dependent vs. independent, collectivistic vs. individualistic, or conservative vs. liberal. This inherent dualistic thinking pattern has much to do with the neurology of human emotions.[43] Any stimulus entering our central nervous system is immediately relayed in two directions towards the *cerebral cortex* – our rational brain, and the amygdala – our emotional detective device. What is interesting is that despite being activated simultaneously, the amygdala decides whether we like the object or not *before* the cortex has managed to figure out what the object actually is. This "quick and dirty" emotional assessment aids survival skills, since we can save time and escape danger without too much thinking. However, it also means that evolution has created a neural machinery that supports instinctive "good or bad" binary thinking.

To this day, the binary mechanism of neurology still influences the foundation of our worldview. It has become our habitual and instinctive psychology for dealing with complexity.[44] We tend to speak in "opposites," such as day and night, male and female, creator and created, sun and moon, without much awareness that these are just two positions of a complex structure – a structure that is more multi-dimensional than binary. The same is true for values. We find it easier to label a society as *either* conservative *or* liberal and, hence, disregard the fact that a society never positions itself only at one of these points, but always intrinsically and dynamically at *both* points,[45] as attested by paradoxes and, possibly, also *other dimensions that we are unaware of*. A good example is the widely used binary construct masculiny-femininity in intercultural studies. The static paradigm posits that societies vary on this spectrum, leaning either towards (1) femininity, with both men and women are modest and caring, or (2) masculinity, with men are competitive/assertive, women are modest and caring.[46] The latter can be confusing, since a masculine society – if we follow the logic of the former – is supposed to see *both* men and women being competitive and assertive. The static paradigm struggles to label a society with two contrasting values, where men are masculine and women are feminine. And in an effort to fit the binary spectrum, it makes such a society a masculine one.

If we can comprehend the normality of paradoxes and the dynamic nature of culture and context, we can rethink the assumed binary structure and question its simplicity. Think about how often we label a person as good or bad. Is this person entirely good or entirely bad? Did (s)he just show some socially perceived good or bad behaviors because (s)he happened to be in that specific situation? Have we considered that this "good" or "bad" character can change over time? If a human being is this complex, how complex is a society, especially a multicultural society consisting of many sophisticated and interconnected communities and cultures?

In our metaphorical tree of culture, values are represented by branches of the tree. They are not binary, i.e. one end is "conservative" and the other is "liberal." Each value can be a separate branch of the tree, either the same size or a different size. Depending on a particular context, a value will prevail. For example, a culture can be conservative when it comes to gay marriage but quite liberal when it comes to abortion. This is the case in Vietnam, where "pro-choice" is rarely questioned, but homosexuality remains taboo. Multicultural societies can be both "liberal" and "conservative" as national, organizational and different group cultures may show opposing values. Over time, circumstances constantly impact these values and drive them towards responsive changes, very much as a tree changes according to its environment.

This non-binary view of values also reflects the variation *within* a society, since within-group diversity is often greater than between-group diversity.[47] In other words, the difference between any two random people from the same culture, say, from Niger, is *greater* than the average difference between this Western African country and Palau – a Pacific island nation thousands of miles away. If all the diversity in a country is reduced to a numerical "average," we risk glossing over fundamental patterns and differences that characterize many co-cultures that exist within a socially constructed boundary. Take Togo, where 37 tribal groups speak 39 languages and Argentina – which ranks among the least diverse countries in the world due to a population of mainly white European descendants.[48] An average ranking for Argentina may make some sense due to its homogeneity, but the same cannot be said for Togo.

Context is the main indicator for predicting change within and between cultures. Paradoxes and contrasting values/outward expressions co-exist, manifesting themselves depending on particular contexts.

2.2.3   The Dynamics of Change and Stability

At this point, we have discussed extensively the changing nature of culture. However, we have not rejected the notion of stability. In fact, we can even take a holistic view and see "stability" and "change" as the yin and yang of culture, which co-exist, recreate, encompass, and succeed each other over time.[49] Adopting this perspective, we will look at the relative degree of change that occurs to different components of the "tree of culture."

2.2.3.1   *Different Speeds of Change*

Does a tree stay the same all the time? Of course not. Does a tree change itself drastically every minute? It is highly unlikely. Without an exogenous shock from internal or external environment, every part of a mature tree is constantly on the move, albeit each part at a different speed. The leaves change regularly and quickly, the twigs and branches change more slowly, and the trunk and roots change slowest of all. Factoring in the context (e.g. the weather), these changes may occur with greater variations.

Like a tree, culture is a constant process, a source of accumulated knowledge that has replaced our genes to guide us through life. However, not all parts of culture change at a similar rate. Our fundamental concerns are subjected to the least amount of change. Compared to ancient times, we have many more concerns, but it is safe to say that despite our apparently rapid development, the core of our worries and interests remain, on the whole, essential issues: from health and security to natural resources and education, from freedom and power to law and governing structures, from family and reproduction to marriage and religion, etc. These are the building blocks of culture as a survival strategy, the very foundation of our secret to advancing as a species.

In the second layer of our metaphorical tree, values indicate a moral position towards a fundamental concern, or how important we perceive a concern ought to be, i.e. low, average, or high. These moral positions change, some slowly, some a bit faster, depending on the context. For example, family bonding is a fundamental concern in all societies. However, urban and modern societies tend to see this value changing *faster* than in rural and remote areas of the world. At the same time, all communities around the world are moving, albeit at different speeds. Remembering this point enables us to avoid one of the most common mistakes we make in discussion: "Oh, but everything there is changing so fast, people are not the same anymore." That may be true, but don't forget that our values are also not the same anymore when compared with our own past. The world does not just stop still to watch some of it parts changing. What matters most in this conversation is the context: what kinds of circumstances and situations that drive the change? As contexts differ, so do the speed and nature of the change.

Of all three levels, the top layer of our "tree of culture," changes the fastest. We are constantly experiencing new things and we do different things on different days. Let's stick to the example of family bonding. While our fundamental concern of family bonding is stable, the value we attach to a strong or weak family bond can change over time. However, the way we express our bond changes rapidly in terms of specific words, symbols and behaviors. Some practices may change at a slower rate (e.g. having a family dinner every day), but there is a constant stream of different things we tell people in our family every day, and there are specific things we do for them every day. It can hurt, it can heal, it can build, or it can crash. But, above all, it is a fast flow of endless words, things, and actions that we use to express how bonded we are with our family. In short, these outward expressions constantly create our tangible world, the living cells of our life.

Context aside, fundamental concerns are pretty stable, values (i.e. the degree of importance) are dynamic, but outward expressions change fastest of all.

2.2.3.2   *The Illusion of Change*

Looking at the tree metaphor, which group of elements do we observe most in our everyday life? Clearly, it is the top one. We do not see a "value" such as the "high degree of secular political system," but we can point out its outward expressions: specific laws, certain practices and the people who advocate for it. Can what we see deceive us? Yes, unfortunately most of the time, because what we see is just the outward expression of the whole system. When looking at this tree from a birds-eye view, flying over it, we assume "Yes, I've seen the (whole) tree!" even though, in fact, we have only seen the leaves.

The underlying message is: What we see is just a very small part of the whole. Fundamental life concerns and values are deep under the forest canopy. We cannot rush above it and expect a thorough understanding. You need to be "down to earth," on your feet, standing next to the tree to observe it. More importantly, this warns us that the superficial embracing of food, music, or clothes does not mean someone has changed her/his cultural values. Of course, repetition of behaviors can eventually change a deep-seated value (see Chapter 1 and the bi-directional interaction between culture and behavior), but we are never sure if the change is *complete or not* just by looking at the outward expressions. We can be so wrong when assuming that the vibrant Christmas decorations and festive atmosphere in predominantly Buddhist countries such as Vietnam and Thailand mean people there have adopted Christian beliefs. An urban Sri Lankan boy who has tattoos, skates to school, and frequents Western fast-food chains has not automatically embraced Western values. We may be surprised that Christmas is seen as an excuse for social entertainment or opportunities for commercial marketing, and the Sri Lankan boy may leave his skateboard neatly outside and kneel down to kiss the feet of his teacher to express his gratitude according to the local custom. Why? Because the outward changes we see don't reflect, or have not yet led to a genuine change in values.

What can we say about the values of this man by looking at his outfit?/ "A pedestrian in Tripoli, (Libya)," MAI NGUYEN-PHUONG-MAI.

Now let's consider a reverse example. Many Muslim girls may fully veil themselves and pray five times a day, but it is possible that they are just as progressive as women who have chosen more casual and generic outfits. In fact, some of them may consider a simple and modest style of dress the epitome of progressiveness, since it empowers their inner beauty, channels attention to their ability, and reduces subconscious stereotypes based on appearance.

Yemeni men and boys usually wear a dagger (jambiyas). This custom, together with the excessive amount of weapons in the country and the constant conflicts are outward expressions that often mislead outsiders into thinking of Yemenis as "aggressive" people. On the contrary, Yemen's revolution was the first and the only transition of power in the Arab Spring in which a dictator was patiently persuaded to peacefully withdraw from office with a mutual agreement. Yemeni protesters wrapped a pink ribbon around their heads. Pink represents "love" and hence it was a signal of peaceful intent. Yemen also presents to the world Tawakkul Karman – the first Arab woman-, the second Muslim woman- and the second youngest Nobel Peace Prize winner to date.. The daggers were historically instruments of hunting, but now are symbols of social status, prestige, power, manhood, responsibility, honor and, to a certain extent, are similar to the wearing of swords in Europe/ "Yemeni boy with dagger," MAI NGUYEN-PHUONG-MAI.

This example reminds us of a crucial point when we evaluate a culture, especially a culture in this fast-changing world: Outward expressions do *not* always match values, a change of outward expressions does not readily reflect a genuine change of values, and vice versa. This awareness should be coupled with the possibility that outward expressions and values can change and be adjusted depending on the context. In fact, we should always question what we see and ask ourselves: "What does this practice mean?" In the GLOBE project, researchers reported that cultural practices (as is) may *contradict* cultural values (should be).[50] What people do can be the *opposite* of what they believe. Knowing the values of a culture cannot guarantee that we will know about the practices in that culture, because culture is more than a set of values.[51] Observing the practices of a culture cannot guarantee that we will know about the values in that culture, because the outward expressions can mislead us.

Outward expressions can be misleading as they do not always match values. A change of outward expressions does not readily reflect a genuine change of values, and vice versa.

CASE STUDY

There have been many metaphors of culture in the history of intercultural communication. Three popular ones are the "iceberg,"[52-53] the "software of the mind" and the "onion."[54] The floating iceberg has its tip visible above the water and can be seen as representing outward expressions. Most of its mass is submerged under the water. These are the values that we cannot see. The metaphor implies that we are misled by what we can see with our own eyes (i.e. the small tip of the iceberg) and catastrophes can happen when we collide with the mass, deep underwater.

The software metaphor posits that culture can be seen as a program hardwired in our mind. Our culture dictates our values, behaviors and outward expressions. Once "installed," this cultural software runs our psyche with distinguished traits that are persistent and difficult to change.

An onion has four layers. The three outer layers are practices that are easy to change, similar to the outward expressions in our tree metaphor. The core of the onion, which is very stable, represents values.

1. Which cultural paradigm do these two metaphors belong to?
2. Metaphors are powerful in guiding behaviors.[55-56-57] For example, when you tell people that *Crime is a Virus*, they propose solutions such as: finding the root causes, eradicating poverty and investing in education. Why? Because when "crime" is framed as a "virus," our brain connects it with an illness that needs care and treatment. However, when you tell people that *Crime is a Beast*, they want to solve the problem by trying to catch and imprison the

criminals, and by enacting harsher enforcement laws.[58] A beast needs punishment rather than care and treatment.

Bearing this in mind, what are the advantages and disadvantages of the iceberg, the software, the onion and the tree in presenting the concept of culture? What could be the behavioral consequences of these metaphors?

3. Let's be creative and develop your own metaphor of culture. In doing so, take into account fundamental factors such as the dynamic of culture, context and the power of metaphors in guiding action.

2.3   The inverted pyramid model

One of the major points for debate in the study of cross-cultural communication is the skewed focus on culture as a purely group phenomenon. This approach underscores the roles of what we all share as humans and the role of individuals. With regard to the former, it is crucial to remember that from a biological point of view, culture has evolved fundamental components that all human groups on earth share and are motivated to care about. This is the trunk and the roots of our metaphorical tree. With regard to the latter, we may argue that the end point that internalizes and externalizes cultural values in any cross-cultural incident is related to the *mind*, which, in every case, is individual.[59] Hence, to avoid the group-orientation bias, in this section, we will construct a framework called the *Inverted Pyramid Model*. This enables us to achieve a holistic and systematic view of culture across all three levels of analysis: universal, collective, and individual.

2.3.1   The Universal Level

Inspired by a work of Hofstede (three levels of mental programming),[60] figure 2.3 shows us an inverted pyramid with three layers. We will start with the bottom one, where we will incorporate our metaphorical tree of culture. The universal layer of culture indicates concerns, values and outward expressions that we all share as human beings, regardless of our background. It signals similarities as the starting point, springboard and foundation for communication. However, this approach is not a conventional one. In cultural trainings, differences have been the driver in motivating people to understand intercultural exchange. So why are differences, and not similarities, considered the starting point? The answer can be found in history.

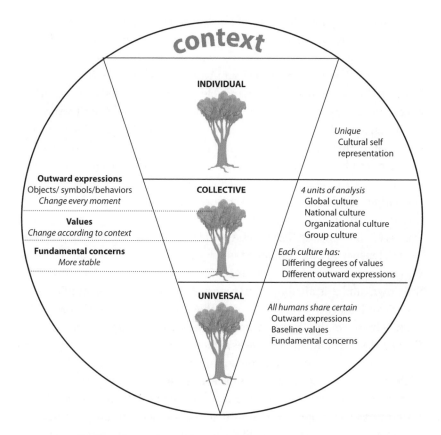

Figure 2.3. The Inverted Pyramid Model

2.3.1.1   *Differences as Starting Point*

After the Second World War and as the Cold War began, two major powers emerged with fierce competition between opposing ideologies, led by the Soviet Union and the US. International diplomacy was characterized by distrust, tension and readiness for reprisal. In *Beyond Culture*, Edward Hall, the founding father of intercultural communication, opened his classic book with alarming crises, conflicts and potential turmoil. The relationship between the different sides was so hostile that he even described the emergence of China, Japan and Latin America and their "[...] demand to be recognized in their own right" as a "crisis."[61]

In this context, the history of intercultural communication study began at the US Foreign Service Institute in the 1950s. At this time, it was clear that the Americans had shortcomings on the diplomatic front compared to the Russians. While 90 per cent of all Russian diplomatic staff, including secretaries and chauffeurs, spoke the local language where they were posted, the American diplomatic corps seldom learned the language or the culture of the country to which they were assigned.[62] Hall was employed to educate American diplomats about how and why cultural differences could contribute to the failure of their missions. And thus, a new discipline was born.

Given this context, it is understandable why Hall regarded cultural differences as a starting point. Here, the "difference" is far from the positive impact of "diversity" or the joy of "curiosity and exploration," but the kind of difference that implicitly tells you: "Here is the list of potential problems that you should be ready to deal with. Good luck!" Accordingly, his iceberg metaphor for culture (see case study in the previous section) has a psychological basis that emphasizes the "dark side" of culture and the adverse consequences of differences. By indicating that the hidden part of the iceberg is also the most critical component and the true essence of a culture, this metaphor prepares for a defensive and reactionary state of mind, typical of the Cold War era. Culture is important, but it is a danger and a mystery. It is hidden, invisible, unknown, and it is all about differences. For those who are familiar with American historical events, the metaphor triggers a connection with the sinking in 1912 of the Titanic, after colliding with an iceberg in the Atlantic Ocean, which resulted in the deaths of more than 1,500 passengers and crew.

The "difference and problem-focused view" of culture has guided much of the theory development and empirical testing in the literature of intercultural management and communication. The result is that research and training have been dominated by problems and such terms as "cultural distance,"[63] "cultural misfit," "liability of foreignness," or the "consequences"[64] when cultures "collide."[65] A content analysis of 1,141 articles from 1989–2012 reveals a 17:1 imbalance of negative over positive theoretical research assumptions on the role of culture in international business contexts.[66] Liabilities are associated with cultural differences by the underlying assumption that differences are a source of problem, cost, risk, danger, and difficulties. In the same vein, a prominent theorist in the field clearly stated that "culture is more often a source of conflict than of synergy" and "cultural differences are a nuisance at best and often a disaster."[67] Consequently, the focus of intercultural training has been mainly about helping clients to navigate around dangerous icebergs. It is no coincidence that most books on intercultural management are illustrated *entirely* using mishaps and blunders in which cultural differences are the culprit.

This approach is not always helpful. As we briefly discussed in the case study above, metaphors and their associated theories are powerful in guiding behaviors and collective experience.[68] In a self-fulfilling prophecy, the way we describe cultural differences as problems may lead to the way we subconsciously create exactly the kind of culture that sees "others" as potentially problematic.[69] Furthermore, it runs counter to the purpose of inspiring people to explore the world, to engage willingly, and to see the benefit of diversity. While evidence of the positive impact of cultural differences is abundant,[70-71-72-73-74] focusing on the dark side of the interaction may do our brain a disservice, by preparing us to be reactive rather than proactive, defensive rather than cooperative, viewing differences as problems rather than opportunities.

2.3.1.2 *Similarities as Starting Point*

In Chapter 1, we discussed how cultural diversity plays a critical role in helping us recognize our own ingroups. Seeking similarities is natural in interpersonal communication since they form a basis for trust and provide signals that cultural resources will be shared fairly. This tendency happens so early that two-day-old infants prefer their mother's face to that of a female stranger.[75] Since culture is our survival strategy, ingroup bias is rooted in our evolution and we have evolved to love our culture and those who look and think in a similar way to us.[76-77]

From a psychological point of view, the "law of attraction"[78] suggests that "birds of a feather flock together."[79] We are attracted to and favor those who share similar traits, be it physical appearance,[80] attitude,[81] or personality.[82] Similar others are more likely to have opinions and worldviews that *validate* our own; thus, interaction with similar others is an important source of social reinforcement and self-affirmation. The "just like me" bias[83] in hiring is a good example, which shows how employers (sub)consciously search for cultural similarities in job candidates and favor those who share similar traits and backgrounds.

Does that mean we are unable to recognize the benefit of differences? Of course not, but it takes strategies and time. As we know, our fear detective device (amygdala) decides whether we like a subject or a person before our rational brain (cerebral cortex) has time to step in.[84] *But,* if we can strategically give the amygdala as few reasons as possible to be alarmed, with time, the cortex can then communicate nicely with the amygdala and exchange finer, richer information for a more thorough understanding and in-depth exploration. Consider this example: Soon after taking office, your new manager starts talking about restructuring the work process. Your amygdala immediately screams: "Watch out! (S)he is going to turn my whole world upside down!" Hopefully, your cerebral cortex will have the time and receive further information to bring you back to the ground: "Oh wait, but maybe (s)he has a point about *why* we need to do so! Maybe we share some baseline of values in having to change the way we normally do things around here!" Knowing how the amygdala and the cerebral cortex work, what would you do if you were the manager? Would you seek shared goals and consensus first, or would you declare a revolution?

In sum, it is not differences, but positive similarities that can initially trigger cooperation and a potential relationship. Consequently, identifying mutual objectives, backgrounds, practices and interests should be an essential skill when communicating internationally. At this level, the tree metaphor represents those "universal and fundamental" [85-86] concerns, *baseline values and similar outward expressions* that are shared by all, understood by all and agreed by all, regardless of our cultural backgrounds. We are essentially the same in the sense that we have to deal with basically similar problems, with more or less the same inherited biological capacity as human beings, supported by more or less the same basic social structures that are our survival strategies, motivated by more or less the same willingness to get them solved. We may choose different ways to deal with these issues, at the roots and deep from within, at this universal level, we are the same. The emphasis on knowing cultural differences should be balanced with the need to establish a foundation of fellowship, sameness, like-mindedness and connection. It is a springboard from which to approach differences more effectively, with the fundamental understanding that *we are not different in kind, only in level.*

The European Union received the Nobel Peace Prize in 2012 for its achievement in transforming Europe "from a continent of war to a continent of peace." Starting with the Coal and Steel Community, six formerly rival countries (Belgium, France, Germany, Italy, Luxembourg, and the Netherlands) were bonded by mutual interests that would make any wars among them not merely unthinkable, but materially impossible/"Café in Baarle-Nassau" – This border town comprises 22 enclaves that belong to Belgium and 8 enclaves that belong to the Netherlands, the borders are marked on the ground – JÉRÔME.[87]

The starting point for fruitful intercultural exchanges should be built upon similari-
ties at the universal level. This creates a foundation of trust, acting as a positive
springboard that helps us to see diversity and differences in a positive light.

2.3.2   The Collective Level

The second layer of the Inverted Pyramid model is *collective*. At this level, we start to differ from each other to various degrees. Most intercultural studies focus on this level with a strong emphasis on the diversity among different national cultures. We will discuss here what the "tree of culture" looks like at this level, and whether nation/country is the only unit for identifying culture.

2.3.2.1   *Culture at the Collective Level*

While the universal level represents the baseline on which we all agree, the collective level differs from that *baseline*. Let's take "fidelity" as an example. At the universal level, fidelity is a concern for all societies. There is also a degree of importance attached to fidelity, which means we can all agree that fidelity should at least be placed on the baseline level. Further, there are some universal outward expressions of fidelity that we can all agree upon, for example, fidelity may express itself through partners being physically or spiritually together.

At the collective level, while this concern persists (the trunk and roots of the tree), each culture or context differs from the universal baseline by placing differing degrees of importance on this concern, projecting "low," "average" or "high" values for fidelity (the branches of the tree), which are manifested in different outward expressions (the leaves of the tree).

Here is another example: Historically, polygyny (one man with multiple wives) is popular in societies with abundant low-yielding communal land farmed by labor-intensive technologies. This type of family structure takes advantage of the significant agricultural surpluses. The more wives and children, the more land can be tended, the larger and more affluent a family can become. Sexual fidelity of the wives is not a top priority, as all children born to a man's wives are legally his. In this model, childbearing is much more of an essential concern than it is in other societies, since each additional wife and her children permit the family to farm more territory and to achieve economies of scale in domestic labor and trade. Compare this with other societies that have traditional subsistence agriculture on privately owned farms. They tend to practice monogamous marriage (one wife and one husband) with stronger cultural safeguards for the sexual fidelity of women, because it is important that limited family lands be passed on to those who genuinely share a bloodline.[88]

This example shows us that the collective level differs from the minimum baseline that we all share at the universal level. At the same time, we should bear in mind the deciding factor of context. For "fidelity," the observation of this value and its outward expressions only apply in this specific case of family structure, during a specific time in history. It is not an absolute rule, and it is changeable, since particular contexts in different parts of the world must be factored in, and culture can be very dynamic.

2.3.2.2   Four Units of Analysis at the Collective Level

When we talk about a culture, many of us tend to associate it with a nation. However, we can broaden this view and take a more sophisticated approach to culture. Imagine at this level of the Inverted Pyramid model that there are at least four trees of collective culture:

Global Culture. As the world becomes increasingly interconnected, exposure to global cultures affords many individuals opportunities to develop global identities.[89-90] Interestingly, "citizen of the world" is not a new concept. The first person who claimed to be a "global citizen" is probably philosopher Diogenes (412 BC), who was born in Sinop, modern-day Turkey, and became famous in Athens (Greece). He shares with the global citizens of our modern era the idea that personal identity can transcend geography, religious, and political borders.

The fundamental concerns that global citizens hold dear are universal: education, self-confidence, pragmatism, flexibility, diversity tolerance, democracy, social justice, sustainability and global awareness.[91-92-93] However, among the members of this global culture, these concerns project a *higher degree of importance* on the associated values. Imagine a tree for this "global culture" at the collective level of the Inverted Pyramid model: the branches for these values are big and strong, so to speak. The leaves of the tree for global culture would represent their specific practices, such as advocating for women's right, fighting against climate change, engaging in social enterprise, supporting corporate social responsibility, building a caring economy, etc.

In comparison with other collective cultures, global citizens are self-selected, choosing to attach, and thus they differ from other cultural memberships in the sense that they are involved in enculturation, by consciously adjusting their values and behaviors. However, global citizens do not abandon their other identities such as being a member of a country, an ethnicity, an organization or a social group. These identities continue to give meaning to their lives and define who they are. That is why, at the collective level of the Inverted Pyramid model, we have more than just one unit of analysis.

National Culture. Cultural diversity has been strongly associated with national borderlines, i.e. "the Lithuanians" are this way and "the Macedonians" are that way. This is because most available literature is organized around the concept of the nation state. However, the practice of using the nation state as a proxy independent variable has been criticized, because it underestimates variations *within* a culture.[94] In fact, "country" only explains 20 per cent of the differences, leaving 80 per cent of the variation for individual diversity and circumstances.[95] Besides, associating a culture with its geographical territory implies that each culture or civilization has its own genealogy by developing separately and independently from others.[96] The current borderlines are more man-made than culturally defined. After all, "nation state" is a new concept that dates from the 19th century. Before that, much of the world was dominated by multi-ethnic societies such as the British-, the Mongol-, and the Ottoman Empires, the Abbasid Caliphate, or the Qing dynasty, etc. with a population belonging to many ethnic groups and speaking many languages.[97] Nowadays, old countries disappear and new countries announce their independence more regularly than one would expect. We saw a burst of 16 new countries after the fall of the Soviet Union and Yugoslavia. The possibility of splitting is inherent in many other multicultural societies, such as the UK, where a referendum in 2014 nearly resulted in Scotland becoming an independent country, with 44.7 per cent of voters favoring their own, separate nation state.[98]

While it is problematic to use "country" as a proxy independent variable, it is arguably still the most practical and convenient method due to the availability of national data. For this reason, we still employ the concept in this book as *one* way to identify cultures.

Organizational Culture. Most of us are members of one or several organizations. The tree of an organization has all the components of a typical culture. While fundamental concerns universally exist (roots and trunks), each organization places a differing degree of importance on them, creating differing values (branches) and different practices (leaves).

The notion of culture as a survival strategy (see Chapter 1) is clearly visible in this unit of analysis. Many studies have proved that a strong organizational culture is the powerhouse for driving performance,[99] a weapon for competing with other companies and the glue that brings every employee together. People work for money, but they also work for what they truly believe in.[100] How one feels is often more important than how much one earns. A congruence between the values/practices of the organization and that of the employees (Person-Organization Fit) results in a source of pride, motivation, work effectiveness[101] and creativity.[102] For example, a study of Indian IT workers shows that they are more loyal to the company because it values their heritage and uniqueness.[103] In contrast, a weak and negative organizational culture is a barrier to growth and performance.

Since culture is seen as a tool to boost performance, organizational culture can be very dynamic. Strategic management policies often aim at promoting innovation and adjustment in order to respond to constantly changing environment.[104] Mergers, acquisitions, new markets, disruptive technologies, social and political changes, etc. are among many forces that demand organizations to be versatile and adaptive. For example, with the majority of the modern workforce comprised of millennials, organizations should foster values that this demographic find important: flexibility, creativity and social responsibility. Since they are also digital natives, outward expressions such as technology-based tools and platforms should replace traditional working environments. This means virtual cooperation, wireless workplaces and creative ways to foster relationships instead of face-to-face contact.

CASE STUDY

FPT is a multinational information technology company in Vietnam with branches in 20 countries and an annual revenue of more than 2 billion US dollars. On its website, FPT emphasizes that culture is the power of company.[105] Its top executive cites an example when FPT was disqualified from an important business deal. Instead of giving up, the CEO invited the contractor to join one of the company's communal gathering. Witnessing how managers and staff were closely bonded as they sang cheerfully with each other, the contractor changed his mind: "This wonderful spirit will overcome any shortcomings. I want to re-open the deal with you."[106]

So what is the culture that FPT sees as a weapon for growth and development? The company is famous for having an extremely casual and satirical way of communication. Employees confront managers directly and openly in staff meetings. They also make fun of managers in a series of parody songs and stunts. Satire reigns during the regular company parties, flying in the face of social taboos. In a famous incident, employees congratulated a bride – also an executive – with a parody toast, adopting a funereal tone and satirical wishes.[107]

While many outsiders consider this culture disrespectful and inappropriate, FPT employees and managers seem to regard it as a sign of intimacy and an effective tool for building camaraderie.

1. What are the concerns, values and outward expressions of FPT's organizational culture?*
2. What are the stereotypical values and outward expressions of Vietnam as a national culture with regard to those issues mentioned in (1)?
3. What conclusion can you draw from comparing (1) and (2)?

(*) See again an example of identifying concerns, values, and outward expressions in the first summary box in section 2.

Group Culture. Each of us belongs to many different communities. It can be *ethnicity* (e.g. almost 20 per cent of the Dutch population are immigrants or children of immigrant parents), *religion* (e.g. Muslims account for 18 per cent of the population in Israel), *sexual orientation* (e.g. 2.5 per cent of Australia's men and 2.2 per cent its women self-identify as gay, lesbian or bisexual[108]), *location* (e.g. regional culture), *profession* (e.g. army culture), *age* (e.g. teenage culture), *capacity* (e.g. deaf culture), *lifestyle* (e.g. gothic culture), etc.

Group culture can either be a *co-culture* or a *dominant culture* (mainstream culture). The dominant culture refers to a group that usually has the greatest amount of control, but not necessarily the biggest group in size. Take Bahrain for example: 70 per cent of the population in this oil-rich Gulf kingdom are Shia Muslims, but the rulers, the majority of the government officers, military, and influential businesses are Sunni Muslims. Similarly, white males now constitute only 34 per cent of the US population, but their positions of power allow them to control most of the cultural messages and the political decision-making process, and thus they influence others' thinking and doing.

2.3.3   The Individual Level

The third layer of the Inverted Pyramid is *individual*. At this level, we not only differ from each other in group-pattern but every single one of us differs completely from one another. Each person is unique and different, even among those who share the same collective system. A man born and raised in Saudi Arabia may not embrace the stereotypical collective values and practices such as having a strong tribal attachment, being an ardent believer, wearing the traditional *thawb* and *bisht*, etc. It is hard to overemphasize that *people are more than their cultures*. No matter how dominant and pervasive a value is within a society, you will always see individuals whose values and outward expressions completely contradict what the majority in that culture appear to adhere to.

A person can be a member of multiple collective cultures, have *multiple identities*, and is able to self-develop in a culturally selective way. A French citizen can be French, Moroccan, Muslim, Arab, Parisian, police officer, mother, vegetarian and a pro-choice activist… all at the same time. And this particular person can relentlessly develop her own profile, selecting her most responsive identities, even constructing new identities or adding layers to existing ones in order to deal with a myriad of situations in her daily life. The same goes for everyone else. At this point, it is useful to remind ourselves of the plasticity of our brain (see Chapter 1), and the dynamic way behaviors influence our values, and vice versa. People change, culture evolves, hence, the best label for any individual is her/his name, and not her/his culture.

2.3.4   Observing Culture from all Three Analysis Levels

Any attempt to understand cross-cultural issues should take into account a holistic view of all three analysis layers, since they provide us with a big picture and, at the same time, keep track of important details. Consider this example: Many of us tend to blame certain business cultures for being corrupt and prone to bribes – a criticism that indirectly assumes that we are the opposite. In fact, the Inverted Pyramid model tells us that corruption exists everywhere (universal), but that it is more obvious in a particular culture and less in others (collective). There is also no absolute foundation for assuming that a business partner, despite coming from a culture with a reputation for practicing bribes, is going to accept bribes (individual). Everyone can differ from the cultural baggage (s)he was born into, to the point that there is no such thing as, say, a 100 per cent typical Croatian or Moldovan.

Moreover, the differences between us can all be traced back to the baseline of similarities we share at the universal level. We may obey authority in different ways but, ultimately, obedience towards authorities is universal. We may express love for our country in different ways but, ultimately, patriotism is universal. It is impossible to overemphasize that *we are not different in kind, we are just different in level*.

The Inverted Pyramid model of culture analysis has three layers:

- *Universal: The tree metaphor here indicates fundamental concerns, a baseline of values and outward expressions that we all share and agree upon.*
- *Collective: There are four units of analysis: global culture; national culture; organizational culture; and group culture (dominant and co-cultures). While the nature of concerns remain, the tree metaphor here places differing levels of importance on those concerns, leading to a diversity in values and different outward expressions.*
- *Individual: Each person is both a product of a culture AND an active agent in shaping her/his culture. Each person's "tree of culture" is unique, and is never a perfect representation of any of her/his collective cultures.*

CASE STUDY

Simon is the English name of Ahmad – a 45-year-old single man born and raised in Egypt. He comes from a Shia family – a Muslim sect that accounts for around 8 per cent of the Egyptian population. He is currently in Canada, on a six-month business assignment with a partner company. He quickly fits into the Canadian culture. He feels at home and often drinks wine with his host family. He openly admires the way Canadian people embrace freedom of speech and the effectiveness of social welfare. He wishes that Egyptians would voice their opinion more liberally, and that Egypt would close the inequality gap with a more caring economy. At the weekend, he regularly cooks for friends and his host family, proudly showing that hospitality is a wonderful aspect of the Egyptian culture, something that other cultures are short of.

To analyze this case, we need to take a holistic and systematic view. Here is an example with "freedom of speech":

Universal level
- Concern for "freedom of speech"
- Value is held at an abstract baseline that we all agree upon
- Outward expressions can be verbal expression of personal opinion such as "I think…"

Collective level (national culture of Egypt)
- Concern for "freedom of speech"
- Stereotypical value can be "low," "average" or "high" depending on your argument, bearing in mind particular contexts
- Outward expressions are not included in the text. You can find examples to back up your arguments

Individual level (Simon)
- Concern for "freedom of speech"
- Value is "high"
- Outward expressions include "verbally praising"

1. Continue to analyze this case study according to the tree metaphor and the Inverted Pyramid model with other universal concerns such as "social welfare," "differences in gender's role," and "hospitality." You are encouraged to use the internet for more information.
2. At the collective level, how many cultures are there that Simon can be a member of?
3. Imagine that Simon and someone have a disagreement on the fundamental concerns of "freedom of speech" and "hospitality," what can you say to bring them closer to each other and bridge their differences?
4. Imagine that you are going to start working with Simon next week on a project, please make a list of what you should do to prepare for a good working relationship. Use theories to explain.
5. Bearing in mind the plasticity of culture, the dynamics of values and outward expressions, what are the advantages that Simon has while working in Canada? What are the advantages that his partner company has by hosting him?

2.4   Culture and international business

In Chapter 1, we learned that globalization is not new, but that in the modern era it is driven by different factors, such as the speed of technology, rapid changes in global demography and the emergence of a global economy. However, globalization does not necessarily erase diversity. From a biological perspective, diversity is a regulator for: (1) safeguarding cultural resources, recognizing who we can trust; and (2) negotiating cultural resources with other groups for mutual interests. Effective resource management can lead to both a dividing and a merging of cultures. Reviewing the history of mankind, while the merging of cultures seem to be winning the race over a *long* period of time, diversity persists. Local cultures interact with the force of globalization in a very dynamic and complex way, a tug of war, *a negotiation rather than a straightforward linear process*. That is why despite the overwhelming power of globalization, we still need to pay attention to collective cultures and the role of individuals.

2.4.1   The Persistence of Diversity

While the merging of cultures is easy to see in the process of globalization, the dividing of culture is an interesting aspect. The global economy has unfurled a closely interwoven network of interdependent business and trade. However, it is wrong to assume that we are already living in a global village and globalization is nullifying cultural boundaries. On the contrary, globalization can be the very reason for the revival of local culture identities.

At the collective level of the Inverted Pyramid model, when different values come into direct contact they can either merge or clash with each other. In many cases, the latter would lead to a reinforcement of their own distinct traits. The first reason is that cultural values can change, but not as fast as outward expressions. For example, it has been pointed out that we tend to converge until societies reach a tipping point, and from this point we start to diverge according to our local culture's norms and values. Most poor countries share a preference for low-priced, high-quality products rather than high-priced, added-value brands. However, as such countries become richer and more educated, consumers start to pick products that fit more with their own cultural preferences and tradition.[109] For example, after reaching the tipping point, the spread of satellite TV in India actually increased the popularity of regional channels and, consequently, led to local cultural awareness.[110] When people possess a sufficiency of everything, they will spend their discretionary income on what most *fits their value patterns*.

Even when people seem to buy the same products (read: outward expressions), they may use it for different reasons (read: values). Billions of people use Facebook, but this social media channel is a private friend-and-family zone in some cultures, while it is fully interwoven with business in others. In Shanghai, IKEA managers had to ban old people from turning its café into a dating club.[111] These lonely, divorced or widowed elderly people could not find their peers in KFC or McDonald and so, IKEA became an ideal place to hang around. This example shows that a global brand and its facilities may look the same everywhere, but they sell localized products and carry different status and meanings in different contexts.

While globalization can homogenize values and cultures, in many cases they are merely the frequency of similar outward expressions in our tree metaphor across the whole world. Change can be an illusion, as we can never be sure if external changes also reflect a change of values. Business people who think customers are a globally homogenized mass of consumers are simply the birds that fly over the forest, seeing many trees that have similar patterns of leaves and canopies, and think to themselves: "Yes! I have seen the trees. They are all the same!"

The second reason for the revival of local cultures despite globalization has to do with the conscious appreciation of our own culture when the contrast is *overwhelming*. When we are safely inside our own culture, we tend to take it for granted, like the air we breathe. But imagine that you are in water. The moment we submerge our heads in the water is the moment we realize what our own culture means to us, what our air means to us. Similarly, a fish will not understand the meaning of water until it finds itself on the ground. This is the moment where the differences between our culture and the new culture are obvious, undeniable and striking. The contrast put things into perspective. We start to realize who we actually are, what norms and values we actually have. Many expatriates profess that they understand their culture better during the times they are living abroad. Therefore, in order to be culturally competent, knowing one's own culture is not really a good starting point, but having a chance to compare and experience both similarities and differences of diverse cultures.

While many of us are able to see the benefit of coming into contact with new cultures, others may feel an imbalance of power and regard this cultural contact as a *threat* to the stability and order of society. They may choose to react conservatively in response to the unfair trading of cultural knowledge. We have witnessed many communities with a tendency to shield and protect their traditions by distancing themselves from modernity. Here is an example: In 1948, a devout Muslim teacher from Egypt by the name of Sayyid Qutb was granted a college fellowship in the US. He arrived with a benign view of the country, but witnessed what he saw as a society devoid of ethics, a clash between the sacred Old and the immoral New world. He returned to Egypt, where he refined a radical political theology that sees the solution for the modern era in what happened in the glorious past, inspiring and laying the foundation for an ideology that has become a global headache: jihadism.[112]

The third reason why local culture revives in the face of globalization has to do with the issue of identity. This is best understood by looking at The United Arab Emirates (UAE). As a barren desert, the UAE has never been a major stage of civilization. In 1971, seven autonomous sheikhdoms, consisting of several tribes from all around the peninsula, were challenged with the task of establishing a national identity based on a thin desert history. Islam was seen as the primary binding force to the newly formed nation, lending moral and legal substance to the fragile national culture.

The author of this book witnessed a start-up in Dubai whose founder actively donned a *hijab* because she wanted to convince customers that she was an ambitious *Emirati* woman. When the search for an Emirati identity ended up pretty swiftly on Islamic ground, she took a dramatic turn and completely changed her way of life. Her entire wardrobe was thrown out and replaced with a new one, all previous pictures on Facebook were erased. The young entrepreneur set out on a greater mission to show people how a true Emirati woman can also be progressive, liberal, honest and advanced: "If I appeared like I used to be, nobody would take me serious. They would immediately regard me as a non-Emirati. If I want to influence, I need to be seen as an Emirati. And being an Emirati means being a Muslim." As we can see, religion does not just replace the UAE's national history, it defines it and is a source for the people to dwell on in their search for identity.

Outnumbered by an expat population that is seven times larger than the local population, many Emiratis are conscious of not losing themselves in the melting pot. Instead, they shun foreign values and outward expressions, adhering to Islamic traditions as a way to reinforce the newly constructed national identity/ "Dubai market, (UAE)," MAI NGUYEN-PHUONG-MAI.

Combining the reasons, it is understandable why co-cultures can be persistent and powerful, despite the influence of the dominant culture. In many African and Middle Eastern countries, tribal and ethnic groups still define people's identities. Countries with an immigrant history often have ethnic enclaves or pockets of co-cultures, such as a vibrant Asian district, Slavic village, French quarter, Little Saigon, Lithuanian plaza, gay village, Mormon corridor, retirement community, hippie haven, etc. International business is not going to be homogenized in a global village. In fact, we cannot talk about global business without making it *glocal* business. As Kevin Roberts, CEO of Saatchi & Saatchi said: "Anyone who wants to go global has to understand the local. People live in the local. I've never met a global consumer. I never expect to. We define ourselves by our differences. It's called identity."[113]

The top two layers of the Inverted Pyramid model (collective and individual) interact with globalization in a dynamic way, a contextual give-and-take negotiation rather than a straightforward linear process towards a merging of cultures. Factors that reinforce collective culture and individual identities include, but are not limited to:

- *market activities that fit stakeholders' values*
- *reaction to cultural contrast*
- *reinforcement of identities*

2.4.2   Think Global – Plan Local – Act Individual

Savvy business people know that it's easier for their product to win if it taps into a human motivation or interest that is universally shared across cultures, regardless of the context. This notion of "think global" resonates with our Inverted Pyramid model and the tree metaphor in the sense that it regards universal concerns and similarities as the starting point of communication. Of course, universal concerns may still demand different expressions and carry differing degrees of importance across cultures and contexts, manifesting in a dynamics of values. This is where "plan local" needs to align with cultural identity and local engagement. To win people's hearts, you must engage them on their own terms and in their own languages. "Think global" and "plan local" go hand in hand on the road to success. Companies that move too far in the direction of global consistency may be disadvantaged when competing with local brands and, vice versa, companies that rely heavily on culturally specific identities and connections will be ill-equipped to expand their market beyond borders.

However, business does not stop at the "local." The end contact is always a specific person: a customer, a partner, or a colleague, etc. Each individual engages in social interaction with an incredible complexity, since (s)he is both a product and a creator of her/his culture. This person may subconsciously follow the values of any collective cultures that (s)he is a member of, but can also react in a contradictory way, depending on a particular context. Most of us choose to overcome this complexity by employing a very natural mechanism called *stereotyping*. In our Inverted Pyramid model, it equates to an erroneous attempt at understanding the individual level by using the collective level. Utilizing an incorrect level of analysis means we falsely assume everyone in a particular cultural group is the same (he behaves like that because he is a "man," "atheist," "Liberian," "black," "old," "expat," "artist," etc.), or we falsely assume some particular action represents the whole group (the Asians in movies knows martial arts, so Asians can fight). Of course this is wrong, but most of us are prone to do it anyway, because of our fear of everything we cannot control and understand. The fact that we can give this unknown element a collective name makes it less threatening and manageable.

We will discuss more about stereotyping later in this book. We will also delve deeper into different mechanisms and processes such as *cultural intelligence* to overcome the need to stereotype, to deal with cultural shock in the long term. Competent business people will skillfully develop themselves through the process of cultural sensitivity, and interact mindfully with the social context in which they operate. At the starting point of any business endeavor, they will begin by building a crucial foundation of *universality*, which connects all stakeholders, seeks similarities, recognizes fundamental sameness, and nurtures a willingness to tackle shared concerns and benefits from mutual interests.

From this solid platform, they move on to plan for the unavoidable diversity in various local *collective* cultures that they will encounter. They are enriched with knowledge about general trademarks of the activist culture, Hispanic culture, academic culture, hip-hop culture, LGBTQ culture, etc. They may prepare their marketing campaigns, sale strategies and social responsibility programs according to this repertoire of knowledge about local collectivities. However, the moment they are confronted with an *individual* interaction, such as greeting a colleague, discussing with the team, convincing a customer, emailing a partner, etc., they are ready to strip off much of the collective navigation and cultural baggage. Because they know each individual is very different, capable of carrying on along opposing values and practices, acting dynamically and even contradictorily, depending on particular contexts.

We can term this process of cultural competence as "Think global – Plan local – Act individual," which corresponds with the three layers of our Inverted Pyramid model. It may sound easy, but it is not. The fact that up to 40 per cent of expatriates return home before the completion of their foreign assignments, mainly due to their failure to adjust to the host culture, shows that working in international business can be challenging.[114] And it is costly too, as for each failed assignment, the damage for multinational enterprises is between $40,000 and $1million.

None of us want to be one of those 40 per cent who return home before the deal is sealed. Nor do we want to be the reason for costing our organization resources because a working term is cut short. Our goal is to be successful in the new age of management, which is no longer the management of work, but is now the management of people. And if people are both products and producers of their cultures, then this interaction between people and culture is what we will need to know.

Summary

1. The "tree of culture" metaphor has three main components: *Fundamental concerns* are many cultural notions that act as building blocks of a culture, such as "hierarchy." *Values* are the degree of importance each society, individual or context places on these concerns (e.g. low, average or high on "hierarchy"). *Outward expressions* are visible manifestations of these concerns and values (e.g. respectful behaviors towards authority). Context aside, fundamental concerns are stable, values are dynamic, but outwards expressions change fastest of all.

2. Context is the main indicator for predicting change within and between cultures, for understanding paradoxes and contrasting values/outwards expressions that simultaneously co-exist.

3. Outward expressions can be misleading because what we see can be both "what it is" and "what it is not." A change in outward expressions does not readily reflect a change of values, and vice versa.

4. The Inverted Pyramid model has three layers:
   - *Universal:* The tree metaphor here indicates concerns, baseline values, and outward expressions that we all share and agree on.
   - *Collective:* There are four units of analysis (global culture; national culture; organizational culture; group culture [dominant and co-culture]), each can be represented by a metaphorical tree that has differing levels of importance placed on concerns, projecting a diversity of values and outward expressions.
   - *Individual:* each person is unique, with a tree metaphor that is never a perfect reflection or representation of any of her/his collective cultures.

5. Collective cultures and individual cultural identities (top two layers of the Inverted Pyramid model) interact with globalization in a dynamic way, a contextual give-and-take negotiation rather than a straightforward linear process heading towards a merging of cultures.

6. In international business contexts, factors that reinforce collective cultures
   and individual identities vary, including:
   - market activities that fit stakeholders' values rather than just financial
     capacity.
   - reaction to cultural contrast and clash.
   - reinforcement of identities.
7. To cope with the complexity of international communication, a general
   guideline is: *"Think global – Plan local – Act individual."*

3.   Stereotype – A Necessary Evil

Objective

At the end of this chapter, you should be able to:

·   Explain the origin of stereotypes and prejudices from biology's point of view.
·   Explain the pitfall of stereotypes and prejudices with accurate examples.
·   Given a specific case, recognize stereotypes, prejudices and explain the reasons.
·   Given a specific case, propose alternative solutions.
·   Describe strategies to live with stereotypes and reduce prejudices.

Chapter outline

Everybody knows a joke that stereotypes a cultural group. The most common is the one about "Heaven and Hell":

> Heaven is a place where: The police are British, the chefs are French, the lovers are Italian, and everything is organized by the Germans.
> Hell is a place where: The police are French, the chefs are British, the lovers are Germans, and everything is organized by the Italians.

The fact that people in each cited country can laugh about this suggests that there is at least a grain of truth in this joke. In general, many of us have an overwhelmingly stereotypical perception that the Italians are both erotic and chaotic, and that the Germans are slightly better than the Italians at structuring their lives, but at the same time can be quite uptight about expressing emotion. As for the British, their gastronomy is not quite on par with that of the French (in fact, French cuisine is so tasty that it has been awarded World Heritage status by UNESCO), but the British are known for seeing authority as a professional privilege, while the French may perceive authority more as a right and make it less open to question.

Jokes aside, why do we form stereotypes? Are they all bad? How do stereotypes lead to prejudices and discrimination? What are the consequences? What can we do to deal with this tendency to lump people together, to judge? And what can we do to make sure this inner voice does not transform into discriminatory behavior? These are the questions that we will address in this chapter. These issues are essential in cross-cultural communication, not only because *nobody* can avoid stereotypes, but also because the biological mechanism behind them can both enrich and impede us, and, when stereotypes escalate to prejudices and discrimination, they can destroy us and others.

3.1   Stereotype

A stereotype is a fixed, oversimplified idea about a particular social category or collective culture that strongly influences our expectation and behaviors.[1]

At the second level of the Inverted Pyramid model, all units of analysis (global, national, organizational and group culture) are subjected to this tendency of being seen as a homogeneous mass: what "men" and "women" can do, what "young" and "old" people can achieve, or how a particular "profession" can be an indicator of an individual's personality. This is not a new phenomenon, and it is there for a reason.

3.1.1   The Origin of the Stereotype

We will incorporate insight from evolutionary biology and neuroscience to gain a more thorough understanding of what stereotypes are really about.

3.1.1.1   A Survival Skill

At the origins of the human race, in Africa, our ancestors were constantly coping with situations that required them to react quickly and avoid danger. A rattle in the bush signals a poisonous snake or a dangerous predator, and it would be much wiser to run away, rather than stay and investigate what the curious noise is. Better safe than sorry. Such a cautious reaction is probably the *wrong response* 99.9 per cent of the time (there is, usually, no snake), but it only takes a single occasion for the guess to be correct to save a life. This tendency to make such a systematic error is called *bias.*

Thus, stereotyping has evolved as a survival mechanism that allows our brain to make a snap judgment based on the immediately visible characteristics of a situation. We are in the "bush," the territory is known to have "predators," and we can't see what/who caused the "rattle." These bits of information (bush, predators, rattle) are sent to our brain, where they reach first the amygdala – a subcortical structure in the anterior-temporal lobe that acts as a danger detector or warning system.[2-3] Here, these bits of data are connected, creating a big picture from the separate pieces of information. If the outcome of the connection fits a *pattern*, the amygdala immediately ignites a fight-or-flight reaction. The whole process is extremely fast and does not involve any thinking, it is conducted completely by the subconscious. From an evolutionary point of view, those who failed to stereotype by making this kind of quick call were much less likely to leave behind offspring.

As humans, we are often put in a situation where we fail to see any similarities or where we lack relevant experience. At the same time, we still need to make sense of the situation and react in short space of time. Stereotyping is the result of this mismatch. Our mind forms a stereotype by connecting bits of *loose information* in order to reach a significant *whole* – something that gives us a meaning that enables us to make a decision and react quickly. It is not for nothing that sales pages are often very long, with a lots of bullet points, experts' recommendations and testimonies from satisfied customers. This is done in the hope that our mind will connect the loose information and create a big picture of "a good product," prompting a swift decision to buy it without having used it first. This mental shortcut of "judging a book by its cover" helps us to retain knowledge using minimal thinking effort and provides us with a sense of structure to deal with an otherwise chaotic universe.[4] Thus, stereotyping is bad, but it is also crucial. Some call it a "necessary evil," and that is a pretty good way to describe it.

3.1.1.2   A Social Mechanism

Our brains categorize objects and people in more or less the same way. Suppose you have never had a chance to get to know the Italians. There are about 60 million of them, thus at least 60 million sets of information – a number that is impossible to process. This is where stereotypes step in, using categories to help simplify and systematize information and, in this case, attributing a fixed set of characteristics to *all* Italians. For example, in our "heaven and hell" joke, they are portrayed as having a chaotic approach to work and a passionate approach to love affairs. In a nutshell, stereotypes maximize the differences *between* cultures (the Italians are completely different from the British, etc.), and maximize similarity *within* a culture (all Italians share this characteristic). Now that things have been "sorted out" and put into boxes, the world should look much simpler, and thus easier to understand. We can save time and energy to act more efficiently. Next time we meet an Italian, we can quickly draw on this stereotype (e.g. [s]he would make a great lover; [s]he would mess up the whole project), and consequently make a decision or form an opinion.

Stereotyping as a social mechanism has some disadvantages in our modern time. While this survival skill saved our ancestors from being bitten and eaten, in today's world, it is not poisonous snakes that we constantly have to worry about. Our everyday decisions do not always involve matters of life and death. However, the automatic reaction meant to save our life is still being used, including for very *complex* tasks such as negotiating a contract with a business partner. The ability to make a snap judgment is not very useful here, because your important decision will be based on subconscious instead of actual thinking; on gut feeling instead of rationality; on a lack of information rather than a clear bigger picture; and on the perceptions formed by *others* in the society, instead of the situation's uniqueness.

Furthermore, modern life *overloads* us with information, something that our ancestors didn't have to experience. In any given moment, we receive 11 million bits of information, but we can only consciously process 40 bits,[5] which leaves 99.999996 per cent of the information for the subconscious to take care of. This means, like it or not, we are biased. We tend to think of stereotypes as a bad thing, and that only racists and bigots engage in pigeonholing others. Despite the fact that our knowledge may be based on nothing more than a grain of truth of a half-truth, all of us are guilty of putting others in a box. When things do not fit the boxes, we are surprised. Whenever we are surprised, it probably means we have just stereotyped.

Stereotyping is a survival mechanism that helps us to make quick judgments based on limited information. However, in modern times, decisions do not always involve "survival" matters, and we are "overloaded with information." Hence, quick calls based on subconscious thinking can have shortcomings.

ACTIVITY

Are you racist, sexist, homophobic or discriminatory? Many of us would say no, and it is probably true in terms of any *explicit* bias. Those with explicit, overt and ideological bias have a *conscious* belief that race, age, religion, ethnicity, gender, etc. are the determinants of human traits and ability. They also say it out loud, advocating this idea, even killing for it, as we have seen with right-wing or supremacist groups such as the Ku Klux Klan, the Aryan Nation, neo-Nazi groups, etc.

The second type of bias is implicit, conditioned, subconscious or covert. It is not visible. We don't know we have it. We even deny we have it. We get extremely offended when accused of it, because we oppose such an idea. This is exactly the reason why *implicit* bias is more harmful and widespread, since we hurt others unknowingly. The truth is, all of us harbor more biases than we think. This comes from our brains' automated response that has been conditioned and shaped by various social cues.

Please take the Implicit Association Test[6] (free on the internet), but be prepared to be surprised at how racist or sexist you actually are.

3.1.2   The Methodological Flaw in Stereotyping

Looking at stereotyping from the perspective of cognitive function, there is nothing wrong with the act of categorizing. Our mind has evolved to conduct this vital process so that, as humans, we can effectively manage our life, develop our skills, and conquer the world that is otherwise too big, too complicated, and impossible to know in all its details.

However, the major problem with this seemingly natural process is that while our brains can be adept at categorizing inanimate objects, we run into problems when categorizing people, because people are much more complicated than objects. In this section, we will look at two basic methodological mistakes in the process of stereotyping people.

3.1.2.1   *Applying Collective Norms to Unique Individuals*

The primary problem with stereotyping is the tendency to put every single person into a fixed category. This pigeonholing measures the wrong level of analysis on the Inverted Pyramid model. Starting at the *collective level*, we assume that certain groups may share some outward expressions and values. We then jump to the *individual level* and assume that every single person at this level also shares exactly those same expressions and values: you are a man, so you should be tough; you are a nurse, then very likely you are a woman in a white outfit with a little cap; you are Irish, well, for sure you drink like a fish, etc.

Let's unpick the stereotypes we have just listed: It may be true that, in general, men are *expected* to hold back emotion, but a study has found that young men are more emotionally affected by relationship woes than women.[7] Similarly, it may be true that many nurses are female, but 21 per cent of nurses in Italy and 32 per cent of nurses in Saudi Arabia are male, and these numbers are rising.[8] To make matters even more interesting, the patron saint of nursing is a man: St. Camillus de Lellios.[9] Finally, the Irish may drink a lot, ranking 21st with regard to total alcohol consumption per capita, per year,[10] but only 3 per cent of Irish people consider themselves heavy drinkers, and a quarter of all Irish adults do not dink at all.[11] If drinking were an Olympic sport, the Irish would probably come home empty-handed.

Obviously, a trait at the collective level, no matter how pervasive it is, let alone how wrong it can be, should not be applied to everyone at the individual level. A person is not her/his culture or nationality. In fact, the cultural background of a person tells us very little about her/his personality. To make matters worse, when we use stereotypes, we *deny people their individual identity*. By insisting that a person is just a random unit of many similar copies from a mass collection, we deny this person a sense of self and personhood, the right to be special and unique. We appease our minds and turn a blind eye to the complex reality. Edward Said, the founder of postcolonial studies, reflecting on his Palestinian origin, has put this to words: "An Oriental man was first an Oriental and only second a man."[12]

In Chapter 2, we emphasized the nature of multiple identities. Everyone is a member of many collective cultures. Under the impact of globalization, technology, immigration and interracial marriages, individual identities can become *lego identities*, which can be both ascribed and situational. Behavioral[13-14] and neural studies[15-16-17-18-19] have showed us that we are capable of a multicultural mind,[20] (sub)consciously changing our perspectives and switching our value frames when the context requires it. Hence, using stereotypes not only risks pigeonholing people in a simplistic box, but also risks pigeonholing them in the *wrong box*, which is what we will look at in the next section.

This is a stereotypical image of video game players, who are all boys. In reality, the ratio of female to male gamers is balanced, mirroring the population at large: Australia (47:53),[21] New Zealand (46:54),[22] Finland (49:51),[23] etc., with Japanese female gamers surpassing males (66:34).[24] By being trapped in this stereotype, oblivious to sexism in video gaming and the underrepresentation of women as characters in games, the industry has failed to capitalize on a massive potential market. However, the tide is changing fast. In 1989, women constituted only 3 per cent of the gaming industry. It is predicted that by 2020, the games development workforce will be 50 per cent female[25] / "Children playing video games," GAMESINGEAR.[26]

3.1.2.2 Creating Incorrect Group Norms from Individual Information

The process of stereotyping can go wrong the other way around too, i.e. using the individual level to judge the collective level of the Inverted Pyramid model. This is due to the influence of misleading information. This incorrect data then forms a framework that we apply to the whole group, assuming that it is representative of *typical* values and outward expressions of that group: Some black people commit a crime, so black people are criminals, and being criminal is a typical trait of black culture; some Muslims are terrorists, so Muslims are terrorists, and being a terrorist is typically Islamic; some white people are racist, so white people are racists and discrimination is a normal part of being white, etc.

The danger of creating incorrect norms has been exacerbated by media and social networks. Many stereotypes spread by mass media are exaggerated and based on half-truth. What should be seen as a non-typical and exceptional incident is blown out of proportion, creating the illusion that it is the *actual norm*. A good example of this phenomenon is the connection between air travel and fear of a plane crash. Although flying is the safest of all transportation modes, each time a plane comes down, the whole world is shaken by the constant and excessive amount of news and reports, creating an impression that it is dangerous to fly. Similarly, the abundance of media attention on a certain topic can trick many of us into making a wrong assumption, such as, people from the Gulf are oil millionaires, the standard beauty of modern women is exactly the same as that of a catwalk model or a Barbie doll, or the entire Middle East is an everlasting war zone, etc. The incredible network of media and literature is partly responsible for creating a distorted image of many collective cultures, focusing on *irregular traits* and turning them into *typical trademarks*. When exceptions become the norm, stereotypes that stem from this categorization can be destructive, since they are incongruent with reality, and yet, they are considered to be the standard.

The media often focuses on irregular traits and turns them into typical trademarks. Regular women rarely look like these models, but the normalization of extremely skinny figures has made many women believe themselves to be "not good enough," causing insecurity and reinforcing sexism. Young women put their health in danger by attempting to slim down to the unrealistic body image portrayed by the fashion industry. Size 0 and 00 were invented due to changing clothing sizes over time. For example, a size 0 in 2011 is the equivalent of a size 2 in 2001 and is larger than a size 6 in 1970 and a size 8 in 1958. In other words, a regular woman in the past could be seen as a plus-size woman by today's standard. The social effect is so destructive that France followed the example of Israel and banned ultra-skinny models in 2015, requiring a minimum healthy BMI of 18.5/ "Modern fashion standards," JULIA KISHKARUK.[27]

When stereotyping people, we risk making two mistakes:
- *Using the "Collective level" to evaluate the "Individual level": Group norms are applied to every unique person.*
- *Using the "Individual level" to evaluate the "Collective level": Exceptional cases become incorrect norms for the whole group.*

3.1.3   The Pitfalls of Stereotyping

In this section, we will discuss the "evil"'s side of stereotypes.

3.1.3.1   *Stereotypes can be Stronger than Fact and Rationality*

When our ancestors lived in small bands of hunter-gatherers, analyzing what was right and what was wrong didn't add too many advantages. In contrast, winning arguments helped to bolster their social status. Hence, humans embraced the tendency to accept facts and opinions which reaffirm our view, and reject those which challenge it, especially when we do not have the resources to counter such information.[28]

Stereotypes are persistent. They can trap us in a frame that filters out all information that is not consistent with our assumptions. Even when we are confronted with instances that contradict stereotypes, we tend to assume that this is just a special case. For example, if we hold the common stereotype that gay men are soft and unathletic, when meeting an athletic and assertive gay man, we are more likely to conclude that this person is *not* a typical gay man, and that gay men, in general, are *still* soft and unathletic. Further, this selective filter *only* reinforces information that suits our assumption. In a nutshell, we only see what we want to see. It is a solution for so-called "cognitive dissonance" – a dilemma between our own belief and facts. Consequently, we are misled into making decisions based on half-truths.

To make matters worse, neuroscientists tell us that the brain even *distorts* facts to fit our stereotypes.[29] For instance, female faces are perceived as "happy" and male faces as "angry," even when the opposite is the case. Black faces tend to be seen as "angry," even when they are objectively happy. This is the result of a society where women are constantly told to smile and men, especially black men, are associated with masculine aggression.

This helps to explain why people tend to have an even *stronger* belief when they are confronted with facts and overwhelming evidence against their point of view.[30] This "backfire effect" happens when facts threaten a worldview or self-concept. In a series of studies,[31] researchers reported that those who held a negative belief about Aboriginals didn't change their view when provided with correct information. Similarly, those who believed the misinformation on weapons of mass destruction in Iraq *strengthened* their belief after being made aware of the correction that suggests otherwise.[32] The power of information and transparency is not always guaranteed and can even be counterproductive. Like an underpowered antibiotic, facts can actually strengthen misinformation and false belief.

This is not the end of the story. The failure of facts and rationality can be accompanied by the "I know I'm right" syndrome. A political study shows that not only will most of us resist correcting our stereotypical belief despite the facts, it appears that misinformed people also often have some of the strongest opinions. In this study,[33] half of the participants indicated confidence in what they know, but only 3 per cent got half of the questions right, and the ones who were the *most* confident were also the ones who knew the *least* about the topic.

3.1.3.2   *Stereotypes Exclude Those Who Don't Fit*

Since stereotypes put people in boxes, they deny the existence of those who do not fit those assumptions. The story of this blogger vividly illustrates his frustration:

> I'm a black man who grew up surrounded by white people. Growing up, I was the only black person in my neighborhood, my school, and sometimes it felt like the entire town. I never played basketball. I can't rap or dance well – I don't even like hip hop. I'm really good at video games and I watch baseball. When I got to college, my skin made me too black to fit in with the white kids, and my skills/hobbies weren't black enough to fit in with the black kids.
> It sucks to feel like you're in the minority sometimes. It sucks even more to feel like you're not even good enough for the minority.[34]

In fact, every single one of us doesn't fit. The reason is simple, boxes don't mix, but identities do. You may fit the stereotype of how someone from Brunei looks like, but at the same time, you are not just a Bruneian but a Buddhist, an entrepreneur, a global citizen, single father, a wannabe rockstar, etc. Within and between each of these identities, there will always be something about you that does not fit the stereotypical assumptions. Sooner or later, you will face a few options: being forced into a box, being left out of the picture, or struggling to fit in a box that is not "meant" for you.

A good case in point is women and the numerous stereotypes they have to struggle with. The overwhelming stereotype is that they are homemakers, i.e. generally, women want to be, should be, or have to be a care-giver. This social expectation hampers women and they have to struggle much harder than their male counterparts to advance in the workplace. Popular profiles present girls and women as young, thin, beautiful, passive, dependent and often incompetent. At the same time, boys and men are portrayed as active, adventurous, powerful, sexually aggressive and largely uninvolved in human relationships.[35] This stereotype has popularized the meme "game over," which variously depicts a bride victoriously or desperately dragging her groom into a wedding while the man shows a sad and helpless face. It perpetuates the false idea that a woman's purpose in life is to get married and make a home, and a man's mission is to escape this. It is not true, of course, but it has become something that few of us bother to argue against. Societies trapped in this stereotype fail to pay due respect and give equal opportunities to half of the workforce. There are countless women who are active citizens, who want to pursue serious careers, who strive to be executives, who desire to lead and make an impact, and who just want to be single or child-free.

3.1.3.3   *The Threat of Stereotypes and Self-Fulfilling Prophecies*

The stereotype threat is a situation where your performance is influenced by negative assumptions that others have about your collective culture, and hence, indirectly about you.[36] For example, if you told white men that, generally, they have *lower* athletic ability than black men, consequently, they would perform *worse* than those white men who were *not* made aware of this stereotype.[37] Similarly, women would perform math tasks worse if they were reminded of the stereotype, but perform equally well in comparison with men if free from this threat.[38] This effect of stereotyping is so detrimental that it can drive us away from putting more effort into solving a problem. Instead, we start to question our own ability and attribute this temporary failure to our age, race, gender, nationality, skin color, etc.: "Why can't I do it? Is it because what people say is correct? Maybe the stereotype is correct! Oh dear! It *is* indeed correct!" In a self-fulfilling prophecy, this belief begins to guide our behaviors and, eventually, we create the reality that originally was just an idea, an idea that was not even correct. This phenomenon also works in our interaction with others. If you stereotype someone as intelligent, you will subconsciously act in a way that encourages an intellectual response. If you expect them to be dull, your behavior is likely to elicit this trait.

With Functional Magnetic Resonance Imaging (fMRI), we are able to know what really happens when people experience a stereotype threat. Women free of such a threat showed increased recruitment of neural activity in the regions that are associated with math performance, including the inferior prefrontal cortex and bilateral angular gyrus.[39-40] In comparison, this increase was absent among women who had been reminded of their inferiority. Instead, there was increased activity in the ventral anterior cingulate cortex, a brain region associated with emotional self-regulation and processing social feedback.[41-42] This means that valuable cognitive resources are spent on emotional regulation, *rather than on the task at hand*; this, in turn, results in poorer performance.

3.1.3.4   *Positive Stereotypes*

Logically, one would think: "If a negative stereotype makes people perform worse than their actual ability, then a positive one would make them perform better." That is partly true. However, no matter how positive they are, stereotypes are still stereotypes, and we will always fail to grasp the whole picture by using them. Further, positive stereotypes can be detrimental since they set the bar unrealistically high, causing holders of stereotypes to be disappointed when confronted with the truth and, at the same time, loading unnecessary burdens on those viewed through such stereotypes.

A classic example is Model Minority – an assumption that Asians in Western societies achieve a higher degree of socioeconomic success than the population average. Despite the fact that Asian minorities have also been marginalized and face racism like other collective cultures, this positive stereotype creates an illusion that Asians do not suffer from social inequality. This dismisses problems and denies chances that the disadvantaged deserve. Worse still, this positive stereotype has been used to justify the exclusion of those in need in the distribution of government support.[43] In the 1980s, several Ivy League schools admitted that they chose other minority groups over Asian applicants in an attempt to promote a national agenda of racial diversity.[44] Holding Asians to a much higher standard also presses them to live up to unrealistic expectations, resulting in tremendous stress and mental illness, even suicide attempts among young people unable to deal with pressure from parents and society to be exceptionally high achievers.[45]

In a multicultural society, maintaining positive stereotypes about one specific group accentuates negative stereotypes about others. It can actually promote legal injustice, social hostility and racial hatred, creating platforms to blame other groups for not being a model, falling short in terms of their contribution. In her book *Murder and the Reasonable Man*, Cynthia Lee argues that the verdict on the shooting death of a black teenager by a Korean shop owner was influenced by the positive stereotype of the shooter as "unfortunate victim of 'bad' African or Latino looters."[46] This event contributed to the 1992 riots in Los Angeles and has left a tension between the two communities until this day.[47]

The pitfalls of stereotypes are:

- *Stereotypes can be stronger than fact and rationality. People will strengthen their false belief if deep-seated values are challenged. Our brain can also distort images to fit our stereotypes.*
- *Stereotypes exclude those who don't fit the boxes.*
- *Stereotype threats create anxiety that results in lower performance and self-fulfilling prophecies (we become what we believe we are).*
- *Positive stereotypes create burden, dismiss problems, and deepen group conflicts.*

African immigrants are described as an "Invisible Model Minority" because their high degree of success has been overshadowed by negative stereotypes. In the US, 48.9 per cent of all African immigrants hold a college diploma, more than double the rate of native-born white Americans.[48] Immigrants from Egypt, Nigeria, Cameroon, Uganda, Tanzania and Zimbabwe are among the best educated. A similar situation among different ethnic groups is found in the UK, Australia and Canada/ "High school students conducting experiments," UNKNOWN PHOTOGRAPHER, NATIONAL CANCER INSTITUTE.[49]

3.2   Prejudice

If stereotypes can be both positive and negative, prejudices are often deeply held negative feelings associated with a particular group. Built into the notion of prejudice is a sense of hostility and judgment. While stereotypes may be free from value and evaluation (e.g. people from Latin America are Catholics), prejudices are loaded with feelings about what is good and what is bad, what is moral and immoral (e.g. "my religion is the only true one, and my God is the only true God.") Consequently, people with prejudices are likely to end up in hostile encounters where each side believes that their view is the right one.

3.2.1   The Origin of Prejudice

Similar to stereotyping, the tendency to form prejudices is the result of 25 million years of primate evolutionary heritage.[50]

3.2.1.1   Group Categorization

In Chapter 1, we discussed how human beings are the only species capable of moving beyond family boundaries and forming different non-kin groups in order to maximize chances of survival. In fact, many think that our big brain evolved, in part, to cope with group living conditions. Since group living is directly connected to survival, our brains have evolved to be adept at recognizing who belongs to our ingroup (i.e. who we can trust) and outgroup (i.e. who we should watch out for or fight against). We do this by placing people into different categories. The tendency to categorize people into ingroup or outgroup is so pervasive that we often automatically locate others along simple dimensions such as skin color, gender and age. However, while this process can be quite accurate when categorizing inanimate objects, it can be faulty when categorizing people, since factors that define ingroup-outgroup are much more complex than visual elements such as skin color, gender and age.[51]

3.2.1.2   Group Love

Our ancestors spent thousands of years in close-knit communities, where the group was their source of help, comfort and survival, protecting them against human and non-human enemies. By contrast, outgroup members can mean "threat." Until today, the culture of our group provides us everything we need to survive: what to eat, how to seek support, where to study, when to start a family, how to become successful, and why doing all those things in a certain cultural way is important. Naturally, we have evolved to build a strong affection for our ingroup and our culture. It becomes the center of everything, a yardstick that all other groups/cultures are measured and judged by. Our pride and sense of superiority leads to a tendency to look down on and distrust outgroup members (Social Identity Theory)[52] as we start forming certain prejudices towards others. In a nutshell, the love for our ingroup and culture automatically causes us to have negative attitudes towards outsiders.[53] Our cruelty to "them" is the result of our kindness to "us."

Because we naturally feel safer among our ingroup, the contact with outgroups consequently triggers the nervous system to go into an automated fight-or-flight mode, similar to the stereotype mechanism. Again, better safe than sorry. That is how the brain has evolved, to protect us against any possible danger as it constantly gauges whether people are "friends" or "foes." Physical traits (e.g. race, gender, age) and social cues (e.g. employees of the competing firm or members of other political parties) can be indicators that signal threats. For example, the amygdala becomes more active when we see someone who racially looks different from us, indicating a potential threat.[54-55] Not only is the fear-detector alert, evolution has also prepared us to feel less empathy towards outsiders. Watching people in pain, we tend to have more sympathy for those in our ingroup rather than outsiders,[56] even when they are just supporters of a rival team.[57] This makes sense, if we think about the moment we need to wield the sword to kill enemies. If we were to empathize with them as much as with our ingroup, we would likely stop and think, which would do us a disservice. In fact, demonizing others is a frequent practice to trick our brain into a prejudiced mode, enabling us to hate, discriminate, and destroy others without too much feeling.[58] In the end, killing people who have been made to look bad is easier than killing someone who is the same as us.

However, while being helpful in basic and closed societies, the machinery of detecting us vs. them and automatically treating "them" as a potential threat has become increasingly disadvantageous as we cross ever more borders throughout history. Furthermore, our environment is filled with racial stereotypes and prejudices, and the amygdala can wrongly adapt to prejudicial information about those who look different and, consequently, put us on *false alarm*. The amygdala operates extremely fast, long before our conscious thoughts have time to react.[59] Obviously, if left unchecked, the combination of all three factors (our tendency to categorize people into ingroup and outgroup; our love for ingroup; and our constantly [and falsely] alarming amygdala) can result in quite a nasty cocktail.

Prejudices are rooted in the biological need to categorize other groups and to love our own ingroup/culture – the source of our survival strategies.

3.2.2 The Expression of Prejudice

The attachment that we naturally have towards our ingroup is so strong that we not only favor our own group based on skin color, ethnicity, class, age, religion or gender, but we are even capable of feeling attached to a group that is *randomly* formed and based on something trivial. Divide any number of people into two different camps and, after no time, participants will exhibit ingroup favoritism, giving preferential treatment to their own members. Prejudices stemming from this group-based environment can escalate to *acts of discrimination* through the following forms and factors:

3.2.2.1 *Conflict of Resources*
According to Realistic Conflict Theory, prejudices are formed when one group perceives the other(s) as a threat to their economic, political or cultural interest.[60] If one group has the potential to compete in the job market, and the other wants to maintain their privilege, power and status, a frequent strategy is to exploit or put down the minority group in order to maximize profits and to justify the hostility.

Understandably, prejudice often finds its peak during crises. In the recent global economic downturn, many minority groups in the West became victims of suspicion or hatred. A historic case in point is the "roller coaster" of prejudice suffered by Chinese immigrants in the US. This is what happened to them before they were lumped together with other Asian ethnicities as a Model Minority of exemplary citizens:

> In the nineteenth-century American West, Chinese immigrants were hired to work in the gold mines, potentially taking jobs from white laborers. The white-run newspapers fomented prejudice against them, describing the Chinese as "depraved and vicious," "gross gluttons," "bloodthirsty and inhuman." Yet only a decade later, when the Chinese were willing to accept the dangerous, arduous work of building the transcontinental railroad – work that white laborers were unwilling to undertake – public prejudice toward them subsided, replaced by the opinion that the Chinese were sober, industrious, and law-abiding. "They are equal to the best white men," said the railroad tycoon Charles Crocker. "They are very

trusty, very intelligent and they live up to their contracts." After the completion of the railroad, jobs again became scarce, and the end of the Civil War brought an influx of war veterans into an already tight job market. Anti-Chinese prejudice returned, with the press now describing the Chinese as "criminal," "conniving," "crafty," and "stupid."[61]

In the US, the Asian threat, presented as the "Yellow Peril," would later also be associated with the Japanese, as a result of their military ambitions and the Second World War; other South Asian immigrant groups were labeled as the "Turban Tide" and the "Hindoo Invasion." Similar prejudice towards blacks were found in white groups that were just *one rung* above the blacks socioeconomically, implying a close competition for jobs.[62]

Even when there is no conflict, resources can also be a factor that triggers prejudice. Many people justify discrimination against other groups because it helps maintain their own economic advantage: "These immigrants have little education, so they are lucky to have the jobs we offer. We really don't need to pay them more." In this case, assuming immigrants are ignorant people is useful, because it justifies the discriminatory act of paying them less.

3.2.2.2   The Blame Game

As hatred rises, society becomes destabilized, and people then start looking for a way to ease their frustrations. This is the point where an individual or a group is singled out and given all the blame. This unfortunate individual or group is called a *scapegoat*. If a scapegoat is killed, social order will be restored, since everyone believes that they have removed the cause of the trouble. Scapegoating acts as a psychological treatment, much like sacrifice in worship rituals.

Due to the snowball effect of antagonism, the original and genuine cause of the problem is often too big or too vague for direct retaliation. Situations such as a bad economy, unemployment, loss of status and confidence or failure in management can cause unhappiness and frustration. However, it is not possible to strike out against the whole system. Instead, people lash out at something or someone more specific, ideally a minority. Tarring an individual or a group with negative prejudice convinces us that they are the bad people and they deserve their fate.

History is replete with horrific cases of scapegoating, at all levels of society. We love the blame game and love to hold someone responsible for our problems. In Greek mythology, it was Pandora, who opened the box of trouble; in Christianity, it was Eve who asked Adam to eat from the forbidden fruit and, consequently, we still bear the brunt of original sin; in Nazi Germany, it was the Jews; when an economy struggles, nationalists tend to scapegoat minorities for economic woes and immigrants are quickly seen as those who "steal our jobs";[63] when confronted with domestic problems, country leaders are adept at using a "perfect enemy" to divert public attention elsewhere.[64] At the micro level, scapegoats are individuals, such as a staff worker who gets the blame for mismanagement.

Homosexuals have frequently been made scapegoats and blamed for AIDS, natural disasters, even terrorist attacks. Pastor Jerry Falwell is believed to have said: "Thank God for these gay demonstrators. If I didn't have them, I'd have to invent them. They give me all the publicity I need"/ "Shah Abbas 1 of Persia with a boy," MUHAMMAD QASIM.[65]

Scapegoats are not always a person or a group. Many believe the 2008 financial and economic collapse was due to "greed," and that the desire to accumulate more than we need was the root of the crisis. Facing economic problems in Europe, another study in 2014 reported that governments made "public sectors" scapegoats and punished them with wage cuts and retrenchment.[66] According to the authors, the real culprit is inequality and the dysfunctional regime of financial accumulation. By cutting public expenditure, governments allow more inequality, more debt, and further bubbles, continuing the vicious cycle.

3.2.2.3   Institutionalized Discrimination

A great deal of prejudice is embedded in the social systems of our societies through laws, regulations, operating procedures, objectives of governments and targets of corporations and other large entities. Together, they help "maintain the power of dominant groups over subordinate ones."[67] The unjust treatment can be conscious or subconscious, but it is always codified in the process of the institution.

Conscious discrimination. To this day, a number of countries maintain a pronounced system of disparity among various groups. For example, Saudi Arabia still does not allow women to drive and open their own bank account. Every woman needs to be in the presence of a male guardian, regardless of their age, whenever they go out, and the King only granted Saudi women the right to vote in local elections in 2015. The system also extends to foreign workers. They need sponsors to provide entry and exit permission, and cannot keep their passports during their stay – a control practice that makes them greatly dependent on the mercy of employers. In Dubai, where foreigners make up almost 90 per cent of the population, nationality largely decides one's salary rank: Europeans on top, Arabs follow, and different Asian and African groups cover the middle and lower rungs.[68]

Subconscious discrimination. However, institutionalized discrimination is often much less obvious, but still pervasive. Those with prejudices even twist merit to justify job discrimination. Recruiters can *redefine* criteria for success and use these new requirements as an excuse for rejecting the applicants they don't like.[69] In the Netherlands, more than half of recruitment agencies complied with clients' requests not to accept candidates of Moroccan, Turkish or Surinamese origin.[70] Even when applicants don't have to endure this discrimination, their non-Western names and addresses, which signal non-White neighborhoods, can subconsciously influence the selection process. In the UK, people with foreign sounding names are a third less likely to be shortlisted for jobs than people with white, British sounding names.[71] Emily and Greg are more employable than Lakisha and Jamal, even when they have exactly the same curriculum vitae.[72] The Dutch Prime Minister, Mark Rutte, was apparently oblivious to this fact when in 2017, he called anonymous job applications, which omit the name and country of origin, "terrible."[73] As a country leader, his remark used the cover of "sameness" to justify a policy that disregards subconscious discrimination, rubbing salt into the wound of many whose inequality is part of everyday life.

Business owners also suffer from institutionalized economic prejudice. Women of color start businesses at rates three to five times faster than all other businesses. However, once in business, their growth lags behind all other firms due to the negative impact of race and gender.[74] In capital investment markets, banks are often accused of not providing loans and other financial instruments for minority owned businesses, abusing the legal system in order to avoid clients perceived as "high risk" while failing to provide reasons to back up their denials.[75] Minority business owners pay interest rates that are 32 per cent higher than the rates whites pay for loans.[76]

In the same discriminatory way, prejudices subconsciously influence decision making processes in other social aspects. For example, in many multicultural societies, racial profiling has been blamed for much harsher punishment of non-white people. In the US, black men are reportedly 12 times more likely to be incarcerated for drug offenses, even though both blacks and whites use and sell drugs at almost the same rate.[77] Black drivers are 31 per cent more likely to be stopped by police than a white driver and twice as likely to be searched during routine traffic stops.[78] Criminologists have proved that the disproportionate number of marginalized groups in prison is linked to their socioeconomic disadvantages. In a vicious cycle of poverty, discrimination and negligence, it takes more than a strong will to wrench oneself out of the orbit of endless problems.

Similarly, many of the social issues we are facing today are the indirect consequences of institutionalized discrimination: gender pay gap, shortage of women and minorities in leading positions, achievement differences in education, higher suicide rate among men and marginalized groups, etc. It's easy and convenient to attribute these disparities to factors such as inherent capacity or particular cultural values (e.g. "they don't get there because they simply can't," "they don't try hard enough"). This is a form of *symbolic* racism/discrimination where we assume the problem is "lack of effort," rather than external disadvantages. The focus is switched from visual traits such as skin color to an abstract value, staying away from the direct racial slurs and hiding behind "value" as a justification, which is more politically correct in liberal democracies.[79] Here is an example: Support for Obama would have been 6 per cent higher if he were white. In fact, he lost votes from those well-educated whites, who genuinely believe in racial equality, but unconsciously have no intention of voting for a black president. They may have criticized him for lack of experience, but this would not have been an issue if he were white.[80]

Using value as a justification to discriminate is so pervasive because it sounds like common sense. At the same time, it disregards many burdens and disadvantages that are out of a person's control. The root cause always has a lot to do with the systematic, institutionalized inequality that is built upon (sub)conscious prejudices. We may think a tiny little bias can't possibly lead to such a huge setback, but a computer simulation has proved that an edge of just 1 per cent given to a particular group at the starting line will quickly lead to 65 per cent of the advantages at the finish post.[81] It is often the case that someone who is not a member of the dominant culture will need to try many times harder than those with privileges (e.g. native, white, male) in order to reach the very same position.

Those with privileges often unknowingly benefit from institutionalized discrimination through biases. It's easier for them to be recognized, to be chosen, to be employed, to make an impression, to be pardoned, to be accepted in a circle or network, etc./ "Bob's privileges," BARRY DEUTSCH.

ACTIVITY

When Johana Brurai – a graphic designer from Sweden – searched for pictures of "hands" on Google, she found that most of the images were white. When she searched for "black hands," they often came with added information, such as a white hand reaching out to offer help. White images also dominates search results for "man," "women," or "child." Even the search for "beautiful dreadlocks" – a hairstyle strongly associated with African culture – yields images of white people with dreadlocks.

Do a Google search for other concepts such as "leadership," "business" or "expert."

1. Who are the majority in the images? What is the environment? What are they doing? What is the hidden message?
2. Why does this group dominate Google's search results?
3. What can you do to balance the situation?

Media. Institutional discrimination can be amplified through media.[82] In fact, journalists in both the Nazi Holocaust and the Rwandan Genocide were convicted of charges related to inciting genocide. Although journalism is expected to be objective, it is conducted by humans, and humans are biased. Reporters reflect reality through their own eyes and are not completely free of stereotypes and prejudices. More often than not, newspapers tend to identify the racial or religious background of a suspect who belongs to a minority or scapegoat group (immigrants, guest workers, gays, women, religious or ethnic minorities, etc.). At the same time, they *ignore* the wrong-doer's background if this person belongs to a dominant culture. This selective exposure undoubtedly creates a distorted picture of the number of bad things committed by non-dominant groups. If a man parks his car badly and hinders others, he is just a bad driver. But if a woman parks her car badly, it is because she is a *woman*. If an employee fails to reach the target, it is because (s)he is simply not an effective worker. But if an immigrant fails to reach the target, it is because (s)he is *not from here*. After the French satirical magazine *Charlie Hebdo* was attacked in January 2015, a tweet from political commentator Sally Kohn snowballed into a trend because it attacked exactly this hypocrisy and prejudice:

Muslim shooter = entire religion guilty
Black shooter = entire race guilty
White shooter = mentally troubled lone wolf.[83]

So, white people see such white criminals as exceptional individuals who do not represent their white identity. But Muslims also strongly condemned these attackers as not Muslims. They were simply horrible and exceptional individuals who do not represent their identity. Thus, it is clear that also for Muslims, these bad guys = mentally ill lone wolves.

Obviously, all of us are influenced by the tendency to stereotype a whole group of outsiders as a one-dimensional group, based on the acts of some individuals. At the same time, we also want to protect our own group's interest and to isolate the bad individuals as non-group members. This double standard is endemic in all cultural groups, without exception. In essence, it is evolutionarily part of our fundamental need for group love and cultural attachment. The viral power of media accentuates this tendency and turns a group's self-defense mechanism into an ugly battle of prejudice and discrimination towards others.

CASE STUDY

Racism is the idea that genetic endowment implies the inherent superiority of a particular race and defines success or failure of a group. Nowadays, the concept of race has moved on to imply a culture, at the same time focusing on simplistic and visual signals of race and culture, such as skin color, attire, body features, national origin, ancestry, religion and sexual preference. Consequently, racism is easily ignited, even as a result of very superficial contact.

Racism directed at the Jews was used for economic gain. Today, the practice of lending money at a rate of interest is the basis of our economy, but before capitalism emerged, usury was seen by many as a sin or inferior work, practiced mostly by Jews who were excluded from many professions and trades and had no job alternatives. This is one of the reasons why Jews excelled in business and finance as merchants and middlemen, but they also suffered from hatred of those who borrowed money.

In fact, even this "sinful" job was given to the Jews out of economic interest in the medieval European economy. From the 11th century, greater commerce and urbanization became possible due to new agricultural surpluses, which made the economic function of lending money more important. However, lending money was condemned. The church solved this dilemma in the early 12th century by allowing Jews to practice this "sinful" activity, since Jews were not subject to Canon law. Medieval Kings exploited the new situation, now that they were able to exact heavy taxes from Jewish usurers in exchange for protection.[84] In the 14th and 15th centuries, the medieval economic landscape changed as cross-border trade flourished. Jews became economic rivals of the new merchant class. Together with the rise of capitalism, anti-Semitism was cultivated in order to eliminate economic competitors, turning Jews into scapegoats for popular discontent and they were blamed for all social problems. Although there is no Jewish race, they were portrayed as a people of "greedy," "self-interest," "cheating on non-Jews," "secretly dominating the whole economic system," or "cooperating with their communist counterparts to topple Christian civilization."[85] The 18th and 19th centuries saw the expansion of industrialization, with many people being driven from the land and forced to work in factories. Anti-Semitism was used to shift the blame from those who actually profited from their suffering. Later, in the 20th century, the Nazi's creation of a "master race" condemned Jews as an inferior race, leading to the genocide of six million Jews whose confiscated wealth paid for 30 per cent of the wars waged by the Nazis.[86] Even today, Jews are identified with the nation of Israel, mixing political grievances with racism, creating a "perfect enemy" to seek unity, to divert criticism away from the country, or to blame Jewish conspiracies for homegrown problems.

1. Collect at least five stereotypes and prejudices about the Jews and explain the root of these assumptions, based on the history provided in the text.
2. Compare the discrimination against Jews with the Yellow Peril, Turban Tide and Hindoo Invasion (section 3.2.2.1).
3. Conduct a quick research and discuss why immigration is essential for an economy, yet immigrants are often the scapegoat in their new country.

3.2.2.4   Positive Discrimination

Tokenism. Like positive stereotyping, positive discrimination can also do harm. A "token" is someone who is employed or placed in a certain setting as a symbolic representation of the entire minority group. Tokens often feel very visible and suffer from stereotype threat, because they stand out from the rest of the group.[87] In addition, others view them not as unique individuals, but rather in terms of the collective culture they represent: as *the* transgender or *the* millennial, which allows stereotypes to easily be formed or connected. Tokens, therefore, are under great pressure to behave in an expected, stereotypical way. Yet, at the same time, they have to perform and any mistakes they make will be more likely to catch attention. This leads to more frequent reprimands and more severe punishments. And because tokens are perceived as representatives of a collective minority group, they are stripped of their individual identities and their failures will be perceived as inherent weaknesses or characteristics of the whole collective culture.[88]

Affirmative action. The quota system of affirmative action is useful for creating a level playing field, but if not done carefully, especially when institutions are forced to implement it without full understanding, it can be seen as reverse discrimination and backfire. In South Africa, where the past has left a legacy of racial hostility that still leads to violence,[89] such a quota system is believed to discriminate against white people.[90-91] As a consequence, skilled laborers, know-how, and capital are leaving the country,[92] resulting in a lack of economic growth and fewer international companies wanting to invest. While working in Cape Town, the author met an Asian colleague who bitterly complained: "During Apartheid, I was not white enough. Now I'm not black enough."

Further, the categorical recruitment based on race, gender, ethnicity, age, etc. may undermine merit. In a rush to conform to a quota, we may put not-fully-ready people in positions that are constantly under the spotlight and rigorous scrutiny from others. Such a situation can lead to both tokenism and stereotype threat, which is a double disadvantage for the individuals. It can also perpetuate prejudices against the collective cultures of those individuals unfairly.

- *Prejudices prevail when there are conflicts of resources. The victims of prejudices are scapegoats and can suffer from both conscious and subconscious discrimination.*
- *Institutionalized discrimination is embedded in rules, process and operating systems. It creates barriers through (sub)conscious biases, tougher selection processes, increased caution, more blaming, and quicker rejection.*

3.3   Strategies for living with stereotypes and reducing prejudices

The world is changing fast, and it seems genes do not co-evolve fast enough to support useful cultural traits. In the era of globalization and cooperation, we still carry some part of the psychological and biological baggage of our hunter-gatherer predecessors. However, with the capacity for culture, we are not prisoners of these *lingering traits*. By the means of social learning, we have overcome the worst aspects of our nature. We may not be born ready to assess facts and arguments carefully, but we are capable of learning from mistakes, choosing from the best ideas, and reducing the impact of impulsive reactions.

3.3.1   Training Our Brain

It is wrong to say that our brain is racist or sexist. The brain does not see skin color or gender, but rather information that fits various patterns of stereotypes and "fight-or-flight." Most patterns of stereotyping people and "fight-or-flight" are socially constructed by our cultures. This means, we can change the patterns and train our brain.

3.3.1.1   Acknowledging Stereotypes

The first step to cope with the disadvantages of stereotypes is to acknowledge that, despite awareness and good intention, we all stereotype. Let's look at a neural study that used the classic scenario of "lawyer-engineer."[93]

Imagine you are in a room with 995 lawyers and five engineers. Then you are introduced to Jack, who is 45 years old with four children. He has little interest in politics or social issues, and is generically conservative. He likes sailing and mathematical puzzles. Is Jack a lawyer or an engineer?

Logically, you have only a 0.005 per cent chance of meeting an engineer in that room; yet, many of us would still make Jack an engineer, simply because he fits the stereotypical pattern. The twist is that our brain does not blindly lead us to that decision. In this scenario, there is obviously a conflict between rationality (Jack is more likely a lawyer) and stereotype (He fits the engineer's profile). When we encounter such a conflict, the anterior cingulate cortex (ACC) of the brain's frontal lobe becomes active.[94] The ACC is crucial in helping us to judge and elicit error, controlling emotion and rational thinking.

Researchers watched the volunteers' brains as they tried to decide whether Jack is a lawyer or an engineer, and they found that the ACC lit up in *both* situations: those who rationally think that Jack is a lawyer, and those who give in to stereotypes and think Jack is an engineer. Apparently, *we all detect the stereotype* and recognize that it is completely out of sync with reality. But the comfort of the stereotype is so tempting that many of us choose to listen to it anyway. This experiment shows that even when our brain points out the bias, we still tend to go the easy way.

3.3.1.2   Training the Brain for Goals

There is hope, however. Studies tell us that people with bigger ACC tend to be more liberal thinkers (i.e. flexible, reliant on data, analytic reasoning) and those with bigger amygdala tend to be conservative thinkers (stability, emotion-driven).[95-96] The good news from the aforementioned study is that the ACC lights up regardless of the result, and we *do* see the stereotypes.

The question, then, is, when stereotypes loom and control is needed, how can we increase the ACC's activity and make it win over the amygdala.

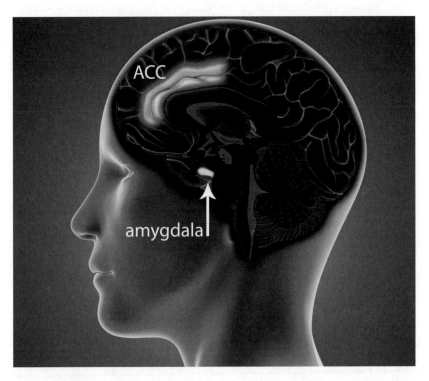

The anterior cingulate cortex (ACC) predicts, detects and reacts to committed errors/ "The ACC and the amygdala," PHAM HOANG MAI.

Neuroscientists suggest that we should focus on the *goal* of the activity. Without a goal, stereotypes reign, but when eyes are on the prize, rationality has a greater chance. In a neural study,[97] participants had to categorize faces according to their race. Since we often stereotype black people, researchers observed greater amygdala activity when participants saw black faces on the screen. However, when participants had a specific goal in which race was not relevant, for example trying to guess what type of vegetable the person preferred, the amygdala response to black faces was *equal* to that for the white ones.

How does this play out in real life? Let's say when companies recruit, here are some suggestions that would help them to focus on the goal of hiring a good employee and *reduce* the impact of stereotypes: Using *recruitment agents* who can be more objective; having a *consensus in advance* about what success looks like; creating a *job description* with clear and measurable selection criteria; avoiding any requirements that relate to age, sex, race, (dis)abilities or religion; declaring *a diversity statement* and commitment to adhering to such a vision; adopting a *name-blind resumé screening process*; having several persons of *diverse backgrounds* on the interview panel for cross-check and balance; *standardizing interview questions* with a clear justification for *why* each specific question should be asked; *recording the interview* and detecting any subconscious bias; justifying the recruitment decision on paper by *matching* each job requirement with the candidate's ability in order to avoid a decision based on gut feeling, etc.

In short, while our brain is evolutionarily conditioned to stereotyping and prejudice, it also has the power to recognize and override those biases. This is a fight we can win. But it requires more than just good intentions. We need to show *explicit* conscious efforts in order to challenge such *subconscious* impulses. We can reduce these automatic mechanisms by purposely looking twice. The more we are aware of it, the better we can overcome it. There is evidence that when we are told "Hey, you are biased" we can self-correct,[98] we will think harder about what we want to say. Our brain's plasticity means we can learn and regulate, since counter-stereotypic training,[99] such as taking the perspective of others,[100] has proven to reduce bias.

CASE STUDY

Two passengers — one Asian-American, the other African-American — boarded a small "hopper" and were told by the white flight attendant that they could sit anywhere. So they sat at the front as it was easier for them to talk.

At the last minute, three white men in suits entered the plane, were told to sit anywhere, and promptly sat in front of the two first passengers. Just before take-off, the flight attendant approached the first two passengers, interrupted their conversation, and asked them to move to the back of the plane to distribute the weight more evenly.

Both passengers were frustrated, sharing the same sense that they were being singled out to symbolically "sit at the back of the bus." When they expressed these feelings to the attendant, she indignantly denied the charge, saying "I don't see color" and that she was merely trying to ensure the flight's safety and give the two some privacy.[101]

1. Were the first two passengers overly sensitive, or did the flight attendant subconsciously stereotype?
2. If you were the flight attendant, what would you have done to avoid the issue and ensure the plane was balanced?

3.3.2   Challenging Available Social Cues

While the capacity to stereotype is an essential part of our survival mechanism, a great deal of what we stereotype is *socially constructed*, based on the available social cues around us. For example, we are not born with the biases that the British have awful teeth and the Venezuelans are addicted to plastic surgery. These generalizations have been created, popularized by various channels of information, and picked up by our brain. In one episode of *The Simpsons*, a dentist scared children into better oral hygiene by showing him *The Big Book of British Smiles*. The stereotype is the material for countless jokes and comedies, including the famous films about Austin Powers, a spoof British super-spy and would be sex-symbol with rotten teeth. Similarly, the idea that men and women in Venezuela are obsessed with plastic surgery is also socially constructed through beauty pageants, documentaries, news articles, and conversations with people, etc. Our brain receives and registers such information subconsciously and the next time that the topic of "British" and "Venezuela" pop up, the brain will do what it does best in the course of survival: make a snap judgment based on available social cues: linking "British" and "Venezuela" with "bad teeth" and "plastic surgery."

While we can't eliminate this impulsive reaction (besides, we still need it), what we can do is consciously regulate the "available social cues" around us. There are a few ways to put this in practice:

3.3.2.1   *Matching the Criteria for Cultural Fact*

Most stereotypes and prejudices are not so straightforward when matched against research and statistics. We soon learn that nuances, grey areas, contexts and changes can turn even the most obvious stereotype into an endless debate and discussions. The act of checking is similar to the neural activity of the rostrolateral prefrontal cortex (RLPFC), i.e. overriding stereotypes, inhibiting subconscious impulses and forcing our mind to listen to facts and logics. For the record, and if you are curious, the UK's dental hygiene is actually second to none,[102] and Venezuela ranked a cool 15th for levels of plastic surgery, behind South Korea, Canada, the US, Germany and many other Latin American countries.[103] Such a check tells us that the "available social cues" around us are not necessarily the reality.

There is a world of difference between a stereotype and an accurate cultural description. It is helpful to remember that stereotypes and prejudice are based on perception, and accurate cultural description is based on research. Here are four criteria for determining whether cultural information is valid and not just a stereotype or prejudice: (1) it is descriptive and not judgmental; (2) it is verifiable from more than one independent source; (3) it applies at least to a statistical majority; (4) it compares between different populations.[104]

Consider the following statement: "The Dutch are tall." The first criterion is justified, because the statement does not attach a moral connotation, good or bad. The second criterion is missing. There must be at least two studies confirming that the height of the Dutch is above the world's average. The third criterion is also not met (What is the percentage? Obviously not *all* Dutch are tall). The fourth criterion is vague, since "being tall" without a frame of comparison is useless (Taller than whom?) Conclusion: the statement in its original form is more of a stereotype than an accurate cultural observation.

The Middle East is stereotypically seen as conservative. However, Syria, Tunisia, Lebanon and many other urban communities embrace a liberal, progressive and modern lifestyle/ "A shopping mall in Beirut, (Lebanon)," MAI NGUYEN-PHUONG-MAI.

3.3.2.2   *Checking Language and the Environment*

Implicit stereotypes are pervasive because they are hidden and invisible. We can't point a figure at them and yet, we are immensely influenced by them. For example, our language can convey subtle signals of stereotypes when we say: "hey *guys*" to a group of both boys and girls, when we say "*Ni hao*" ("hello" in Chinese) to Asian-looking people, or when we are surprised that a woman from Timor-Leste – a poor country in South East Asia – is *leading* a successful business in Europe, etc. These *micro-aggressions* can be so subtle that neither victim, nor perpetrator may entirely understand what is going on, thus making the consequences even more frustrating and toxic.

The power of subtle signals is incredible in the surrounding environment. How a place is designed can subconsciously influence our work productivity and emotion.[105-106] In one study,[107] both men and women chose to work with the science team whose office was not decorated stereotypically (i.e. generic items rather than computer gear, game devices, sci-fi posters, cans of drink, etc.), and more women chose to do so than men (an overwhelming 82 per cent). This means everything around us: the décor of an office, names of the buildings, colors of the walls, objects on the desk, advertisements on the streets, names of the districts, the cleanliness of a neighborhood, the diversity (or the lack thereof) of the pedestrians, etc. can result in an instant appraisal about whether someone will fit into and feel welcome in a certain culture.

ACTIVITY

Here are some examples of micro-aggressions, adapted from a study by Sue Wing and colleagues[108] – the passengers featured in the case study above. Please try to figure out the subconscious messages for each category of examples (the first one has been done for you), and add any examples that you find.

1. Alien in own land
Micro-aggression: Asking someone who looks different from the dominant culture: "Where are you from?" / "Where are you *really* from?" / "Ok, where were your ancestors from?" / "What are you?" / "You speak good Arabic (English/Hindi) …" / "You sound so White" / "How do you say this in your native language?" / "You people…" / "Your kind…" / Presuming that a judge cannot do his job fairly just because of his race (Mexican heritage),[109] etc.
The subconscious messages: No matter what, you are a foreigner here; You are not one of us – the real and original citizens.

Alternative approaches: "Please tell me a little bit about yourself" / "Do you happen to know anyone who can help me with this question?"

2. Assumption of inferiority and ascription of capacity
Micro-aggression: "You are a credit to your race" / "Your achievement is amazing, given your origin and background"/ "Oh wow, you *actually* can write so well"/ "You go beyond those typical girly stuff"/ Asking an Asian to help solve a math problem; or someone from the Middle East to talk about Islam/ Expecting or appointing a male or white person to lead a group / Asking a man to fix electricity / Asking a woman to take care of office housework such as organizing party or making coffee,[110] etc.
The subconscious messages: …
Alternative approaches: …

3. Color/Religion… Blindness
Micro-aggression: "I never see you as a black man" / "There is only one race, the human race" / "Not *black lives matter* but all *lives matter*"[111] / "We are all children of God" / "We absolutely have a culture of equality and transparency here, sexism and racism don't exist in our office," etc.
The subconscious messages: …
Alternative approaches: …

4. Denial of individual bias or the impact of bias
Micro-aggression: "I'm not racist (homophobic), I have black (Muslim/Jewish/gay) friends"/ "Anyone can succeed as long as they work hard enough" / "May the best man win" / "You have only yourself to blame", etc.
The subconscious messages: …
Alternative approaches: …

3.3.2.3   *Exposing Yourself to Counter-Stereotypes*

Because our brain is *subconsciously* tuned in to stereotypes, we need a constant reminder that we can *consciously* override this instinctive tendency. We may challenge that impulsive part of our mind by purposely reaching out to the opposite end of the bias. Studies tell us that female students who see female science professors and experts are more interested and self-confident in STEM (science, technology, engineering, and math).[112-113] The influence of counter-stereotypical examples is so powerful that even a picture of "This is Rebecca. She is a bricklayer" or "This is Christopher. He is a make-up artist" can help to overcome spontaneous gender bias.[114] More interestingly, this can also be done just by *imagining* a counter-stereotype. In a series of experiments, participants were asked to imagine a "strong woman." Their subsequent implicit association test showed that this simple mental exercise *lowered* their level of implicit sexism.[115]

In Oman, it is a norm that men carry children. Reaching out to counter-stereotypes is a strategy to train the brain and change the available social cues around us/ "Poster in a Muscat's hospital," "A man with his child in Muscat, (Oman)," MAI NGUYEN-PHUONG-MAI.

The takeaway is, we can challenge our sub-consciousness by searching for stories that tell otherwise, making friends with those who are negatively stereotyped, finding role models that do not conform to the bias, consciously using non-typical cases and irregular examples in our work, putting an image of such a case on our desk or making it the screensaver on our computer, etc. By doing so, we are actively *alternating* the "available social cues" around us and hence, giving ourselves a reminder and a chance to be objective.

3.3.2.4   Collecting Data

Collecting data is essential[116] because it is hard to improve what we can't measure. In the absence of information, we have a tendency to use stereotypes to fill the empty space. For example, when women and men are evaluated separately, women score equally (7.57) in comparison with men

(7.33). But when they are collectively evaluated, women's work is evaluated with less quality (5.33) than that of men (6.50). This means the less information we have, the more likely we are to rely on stereotypes.[117] Organizations that want to combat biases should build a database with not only the usual demographics, but also continuous surveys and work records, which are useful indicators for areas that need improvement. By doing this, the available social cues that are the *material of biases* will be replaced by available social cues that help to *confront* them.

3.3.2.5   Creating a Vigilant Culture against Biases

If the destructive power of stereotypes is that they are implicit and subconscious, then we need to *purposely make it conscious.* One way to do this is to create an environment where biases can be exposed, where people have to justify their decisions, where everyone is constructively vigilant against any signals of biases. At Google for example, a majority of employees take training on subconscious biases, and it is showing impact, according to Laszlo Bock – the company's Human Resources executive:

> During one recent promotion meeting in which a group of male managers were deciding the fate of a female engineer, a senior manager who had been through the bias training cautioned his colleagues to remember that they were all men – and thus might not be able to fully appreciate the different roles women perform in engineering groups. "Just raising the awareness was enough for people to think about it," Mr. Bock said. The woman was promoted.
>
> Another time, in an all-company presentation, an interviewer asked a male and female manager who had recently begun sharing an office, "Which one of you does the dishes?" The strange, sexist undertone of the question was immediately seized upon by a senior executive in the crowd, who yelled, "Unconscious bias!"
>
> Mr. Bock saw all of these actions as evidence that the training was working. "Suddenly you go from being completely oblivious to going, "Oh my god, it's everywhere."[118]

However, it is important to differentiate between such an open culture with one that is *threatening.* Psychologically, it takes incredible courage to admit that we are wrong. "Backfire" happens when people feel they are being cornered. The more threatened they feel, the less likely they are to listening to dissenting opinions, and the more easily controlled they will be.

3.3.2.6   Being on the Same Side

If group love is the origin of prejudices, it can also be the tactic to fight against it. A neural experiment shows that simply putting people in a mixed group reduces biases.[119] People form ingroup favoritism very easily, at the flip of a coin. The amygdala doesn't see race, gender, or religion. It only sees ingroup and outgroup. The implication of such a study is powerful, because it means we can deal with biases by the idea of *unity*, i.e. that we are on the same team, be it a work group, a company, a country or a planet.

Stereotypes and prejudices are created from available social cues. We can unlearn them, challenge these cues and change the culture around us by:
- *Training the brain to resist the amygdala's impulse and listen more to the ACC.*
- *Matching the criteria to distinguish between stereotype and cultural fact*
- *Checking language and environment for microagressions*
- *Exposing counter-stereotypes*
- *Collecting data*
- *Creating a vigilant culture against biases*
- *Creating and recreating groups to be on the same side*

In sum, we acknowledge the role of stereotypes and our tendency towards group love. But we are also aware that, as human beings, we are capable of creating a culture that supports our own survival. And if our survival in the modern era relies on *cooperation* with different others and the ability to go *beyond the force of subconscious*, then combating stereotypes and prejudices is the right track to follow. By challenging the available social cues around us, we can take an active role in changing the culture in which biases are blown out of proportion and giving our amygdala a constant stream of false signals. By training the brain, we can take an active role in changing our behaviors and values, tapping into the incredible plasticity of our brain to learn and unlearn. After all, stereotypes and prejudices are everywhere and we cannot avoid them. We cannot even escape their immediate impact. However, we have the choice not to act upon them and, even better, to modify our natural tendency, regulate our own behavior and make an impact on society.

Summary

1.   Stereotyping is a survival mechanism that helps us make quick judgments. However, in our modern times, life-threatening dangers are not always around the corner and we are overloaded with information. Hence, quick calls based

on subconscious thinking have shortcomings when we stereotype people: using collective level for individual level, and vice versa.

2. Stereotypes can be stronger than fact. They exclude those who don't fit the box and create anxiety that can reduce performance. Positive stereotypes can cause burden, blurring the real problems while deepening group conflicts.

3. Prejudices are rooted in the biological need to categorize other groups and to love one's ingroup/culture – the source of survival strategies.

4. When there are conflicts of resources, prejudices prevail with a need for scapegoats.

5. Institutionalized discrimination is embedded (sub)consciously in processes, regulations, and operating systems. It creates barriers through biases, unfair selection procedures, increased caution, more blaming, quicker rejection, etc.

6. Stereotypes and prejudices are created from available social cues. We can unlearn them, challenge these cues and actively change the culture around us.

4. Non-Verbal Communication – How You Make Them Feel

Objective

At the end of this chapter, you should be able to:

· Explain the role of non-verbal communication and its root in biology.
· Describe the role of context in non-verbal communication at the universal, collective and individual level.
· Prove the significance of non-verbal cues in communication.
· Identify the limitation of non-verbal communication and its current theories.

Chapter outline

It is a sunny morning and you've been up since 4 am, getting ready for an interview for your dream job. You've spent a fortune on a good pant suit, your shoes couldn't be shinier, and you've tried your best to put on a natural make-up look. You arrived at the company half an hour earlier than the appointment and, at precisely 9:10, you're led to the office of the Human Resources Executive. As you enter the room, three people stand up to welcome you. You reach out to shake hands with each of them, and sit down on a chair that appears to be reserved for you. The interview begins with a friendly question: "How are you today?"

It may take about 45 minutes or less for the interview to end, but the fact is: Employers make up their minds about you in just *four* seconds, starting from the moment you walk through the door.[1] Recruiters only need an extra six minutes to definitely know whether they are going to hire you or not. Their decisions are based on your eye contact, the way you enter the room, shake hands, the way you dress, smile, touch your hair, control your voice, or position your body, etc. It means decisions are made almost as soon as the greetings are over.

In this chapter, we will explore the role of those non-verbal cues and the way they send messages that speak volumes about you, without you uttering a word. We will explore to what extent non-verbal cues can be understood universally, and to what extent they mean different things in different contexts.

4.1   The role of non-verbal communication

Non-verbal communication indicates all non-verbal, intentional and unintentional stimuli that have the potential to convey a communication message. In the metaphorical tree of culture, it belongs to the leaf-and-canopy layer. This includes everything in our surroundings as well as what our body communicates. In general, the surroundings include time and space, while the body includes all five senses in interaction: 83 per cent sight, 11 per cent hearing, 3 per cent smell, 2 per cent touch, and 1 per cent taste.[2] Their role in communication is crucial, and this section will discuss them in depth.

4.1.1   The Universal Role of Non-verbal Communication

The majority of literature on non-verbal communication in intercultural context focuses on the differences across cultures. However, the Inverted Pyramid model reminds us that we are similar at the universal level, and the metaphorical tree of culture reminds us that we all share certain similar outward expressions. For this reason, we should start the discussion at the point we converge, rather than diverge.

4.1.1.1   Primary Means of Communication

Regardless of our diversity, there are certain facial expressions that tell the same story around the world, from the Tongan islanders in the middle of the Pacific to the urban inhabitants of Monaco. These facial expressions are understood across cultures and thus, are arguably biological in origin: anger, disgust, fear, joy, sadness and surprise.[3] The bottom line is, we are one species, with a shared and innate genetic inheritance of the most basic emotions. In *The Expression of the Emotions in Man and Animals,*[4] Charles Darwin attributed human facial expressions to the associated habits in our evolutionary past. For example, if a species attacks by biting, baring teeth was a crucial signal before an assault. With the creation of language, we no longer need to show our teeth to communicate anger. However, the behavior retains its communicative values today, as an *external evidence of our internal state.*

With roots in biology, non-verbal communication has been the primary and the most basic means of expressing ourselves.[5] It has been more fundamental than vocal languages,[6] especially during the period when languages had not yet sophisticatedly evolved. Facial expressions aside, globalization has increased the number of non-verbal outward expressions that many of us can understand, to the extent that we can often follow a muted movie or a conversation in a foreign language and generally understand the main message. Today, whenever there is a language barrier, we automatically use body gestures, costumes and elements from the surroundings to communicate. It is also the reason why body language can have an impact *eight times* more powerful than verbal messages.[7] They are considered the *evidence*, the primary means of communication before language even existed, and thus a more honest, more genuine indicator of true feelings. Consequently, when body language and actual words *contradict* each other, people are more likely to believe the non-verbal cues than the words.[8] Consider a situation when one announces: "We would like to welcome our new manager." Regardless of what it is said, if her/his body language somehow sends a different message, i.e. the smile is not bright enough, the voice is not enthusiastic enough, the hands are not in the right place, etc., the audience will surely take the non-verbal message for the truth. They would clap their hands, but their heart would sink and their mind would think: "Oh dear! This new manager is going to be a disaster!"

4.1.1.2   Indicator for Judgment

Universally, non-verbal cues are essential in guiding our decisions. Some may call it "gut feeling," some may call it "first impressions." Whatever the term, it suggests that non-verbal messages influence the flow of the interaction *before* verbal messages even have a chance to arrive. Link to this what we learnt about stereotypes and biases. The amygdala receives information and immediately and subconsciously categorizes individuals into ingroup and outgroup. This happens rapidly, to the extent that a minimal exposure of as little as 100 milliseconds is sufficient to draw a judgment about a stranger's face.[9] As we know, this is rooted in our evolutionary past, when the ingroup was the primary source of survival and outgroups were often the enemy. It helped our ancestors to quickly and subconsciously decide whether they should fight or flight when meeting a stranger.

Modern day life is not as simple. We are overloaded with information and we often have to cooperate with outgroup people to manage resources effectively. The snap judgment is no longer useful and we know it does us good to resist the first impulse. However, we cannot be totally rid of its impacts yet, because culture has evolved too quickly for our genes to catch up, and the power transition from genes to culture is still in its last stage. In the first few seconds of contact, according to body language expert Eliot Hoppe,[10] we will have already answered four fundamental questions: (1) Do I like you? (2) Can I trust you? (3) Am I safe with you? (4) Who do you remind me of? In short, we size up people literally from the first glance. We use their non-verbal cues, such as body language, clothes, skin color, gender and make-up, to match with stereotypes and our own personal experiences. In an interesting study, two groups of students rated their teachers, one group after an entire semester of class interaction, and the other group only by watching several two-second video clips, without sound, of teachers who they had never met. The rating results of these two groups were very similar. This means first impressions are decisive, taking into account that the second group based their evaluation *solely on body language,* without hearing the voice or attending the lessons.[11]

This tendency to rely on initial non-verbal cues has tremendous influence in recruitment.[12-13] It would be unfortunate if a job candidate pulls her/his legs and arms inwards – a stereotypical sign of insecurity, or if her/his voice happens to resemble that of the recruiter's bossy colleague. Without being aware of these reasons, the recruiter will make a decision without exchanging a single word with the candidate. Employers often trust their first impressions more than objective tests.[14] A survey of 2,500 hiring managers reveals that failure to make eye contact (67 per cent), lack

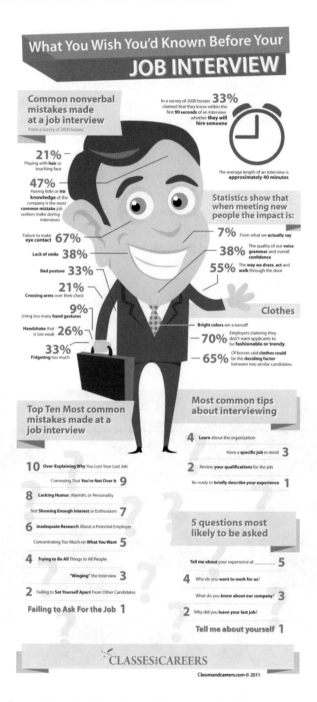

The impact of non-verbal cues in job interviews, with statistics gathered from various sources including Albert Mehrabian,[15] and Career Builder[16]/ "What you wish you'd known before your job interview," CLASSANDCAREERS.[17]

of smile (38 per cent) and fidgeting too much (33 per cent) would make them less likely to hire someone.[18] Among similar candidates, those with non-verbal behaviors that match the expectation of recruiters surely stand out (The Salience Hypothesis).[19] HR executives may make their decision at the beginning of the job interview and spend the rest of the talk *reinforcing* their first impression (The Reinforcement Theory).[20] In a vicious circle, the recruiter's behaviors will cause the applicant to interact in a manner that *confirms* the recruiter's impression.[21] This means a candidate will show competence if s(he) is treated as a competent applicant with approval cues (smiling, nodding, eye contact, hand gestures, etc.), and vice versa. Although these studies were conducted among Western participants, and hence, should be taken with caution at the universal level, it does give an indication of how influential non-verbal messages are.

4.1.1.3   Creating Identity

Non-verbal communication is also a major source for establishing identity. Our hairstyle, way of walking, or even means of transport, etc. are influenced by the kind of collective identities we want to belong to or are supposed to be part of.

In 2014, Conchita Wurst won the Eurovision Song Contest for Austria. As an artist, Wurst is a "she," but as an individual, Wurst is a "he" with his birth name Thomas Neuwirth. The persona of a bearded woman – Conchita – is central to his identity, as Neuwirth visually communicates this information through his grooming and dressing style/ "Wurst holding Eurovision trophy after winning the contest," ALBIN OLSSON.[22]

Fashion, for example, provides one of the most ready means for individuals and collective cultures to make expressive visual statements about their identity, especially in metropolitan cities where diversity is a norm and people have only fleeting moments to impress others.[23] It reflects the wearer's personality, ethnicity, sexual orientation, profession, economic status, educational level, power, etc. Each of us either confirms or subverts the conventional norms in our society by making a choice of what to wear. When a Muslim woman challenged France's full-face veil ban at the European Court of Human Rights, she was seeking to connect the veil with her religious identity.[24] In a reverse situation, when a number of men in Iran wore headscarves and posted on social media, their message was one of solidarity with the women who are forced to cover their hair.[25] When Singapore's first lady Ho Ching carried an $11 purse made by an autistic designer, she wanted to support the country's first autism-focus school.[26] When the Punks put on their anti-fashion style of dress, their creativity communicated the anger and frustration at the changing political and economic structures of their time.[27] When Bhutan imposed its strict dress code (men with *gho*, women with *kira*) on every governmental office, school and monastery, the intention was to reinforce a national identity that is at risk as Bhutan is squashed between two strong cultures: India and China. Thus, regardless of cultural level and background, universally, every individual and group uses non-verbal communication as a means to construct identity.

4.1.2   Non-verbal Communication at the Collective Level

While the roles of non-verbal communication are universal, not all non-verbal messages are universally understood and recognized. Collective cultures influence the way we use non-verbal outward expressions to communicate, to judge and to establish identity. At this level of the Inverted Pyramid model, we learn from our social surroundings how to convey, decode and react to a certain non-verbal cue. For example, a smile is a universal sign of non-threat, but in Russia, the equivalent words for "grin" have negative connotations (оскал, оскалбиться, скалиться),[28] and the lack of social smiles in Russia has been arguably shaped by the Soviet culture.[29] Being beautiful is a universal desire, but it is socially constructed in terms of "the body" in the West (hence, the dominance of fashion magazines) and in terms of "the pretty face" in East Asia (hence, the dominance of beauty magazines).[30] The list goes on.

130 INTERCULTURAL COMMUNICATION

4.1.3 Non-verbal Communication at the Individual Level

At the individual level, each person is unique, and we can only guess that if a person comes from a certain collective culture, (s)he *may* have similar collective outward expressions as the majority of the people living there. Thus, if your new colleague comes from the Gulf, you can only make a general prediction that (s)he *might* dress in loose outfits according to the Islamic modesty rule of not revealing physical curves. However, this can never be guaranteed, since it is not uncommon that Gulf woman and men purposely dress with modern and progressive fashion style to communicate their identity.

While we are on the topic of dress codes, it is noteworthy that many Muslims use different layers of attires, literally, to communicate their identities. Western and fashionable clothes are often hidden under the flowing black or white cloaks that can be taken on and off depending on the social situation. In the conservative culture of Yemen, young women cover themselves in black *abaya*, but show off their most extravagant and sensual costumes, which reveal much of their body, in gender-separation weddings as a way to communicate their beauty and attract marriage prospects.

- *Non-verbal cues belong to the canopy of the tree of culture and the context circle around the Inverted Pyramid model. Universally, they have crucial roles in:*
  1. *being the primary means of communication*
  2. *being indicators for judgment, even before verbal exchange starts*
  3. *being a means to create identities*
- *While a number of non-verbal cues are understood universally, most of them should be interpreted from cultural and individual perspectives.*

4.2 The role of context in non-verbal communication

Non-verbal communication is a sub-component of the tangible context (Figure 4.1). In the job interview scenario at the beginning of this chapter, the context that constantly sends out messages comes from both the environment and the body language of those involved. This context is crucial to interpreting non-verbal messages correctly; for example, the attire or seating position that are proper for an interview could be awkward for a social gathering. In this section, we will discuss the role of context in understanding and communicating non-verbal cues.

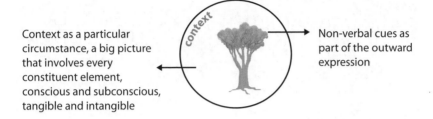

Context as a particular circumstance, a big picture that involves every constituent element, conscious and subconscious, tangible and intangible

Non-verbal cues as part of the outward expression

Figure 4.1. The position of non-verbal communication in the metaphorical tree of culture and the role of context.

4.2.1 Context at the Universal Level

In Chapter 1, we learned that culture is at the last stage of replacing genes to become the resource of life instruction for humans. While genes are more fixed, culture is malleable, evolving and constantly on the move. As a result, the instructions we receive from culture are not a fixed set of rules of the type that animals get from genes, but situational, contextual, depending on various circumstances and interactions. Culture is always encapsulated in *context* – illustrated by a circle that envelops the whole Inverted Pyramid model, the metaphorical tree and the Diagram of Diversity Pathways. Our behaviors are determined by factors such as: who we communicate with, when, where, why and how. A concern, a value, or an outward expression has little meaning without a story behind it.

Similarly, non-verbal communication should be seen through the lens of context. Imagine a close-up photo capturing a couple kissing. We need a specific context to decide whether the kiss is appropriate or not. For instance, many people may find a public kiss improper, but those same people may tolerate a kiss from a newly wedded couple in their wedding ceremony in front of many onlookers. *Different contexts call for different rules.* In comparison, animals, which take their life rules from genes, do not rely on cultural contexts to gauge their thinking and doing. They would be most likely to listen to their instinct, obeying their genes' instruction and therefore, they basically mate (or "kiss" for that matter) whenever their biological body feels ready for it. In sum, context is crucial to understanding the meaning of non-verbal messages. Context to culture is like location to real estate properties. It does not matter what kind of house, it is all about location, location, location.

The face veil is an outward expression that carries different meanings in different contexts for different wearers. For example, it is regarded as a tool to protect women from people with bad intentions, as a religious garment that has been imposed on women, but also as a way for some other women to be liberated from being a sex object, or as a religious symbol such as the cross. Covering one's face has a strong political connotation as well, as with the Global Justice Movement, the Million Mask March, the Occupy, the KKK, or the Anonymous. In this picture, the Zapatista – a revolutionary leftist group in Mexico, which fights for indigenous rights – cover their face in order "to be seen"/ "The Zapatista in Chiapas, (Mexico)," MAI NGUYEN-PHUONG-MAI.

4.2.2   Context at the Collective Level

While our concern for context and our dependence on context is the same for all human beings at the universal level, the importance we place on it and our dependence on it vary at the collective and individual level of the Inverted Pyramid model. Edward Hall coined this degree of divergence "low context" and "high context." To be consistent with our framework, we should understand these terms correctly as *Low Context Dependence* and *High Context Dependence*. The former refers to those who are less dependent on context (including non-verbal cues) while communicating, hence, "low." The latter refers to those who are more dependent on context (including non-verbal cues) in their communication exchanges, hence, "high." Some collective cultures, individuals and situations prefer high context, others prefer low context.

4.2.2.1   *The Characteristics of High and Low Context Dependence*

In low context dependent communication, "the mass of the information is vested in the explicit codes."[31] A large part of the message is spelt out with clear words, symbols and actions. The mode of communication is also direct and to-the-point, leaving little doubt and little need to rely on guesswork. When someone says: "Yes, we like your project very much," those who depend on low context at that moment may take the verbal message for the truth, thinking to themselves: "Our project is great." In that situation, they place a low level of importance on the context in which this statement is given.

In high context dependent communication, most of the information is "internalized in the person, while very little is in the coded, explicit, transmitted part of the message."[32] The mode of communication is indirect and implicit, asking communicators to read between the lines and rely on the context to understand the real message. The same statement "Yes, we like your project very much!" should not always be taken word for word to be the true meaning; rather, the environment (context) of this statement, with *every non-verbal cues possible*, should be taken into account: How was this statement spoken? What was the facial expression? What was the tone in which it was expressed? What was the posture of the body? What was the relationship between two parties at that point? Had there been any ups and downs in the recent past? Who made the statement? Could the status of the speaker influence the way (s)he spoke? What is the personality of the spokesperson? Is (s)he known for being direct or politically correct? Was there a third party present at that moment who might have influenced the context? Where was the statement made, in a formal meeting or a casual gathering? When was the statement made, after a rigorous evaluation process or before the decision maker had a chance to look at it? Is it possible that this statement should be read as: "We like your project, but we are not going to approve it," or even "We actually don't find it interesting at all"? In short, non-verbal cues from both setting context (time and place) and the body context are evaluated to reach the final interpretation.

Public signs can expose differing levels of context dependence. The Dutch translation reads: "Keep passport ready," which has a slightly different tone than the English one/ "A sign at Schiphol airport, (The Netherlands)," MAI NGUYEN-PHUONG-MAI.

Many cognitive studies have shown that when assessing an incident, for example, looking at a picture of a tiger in a jungle, low context dependence makes people focus on the central image, but the eyes of high context people tend to dart around, taking in the background,[33] and when asked to recall the scene, they remembered more secondary details.[34] Low context children learn nouns easier than verbs, and high context children pick up verbs – which naturally relate objects to each other – more easily.[35] In tests of categorization,[36] those who rely less on context are more likely to group items based on how well they fit into categories by types. For example, given three words, "train," "bus," and "track," low context dependent people tend to group "train" and "bus" together because they are both *vehicles*. Those who rely more on context tend to group items based on relationships, so "train" and "track" go together, because *trains run on tracks*. Another study[37] reported that when explaining other people's behavior, low context dependence influences how we emphasize the personal attributes (e.g. "He failed because he was not smart"), but high context dependence made us focus more on situational factors (e.g. "He failed because his family didn't support him"). Interestingly, while low context dependent people need to talk out loud in order to work things out, forcing high context dependent people to talk actually *impairs* their performance.[38] For low context dependence, it is "we talk, therefore we think." For high context dependence, it should be "we *observe*, therefore we think."

This differing level of context dependence can have significant impact on all aspects of our life. Think about the next time you design an advertisement, would you have a picture of the product that highlights all its qualities, or a picture of a person using the product to enjoy a better life with her/his loved ones, in a nice, relatable and homely setting? Think about the next time you introduce a project, would you focus on the content of the work, or would you draw a big picture of the historical context that has led to this project, the wonderfully cooperative team of people behind it, and the close relationship with other stakeholders? Or think about the next time you run a meeting, would you judge those who verbally contribute more favorably than those who quietly sit and contemplate, or would you try to create other channels for opinions to flow without the need to speak out?

Table 4.1. Typical outward expressions in Low and High Context Dependence

Low Context Dependence	High Context Dependence
Rely less on non-verbal cues	Rely more on non-verbal cues
Communication is explicit, direct, and rational	Communication is implicit, indirect, and intuitive
Rely more on words	Rely on both words and non-verbal elements
Start with main points, end with details	Full of details, main points are implied
More content-oriented	More context-oriented (body language and surrounding)
Information should be abundant, detailed and specific	Information is embedded in the surrounding
Concerned with patterns of events, details of the picture	Concerned with the "shape" of events, holistic picture

4.2.2.2   The (Dis)advantages of High and Low Context Dependence

Generally, members of a co-culture, such as people of the same age, sexual orientation, ethnic background, or even a group of friends will tend to be high context dependent for the obvious reason that they are *insiders*. As part of the group, they know the ins and outs of the usual communication, and hence can decode the real message much quicker than outsiders. For instance, those with an accounting background form a high context community where members use their own non-verbal cues, terminologies, slang, symbols and actions to reflect their particular values and concerns. Their codes of conducts are mutually understood and shared. Their information networks are liquid and easy to absorb so that without much being explicitly spelt out, they can still understand each other and cooperate effectively. Hence, communication within high context dependence cultures is very efficient and fast, since its individuals know the cues, the signals, and the true meanings behind them. At the negotiation table, a brief exchange of eye contact among colleagues of the same team is enough for mutual understanding, or a careful choice of word is sufficient to convey a message without having to wait for another lengthy explanation of the details. This makes the decision making process much more effective and time saving, especially if the team is working under pressure. However, to reach this point of "syncing," time must have been devoted to building a mutual connection with each other in the past, effort must have been invested in understanding each other long before the cooperation started, and a relationship must have been established to the point that people are connected naturally without even having to utter a word. For outsiders as well as newcomers, the only way to get things done is to be part of this co-culture. This means learning to look for the holistic picture, to recognize the hidden details of communication, to interpret the non-verbal message correctly, and to react accordingly. This takes time, but for those who are open-minded, things can happen faster.

Space and subtlety reign supreme in Japanese architecture culture. Paper doors, emptiness, and gaps act as features of the house, enabling hidden borders and defining a sophisticated relationship between the house's occupants and the visitors, between soto (outsider) and uchi (insider), between the external world and the home sanctuary. Stepping inside a traditional Japanese home is a test of your honesty, dignity, manner and social ranking/ "A traditional Japanese tearoom with a small and low entrance at the left corner, which one needs to bend down to pass – a subtle request to ask people to leave their ego outside," MAI NGUYEN-PHUONG-MAI.

Communication with low context dependence has different characteristics. The structure that reduces the importance of context has to be simple, systematic and clear. As a result, it is easy to change[39] as long as the change is transparent and logistic in nature. Eliminating context also leads to a tendency to create systems that have high levels of replicability, and instruments that can be universally applied, regardless of the local context. This partly explains why many low context Western multinational companies quickly gain success in emerging markets with low level retail saturation, where customers enthusiastically embrace new Western products. However, they have to cope with the extra challenges of localization[40] when high context dependent customers become picky once there are more choices available. In comparison, high context Asian multinational companies may have an advantage when going global, thanks to their holistic tendency. Whereas Western multinationals have developed in a linear and methodical manner, Asian trailblazers have made up for lost time by embracing flexibility, multi-tasking, diversity, being attentive and learning quickly on the job.[41] In 2015, Asia Pacific-headquartered companies accounted for 40 per cent of the firms in the Fortune Global 500, outnumbering those headquartered in Europe (30 per cent) or North America (28 per cent).

4.2.2.3   When High Context Meets Low Context

Context provides a big picture. When embracing high context dependence, people try to take in all hidden details and non-verbal cues in order to decode the true meaning of communication. When embracing low context dependence, people tend to focus on the explicit message that is clearly spelt out. When these two levels of context dependence match up without sufficient preparation, misunderstanding may occur, often leading to confusion for those who relied less on context (why and where did it go wrong?) and irritation for those who relied more on context (why couldn't they just understand? It is *so* obvious!). At one point in our careers, we are all likely to experience a low context dependent manager trying to impose a new way of working, more or less ignoring – or at least failing to acknowledge – the unique context of the new working environment. Similarly, high context dependent managers may take too much time to understand the new working environment, and may initially appear, in the eyes of the low context dependent staff, as indecisive or disorganized. Another example is the ambiguity of responses such as "Maybe!" which confuse high context dependent people. The reasons behind this answer vary. It can be a subtle promise, a genuine belief in the possibility, a polite rejection, or a sign that the person does not want to let others down by promising something they can't guarantee.

Studies that follow the static paradigm of culture posit that low context dependence is the prevalent form of communication in German-speaking countries and North America.[42] For example, the low context dependent Dutch are often criticized for being too direct, rude, and upfront, sometimes even insensitive in their comments and opinions.[43] High context dependent cultures are usually in Asia, Africa, South America and the Middle East, thus covering a much larger part of the world. Those who are not aware of their high context mode of communication would wrongly blame their counterparts from these regions for being inscrutable, mysterious, vague, and sometimes dishonest with their words and feelings. Squeezed in the middle of these two levels are islanders such as the UK and Southern European countries. Without proper knowledge of your individual counterparts, your *first best guess* when attending a negotiation process with people from these cultures is that: the Dutch will quickly approach a point of talking about price, the English will painstakingly and politely create a whole story before getting down to the main issue of why they set such a price, and the Macanese, who are not as expressive as their counterparts, will make polite, generic comments or meaningful facial expressions of approval or disapproval that may go completely unnoticed by other parties.

ACTIVITY

Predict the meaning behind these statements and techniques in high and low context dependent culture:

1. "I have a small suggestion"
2. Changing the subject
3. Saying yes
4. "I have to inform my manager and wait for her opinion"
5. Telling a story that seems to be off the subject
6. Asking a question about or returning to a point that was previously agreed upon
7. When you ask for opinion, the person responds with "What do YOU think?"
8. Smiling
9. "Probably"; "I think so"; "I'm almost sure"; "There is a good possibility"
10. Mentioning someone who used to be in charge of the negotiation, but who has since left the company

CASE STUDY

Customer service

In countries with a saturated retail market, such as South Africa, UAE, Philippines or Malaysia,[44] there is an intense price competition. The only sustainable advantage that companies can work on is to focus on customer services.[45] Customers in high context dependent cultures tend not to express their dissatisfaction and avoid dealing with problems.[46] This is in stark contrast with low context dependent cultures, where customers are more likely to express their anger and ask for compensation.[47]

1. As head of a customer service department, what would you do to deal with this cultural characteristic of high context dependence?
2. How can you take advantage of the tendency of customers with high context dependence to maintain harmony without overlooking any problems?

Web design
International marketing requires interface design to include culture-specific color connotations, preferences in layout, animation, sound, etc.[48] In which market (low, average or high context dependence) is each of the following websites more appealing? Provide your explanation.

1. There are animations of young people dancing, greeting each other, or showing the site orientation. There are videos that provide the impression that a visitor is virtually welcomed by the staff. There is sound or a jingle in the background. There is limited amount of text. The layout uses many bright colors, fonts and shapes. The website encourages exploration.
2. The images are more static and sedate. The home page has a large collection of links with the use of headings, subheadings and illustrations. There are no pop-up windows. The website encourages quick decision making.

(*Case adapted from a study by Elizabeth Würtz [2005]*[49])

4.2.3   Context at the Individual Level

While all cultures rely on context, most cultures can be quite dynamic, with changes and paradoxes inherent in the process, depending on circumstances. Meanwhile, every individual is unique and capable of adapting and evolving. It is not unusual to see a blunt Cambodian, an ambiguous German, or a direct Burmese, etc. It is also not unusual to see a high context dependent person gradually becoming low context. The brain's plasticity and the demand of each particular situation can have significant impact on how people adjust and change their behavior. For example, if the everyday working environment or a particular circumstance requires someone to take a holistic approach, to have an extensive use of symbolic and body language, to read between the lines, to rely more on experience-based and intuitive knowledge rather than details, rules, and formal logic, etc., then the best way to deal with this new situation is to attempt a shift in thinking style from low to high context dependence. It is not easy, but as the old wisdom goes, practice makes perfect.

In the next two sections, we will focus on two main categories of context: messages that deal with the *setting* (time and space) and messages that are produced by the *body* (touch, body movement, facial expression, etc.). It must be noted that although Hall coined the term "context," his theory intensively focuses on the former and not the latter.

- *High context dependence contributes to situational efficiency, flexibility and holistic policies. Low context dependence contributes to universal efficiency and change processes with a transparent and logistic nature.*
- *Context dependence can dynamically change with paradoxes at both collective and individual level, depending on circumstances.*

4.3   Context in setting: time and space

In the interview scenario at the beginning of this chapter, non-verbal cues, such as how early or late you arrived, how your seat and those of the interviewers were arranged, how the office was decorated, and how the interview topics were organized, etc. send certain messages about you and your potential employer. This section will explore the possible meanings behind these seemingly irrelevant, but influential and significant details.

4.3.1   The Language of Time Setting: Chronemics

The term "chronemics" (derived from the Greek word *chrónos* [time]) was coined by Thomas J. Bruneau to describe the study of human tempo in communication.[50] Similar to other cultural aspects, chronemics converges at the universal level and diverges at the collective and individual level.

4.3.1.1   *Chronemics at the Universal Level*
At the universal level of the Inverted Pyramid model, *time* has always been an indispensable dimension of human life and a fundamental concern in the course of survival. It is a special concept, since it can be both an instrument with which life is organized and the environment in which life occurs. As a consequence, time can be seen as a structural framework

for life (e.g. "Time is money") ,[51] or as a natural course of life (e.g. "There is a time for everything"). Hall clarified this level of difference with the concept *chronemics*, referring to a spectrum ranging between *Monochronic* (M-time) and *Polychronic* (P-time). The former indicates lineal and segmented time where it is seen as a "scarce resource which must be rationed and controlled through the use of schedules and appointment, and through aiming to do only one thing at any one time."[52] The latter indicates time as a "support system," meant to be "flexible in order that we do right by the various people to whom we have obligations."[53] No cultures or people are exclusively monochronic or polychronic. All of us need both to survive.

Context dependence and chronemics do not always correlate with each other. Low context Ireland tends to be M-time/strict with time, while low context Israel tends to be P-time/flexible with time. Similarly, high context Finland is M-time/strict with time, but high context Colombia is P-time/ relaxed with time. The bottom line is, high context dependence *relies* more on non-verbal cues *regarding time*, while the reverse is true for low context dependence.

How we use time sends a certain non-verbal message about ourselves, thus helping others to predict the relationship, whether we are ingroup or outgroup, trustworthy or suspicious, conscientious or unreliable, etc. For example, when you turn someone down for an appointment the next day because your agenda is full, without asking why the meeting is necessary, you are indirectly communicating your values, personality and expectations.

4.3.1.2   Chronemics at the Collective and Individual Level

The characteristics of M-time and P-time. However, at the collective level, time is a language of its own, and different cultures and individuals may have their own language of time, differing from one another in seeing time as being at either an M-time or P-time level.

The most important characteristic of M-time is a *sequential approach*. This view of time as a resource emphasizes punctuality, rigid, step-wise organization, detailed schedules, and doing one thing at a time.[54] Time can be spent, saved, wasted and lost.[55] An appointment needs to be set up in advance, meetings start more or less on time, a daily agenda tells people what tasks are important. Time is a framework that controls people's lives. There is a structure that tells people when to commence their activities: the work agenda tells them it's time to run to the next meeting, the bell tells them to leave for the next class, and the marks on the calendar tell them which social gatherings and appointments to attend. It is not uncommon for two good friends to make a social appointment months in advance.

Changes are fine, but should be planned ahead. Spontaneous events are not always welcome. Certain activities have designated time slots. Bearing this in mind, the best way to get someone's attention (your M-time manager for example) is to schedule a meeting, rather than spontaneously knocking on her/his office door or stopping her/him on the way to the coffee machine. In doing business, "time is money," so people should minimize their small talk and get down to business as soon as possible.

For those who lean more towards P-time, the most obvious characteristic is a *cyclical approach.* Embracing P-time means people tend to do many things at the same time, constantly weighing what should be done *in the moment*, constantly adjusting to the circumstances, being spontaneous to the current situation and the big picture. For them, time is not a framework that controls people's lives, but an instrument to serve people's relationships. As the Nigerian proverb goes: "A watch did not invent the man." The emphasis on getting a certain thing done is not as important as maintaining a certain relationship.

In contexts where P-time prevails, people tend to organize their activities in blocks of time, i.e. in "an hour," "half a day," or a "week." As long as they can achieve what they need in that block of time, the exact moment when they do it is less important. It does not mean they are less efficient, but rather that they work at their own pace. As a result, punctuality is not as strongly emphasized as it is at the M-time level. Many business people encounter P-time when they are confronted by a long wait outside governmental offices. It seems hard, but they need to learn to see this less as an insult and somehow convince themselves that their counterparts are still interested, despite the fact that they are kept waiting.[56] In Fiji, for example, people speak of "Fiji time" to indicate a relaxed lifestyle, what cannot be done today can be done tomorrow. In Vietnam and Indonesia, it is "rubber time," where social appointments can be stretched far beyond what seems to have been agreed upon. We also have "Latino time," "Hawaiian time," "BPT" (Black People's Time), or Samoan "coconut time," meaning that it is not necessary to pick coconuts because they will fall when the time is right.[57] We also have the famous Spanish phrase "*Hasta mañana*" (until tomorrow), which, in most cases, does not indicate at all that something will get done tomorrow. Many novices in doing business with the Arabs can have a hard time getting used to their constant expression "*In sha'Allah*" (if God wills it) whenever a plan, a promise, or an appointment is set. Imagine this conversation: "Will you get this document sent next Monday?" – "If God wills, I will!"

When living according to P-time, guests arriving on time (i.e. M-time) can be problematic, since the hosts may still be in the throes of preparation. In Chile, it is considered rude to be on time for social events.[58] Being late is even a sign of dignity. The author of this book was advised at a young age to arrive on a date at least fifteen minutes late, since a decent lady does not hurry to meet a man and should not show excitement about meeting him by arriving on time.

When embracing P-time, people tend to incorporate many activities at the same time. Here are some examples of P-time's multi-tasking: A crowd at the payment counter; an office worker who signs the paper, consults with the clients, and picks up the phone simultaneously; a conversation being interrupted continuously; a social gathering with serious discussion about contracts and business deals, etc.

Table 4.2. Typical outward expressions in monochronic and polychronic time settings

Monochronic (M-time)	Polychronic (P-time)
Time is money	Time is the servant of people
Time is a commodity and can be gained or lost	Time is not a commodity, there is always more time
Structure and order are central	Relationships and people are central
Strict schedules and plans	Flexible schedules and plans
One task at a time, linear order, no interruptions	Multi-tasking, cyclical order, priority adjustable
Emphasis on punctuality, task-orientation	Emphasis on a harmonious relationship

The (dis)advantages of M-time and P-time. With a strong sense of order, embracing M-time means people have a great ability to prioritize, to implement and to get things done. However, their inflexibility when it comes to accommodating new information and the tendency to value time above all else, in turn, are the strengths of P-time. Those who multitask and switch their focus easily can be highly adaptive and responsive to change, but also risk overloading and missing deadlines.

Both practices can be highly effective, as long as we know how things work. For example, the process of repairing spectacle lenses can take weeks or months in some M-time dominant cultures, such as Scandinavia or Australia, which requires you to plan in advance. But in Vietnam and India, your spectacles can be replaced while you wait, and are ready before you take your last sip of tea. For systems that embrace M-time, the best way to speed up an approval process is preparing well in advance and following the procedure. For a P-time system, spending time building trust and cultivating relationships will come in handy when you pick up the phone and expect a P-time friend to drop whatever (s)he is doing to help you put the proposal on the desk of the decision maker. The book that you are reading was finished on time thanks to many people, both from M-time and P-time cultures, who flexibly changed their priorities and extended a helping hand with many different tasks at the last minute. After many years living in Southeast Asia, an entrepreneur concluded: "Doing business in Asia is like doing both a marathon and sprinting: Most of the time you need to work patiently towards a goal (marathon) and adopt a great tempo only when the opportunity is ripe."[59]

CASE STUDY

The shadow economy (underground/informal economy or black market) also has a fancy name: System D. The "D" comes from the French word *"débrouillard"* – meaning someone who is effective, motivated, resourceful, ingenious and can adapt to any situation. System D includes simple street merchants, pop-up stores, opportunistic businesses, vendors at flea markets, roadside farm stands, workers from home, many family and self-employed businesses, non-wage workers in agriculture, or kids selling lemonade in front of their houses. In 2009, the OECD estimated that System D employed half of the world's workers, and this number will increase, to account for two thirds of the world by 2020.[60] The size of System D is approximately 30 per cent of the world's economy and is considered the wave of the future for the global economy.

System D often started as an economy of desperation and, in some ways, it is a free market. More often than not, it was born because governments needlessly intervened with asinine regulations and bureaucracy, price-control, occupational licensure, and corrupted authorities.[61] The Swedish NGO (SIDA) also listed "excessive cost and regulatory barriers of entry into the formal economy," "weak institutions," "limiting education opportunities" and "difficulties faced by women in gaining formal employment" as key drivers for the growth of System D.[62] In sum, System D emerged to give workers an avenue to embrace their entrepreneurial spirit and better their lives. More often than not, System D is the bloodline of the economy, bringing basic infrastructure such as electricity into households or giving the poorest people a chance to benefit from technology such as a mobile phone.

System D can also be a mechanism to deal with financial crises. A study by Deutsche Bank suggested that European countries with the least (e.g. Austria, The Netherlands and France) and the most robust System D (e.g. Greece and Portugal) fared better in the economic meltdown of 2008 than countries with an average intensity of System D such as Germany (15 per cent).[63]

The top 10 countries with the biggest System D and the percentage of its capacity in their economies are: Bolivia (66.1); Georgia (65.8); Panama (63.5); Zimbabwe (61.8); Azerbaijan (58); Peru (58); Haiti (56.4); Tanzania (56.4); Nigeria (56.2); Thailand (50.6). In comparison, in 2007, System D accounted for 25.1 per cent in Greece, 22.3 per cent in Italy, 19.3 per cent in Spain, 19.2 per cent in Portugal, and 18.3 per cent in Belgium.[64]

1. In a 2016 study, Vanessa Ratten hypothesized that a P-time tendency has a positive impact on System D.[65] Discuss this argument and give your opinion.
2. Why did countries with the least and the most robust System D fare better than average in the economic meltdown?
3. Bearing in mind the dynamics of the world's economy, what implications can we draw about P-time and M-time habits in the future global economy?

When P-time meets M-time. Without proper understanding and preparation, the matching of these two habits can cause confusion. When embracing M-time, people may perceive others as lazy, chaotic, uninterested, unprofessional or unreliable. When embracing P-time, people may think of their counterparts as insincere, trying to cheat or take advantage, machine-like, control freaks, rude and bossy.

The static paradigm of culture tends to see North America and northwestern Europe as M-time cultures, the P-time end includes Africa, Asia and the Middle East, while Southern European countries lie somewhere in between. However, the dynamic paradigm allows us to see that paradoxes are the norm rather than exceptions. In France, for example, meetings can commence 15 minute late, but meal time and restaurants reservations are sacred, so much so that the French are said to be "born with a clock in their stomach."[66] In Japan, people are more M-time with foreigners but P-time with their compatriots.[67] In business, Japanese people are extremely M-time with regard to appointments, but quite P-time in the way they spend a lengthy period of time gaining trust and building relationships before a partnership commitment. Similar situations can be seen in Singapore, Korea and, to a lesser extent, Vietnam.

Within a dominant culture, co-cultures have their own habits. Many of us have experienced waiting for a long time at our doctors' office. They often seem to be late, the reason being that they never know how long it will take to deal with a patient's problem. If (s)he needs some more time, it is then ethical for doctors to do something about it, which is obviously a P-time practice of putting people at the center of time arrangements. One can wonder: "How can they do this at the expense of other patients?" But the fact is, when we step inside the doctor's waiting room, we also switch our perception and turn on our P-time system, one that emphasizes the well-being of other people, because each of us, in turn, is potentially the patient who needs more time. Does that remind you of the *multicultural mind* we discussed in Chapters 1 and 2? Our neurons are capable of accommodating different cultural systems, and the brain's plasticity enables us to adapt. Specific situations and occasions can prompt us to act in an M-time or P-time way. This explains why we can live with paradoxes and accept that superstars can arrive late, but the warm-up bands should not; a CEO and very important managers may arrive late, but not the staffs; technical people, event and project managers can gain a competitive edge from M-time, but not necessarily other professions, etc.

As we conclude this section on how time communicates, it is important to remember that the M-time perception is new, rooted in the Industrial Revolution of the 18th and 19th centuries. The construction of railroads, for example, forced people to adopt an on-time attitude. Before that, each individual town tended to keep their own time zones. Many pre-industrial cultures appear to have no time orientation at all, such as the Pirahã tribe of the Amazon rainforest, the Hopi tribe of Arizona as well as some other Native American tribes whose languages have no past tense or lack verb tenses altogether. Their sense of time is limited to words such as "sooner" or "later." That is to say, the situational nature of time perception cannot be undermined. In this case, modernization can significantly change our approach to time. The circle of context around our Inverted Pyramid model reminds us that context is a major indicator of change, as it can transform a cultural habit, create endless paradoxes, while allowing each individual to adjust and develop her/his attitude as the circumstances demand. The crucial question is not whether you are M-time or P-time, but whether acting M-time or P-time will bring fruitful outcomes; whether you want to be an expert in working internationally; and whether you are dedicated to developing a multicultural mind to respond effectively in each situation.

- Monochronic time (M-time) contributes to the ability to prioritize and to implement. Polychronic time (P-time) contributes to high level of adaptiveness and relationship building.
- Chronemics can dynamically change with paradoxes existing at both collective and individual levels, depending on circumstances.

4.3.2   The Language of Space Setting: Proxemics

Hall coined the term "proxemics," laying the foundations for a field that studies human use of space. In this section, we will explore the meanings of distances when people communicate with each other, the way their seating is arranged, and the environment in which their communication takes place.

The preference for personal space is not neatly correlated with the high and low context. Generally, high context dependent people pay more attention to the hidden message of personal boundaries, and low context dependent people would be less attentive.

4.3.2.1   Proxemics at the Universal Level

Both humans and animals are concerned with a home range. Some animals defend their territories by raising tails high in the air, like ring-tail lemurs, by using auditory signals, like birds and frogs, or marking with urine, like dogs. At the universal level, human beings are territorial too. We use furniture, walls, fences, etc. for the same purpose.

In addition to these visible borders, we also maintain our personal territories with *invisible borders*. These invisible lines indicate who can come close to us, how close, and what we should do when they are violated. For animals, these lines mean "fight" or "flight" when their space is invaded. For human beings, they may also result in "fight" or "flight" as well, but mostly, in such situations we would feel awkward, embarrassed, or angry, either consciously or subconsciously. Have you ever wondered why we are often uncomfortably silent in a crowded lift, and that our eyes seem fixed on the indicator lights to see which floor we are at? It is because our personal space is being violated by those who are instinctively not supposed to be allowed to so close to us.

Similar to time setting, the non-verbal messages of space are crucial in intercultural communication. How close you stand next to a person, whether you sit next to her/him or opposite her/him, and the way you decorate your office with family pictures and abstract paintings, etc. send a certain message about your personality and your view of the relationship. Thus, *distances, seating* and *surroundings* all contribute to communication with their non-verbal cues.

Distances. According to Hall, distance can be categorized into four groups: *intimate* (up to 45cm or 18 inches), *personal* (up to 1.2m or 4 feet), *social* (up to approximately 3m or 12 feet), and *public* (larger than 3m).[68] At the universal level, all of us divide others into these groups and constantly judge whether our home range is being invaded. Our amygdala is activated when people are physically too close.[69] When treading on unknown territory, we should be aware of these invisible borders and think twice before approaching someone to talk, when we deliver a speech, when we share a table with a stranger, when we lean on or touch other people's property, when we come into the room or sit down without permission (you really don't want to sit in the host's favorite chair), etc.

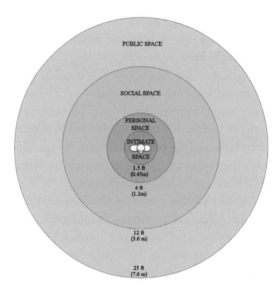

Figure 4.2. We constantly categorize people into different zones, both physically and digitally. For example, many of us have to accept that modern life means those who belong to public or social space will be in the intimate space (e.g. in the public transportation). Digital advancements also come with frustrations that your email or social media is filled with advertisements,[70] or a brand page will appear on your Facebook news feed[71]/ "Interpersonal distances," WEBHAMSTER.[72]

Seating. Our ancestors didn't take seating positions lightly. The best way to avoid attacks is sitting with one's back against the wall, facing the entrance. Since we are mostly right-handed, the person on the right is the least likely to harm you with her/his left hand, hence the phrase "right-hand man" meaning the person you trust and who helps you out the most. Danger is more likely to come from the "gunslinger" position directly opposite.

We are no longer cave dwellers, but these psychological traits linger. In a meeting, the most powerful person will sit at the head of the table, against the wall, facing the door. People will give more credit to those sitting on their right, with influence declining as they reach the defensive point directly opposite. Unless you seek to emphasize a contrast, to be competitive, or to reprimand others, consider this seating position carefully since it can subconsciously create negative energy. By contrast, sitting side by side[73] or at the corner of the table allows friendly engagement, good eye contact and better chances for cooperation. It subtly sends a message of "I'm working *with* you."

At a big gathering, where the audience chooses to sit has a profound impact on communication, something known as the Funnel Effect. Those who sit in the front can develop better rapport[74] and they tend to be high performers[75] or high status individuals. Those who sit in the middle are more likely to ask questions, because they are "safe," surrounded by others. Those who sit in the side areas and at the back are less attentive and engaged. A 2013 study of 1,907 students in Kenya shows that those who sat in the front row could learn up to 27 per cent more than those seated elsewhere.[76]

Surrounding. In Chapter 3, we learned that the surrounding environment can be powerful in sending subtle signals, influencing people and speaking volumes about an individual. Interior design subconsciously influences our work productivity and emotions,[77-78] to the extent that we prefer to cooperate with teams whose offices are decorated in the same taste as ours.[79] Take the office layout, for example, corner offices, windowless rooms, frosted glass partitions, transparent glass walls, or cubical desks, etc. can all be indications of a company's collective culture. If you work in an open office, the overall message is collaboration and transparency, but it also means privacy and focus are a real challenge.[80]

Colors are an important part of our communication. Signals from natural color have historically helped the brain recognize edible and poisonous food and improved the survival of early humans.[81] In ancient Egypt, doctors bathed patients in colors of light to heal ailments. The colors around us don't just change our moods, but profoundly impact our productivity.[82] For example, low-wavelength colors such as light green and blue aid concentration,[83] their calming effect[84] coming from stimulating natural tranquilizers in our brain. Formal restaurants use blue to relax customers and get them to stay longer. High-wavelength colors such as red and orange increase the heart rate, the blood flow, and the appetite by revving the metabolism, so are good for decorating food packages and fast-food restaurants, to attract attention, boost emotion, and prepare for action. Yellow is a mid-range color that can trigger innovation and creativity, giving a brand or a place a warm feeling of happiness and fun. White is a mainstream color as it is less distracting, but the induced feelings of depression are likely to cause people to perform worse than any other colors.[85] The studies of colors and their impact have been conducted mainly in the West, but the implication is universal, i.e. colors are a non-verbal means of communication.

The aesthetic of our surroundings also sends different messages. Art in the workplace for example, helps to reduce stress, increases productivity by 14.3 per cent, enhances morale, sparks dialogue and broadens people's appreciation of diversity.[86] Green offices (biophilia) also generate physiological responses such as increased brain activity and lower stress hormones. The cognitive performance scores for workers in green buildings doubled compared to those who worked in conventional environments.[87] Art works and the design of a place can connect with visitors on an emotional level by subtly communicating values, creating a certain feeling, and guiding the state of mind.

Finally, the combination of all elements in the environment is essential for giving people a big picture. One manager in Asia insisted that his company would only do business with Western counterparts if their top managers were willing to first fly into his city, to drive to the manufacturing plants – a distance of only 20 kilometers, but a journey that takes almost three hours – and see how things work. If they see the whole process, they would think twice before accusing the Asian side of incompetence or treachery if delays and disruptions occur, or if something needs to be renegotiated.[88]

Non-verbal cues from the space setting, such as distances, seating and surroundings are not only a crucial means of communication, but also influence those involved. High context dependence relies more on these cues, while the reverse is true for low context dependence.

4.3.2.2 *Proxemics at the Collective and Individual Level*
Distances. Intimate, personal, social and public distance is a universal framework, but the criteria for who can enter it vary in each collective culture and for each individual. For example, many Arabs find it very natural to be in the intimate zone with same-sex friends and colleagues while in Northern Europe, friends and colleagues are normally kept within

the personal or social zone. This story vividly illustrates various concepts of proxemics in personal space:

> It is the beginning of a negotiation process in Saudi Arabia and this is the first time you meet your counterpart Josef. After the first five minutes, you know it's going to be a long day.
>
> Josef comes on way too strong. He stands so close that his face is only a foot away from yours. There's no letup in his penetrating gaze, and his voice is too loud. The smell of his breath is even more disconcerting, and you shudder at the feel of his hand on your arm. He strikes you suddenly as a pushy rug merchant. As for Josef, he sees you as devious and aloof because you avert your eyes, deny him your breath, and cover up your natural body scent. Despite his overtures of friend-ship, you coldly back away and hold him at an arm's length. He begins to picture you as an ugly American. He thinks it'll be a long day too.[89]

Men in the Middle East tend to be physically close with each other as a way to show brotherhood and male-bonding/ "Two resistance fighters in the Arab Spring, (Yemen)," MAI NGUYEN-PHUONG-MAI.

Both the advancing Arab and the retreating American in this story are typical of their collective dominant cultures. However, they differ in terms of adopting the appropriate zone for their current relationship. In the Middle East as well as many parts of Latin America, distances which almost have sexual connotation[90] or evoke hostile feelings[91] are seen as the ones in which people can talk comfortably. Hall concluded: "If you are a Latin American, talking to a North American at the distance he insists on maintaining is like trying to talk across a room."[92] In a conversation, we can observe that those whose space is being intruded may withdraw physically by stepping back, standing behind a desk or a chair, subconsciously using different objects on the table to create barrier, tucking in their chins toward their chest in an instinctive move of protection, or even rubbing their neck so that their elbow protrudes sharply toward the "invader."[93] These non-verbal body movements are mostly subconscious, but they show how important it is for us to correctly read the unspoken message: "You are violating my space. I am uncomfortable and I may not want to do anything with you."

Seating. In 2010, the Turkish ambassador to Tel Aviv arrived for a meeting with an Israeli government official, and was invited to sit on a sofa that was several inches lower than the one for the host. According to the ambassador, it was a deliberate act, because Israel was angry over a Turkish TV show that portrayed Israeli secret agents as child snatchers. This tit-for-tat escalated into a full-blown diplomatic incident and Israel had to issue a formal apology.[94] This real-life example vividly demonstrates that seating positions can be a powerful means of communication, especially among high context dependent cultures.

In many Asian, African and Middle Eastern cultures, subordinates keep a distance from authorities out of respect. Seating positions, sizes and designs of seating are seen as strategies to enhance or indicate status and power. Leaders sit more frequently at the head or the middle[95] of the table than other cultures. In some cultures, their chairs are bigger, higher, with more sophisticated or unique designs. In many Western offices, the power and status are communicated more subtly with managers sitting in a wheeled chair so they can adjust the height and move around while visitors are invited to sit in a less comfortable stationary chair. Meanwhile, many other cultures choose frequently for a neutral approach, for example, using a round table or having a stand-up informal gathering where people can move freely among different standing tables.

Surrounding. The atmosphere surely communicates, but it may communicate differently in different cultures and for different individuals. In general, its role in communication is more critical in high context dependent cultures.

Entering a space in each culture, an attentive observer can decode the values its inhabitants holds dear. For example, the first sight one catches when walking into a typical office for small businesses in Vietnam is an altar near the entrance to worship the God of Earth, signaling a desire for wealth and prosperity.[96] When communication and social interaction are important, the kitchen becomes the main feature of the house,[97] and that may explain the recent popularity of kitchen islands in interior design. In many parts of Asia, the Chinese philosophy of *feng shui* (wind and water) has influenced how people attach significant values to the position, the direction, the material and the colors of every facility in their working and living space. Main doors, windows, paintings, and plants are chosen carefully to ensure the balance of energy and harmony.

Office arrangement often indirectly communicates the working atmosphere and the hierarchy of power. In France, a supervisor will ordinarily be found in the middle of her/his subordinates, from where (s)he can control them.[98] In Germany, offices are often compartmentalized and sealed off from interference with managers isolating themselves in private offices. In Japan, where group participation is encouraged, and new employees learn by silently observing their senior colleagues, desks are arranged hierarchically in the center of a large, common room, absent of walls or partitions.[99] Occupational and organizational cultures can have an impact too, as many companies who aim for creativity choose to have a huge open atrium where firm members run into each other throughout the day and interact informally, while others prefer their staff to sit in a cubical style office. Managers who want to send out a message of equality and openness will not speak to clients, customers or employees from behind their desk (i.e. a barrier), but instead come around and sit next to them. A frequent practice in pediatrics is that a desk should face the wall, so that the pediatrician can turn to talk with patients without having the desk between them, thus, creating a more friendly and cooperative atmosphere.[100] Office design can send a powerful message and even help to build a positive team spirit. At Caterpillar's European headquarters in Geneva, a central communal square was created in the top floor cafeteria with walls painted in a village theme where villagers portrayed in the panoramas were actual employees. It quickly became a center of culture and casual business, helping to create a common sense of purpose.[101]

Colors are strongly associated with culture.[102] For example, green is sacred in Islam because it's said in the Quran that the dwellers of paradise wear green garments.[103] For this reason, using green as part of a label should be carefully considered. Gender is another crucial category for color association. As a social construct, gender preferences for color are learned. Babies don't care about colors,[104] but after the age of two, girls started to opt for pink and boys for blue, no wonder if we see the way toys and clothes stores are designed. Gender stereotypes grow subconsciously as adults would treat the exact same babies differently depending on whether they were dressed in pink or blue. In an experiment, blue-wearing babies were encouraged to play more physical games, while pink-wearing babies were gently soothed and given a doll.[105]

As a part of culture, colors dynamically change their meanings throughout the history. For example, white represented holiness in ancient Egypt, citizenship in ancient Rome, purity and virtue by the early Christian church, and mourning and death during the early modern era in Europe. In Japan, Vietnam and many other parts of Asia where tradition mixes with Western influences, white is worn by both brides at weddings and mourners at funerals. White is associated with "masculine" in the yin-yang system, but it is associated with "feminine" in the West, and thus ignited a discussion about whether white gadgets are too "girly" for men.[106] White has deep political meaning too. The White Movement in Russia was against communism, the Ku Klux Klan wore white robes and violently murdered black people, the White Revolution in Iran was a series of reforms from the Shah, and British women wore white to fight for their right to vote. That is why many famous politicians, including Hillary Clinton, choose to dress in white to subtly communicate their message.[107]

Similar to chronemics, the characteristics of proxemics across cultures are not static and can dynamically change under the impact of circumstances, resulting in numerous paradoxes, as we see in the case of white as a communicating tool. At the individual level, each one of us has an incredible capacity to observe, to decode the right message, to respond appropriately and to change ourselves as the situation demands.

Non-verbal cues from space setting (distances, seating, and surrounding) have different meanings across cultures, but can be very dynamic depending on circumstances.

CASE STUDY

Conduct research and find out why Disneyland is not the same in different locations across the globe:

1. In Tokyo, the castle at the center of the park features Cinderella and not Sleeping Beauty.
2. In Hong Kong, the main gate faces the north-south direction. There are two gigantic boulders and a large fountain featuring Disney characters at the entrance. Lakes, ponds, and streams are carefully positioned throughout the park.
3. In Paris, the arcade features a small replica of the Statue of Liberty. It is also the only Disneyland in the world where meals can be served with an alcoholic drink. However, this Disneyland has been criticized as a "cultural Chernobyl."

(*Case adapted from Tang [2012]*[108])

4.4   Context from the body

In the previous section, we discussed the importance of context in terms of what is produced by the setting (time and space). In this section, we will delve into the messages that our own body produces: silence, eye contact, touch, gestures, etc. This list of non-verbal elements is extensive, however, their characteristics can be grouped into two levels of outward expression: *Neutral* and *Affective*. The authors who came up with these two concepts are Trompenaars and Hampden-Turner.[109] In essence, people who lean towards neutrality tend to hold their emotions and control their body movements. Those who lean towards affection tend to find an outlet for their feelings, and their body language is also more animated. Regardless of the tendency, in general, high context dependence relies more on body language to understand the hidden message, while the reverse is true for low context dependence.

4.4.1   Silence

The value of silence is universally credited. Similar proverbs can be found in many cultures: "Even a fool, when he keeps silent, is considered wise" (The Bible 17:28); "The tree of silence bears the fruits of peace" (Arab proverb); "Fear a silent man. He has lips like a drum" (Beninese proverb); "If speech is worth a shilling, silence is worth a pound" (Jamaican proverb), etc. While all cultures acknowledge the crucial role of silence at the universal level, the meaning of silence and the level of importance each culture places on silence differ from one to another.

Firstly, silence should not be interpreted similarly across cultures. In low context dependent cultures, it probably means "lack of attention," "not interested" or downright "rejection." But in Scandinavia, silence can be an indication to the other person that they want you to continue talking.[110] The true meaning of silence can be hard to know in high context dependent cultures, where people really have to read between lines, to rely on non-verbal cues and the history of the situation that stretches backwards and forwards in order to understand what silence really communicates in each particular case.

Secondly, not every culture puts silence on the same level of importance. Silence is more meaningful for neutral cultures as people use it to seek answers, to interpret, to encourage talking, or to think of new topics, etc., so they are occupied with certain activities and not just waiting awkwardly during an empty message.[111] For affective cultures, pauses are more empty messages. One only has to watch a typical Arab or Southern European TV show to recognize the busy speaking pattern, with participants talking over each other and sounding as if they are having a fight. In negotiations, the urge to keep a conversation going and to avoid silence can bring disadvantages, since one may unwittingly disclose unnecessary information.

4.4.2   Eye Contact

Universally, eye contact has evolved as a human survival skill. Children with more acute ability to maintain eye contact with parents can attract more attention and care, hence, a better chance of survival.

The eyes have been described as the "gateway to the soul." They convey more messages and feelings than any other part of the body. Generally speaking, lack of eye contact indicates lack of interest, honesty, or suggests the person is discussing something intimate or difficult. Waiters and waitresses who squat down next to the table to bring their eye level on par with the customers' receive more tips.[112] Generally speaking, prolonged staring can be considered rude or threatening, darting eyes are linked to deceit or insecurity, and wild eyes signal approval or pleased surprise. The pupil size also tells us more than we think. Under the same light conditions, they unconsciously dilate when the eyes see something pleasant, exciting or arousing. The pupils widen to allow us to see more, and that is why romantic dinners are often in a dimly lit environment. By contrast, pupil contraction signals resistance, anger or negativity.[113] Females are normally judged to be more attractive if their pupils are wide open. Indeed, Revlon increased its lipstick sales by 45 per cent using the technique of enlarging the pupil size of their models.[114] Further, a lowered gaze is generally a sign of submission. Looking up in combination with a lowered head mimics the upward gaze of little children, and therefore can touch a parental instinct in the audience, attracting sympathy and affection.[115]

Eye movements are closely linked to brain activities too. According to neuro-linguistic programing theories, most right-handed people, i.e. most of us, when visualizing a "remembered" memory, look up to the left ("That market exhibition was really interesting!"). When we are "creating" an image, we often look up to the right ("I wonder what our product stall would look like!"). Gazing also indicates a spirit of the conversation. When you mean business and want to do business, employ the "business gaze," which focuses on the triangle connecting the forehead and the eyes. If your eyes drop a notch down to the "social gaze," which is the triangle connecting the eyes and the mouth, then the relationship has shifted. Take extra care when your eyes venture within the "intimate gaze," which forms a triangle from the eyes to both sides of the chest or breasts. Successful salespeople, negotiators and gamblers alike monitor and read pupil dilation and eye contact to gauge their partners' and competitors' emotions and feeling.

Diana, Princess of Wales earned her nickname "Shy Di" partly because she was often photographed using this gesture, which also triggered people's compassion and support/ "Princess Diana," AUGUEL.[116]

At the collective level, different societies may attach differing levels of importance to eye contact, as well as different meanings to eye gazes and movements. High context dependent and neutral cultures are more likely to embed messages in eye exchanges. Koreans even have a specific term for it: *nunchi* means communicating with the eyes. Low context dependent Germans and affective Arabs of the same sex tend to engage in prolonged eye contact, since it shows sincerity and honesty, with an intensity many from Western cultures may find disconcerting.[117] In some Asian and African cultures, the same way of making eye contact can be considered rude or a lack of respect, especially with senior and elderly people. The augmentative environment of politics also takes eye contact into account, to the extent that American senators in Minnesota are banned from looking at each other during debates in order to keep things civil and reduce aggression.[118]

4.4.3   Touch

Of all the senses, touch is the first to develop in unborn babies. It becomes the most primitive and essential form of non-verbal communication. Newborns need to be in constant skin to skin contact with their care-takers, so much so that premature babies who are stroked grow up to 47 per cent faster than those who do not receive the same amount of touching.[119] A touch is the quickest way to build personal rapport and human bonds, since we have evolved to feel more attached to those we have exchanged physical contact with. A study shows that waitresses who casually touched their customers on their shoulders at the end of a meal received 14 per cent more tips than those who did not. In many commercial settings, casually touching customers can increase their time in a store, the amounts they purchase, and favorable evaluation of their shopping experience.[120]

At the collective level, touching is strongly cultural bound. Affective people employ touching as part of their communication style, hence they touch, hug, embrace, kiss, and pat on the back more frequently and inten-sively than neutral people. The handshake, originally an indication that a person wasn't holding any weapons, has become a popular way of greeting. A study by the Income Center for Trade Shows reports that people are twice as likely to remember you if you shake hands with them.[121] However, even this seemingly simple handshake has its cultural nuances. Some Western cultures prefer a strong grip, while in some other Asian and Latin American cultures, a light, soft, lingering handshake is more common. Further, using the left hand can be seen as an insult for the Arabs and Indian, since it is used for personal hygiene. To show respect, many people from Vietnam will use both hands and lower their head.

Both Bill Gates and US President Donald Trump have made headlines with their handshake manner. The former shook hands with Korean president Park Geun-hye with his left hand firmly planted in his pocket – a sign interpreted by the Korean as "disrespect."[122] The latter engaged in a 17-second-long and aggressive handshake with the Japanese Prime Minister – an experience so awkward that Shinzo Abe rolled his eyes afterward in obvious relief.[123] Note that Abe comes from a neutral and high context dependent culture, where a proper way of greeting is to bow, and the vocabulary does not even have a word for kissing. They borrow from the English and make it *kisu*.

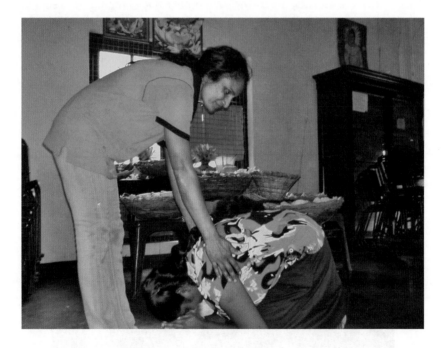

Hierarchy plays a critical role in touching. In collective cultures that emphasize hierarchy, one should refrain from touching people of higher status (managers, parents, teachers, dignitaries, monks, etc.). Those who touched Queen Elizabeth for example, including two Australian Prime Ministers and American first lady Obama, received critic from media/ "Parents touch and kiss the feet of their children's teacher to honor their guidance, (Sri Lanka)," MAI NGUYEN-PHUONG-MAI.

4.4.4   Body Movement (Kinesics)

You must have noticed that many of us talk with our hands in foreign countries, with frequently successful attempts to convey a simple message. It is, however, pointless to categorize body movement, since there can be as many as 700,000 distinct physical signs, of which 1,000 are different bodily postures, 5,000 are hand gestures and 250,000 are facial expression.[124] A majority of these movements are learned by imitation. Our amygdala automatically scans others to categorize people into ingroup and outgroup. Similar body languages signal ingroup, and vice versa. As early as infancy, the mirror neurons[125] in our brain trigger an instant mirroring reaction that helps us to automatically copy the behaviors that we see and imitate.[126] This is an evolutionary solution that allows us to signal that we are part of an ingroup and benefit from its support and collective knowledge.[127] That is why, universally, mirroring each other's body language is a sign of ingroup trust, a way of bonding and a method to establish empathy.[128] In job interviews, candidates who mirrored the friendly body language of the interviewers fared better because they built a better rapport.[129]

Mirroring body languages can create incredible collective power. We see that in a public queue, in the way a person starts a sentence and the other finishes, in a group performance, etc. The haka *ritual dance of the Maoris is originally a triumph of life over death, and is famous for its extreme form of body language. When performing together in sync, it is both fearsome if they are facing opposing teams, and intensely emotional if they use the dance to express group bonding in peace. In a working context, your team can decide to subtly make a gesture in sync with the leader, which will subconsciously give the whole team a powerful appearance of group cohesiveness/* "Haka dance of brotherhood, (New Zealand)," MAI NGUYEN-PHUONG-MAI.

While a great number of body movements can be understood universally, a significant amount are culture bound. A good example of how body movements send a specific message is leg posture. At the universal level, we are more aware of the body parts that are closer to the brain (e.g. our face) than those that are further away such as our feet. Evolved to move us towards what we want and carry us away from what we don't, our legs subconsciously reveal unspoken feelings simply by pointing towards the people we are talking to or the exit. At the collective level of culture, many people have accidently insulted their counterparts who are Muslim, Hindu and Buddhist by adopting the common ankle-to-knee leg crossing, showing the bottom of their feet. This part of the body is considered unclean. Similarly, the feet-on-desk pose may lead to greater feelings of power in certain part of the world, but can be seen as a sign of rudeness in another culture.[130]

Throwing shoes at people is considered a strong statement of discontent. As a form of protest, politicians across the globe are frequently pelted with shoes and socks, including the Presidents of Pakistan,[131] Sudan,[132] Egypt[133] and Iran,[134] Prime Ministers of Mongolia,[135] China,[136] Australia,[137] and the US[138] / "Taiwanese people donate old shoes to support shoe-throwing against Ma Ying-jeou's administration and the ruling KMT party," 美國之音黃耀毅拍攝.[139]

Generally speaking, when embracing affective body language, people employ a great deal of body movements while communicating with others. They use heated, passionate and animated expressions with extensive hand gestures, facial expressions and body postures. As the joke goes, the quickest way to shut an Arab or a Southern European person up is to tie her/his hands together. Jokes aside, the case of Anna Mannino in Italy does make us wonder where the boundary is. In 1996, the hospital accused her husband for beating her, but the Prime Court found that it was not systematic and conscious brutality, and her husband was in a "passionate mood."[140] People who embrace neutral communicative patterns tend to dam up their emotions and often try to look calm or appear stiff. Those who embrace affective style may perceive their counterparts as uninterested or lacking commitment, those who embrace neutral style may see their counterparts as irrational or having a lack of control.

While we are on the subject of body movement, it is interesting to know that body positions can influence our behavior. A study shows that interacting with devices of different sizes (smartphone, tablet, laptop, and desk computer) has an impact on subsequent power-related attitudes. Those who hunched over a smartphone to perform tasks were reported to be less assertive than those who used a full-sized computer. The study suggests that we ditch the tiny smartphone before entering a meeting.[141] Another study shows that adopting a power-pose (hands on hips or clasped behind the head, chin tiled upwards, feet planted wide apart) can change our body chemistry, increase our testosterone, making us feel more confident, and leading to higher performance in job interviews.[142] The connection also explains why the intimidating *haka* dance symbolizes the power of New Zealand's legendary All Blacks rugby team and their alleged invincibility.

- *Non-verbal cues produced by the body such as silence, touch, eye contact and body movement not only send a certain message, but also influence those involved.*
- *With neutral communication style, people tend to control these non-verbal cues, and with affective communication style, people tend to employ them more to express their feelings.*
- *High context dependence relies more on these cues, while the reverse is true of low context dependence.*
- *Non-verbal cues produced by the body have different meanings across cultures, but can be very dynamic depending on circumstances.*

4.5   The limitations of non-verbal communication

Non-verbal communication is crucial, but it has disadvantages as well. In this section, we will discuss these shortcomings.

4.5.1   Ambiguity

Since non-verbal communication is both intentional and *unintentional,* it is fairly easy to misinterpret a cue, even when cultural consideration has been applied. One can never be sure and everything is simply a guess. The second reason why non-verbal communication is ambiguous is because it is always *based on a specific context.* Nobody can have 100 per cent of all the related information regarding a specific situation, including the insiders. Special context can make people react differently compared to their normal collective or individual outward expressions. If we happen to deal with a very loud and emotional client, is that because this person has a very affective character, or is because (s)he is having a tough day? If our new colleague arrives late to a meeting, is that because (s)he is polychronic or (s)he had an unexpected family issue? Hence, we should always remember that "meanings and interpretations of non-verbal behaviors often are on very shaky ground."[143]

4.5.2   Not Necessarily a Value Indicator

Hall's theories on context (chronemics and proxemics) have been strongly connected with values such as collectivism and individualism by scholars of the static cultural paradigm. For example, high context dependent people tend to be group-oriented (i.e. harmony, face, honor and relationship), and low context dependent people are more likely individual-oriented (i.e. ego, independence, free thinking and task-oriented).

   From the dynamic paradigm's point of view, this assumption is problematic. Since non-verbal communication is ambiguous, or frankly, a guess, we will do ourselves a disservice by taking the outward expressions of non-verbal cues such as how a person gives "maybe" as an ambiguous answer, how (s)he organizes her/his agenda, how close (s)he stands next to us, or how (s)he painted her/his office etc. as an indication of her/his individual or collective values. These outward expressions are on shaky ground. Regardless of how much scholarly work backs them up, the assumption of "high context = collectivism; low context = individualism" should always be understood as what Osland and Bird[144] called *sophisticated stereotypes.* An obvious example is Finland – a culture that has individualistic values cloaked in a high context dependent communication style[145] and an M-time way of organizing everyday activities. Finns use silence as a component of communication and employ ultra-taciturnity; yet, despite these trademarks of high context dependence, Finland is an individualistic culture.

4.5.3   Static View of Change, Paradox and Individual Development

Assigning a country as high or low context dependence means assuming culture is static and fixed. In Chapter 2, we discussed the notion of dynamic culture, paradoxes in practices, the non-binary structure of values and the impact of circumstances. Studies have shown that, for example, high context Finland is shifting towards low context dependence and, despite conventional assumptions, India is closer to low than high context dependence.[146] Within a society, both low and high context can simultaneously co-exist. The stereotypically high context dependent Chinese can have quite a blunt and testy negotiation style[147] in which they ignore non-verbal cues and challenge everything and question every clause.[148] The very progressive sex education that China has introduced for children, with explicit illustrations of the penis, vagina, a naked couple making love in bed, and direct talk about homosexuality, could not be any further from high context dependence.[149] In Vietnam, Japan, Korea and Malaysia, karaoke bars serve as an emotional outlet for high context dependent cultures where an entertaining environment allows for expressions of low context behaviors.[150] If we do not bear in mind the dynamic nature of culture, we will tend to look for stories and incidents that fit the stereotypes. Hence, in the absence of proper knowledge, knowing whether a culture is high or low context can only give us a *first best guess*. A competent student of intercultural communication will be ready to deal with changes, shifts, paradoxes, and unexpected outwards expressions that only the uniqueness of circumstances can justify.

One way to benefit from both high and low context dependence is matching goals and cultural tendencies. For example, low context dependence may support tasks of standardization, implementation, technical process, a certain stage of virtual working, or emergency. With relationship building, policy making, negotiation, observatory research and supervision, etc., high context dependence may give some competitive edge. Of course, the best strategy is developing both capacities and being adaptive in any given circumstances.

As emphasized throughout the chapter, the crucial question is not whether you are M-time or P-time, whether your stand close or far away from others while talking, whether you shake hands or bow, etc. Being competent in intercultural communication means you are able to find out which outward expression works better in each particular situation, being direct or indirect, acting M-time or P-time, keeping a distance or touching others empathetically, shaking hand softly or taking a deep bow. You can read high context and take in all the non-verbal cues, but you can also act low context effectively. It may be hard to do so, but never underestimate the plasticity of your brain. Regardless of what you do, one thing remains crucial: non-verbal cues deliver strong messages. People will forget what you say, but they will never forget how you make them feel.

Non-verbal communication can be ambiguous, not necessarily an indicator for values, and its current theories may undermine the dynamics of culture.

Summary

1. Non-verbal cues are part of the canopy in the metaphorical tree and the circle around the Inverted Pyramid model of culture. They are the primary means of communication, the indicators for judgment and the tools to create identities.
2. Universally, we all rely on context to interpret the world. However, low context dependence focuses more on explicit verbal and non-verbal cues, and high context dependence focuses on both explicit and implicit cues.
3. High context dependence contributes to situational efficiency, flexibility and holistic policies. Low context dependence contributes to universal efficiency and change processes with transparent and logistic nature.
4. Two channels of non-verbal cues produced by the context in setting are: time (chronemics) and space (proxemics).
5. Chronemics deals with how we use time to communicate. Polychronic timing (P-time) is flexible and cyclic. Monochronic timing (M-time) is strict and linear. High context dependence relies more on these cues, while the reverse is true of low context dependence.
6. M-time contributes to the ability to prioritize and to implement. P-time contributes to high levels of adaptiveness and relationship building.
7. Proxemics deals with how we use distances, seating arrangements, and the environment to communicate. High context dependence relies more on these cues, while the reverse is true of low context dependence.
8. Examples of channels of non-verbal cues produced by the context of the body are: silence, touch, eye contact and body movement. Those with neutral style tend to control these non-verbal cues, and those with affective style tend to employ them more to express their feelings. High context dependence relies more on these cues, while the reverse is true of low context dependence.
9. Non-verbal communication can be ambiguous, not necessarily an indicator for values, and its current theories may undermine the dynamics of culture.
10. The level of dependence on context (non-verbal cues) can dynamically change with paradoxes at both collective and individual level, depending

on circumstances. Thanks to the brain's plasticity, individuals can develop a multicultural mind and adjust to the demand of the situation.

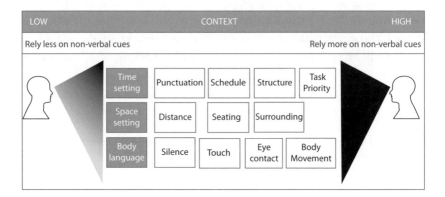

Figure 4.3. Low and high context dependence

5. A Taxonomy Of Diversity

Objective
At the end of this chapter, you should be able to:
· Explain the evolutionary origin and the characteristics of Group Attachment, Hierarchy Acceptance, Gender Association, Uncertainty Avoidance and Time Orientation.
· Given a case or a phenomenon, identify related concerns and values.
· Given a case or a phenomenon, identify the possibilities of paradoxes, the impact of change and the non-binary nature of associated values.

Chapter outline

In Chapter 2, we were introduced to the metaphorical tree of culture, which has three layers: fundamental concerns (the trunk and the roots), values (the branches, i.e. the degree of importance we place on each concern), and outward expressions (the leaves, i.e. objects, symbols and behaviors). We have used religion and art as examples to show how these cultural notions act as universal building blocks for survival from the evolutionary point of view. Groups that failed to acquire them would risk losing out to those who had.

In the field of intercultural studies, Kluckhohn and Strodtbeck[1] asked a similar question: "What are the universal concerns that all societies have to deal with?" They came up with five issues: (1) the relationship between an individual and others; (2) the aspect of time that is our primary focus; (3) the relationship between humans and nature; (4) the prime motivation for behavior; and (5) the moral nature of human beings.

Kluckhohn and Strodtbeck's framework has inspired many theorists to work on different taxonomies to understand the complexity of culture. In this chapter, we will take a look at some of the most cited concerns: Group attachment, hierarchy acceptance, gender association, uncertainty avoidance and time orientation. However, they will be seen through the lens of the dynamic paradigm with insight from interdisciplinary studies. We will explore how these concerns play a crucial role in our strategies for survival, and the ways in which different cultures, individuals and contexts call for different values; or, better put, the differing degree of importance that is placed on a specific concern.

5.1 Group attachment

Humans are social animals and the group is vital for our existence. This explains why interpersonal relationships have been a fundamental discipline in human studies. Two of the most popular concepts in communication studies are *individualism* and *collectivism*. They appeared in the frameworks of many intercultural theorists and classic studies: Kluckhohn and Strodtbeck,[2] Triandis,[3] Schwartz,[4] Hofstede,[5] Trompenaars and Hampden-Turner[6] and GLOBE.[7]

5.1.1 The Terms: Group Attachment, Individualism and Collectivism

In the 19th century, the French revolution washed away the last vestiges of feudal social structures, which had served as intermediaries between individuals and the central government.[8] People became less attached to the community. In this context, the French social theorist Alexis de Tocqueville was believed to have coined the term *individualism*[9] to express concern about how an individual forms "a little circle of his own" and "leave society at large to itself."[10] However, as the term became widely used in England and Germany, the historical contexts of these cultures stripped away its negative overtones and it came to be associated with the positive aspirations of romanticism, utilitarianism, democracy, capitalism and laissez-faire economics.[11] Today, in the context of intercultural communication and even in its homeland France, individualism indicates a degree of independence and self-reliance towards one's own ingroup.

While it is unclear who coined the term *collectivism,* a similar term "communitarianism" came from the British socialist John G. Barmby in the 19th century. However, its use in the academy was limited due to its associations with socialism. The term collectivism has become a popular alternative in intercultural communication.

From the evolutionary point of view, the term individualistic can be misleading, since nobody can survive on her/his own. In other words, we are all collectivistic, albeit to varying degrees. Since the group is vital for our existence as human beings, a new generic term has been coined to indicate this fundamental concern: *Group Attachment.* It is defined as the extent to which one gives her/his ingroup priority over oneself.

5.1.2   Group Attachment in the Inverted Pyramid Model

5.1.2.1   *Group Attachment at the Universal Level*

In Chapter 1, we learned that humans are social animals. We are born with a very perceptive mind, ready to join the first cultural group we see after birth. Group attachment is therefore a fundamental concern, and the *degree* of attachment at the *baseline level* is a universal value in all human societies. Every single one of us has to attach to one or several groups, since the collective cultures we receive from these communities are our source of support, identity and advancement.

Because ingroup culture is our survival strategy, genes have evolved to create a biological mechanism that allows us to quickly recognize our ingroup. In previous chapters, we learned that our amygdala becomes more active when we see someone who looks different from us, indicating an outgroup member, and thus a potential threat.[12-13] Brain images show that we also feel less empathy towards outsiders.[14-15] In sum, genes have co-evolved with culture and prepared us by giving us the biological ability to effectively fit into *any group* at birth, and to be on alert against any outgroup members. In the same vein, the brain's plasticity has also prepared us by giving us the incredible capacity to adjust to *new groups* during the course of our life.

5.1.2.2   Group Attachment at the Collective and Individual Level

Differing in degree of attachment. At this level of the Inverted Pyramid model, cultures and individuals *differ* from the baseline level of attachment we share at the universal level. Some expect individuals to build a strong bond with their ingroups, thus showing more collectivistic or strong group attachment. Others allow individuals to cultivate a degree of independence and have a pretty loose relationship with their ingroups, thus showing individualistic or weak group attachment.

Group attachment is about the relationship between one individual and her/his in-groups. It is the extent to which one gives her/his ingroup priority over oneself/ "An act of selflessness," MAI NGUYEN-PHUONG-MAI.

Individual-group and not group-group. Group attachment is exclusively about the relationship between *one* individual and her/his ingroups. We cannot use this concept for a group or collective culture (e.g. the company is so individualistic that they ignore a customer's requirements); or for an intergroup relation (e.g. the debate between democratic and labor parties has become very individualistic in this issue). When you see a group of people working in teams, joining a protest, or forming a party, etc., it does not mean they are collectivistic; rather, these are universal, average ways of group functioning. The act of forming a group says little about this value if there is no sign of relationship between this group and an individual within it. Without an interaction between an individual and her/his ingroup, we cannot decide whether that individual has weak or strong group attachment. Thus, the description of a person as "independent, freedom-loving, and rebellious" does not automatically indicate that (s)he is an individualist, because we do not know how (s)he is attached to her/his ingroup.

Static ranking. The static paradigm of culture is dominated by a binary view of value. Here are a few samples from the studies by Hofstede, Trompenaars and Hampden-Turner. Scores are taken from the top, the middle and the end of the spectrum:

	Individualistic	Average	Collectivistic
Hofstede[16]	91. US	47. Surinam	13. Colombia
	90. Australia	46. Argentina	12. Venezuela
	89. UK	46. Japan	11. Panama
	80. Canada	46. Morocco	8. Ecuador
	80. Hungary	41. Iran	6. Guatemala
Trompenaars & Hampden-Turner[17]	89. Israel	50. Ireland	32. Mexico
	81. Romania	52. Italy	31. Nepal
	74. Nigeria	53. Germany	30. Egypt

Paradox and change. While the assumption that culture is stable can reduce ambiguity and provide the *first best guess*, the static view undermines paradoxes, changes and other collective cultures, such as organizational culture and group culture. We discussed the neural explanation for this binary tendency in Chapter 2, and have come to an understanding that a culture does not have a fixed position on the spectrum of low-high group attachment. For example, a 2015 study found that values are dynamic: both individualism and collectivism co-exist in Canada, and individualism characterizes Morocco even more than Canada.[18] Another study comparing this value in Vietnam, China, and the US shows that North Vietnam scores high for both individualism and collectivism.[19] In countries with a rich history of immigration, multiculturalism or a fast pace of development, paradoxes and changes are the norm and not an exception.

Two or more separate values. In our metaphorical tree of culture, while group attachment is a fundamental concern (the trunk and the roots), weak and strong group attachment can be presented as two separate branches of the tree or two values. The suggestion to see them as two or more separate values is supported by a number of studies. The GLOBE study[20] identified two types of collectivism: institutional collectivism (which maximizes the interests of the collective) and ingroup collectivism (loyalty, pride and cohesiveness within a group). Triandis and colleagues[21] distinguished four separate dimensions: vertical individualism (individuals want to be distinct and desire special status); horizontal individualism (individuals want to be distinct *without* desiring special status); vertical collectivism (individuals want interdependence and competition with outgroups), and horizontal collectivism (individuals want interdependence but do not submit easily to authority).

Multiple cultures at the collective level. Indexes from the static paradigm should also be viewed with care because they mainly focus on national cultures. Italy, for example, is positioned next to Denmark and Belgium and scores high on Hofstede's scale for individualism (76), while Spain, which has a similar level of individualism is 25 points behind (51). This is probably because the statistics were gathered mainly from people in the North of Italy.

Japan offers another example of the discrepancy between culture, organizational culture and group culture. Scoring in the middle of the spectrum, however, Japanese employees are known for extreme loyalty and dedication to their companies. The term "corporate samurai" refers to ultra-loyal employees, who would rather die than betray the company. At the same time, the importance of family – a trademark of collectivism – is fading in Japan, to the extent that many people refuse to get married or decide to marry their friends for convenience, abstain from sex and the idea of having children,[22] or go a step further by "dumping" their parents on the street.[23]

Similar dynamics among collective groups can also be seen in the Middle East. Here, tribal loyalty is much more influential than religious affinity or even national pride. In a study, 62 per cent of Middle Eastern people expected their governments to do what is good for either Muslims or Arabs generally, while only 31 per cent thought that national policies should benefit their own country.[24] In sum, different identities and affinities with different collective cultures, such as clans, tribes, religious sects, ethnicities, companies, and nationalities, etc., make it problematic to rely solely on a static country index. Rather, in order to know the level of group attachment, the appropriate question should be: "which group?"

Individual level. At this level of the Inverted Pyramid model, the dynamics of group attachment is even more profound. We are reminded of the discussion in Chapter 2, in which both neural[25] and behavioral studies[26] confirmed that a specific context prompts a person to have either collectivistic or individualistic thought, to the extent that simple cues ("I" or "we") trigger us to switch our frame of value. With the brain's plasticity, we can develop a multicultural mind, which will enable us to make the best of culture as a survival strategy in an international context.

The driving factors of diversity in group attachment. The differing level of attachment that various cultures, individuals and contexts place on ingroups can be explained by the theory of culture–genes coevolution. In Chapter 1, we worked on a case study that links the prevalence of pathogens (bacteria and fungus) in the environment and the shorter variant of serotonin carriers (s5-HTTLPR) with the need to develop a culture of group-mindset. Those who followed the cultural rules of group conformity had a higher chance of survival. Simultaneously, those with short alleles (i.e. higher chance of depression) need and fit better into the group-mindset culture, so their gene became dominant to support this value.

The external impact of disruptive or collective behaviors and the dynamics of contexts cannot be emphasized strongly enough. For example, economic development can dynamically increase *or* decrease group attachment.[27] When there is a perceived external threat, a common goal or a strong movement, group attachment can be reinforced. The rise of populism and nationalism in the US and Europe since 2010 illustrates clearly how far-right leaders can unite a large number of voters under the banner of protecting national identity and stability.

5.1.3   Outward Expressions of Group Attachment

5.1.3.1   *Harmony and Face*

Harmony is one of the most salient characteristics of group attachment. Although concern for harmony is universally important in all societies, it is more so among cultures, people and contexts with strong group attachment. The word "no" should be used with care, since it may signal confrontation. "You may be right" or "we'll have a look at it" are examples of polite ways to turn down a request. In the same vein, the word "yes" should not necessarily be seen as approval, but probably: "Yes, I hear you." In this sense, it seems strong group attachment correlates with high context dependence, but don't forget that it is not the rule. Finland is generally high context dependent, but many Finns embrace weak group attachment (see Chapter 4).

In a group setting, where strong group attachment reigns, people may find it uncomfortable to speak up individually for fear of disrupting harmony. A tactic to deal with this is giving the group some time to discuss and then asking individuals to represent the group's ideas at a later stage.[28] In a business context, heated discussions and big decisions may not happen regularly in the meeting. One-on-one and private talks can be conducted with everyone involved *before* the meeting to ensure alignment and to smooth out mismatches in a more harmonious manner. However, it is wrong to assume that this value will definitely put an end to open-minded discussion and hinder innovation. Different context evokes different values. Hence, changing the approach can make a strong collectivistic person embrace individualistic ideas. Studies have shown that those who are stereotypically assigned with strong group attachment can effectively engage in debates and constructive controversies when collaborative goals and safe environment are ensured.[29-30] As a matter of fact, "in the world of ideas," collectivistic "South Korea is king."[31] It has topped the list of the globe's most innovative countries for many years, together with other Asian countries such as Japan and Singapore, where this value also prevails.

The concept of harmony is strongly connected with *face* – the public dignity of a person or a group. Maintaining a positive face is desirable for everyone.[32] It is a social currency and a strategic tool in communication,[33] for it can be lost, gained, built up, given to others in a sense of honor, or taken from others in an attempt to evoke embarrassment.[34] However, the way we maintain face is culture-bound.[35] For example, when embracing weak group attachment, a person may use a more defensive mode, such as blaming external factors to protect her/his own face (e.g. "I missed the deadline because my team didn't cooperate"). By contrast, when embracing strong group attachment, the same person may consider more mutual face-saving (e.g. "I profusely apologize for missing the deadline, despite the fact that the team has tried its best").

5.1.3.2   *Interdependence and Trust*

Universally, nobody can survive without a network of reciprocal support. Similar to face, *relationship* is a crucial currency. "Who you know" is a deciding factor for success. However, this network is more dense and influential for cultures, individuals and contexts where strong group attachment prevails. The circle of favor and reciprocal obligation goes far beyond immediate time and space. You may be expected to help someone because of any of

the following reasons: (s)he is your colleague or relative; you do not know
the person but (s)he is a colleague or relative of your colleague or relative;
(s)he helped you in the past; her/his colleague or relative helped you in the
past; they may help you in the future; they may help your colleague/relative
in the future, etc. Everyone is potentially in debt to everyone else. Many
people even actively want to do others a favor because that means support
can be asked for in the future. This circle of interdependence snowballs
into an immense network of connections within which people perform a
favor or service in accordance with how distant or close their relationship
is.[36] The following business cases illustrate this point:

> Upon learning that China Post Savings Bureau planned to modernize its
> computer network, C.T. Teng, the general manager of Honeywell-Bull's
> Greater China Region, asked his Beijing sales director to approach the
> China Post executive responsible for this project. Because the sales direc-
> tor and the China Post executive were old university friends, they had
> guanxi (relationship). That connection enabled Teng to invite the China
> Post executive to a partner's forum at Honeywell-Bull headquarters in
> Boston. He also invited the CEO of Taiwan's Institute of Information
> Industry to the event. Over the course of the meeting, Teng proposed a
> banking system using Honeywell-Bull hardware and Taiwan Institute
> software to China Post's CEO, and the deal was done.[37]

Whether it is *"guanxi"* (relationship) in China, *"wasta"* (medium) in the Middle East,[38] *"hyvä veli-verkosto"* (dear-brother network) in Finland, *"ksharim"*
or *"vitamin P"* (protection) in Israel,[39] *"quan hệ"* (relationship) in Vietnam,
"shurobadzhanashtina" (brother-in-law of the wife) in Bulgaria,[40] etc., connections plays a vital role as social capital, more so in certain cultures or
circumstances than others. Here is another case of *"enchufe"* (plug in)[41] and
its impact on the economy of a country:

> In Spain, the high-speed train AVE connecting Seville and Madrid has
> been envied by all cities. However, critics complain that politics has
> loomed too large. The first AVE line did not connect Madrid to busy Bar-
> celona but to sleepy Seville, the hometown of the then prime minister.[42]

The visibility of interconnected relationship varies. It can take the shape
of ordinary and petty favors, such as a helpful introduction, but it can also
manifest itself in the form of a powerful "old boys' network" or corporate
elite,[43] as we see in the West. An analysis of the relationship between 43,000

transnational corporations has identified a small number of companies with disproportionate power over the whole global economy.[44]

Interdependence and relationship are strongly connected to the concept of *trust*. Naturally, trust is a universal concern. It can be further distinguished as affect-based trust (derived from the emotional bonds between group members) and cognition-based trust (built up based on the knowledge, skills and performance of individuals).[45] The former is more associated with strong group attachment and the latter with weak group attachment. This explains why, in some societies, nepotism (hiring relatives or friends) is a rule, rather than an exception, because it comes from affect-based trust. Outsiders may judge such a situation differently. Someone embracing strong group attachment would nod his head: "She is doing the right thing. How else can we trust her if she can't even help her own relative?" Those embracing weak group attachment may wonder: "She is *not* doing the right thing. How can we trust her since she is helping her own relative?"

Generally, children everywhere are expected to fulfil certain obligations, such as taking care of their parents or studying well, but this is more so in contexts where strong group attachment prevails. Striving for a good grade at school can have very different purposes, either for the collective goal of high earnings in the future to support the family, or to pursue one's own dream. Similarly, a child may labor for different reasons. They may sell their old toys and lemonade or play music to passers-by to earn money for themselves, but they can also take a serious and active role in labor to contribute to the household's well-being/ "A 3-year-old child carrying wood in Malawi," MAI NGUYEN-PHUONG-MAI.

While both types of trust are essential, some people may need a different order of trust building. For example, in a context where weak group attachment prevails, people may emphasize cognitive-based trust, as in "It doesn't matter who you are, as long as you can do the job" or "Trust me! Everything is written down in the contract." In comparison, when strong group attachment prevails, people may take a long time to build affect-based trust: "Can we trust that these people will go through ups and downs with us?" "Will they sympathize with us if the unexpected happen and we need to revisit some clauses?" "Will they be a long-term partner?" "Is this the right direction for the organization?" etc. Big decisions take time, days, weeks, months or years. While some consider this a waste of time, others see it as a testing period and a good investment in a relationship, so that future business won't even need a contract to bear fruitful outcomes. Indeed, by that stage, the relationship *is* the contract.

- *Group attachment is critical for our survival, because the group is our source of support.*
- *Group mindset was useful in environments with germs and pathogens. Hence, it has coevolved with genes to biologically prepare humans for adjustment. This is the evolutionary root of strong group attachment.*
- *Weak and strong group attachment varies across national, organizational, and group cultures, individuals and particular contexts.*
- *The degree of importance varies with regard to harmony, face, trust and interdependence.*

CASE STUDY

In the following mini-cases, how can we use the values discussed in this chapter and other factors such as behaviors, environment and particular context to explain these outward expressions? How do change, paradox and the non-binary of values play a role? You may want to read about other values first.

1. In Japan, you introduce yourself by stating *first* the name of the organization, and then your name: "From company X, my name is Y." Similarly, Maoris (New Zealand), introduce themselves by identifying their *iwi* (tribe), *hapu* (sub-tribe), etc., and the last thing mentioned is their name.
2. In Vietnam, China, Japan and Korea, the family name comes first, followed by your first name (given name). For example, in the name Chu Minh, the family name is "Chu," the first name is "Minh."

3. In 2009, former President Roh Moo-hyun of South Korea committed suicide amidst a corruption scandal. The accusation had threatened to undo his proudest legacy as an upstanding political leader.[46]
4. In 2014, the captain of a South Korean ferry abandoned his sinking ship with more than 300 casualties, he was later found drying his bank notes.[47]
5. The Queen consort of The Netherlands, Máxima, is from Argentina and is the daughter of Jorge Zorreguieta. As the Secretary of Agriculture, he served during the country's military dictatorship from 1976 to 1981 and was accused of turning a blind eye to the Dirty War – a period of repression that saw 10,000–30,000 people killed or disappeared. Despite months of controversy, her marriage to the then Crown Prince was approved.[48]
6. When extending to new markets, businesses often calculate purchasing power depending on individual income. This practice can be misleading in societies where families pool their resources together for shopping.

5.2 Hierarchy acceptance

All human societies are organized based on social status. That is why *hierarchy* is a universal dimension of human relationships[49] and a major concept in intercultural communication. It was named "relation to authority" by Inkeles and Levinson,[50] "lineal" vs. "collateral" by Kluckhohn and Strodtbeck,[51] "power distance" by Hofstede,[52] and "achievement" vs. "ascription" by Trompenaars and Hampden-Turner.[53]

5.2.1 The Term: Hierarchy Acceptance

From an evolutionary point of view, hierarchy goes hand in hand with the birth of leaders, all for the sake of our reproductive success.[54] Hierarchy can be achieved by either *dominance* or *prestige*. The former is common among non-human primates, with individuals gaining access to resources through threat, intimidation and display of force. Among human beings, leaders are awarded with "prestige"[55] in exchange for expertise, skills, education, personal risks and the time that they give to the community. For this reason, the fundamental difference of hierarchy between animals and humans is that leaders are often highly respected, liked and admired, while alpha males and females are feared.[56] In order to achieve hierarchy, animals use dominance and power, humans tend to use prestige and status.

Because hierarchy can create easier access to more resources, it is often mistaken for power, which is not always the case. We are reminded of the words of Wendell Berry: "The hierarchy of power is not the same as the hierarchy of value. [...] An evil human is high on the scale of power, but at the very bottom of the scale of values." Indeed, power maybe the consequence of hierarchy but not the other way around. Those with power, be it money or official rank, do not necessarily achieve higher positions on the hierarchical ladder. Wizards and fortune tellers can have great influence on people, but do not necessarily command respected. In some traditional Southeast Asian societies, entrepreneurs were placed on the lowest rank of status, behind intellectuals, farmers and artisans. From an evolutionary perspective, hierarchy was born first and associated power was more of a side effect. We will discuss the evolutionary need for hierarchy in the next section. For now, the term *Hierarchy Acceptance* is coined to indicate the extent to which subordinates accept a hierarchical (unequal) distribution of prestige, status, influential power and resources between them and their superiors.

5.2.2   Hierarchy Acceptance in the Inverted Pyramid Model

5.2.2.1   *Hierarchy at the Universal Level*

Hierarchy was born out of evolutionary pressure. This is true at all levels of organization, be it a biological system or a man-made system such as a machine. In essence, the main reason for hierarchy is the *cost of connection*.[57] Connections are expensive because they have to be designed, built and maintained. Imagine you want to a keep good relationship with 20 people on an individual basis. That sounds just fine, especially in a small hunter-gatherer group, but your life in the modern era can't run smoothly if you only know 20 people, since everything from shopping, travelling, cooking, etc. needs thousands, if not hundreds of thousands or millions of people involved in order to produce an end product. Hierarchy came into existence to reduce the number of connections you need to make and maintain, in the same way as you organize files into different levels of folders on the computer. In human societies, this is also the starting point of labor division, which allows for better extraction of resources.[58] Now, you only need to know the shop's owner to get the groceries, and it is *her/his* responsibility to make other connections and ensure a smooth chain of supply. Everyone does not need to know everyone else. For this reason, hierarchy has evolved to become an element of culture – the survival strategy for human beings.

At the universal level, hierarchy is a fundamental concern because it is needed for the advancement of the whole community. Human groups everywhere are organized into a hierarchy, and hierarchical groups ultimately outlived egalitarian groups.[59] Hierarchy acceptance on the *baseline level* is a universal value. All of us accept, to a baseline degree, that we are not equal. No matter where you come from, you will always acknowledge that your tribal leader, your managers, your parents, your teachers, and even someone who is older than you has a degree or two more prestige, status and resources than you do. Put any two persons in a room, in the end we will have a senior and a junior.

5.2.2.2 *Hierarchy Acceptance at the Collective and Individual Level*

Differing in degree of acceptance. While all societies have the same fundamental concern about hierarchy and accept on the baseline level that some people may be a rank or two higher, and hence, may gain more access to status and power than others, the level of acceptance varies from the minimum baseline at the collective and individual level. A leader may have power to influence, but the amount of prestige (s)he receives and the amount of *acceptable* resources (s)he may access vary from one subordinate to another. For example, two workers perform the same job and have the same boss. In principle, the hierarchy gap between the boss and both of the workers is the same. However, the way that these two workers view this gap can be very different. The first worker may show greater respect for his boss, giving this person more prestige, accepting that (s)he controls most of the decision making process and may have much higher salary (high hierarchy acceptance). Meanwhile, the other worker may challenge this gap in prestige and resource by questioning her boss's decisions and demanding a more equal salary (low hierarchy acceptance). In sum, this value is the level of acceptance towards the hierarchical amount of prestige and resources leaders *should* receive in exchange for their service. It is not the reality of prestige and resources, but the perception of what is acceptable.

In general, there are a few signals that prompt us to decide how unequal our relationship with superiors should be. Trompenaars and Hampden-Turner[60] distinguished between *achieved status* that is based on performance and merit, and *ascribed status* that is based on seniority, background or sex. All of us may afford status to those who are more competent and with more years of employment. However, the former factor (competence) is more important in contexts where achieved status prevails, and the latter (seniority) is more important in contexts where ascribed status prevails. Hence, sending a young and talented person to negotiate with a senior and experienced partner may initially hinder the process because their assumptions are confronted.

Ascribed status is based on seniority, background, or sex/ "A sign at Kuala Lumpur Airport, (Malaysia)," MAI NGUYEN-PHUONG-MAI.

Neuroscience offers some interesting insight. While human adults typically respond faster to their own face than to the faces of others, the "boss effect" suggests that those who embrace high hierarchy acceptance respond faster to their supervisor's face than to their own.[61] Of course, this does not mean that some people were born with this mindset. Culture is learned, and the brain's plasticity means one's cultural values can change.

Static ranking. Similar to group attachment, the static paradigm is very influential in the discourse of hierarchy. Hofstede measured the extent to which subordinates were afraid to express disagreement and how they preferred a certain decision making style from managers. Trompenaars and Hampden-Turner's ranking is based on how unlikely an ascribed status such as family background can command respect (the result for this index has been reversed to aid understanding). Here are a few samples from the top, the middle and the end of the spectrum:

	High Hierarchy Acceptance	Average	Low Hierarchy Acceptance
Hofstede[62]	104. Malaysia	55. Pakistan	26. Switzerland
	100. Slovakia	54. Canada Québec	22. New Zealand
	95. Guatemala	54. Japan	18. Denmark
	95. Panama	50. Italy	13. Israel
	94. Philippines	49. Argentina	11. Austria
Trompenaars & Hampden-Turner[63]	50. Israel	27. South Korea	8. Denmark
	50. Romania	26. Russia	6. Ireland
	49. Nigeria	26. Germany	6. Norway

Paradox and change. While these statistics serve us well in imagining a big picture with a strong focus on comparison, the dynamic paradigm of culture reminds us that they are only suggestions and not the rules. Zooming in on details, you may notice that some of the scores do not seem to align with the common observation. For example, Pakistan (55), Japan (55) and Quebec Canada (54) score very similarly on Hofstede's index. But anyone who is familiar with the strong emphasis on social honor in Pakistan and the intricate system of social ranking in Japan will immediately question the positions of these two countries when they are put on par with the French culture in Canada.

Like all other values, high or low hierarchy acceptance is subject to the dynamic change of historical and social context. The influence of class-system offers a good example. During the 60s and 70s of the communist regimes in Cambodia,[64] China[65] and Vietnam,[66] many of those who traditionally received high prestige or enjoy more resources, such as doctors, teachers, priests and entrepreneurs, were considered "class enemies." Subsequently, millions were subjected to forced labor, torture, public shaming, imprisonment and systematic killing. In this period, students physically attacked teachers, children publically disowned parents, young people spit on seniors and intellectuals were forced to address uneducated people as "sir," "madam," "Mr. or Mrs. Peasant." While these are extreme examples, they remind us of how influential context is in viewing collective values. Drastic economic and political changes, modernization, radical or dramatic events, etc. all contribute to both paradoxes and shifts of value.

Two separate values. While hierarchy acceptance is a fundamental concern, low or high hierarchy acceptance can be presented as two separate value constructs.[67] One of them will prevail depending on particular contexts. We are also reminded here of the negative correlation between "what is" (how hierarchy is practiced in reality) and "what should be" (how hierarchy is supposed to be) in the GLOBE study.[68] This means outward expressions and values can be contradictory, you can believe in one thing and act the opposite – a discussion we had in Chapter 2. Context is the main indicator for predicting the change within and between cultures. Paradoxes and contrasting values/outward expressions co-exist, manifesting themselves depending on particular contexts.

Multiple cultures at the collective level. National culture is just one of four collective cultures at the second level of the Inverted Pyramid model. Organizational culture, for example, can diverge widely from what is perceived as a typical value of the whole country. While Brazil scores 69 on Hofstede's index (at the same level as Hong Kong [68], Vietnam [70], and Morocco [70]), the country also gives us Semco – an exemplar of flat hierarchy in the corporate world. Here, your question of "who is charge?" will be answered with: "No one."[69] Semco's famous organizational culture of *holacracy* is compared to Freys – a hotel chain from Sweden (31 on the index) with only two levels of hierarchy.[70]

Next to organizational culture, group culture is also influential. In a study that gathered data from authority-based advertisements in South Korea and Thailand, the author reported that national culture alone is not a good predictor, rather it is the extent to which a *segment* (i.e. a group culture) embraces or rejects their own cultural values.[71] Another example of group culture diverging from national culture is Israel. While it is common to challenge the hierarchical amount of prestige and resources superiors receive (13 on the index), the degree of respect a rabbi (religious leader, meaning "a great one") enjoys in Israel very likely indicates a number much higher than 13. When it comes to profession, military culture everywhere is characterized by a high level of hierarchy acceptance. Orders are not to be questioned. Regardless of national cultures, officers and soldiers tend not to fraternize, so that in a battle, officers can give objective orders without personal feelings being involved. In sum, multiple cultures at the collective level of the Inverted Pyramid model suggest that it can be perplexing to use national scores to compare Estonian accountants and Latvian artists.

Individual level. Non-typical outward expressions at the individual level are endless. In every country where high hierarchy acceptance is the norm, one can always find individual cases that challenge it, and vice versa. In an international context, someone who moves to a new culture will gradually acculturate, and someone who exercises a high level of intercultural competence will adjust accordingly when the context demands.

The driving factors of diversity in hierarchy acceptance. The gene–culture coevolution theory has a similar explanation for the differing levels of hierarchy acceptance as it does for group attachment. During the early human migration, in some parts of the world, the prevalence of pathogens (bacteria and fungus) in the environment posed a risk for our ancestors. Under this influence and the presence of the shorter variant of serotonin carriers (s5-HTTLPR), we have evolved with the need to develop a culture of group-mindset *and* hierarchical dominance. This is especially true in environments with a high level of territorial and resource threats.[72] Those who followed the cultural rules of group conformity and hierarchical order had a higher chance of survival. Simultaneously, those with short alleles need and fit better into the group mindset and hierarchical culture, so their gene became dominant to support these values. Throughout history, the dynamic context of culture, genes and behaviors constantly shapes how we accept hierarchical distribution of status, power and wealth.

As a consequence of the Second World War and the Cold War, Korea was divided into two countries in 1945. The Korean culture in the North and South has evolved differently as the two countries pursue diametrically opposed political, economic and social systems. The leaders in the North are revered, to the extent that people have lost their lives and loved ones to save portraits of the leaders during natural disasters.[73]/ "North Koreans bowing in front of statues of the Eternal President of the Republic Kim Il-sung and his son – Kim Jong Il on Mansu Hill, Pyongyang," J.A. ROO.[74]

5.2.3   Outward Expressions of Hierarchy Acceptance

Because human hierarchy is characterized by *reciprocal* arrangements between superiors and subordinates, the relationship between them is always a two-way street. Superiors are expected to care, protect and guide subordinates. In turn, subordinates are expected to respect, be loyal and obedient towards their superiors. Across cultures and individuals, depending on circumstances, this degree of reciprocity varies.

5.2.3.1   Respect – Care

Respecting superiors is a code of ethics that we all learn from young age. In many cultures, it is embedded in languages. For example, while English has only two pronouns "you" and "I," Vietnamese and Japanese have very specific pronouns for each relationship.[75] In Vietnam, it is sometimes impossible to communicate properly if two people do not know the age of each other, simply because they cannot establish a ranking relationship to address each other. The notion of respect also varies across cultures.[76] A study of Arabs and Israeli Jews shows this difference. Arabs preferred *musayara* speech, which employs avoidance of interruption, topic shifts, effusive use of greetings, and intensification of interpersonal bonds. Israeli subjects preferred *dugri* speech, which emphasizes straight talk, and is direct and sincere in nature.[77]

Respect is given to superiors in exchange for care. The notion of care also varies. For example, when embracing low hierarchy acceptance, a manager would show care by giving her/his subordinates a certain degree of freedom and autonomy. In comparison, when embracing high hierarchy acceptance, a benevolent autocrat or paternalistic/maternalistic manager would act like a family member who is ready to help if her/his employees have to deal with personal struggles. In Nigeria, for example, it is reasonable to ask the company to provide accommodation – a request that some may find hard to justify.[78]

According to the Vietnamese tradition, the parents of the groom-to-be should organize a formal proposal ceremony in which they present gifts and ask the woman's parents for permission to marry. In this picture, the people who lead the delegation are not the groom's parents. In the absence of his parents due to personal circumstances, three executives from his company take on the task and play the parental role in the ceremony/ "Proposal ceremony," TU HUNG.

5.2.3.2 Loyalty – Protection

Subordinates are expected to be loyal to their superiors, but this varies across different contexts. Confucianism, for example, dictates that if the king wants his subordinates to die, refusing to die is a sin. A good example of the reciprocal link between loyalty and protection is the employment system in Japan. The *bushido* philosophy of life has translated the traditional concept of loyalty into a fierce commitment to one's company. In turn, companies reward employees with lifetime employment. Although this policy is now fading,[79] a seniority wage system remains. Salaries are determined by the length of time an employee has been with the organization. An employee who leaves her/his job for a new position will start again from a lower end of the new company's wage scale.

Loyalty varies across other collective cultures as well, such as generations. A study in the US shows that younger people are the least loyal to their employers,[80] but that is probably because they have a different definition of loyalty. Millennials want leaders to earn their loyalty, not just by providing them with a salary but by being an inspiration.[81] Once loyalty has been earned, it will be given fiercely.

5.2.3.3   Obedience – Guidance

A cross-cultural observation in the classroom would quickly reveal a stark contrast between the context where low hierarchy and the context where high hierarchy acceptance prevails. In the former, teachers are facilitators of discussion and are less hesitant to admit "I don't know!" In the latter, teachers are *guru* who are supposed to know everything. In countries under the influence of Confucianism (China, Vietnam, Taiwan, Hong Kong, Japan, Korea, and Singapore), the teacher is ranked below the king and above the father. Students' obedience is given in exchange for teachers' excellence.

A slightly similar situation can be observed in the workplace. Some organizational cultures have broad guidelines and expect staff to manage themselves, such as those with holacracy. Others expect managers to give instruction and guidance, and employees should ask managers or wait for opinions even though they may know exactly what to do.

- *Hierarchy acceptance is critical for our survival because it reduces the cost of connection.*
- *Hierarchical mindset was useful in environments with germs and pathogens. Hence, it has coevolved with genes to biologically prepare humans for adjustment. This is the evolutionary root of high hierarchy acceptance.*
- *We accept that superiors gain more access to status, power and resources. But the level of acceptance varies, depending on national, organizational and group cultures, individuals and particular context.*
- *The relationship between superiors and subordinates are two-way: respect and care, loyalty and protection, obedience and guidance.*

CASE STUDY

In the following mini-cases, how can we use the values discussed in this chapter and other factors such as behaviors, environment and particular context to explain these outward expressions? How do change, paradox and the non-binary of values play a role? You may want to read about other values first.

1. In 2017, a Taiwanese woman wanted to marry her girlfriend of 11 years but her father refused to attend the wedding. When she shared her feeling of rejection at work and a concern that she would lose clients, her CEO reached out and offered to walk her down the aisle. Same-sex marriage is still illegal in Taiwan.[82]

2. In 1977, US President Nixon was interviewed by British journalist David Frost. In an attempt to defend his spying on political opponents and the massive "Watergate" cover-up, he uttered the most famous political lines of the 20th Century: "When the president does it, that means it is not illegal!"[83]

ACTIVITY

1. In a 2006 study, researchers gathered 150,000 parking tickets that were racked up in Manhattan by diplomats from 146 countries posted to the UN. They found that the worst offenders came from Kuwait (246 unpaid tickets per diplomat), Egypt, Chad, Sudan, Bulgaria, Mozambique, Albania, Angola and Senegal.[84] Conduct research and discuss if this outward expression correlates with the scores of diplomats' home countries on corruption, and if it can be explained from value perspectives.

2. In defense of their war crimes during the Second World War, many said they just followed orders. Psychologist Milgram wanted to investigate whether Germans were more obedient to authority figures than others.[85] Conduct research to understand the experiment carried by Milgram and discuss if a willingness to follow and order to kill is universal or cultural. Discuss the relationship between this experiment and hierarchy acceptance.

5.3   Gender association

Sex is fundamentally different from *gender*. While sex (male/female) refers to biological makeup such as chromosomes, reproductive organs, and hormones, gender (masculinity/femininity) refers to two sets of behaviors: (1) traits that are associated with femininity, such as modesty and caring; (2) traits that are associated with masculinity, such as competitive and assertive. Originating from gender's role, these traits have become a fundamental concern for all societies, as they not only express what is expected of men and women, but also the relationship between members of a cultural group and their worldviews.

5.3.1   The Terms: Gender Association, Masculinity and Femininity

The measurement of masculinity and femininity started in 1936 with a 455-item test that declared an individual masculine if (s)he disagreed, and feminine if (s)he agreed with statements such as "I always prefer someone else to take the lead" or "I am often afraid of the dark." It is hard to imagine such a test today, because the social perception of men and women has changed significantly.[86]

That is to say, gender is essentially a social construct. In Chapter 1, we discussed how the brains of women and men do not come in male or female forms,[87-88] but rather changed into different structures as a result of repeating behaviors. A woman's brain may be different from a man's brain, not because she was born that way, but because her brain's plasticity is responding to the demands of her environment. The French scholar Simone de Beauvoir wrote: "One is not born, but rather *becomes,* a woman."[89] Even under the influence of social impact, up to 53 per cent of brains cover both male-end and female-end features.[90]

Because gender is a social construct, what we associate with masculinity and femininity today is different in comparison with a century ago. It should not come as a surprise that if these concepts had existed in some traditional societies, the lists of masculine and feminine traits would have been almost reversed. As anthropologist Margaret Mead described in her classic study of tribes in Papua New Guinea, both men and women of the Arapesh displayed feminine temperaments, but among the Mundugamor, both men and women were masculine. Among the Tchambuli, men were feminine and women were masculine. "Women in charge" was a norm in ancient matriarchal societies in Myanmar,[91] India,[92] Vietnam,[93] Tahiti[94] and among the Hopi Native American tribe.[95] In the modern era, matriarchy is the norm among the Mosuo in Tibetan Himalayas, the Minangkabau of West Sumatra (Indonesia), the Akan in Ghana, the Bribri in Costa Rica, the Garo in India, and the Nagovisi in New Guinea. Among the Mosuo, for example, women are in charge, children don't normally know who their father is, and men are feminine. Choo Waihong, the author of *The Kingdom of Women,* recalled she "was once made to wait before talking business with an elderly Mosuo man until he had bathed his family's twin baby girls and changed their nappies."[96] The change in gender roles and the dynamics of traits associated with them throughout history pose a critical question: How will our current perception of masculinity and femininity change in the future? For the sake of argument, will "tolerance" become a masculine trait?

In Tunisia, a man who wears jasmine on his left ear indicates that he is single. Offering white jasmine is sending a message of affection/ "A man in Tunis, (Tunisia)," MAI NGUYEN-PHUONG-MAI.

Another issue relating to these terms is the (sub)conscious bias that the association with sex may evoke. While women can be masculine and men can be feminine, women may feel pressured to act feminine and men to be masculine. The traits are *unisex,* but the names signal otherwise. If a trait can interchangeably and simultaneously exist in both men and women, it is neither masculine, nor feminine, but a sexless, androgynous trait. This branding problem has not yet been solved, since no terms have been created to address the traits properly.

The masculinity-femininity dyad became popular in the mainstream of intercultural studies through the seminal work of Hofstede. His value is incorporated in this chapter, albeit with interpretation from the dynamic paradigm of culture and insight from other disciplines. The term *Gender Association* has been coined to cover both tendencies towards masculinity and femininity. In this book, gender association is defined as the extent to which people are associated with either masculine or feminine traits. Femininity emphasizes care, modesty and sustainability. Masculinity emphasizes competition, assertiveness and performance.

5.3.2   Gender Association in the Inverted Pyramid Model

5.3.2.1   *Gender Association at the Universal Level*
Looking at the list of masculine and feminine traits, we can quickly recognize that everyone needs both to survive and advance, at least at the *baseline*

level. No human being or societies can survive with only one set of values. It is also important to note that femininity means "care" for everyone and not just one's own ingroup. Here is an example: Taxes can be shockingly high in Scandinavia, up to half of the total salary for an ordinary middle-class employee. It is a feminine practice that aims to ensure well-being for the whole country. In comparison, saving for your own children or showing empathy for your own colleagues shows group attachment and not femininity.

5.3.2.2   Gender Association at the Collective and Individual Level

Differing in degree of association. While all societies and individuals possess both masculine and feminine traits, they differ from the minimum baseline in the degrees that these traits are associated with how things should be. When feminine values prevail, we tend to emphasize modesty, care and sustainability above competitiveness, assertiveness and performance. In contexts where masculine values prevail, priorities are different.

Static ranking. Hofstede considers masculinity and femininity as two extremes of a bipolar construct. Here are some samples from the top, the middle and the end of the spectrum:

	Masculinity	**Average**	**Femininity**
Hofstede[97]	110. Slovakia	52. Canada	19. Slovenia
	95. Japan	50. Luxembourg	16. Denmark
	88. Hungary	50. Malaysia	14. Netherlands
	79. Austria	50. Pakistan	8. Norway
	73. Venezuela	49. Brazil	5. Sweden

Paradox and change. Since gender is a social construct, traits that are socially associated with men and women vary across cultures and become dynamic due to changes in gender roles[98] and social development. Besides, paradoxes are inherent parts of every culture. A person or a group can fight for a feminine cause (e.g. equality) in a masculine way (e.g. revolution) and vice versa. In his 2011 study,[99] Tony Fang offered two examples of masculinity from Scandinavia's feminine cultures. On Hofstede's index, Sweden ranks as the world's most feminine culture with a highly developed social welfare system and a progressive attitude toward the environment. However, in the context of global competition, the success of Swedish multinationals shows a true Viking spirit inherited from their ferocious sailor-warrior forefathers. Likewise, the feminine Finland (26) also deeply embraces the masculine value of *sisu* – a national pride that emphasizes courage, grit and bravery against all odds. Only the logic of paradox can explain why the following description of *sisu* exists simultaneously with the country's feminine value:

> The Finns have something they call *sisu*. It is a compound of bravado and bravery, of ferocity and tenacity, of the ability to keep fighting after most people would have quit, and to fight with the will to win. The Finns translate sisu as "the Finnish spirit" but it is a much more gutful word than that. Last week the Finns gave the world a good example of sisu by carrying the war into Russian territory on one front while on another they withstood merciless attacks by a reinforced Russian Army. In the wilderness that forms most of the Russo-Finnish frontier between Lake Laatokka and the Arctic Ocean, the Finns definitely gained the upper hand.[100]

Two separate values. The bipolar concept of masculinity and femininity has been criticized since the 70s, when researchers became disenchanted with the scale. It was argued that people can be masculine, feminine or both (androgyny).[101] New instruments were created to measure masculinity and femininity on separate, independent dimensions.[102-103] The two scales were not negatively related and this means masculinity is not the opposite of femininity. Those who scored low on both values were classified as "undifferentiated." Those who scored high on both values were labeled as "androgynous." In many traditional societies, men are expected to be masculine and women to be feminine. In some others, such as among the Tchambuli or the Mosuo, men were feminine and women were masculine. Regardless of the gender role, masculinity and femininity coexist. A culture can score high on *both* masculinity and femininity.

Individual level. From the dynamic paradigm perspective, androgyny represents the flexibility of a multicultural mind, i.e. being able to adjust when needed. Personalities that associate with masculine and feminine traits also shift throughout the time.[104]

The driving factors of diversity in gender association. From the point of view of evolutionary psychology,[105] there is a profound difference between the sex cells of women and men. Women's eggs are large and much fewer in number (15–20 mature eggs each month). Men's are small and abundant (100 million sperms each ejaculation). Women also have to carry the fetus for nine months and take care of the child afterwards. If she makes the wrong choice of man, the cost is high. Therefore, men have to compete for sexual access to women. This biological view explains certain gender associations of women being caring and faithful, and men being competitive and risk taking.

In contrast, social construction theory posits that gender roles are caused by division of labor and not biology. Dividing the tasks along the sex line showed advantages in hunter-gatherer groups and women and men become psychologically different to adjust to their social roles. Economists often weigh in this direction. For example, between two forms of soil cultivation, the *shifting* type that uses hand-held devices favors women, and the *ploughing* type that requires upper-body strength favors men.[106] The result is that men dominated the field in plough cultivation, pushing women back home. Masculine traits became associated with market employment, political participation, success and competition, while feminine traits became associated with home-bound activities such as caring. Modern societies with traditional plough agriculture have lower rates of female employment and higher gender inequality.[107]

Women adjust to circumstances, redefining perception of gender roles. In the Dahomey Kingdom (present-day Benin), women were added into the army to make it look larger in battle. They behaved so courageously that they became a permanent corps with high social status/ "She-Dong-Hong-Beh, a leader of the Amazons," drawn by FREDERICK FORBES *in 1851.*[108]

The *biosocial* theory combines these two schools of thought and proposed an interactionist approach that involves both genes and culture, both nature and nurture.[109] An individual is influenced by both social expectation (i.e. what men and women are supposed to be) and biological factors. Despite differences, all three theories emphasize behavioral adjustment to social environment.

5.3.3 Outward Expressions of Gender Association

5.3.3.1 Gender's Role

When femininity prevails, there is no clear distinction between how men and women are expected to behave. In Sweden, a new gender-neutral personal pronoun "hen" was created as an alternative to the gender-specific female "hon" and male "han."[110] Nurturing, caring, tolerance, modesty and sustainability are important to everyone. This not only leads to men and women entering each other's traditional professions, but also means "masculine" jobs are executed in a feminine way. Police in the Netherlands, for example, are famous for being kind and considerate, to such an extent that they have been mockingly called "social workers."[111] In short, femininity has nothing to do with the kind of job, but *how a job is done.*

When masculinity prevails, both men and women may adopt the masculine manner of conduct: competitive, dominant and self-reliant. Look no further than Margaret Thatcher for an example. Masculinity puts pressure on men to live up to masculine stereotypes and it may hurt their emancipation. Many of them would probably be laughed at if they express the wish to become a full-time father or kindergarten teacher.

When both masculinity and femininity prevail, we often see masculine men and feminine women, or vice versa as in the case of the Tchambuli tribe. However, this does not apply at the individual level because a person's value is much more dynamic than a collective value.

5.3.3.2 Modesty and/or Assertiveness

Modesty is a crucial universal norm, but the emphasis placed on this norm is so much stronger when feminine values prevail. People downplay assertive behavior and attempts to excel and stand out. The Dutch, for example, love to ridicule a show off with their favorite saying: "*Doe maar gewoon, dan doe je al gek genoeg,*" roughly translated as "Act normal, because being normal is mad enough." No one culture has the monopoly on boasting about achievement, overpromising in job interviews, or being overtly self-confident, it is just more common in some than others. For masculinity, it is "the bigger the better." For femininity, quality doesn't need to scream out. Do not mistake this for pride. Everyone has a strong sense of pride, but masculinity and femininity deal with how one expresses her/his pride: loudly blowing one's trumpet or modestly mentioning the achievement as if it is the normal thing to do.

5.3.3.3   *Well-being and/or Competitiveness*
Similarly, competitiveness is universally needed in all societies, for everyone. However, it is more of an essential characteristic in contexts where masculine values prevail, typically manifested through the spirit of "may the best man win." A masculine educational system would make the best student the norm. A masculine employer would want to see a candidate with an impressive CV and bold promises. A masculine job seeker would place strong emphasis on high salary, promotion and job opportunities. A masculine politician would be less hesitant to engage in armed conflict. In a different context, a feminine educational system would care more for underdogs and those with disabilities. A feminine employer would prefer a candidate who is down-to-earth. A feminine job seeker would prioritize a good relationship with colleagues and work-life balance. Feminine virtues also nurture teamwork, discussion, negotiation and compromises instead of resorting to win-lose situations or violence.

Another important aspect of gender association is the importance of well-being. All governments have policies on environment, services, education, animal right and social welfare, but these issues will get more attention from a feminine government than a masculine one. For example, same-sex marriage was first legalized in the Netherlands, and the country has the world's only legal Red Light district. Many Dutch executives work part-time in an attempt to balance working and private life.[112] There are political parties that represent animals, senior citizens and those who "don't want to vote."

- *Gender association is rooted in the biological differences between male and female, in the historical division of labor and the dynamics of contexts.*
- *Everyone and every society needs both masculine and feminine values to advance. But the level of importance depends on national, organizational and group cultures, individuals and particular context.*
- *The level of importance varies with regard to modesty and assertiveness, well-being and competitiveness.*

CASE STUDIES

In the following mini-cases, how can we use the values discussed in this chapter to explain the outward expressions? Do the cases reflect the typical values in the cultures where they occurred? You may want to read about other values first.

1. In 1896, Costa Rica became one of the world's first countries to make education both free and obligatory. When the army was abolished in 1949, it was said that the army would be replaced by an army of teachers.[113]
2. The word *karoshi* means overwork-death in Japanese. There is an increasing number of people suffering from fatal strokes and heart attacks due to long working hours.[114] In 2016, a 24-year-old woman reportedly logged 105 overtime hours in one month and later on committed suicide.[115] Japanese workers typically refuse to leave their desks while the boss is still in the office.
3. While most countries' success is measured by Gross Domestic Product (GDP), the King of Bhutan believed that an economic approach dehumanized the development process.[116] The country created its famous Gross National Happiness (GNH) index, which is based on sustainable socioeconomic development and preservation of culture and environment. For example, Bhutan restricts mass tourism by imposing a high tariff of $250 per day for travelers to promote a policy of "high value, low impact." GNH initiatives have developed around the world, including Thailand, Dubai, Canada and the US.
4. Some of those countries defined as masculine according to Hofstede's index, such as Slovakia (110), Hungary (88), Poland (64) and Germany (64), offer long periods of protected parental leave.[117] Conduct research on this feminine policy across the countries worldwide and see if you can recognize more paradoxes.

5.4 Uncertainty avoidance

Trying to predict and avoid the unknown is universal and a basic human instinct. Fear is the result of both strongly innate feelings and social learning. In general, we have several inborn fears, for example the fear of falling and the fear caused by loud noises. These fears are genetically coded in our body and are healthy emotions that keep us from harm. Most other types of fear are learned from the culture of our life, what is good and what is bad, what is safe and what is dangerous. Our fear may have an object (fear of the dark) or no specific object (what will happen to us in the future, when we take a new job, or after we die?) The latter is called *uncertainty*.

5.4.1   The Term: Uncertainty Avoidance

Hofstede borrowed the term "uncertainty" from the work of James G. March,[118] and used it to name a value that emerged from his survey of IBM employees. He argues that every human society has developed a structure to alleviate the ambiguity in life. This structure comes in the forms of three cultural strategies: religion, law and technology.[119] This value was replicated in the GLOBE project, in which *Uncertainty Avoidance* is defined as "the extent to which members of collectives seek orderliness, consistency, structure, formalized procedures and laws to cover situations in their daily lives."[120] Similar to gender association, uncertainty avoidance is incorporated in our discussion, albeit with interpretations from the dynamic paradigm of culture and insight from other disciplines.

5.4.2   Uncertainty Avoidance in the Inverted Pyramid Model

5.4.2.1   *Uncertainty Avoidance at the Universal Level*

The origin of our tendency to avoid the unknown is rooted in our nature as social animals. We need each other in the form of an ingroup for protection, and the culture of this ingroup will provide us with what we need to survive. Rules emerged from the need to keep this ingroup culture effective, to maintain trust among members, to safeguard cultural ideas from outsiders and to gauge between the choice of cooperating or fighting with other groups over resources. Three universal forms of cultural strategy in dealing with uncertainty are: religion, law, and technology.

Religion. In Chapters 1 and 2, we learned that religion is a fundamental concern, and this cultural strategy has been essential to enhancing our chance of survival. Evolutionary biologist Mark Pagel calls religion a "cultural enhancer" because it can "get at minds so hungrily to pursue aesthetic and psychological rewards," and, consequently, enhance our performance.[121] The future is so uncertain, and religion has historically given humans the hope that justice will be served, our enemy will be defeated, rain will come, travel will be safe, or our eternity will be in heaven. Religion as a cultural strategy can *reduce our worries and anxieties*, giving us the motivation to stride ahead – something that genes simply can't. For this reason, according to Pagel, regardless of our subjective opinion of religions, whether they are true, frivolous or hedonistic, human groups have adopted them. The reason is that, in a particular context, groups that failed to do so would risk losing in the competition with those who were more motivated by the force of faith.

Law. Religion is also among the earliest forms of law. With codes of morality and conduct, it has given us some certainty and direction in this arbitrary, capricious and unpredictable world. Traditional religions and beliefs still influence many modern law systems.[122]

Technology. Pagel went on to connect the prehistoric notion of religion with science. For our ancestors, religion was a form of science, signaling an attempt to understand the world and to answer questions such as "why is the harvest bad this year?" or "why do earthquakes happen?" Religion provided a framework for understanding the universe, nature and the logic of life. In the modern era, science and technology seem to have become divorced from religion, but their original purpose is quite similar, to predict the future, to give the unknown a structure and to reduce uncertainty.

5.4.2.2   Uncertainty Avoidance at the Collective and Individual Level

Differing in degree of avoidance. While all societies want to avoid the negative impact of the unknown, cultures and individuals differ from the universal *baseline value* in the degree of avoidance, based on the particular context. When uncertainty avoidance is strong, religion, law, and to a certain extent, technology tend take a more central role, and vice versa.

The strictness of rules and regulations depends on the context. Regardless of how low uncertainty avoiding a culture is, there are always situations where strict rules apply. For example, in Manila (Philippines), due to heavy traffic, the last digit on the car's license plate number determines the days it can or cannot hit the road. On the static ranking, the UK score 35 on the low end, but the country is known for laws from the 1300s that are still in force. In 2007, it was still illegal to die while in the Houses of Parliament[123]/ "Two security signs of strong and weak uncertainty avoidance," MAI NGUYEN-PHUONG-MAI.

Static ranking. Hofstede's index is based on "being nervous or tense at work" (i.e. stress means anxiety about rules to be followed), "rule orientation" (i.e. rules should not be broken, even when it is in the company's best interest), and the "length of employment" (i.e. changing job means venturing into the unknown). According to his interpretation, religion, law and technology have translated into *rules* to deal with ambiguity and the unknown. Here are the samples from the top, the middle and the bottom of the spectrum

	High Uncertainty Avoidance	Average	Low Uncertainty Avoidance
Hofstede[124]	112. Greece	52. East Africa	29. Hong Kong
	99. Portugal	51. Australia	29. Jamaica
	99. Guatemala	51. Slovakia	23. Denmark
	99. Uruguay	50. Norway	13. Sweden
	97. Belgium Flemish	49. New Zealand	8. Singapore

Paradox and change. While the index makes sense for many countries, it can be quite confusing trying to understand the indication for others. One of the reasons is that the score didn't distinguish between *institutional* and *social* rules. The former focuses on regulations, written laws, structured guidelines and formal organized procedures ("How rigid is the legal system?"); the latter is informally agreed-upon codes of conducts and social values ("How much respect one is expected to give to one's teacher?"). To be strong on social rules means values and codes of conducts are expected to be followed strictly (e.g. one is expected to show great respect to one's teacher, and not doing so will be frowned upon). To be weak on social rules means values and codes of conducts are more relaxed (e.g. one can show both high and low hierarchy acceptance towards one's teacher and expect no consequences).

Some cultures, such as those in Scandinavia, tend to be strong on institutional rules, but weak on social rules. Others, such as Vietnam, Laos, Cambodia and Myanmar, exercise strong social rules, but are not so strict in terms of institutional rules. This categorization of "rules" vs. "values" can help us to guess why these countries score so similarly: between Germany (65) and Thailand (64); between Bangladesh (60) and Quebec (60); or between Canada (48) and Indonesia (48). It also highlights the biggest paradox of the index: the champion of dealing with ambiguity – Singapore

(8) – is in fact a country that exercises one of the world's strictest systems of laws and punishment. It bans chewing gum and littering can invoke a fine of up to $1000.[125] As a society made up of three Asian ethnicities, which strongly embrace certain values and codes of conduct (Chinese, Indian and Malay), Singapore is both strong on institutional rules (laws) and social rules.

Two or more separate values. Due to the differences, and the sometimes contrasting nature between institutional and social rules, it is argued that a culture or an individual can be both strong and weak when it comes to avoiding uncertainty. In other words, (strong/weak) institutional rules and (strong/weak) social rules can form four different values. Another compelling reason to see strong and weak uncertainty avoidance as two separate tendencies is the *negative* correlation between cultural practices and value in almost all of the 62 countries where the GLOBE project gathered data.[126] In other words, what you do can be the opposite of what you believe.

The driving factors of diversity in uncertainty avoidance. Studies have been connecting variation in the dopamine D4 receptor gene (DRD4) with financial risk taking,[127] novelty seeking[128] and pathological gambling.[129] The alleles with 7 repeat-variation (7R) of DRD4 show greater ventral striatal activity and are more sensitive to rewards. It originated about 40,000 to 50,000 years ago when humans started to expand their territory across the world.[130] Biologists suggest that migrations have influenced the evolution of genes and culture. That is why the 7R allele is extremely prevalent among native South Americans or other nomadic groups, but extremely rare among East Asians.[131] Historian Frederick Turner in his *Frontier Thesis*[132] also argued that the process of migration, conquering new land, venturing into the unknown and striving for survival has transformed Europeans into a new people: the Americans. In a similar case, the inhabitants of Hokkaido (Japan) tend to have a strong sense of personal achievement and independence, which is different from people living in Honshu just 54km away.[133]

The Diversity Pathway diagram suggests that there are other factors throughout history that can influence the dynamics of uncertainty avoidance. Environmental and social threats can force a group to form a cautious view of the world and outsiders, hence, doubling on social rules and institutional rules as an attempt to safeguard identities and cultures. They can also aggressively invest in technology to fight enemies, or to replace the lack of human force so that there is no need to involve cooperation with outgroups.

5.4.3 Outward Expressions of Uncertainty Avoidance

5.4.3.1 Religion

Since religion is a strategy to deal with uncertainty, being religious can be seen as a signal of uncertainty avoidance. Religious people generally have a strong sense of justice, and that we get what we deserve, either in this life or in the hereafter. For example, the rule of karma warns you that what goes around comes around. This stems from the need to see the world as just and orderly.[134] If you play by the rules, you will be treated fairly. The dark side of this worldview is a tendency to blame the victim. For example, a rich entrepreneur was framed because (s)he was not careful enough in choosing a partner, not because the system was corrupt.

The intensity of following religious practices has more or less faded in our modern era, but its impact lingers in the way people perceive what is moral and what is not. 76 per cent of the world's atheists reside in Asia and the Pacific,[135] but in reality, most people here follow some folk beliefs in combination with a philosophy of life such as Confucianism or Buddhism. These frameworks of ethics and conducts can dictate rigid social rules. For example, a mother whose name is not officially on the management board but who, in effect, has the final voice in most of the business deals. Her influence is indirect, but powerful, not only because she laid the foundation for the business when it was still a small family trading company, but also because, as a mother, she receives ascribed status and a high level of hierarchy acceptance from her children, now executives of the company.

Implicit rules based on values like this govern life universally, but more so in cultures, individuals and contexts where strong uncertainty avoidance prevails. In *Driving Excellence*,[136] Steve Sanghi and Mike Jones distinguished between value-based and rule-based cultures, which illustrates quite well the difference between social and institutional rules in our topic.

5.4.3.2 Law

While a set of values (e.g. high hierarchy acceptance, strong group attachment, etc.) guide individuals' behavior, a set of institutional rules can serve the same purpose. An organization with rules, procedures and specifications ensures that employees know how they are expected to conduct their business effectively. However, an exceedingly rule-based culture can slow down decisions, create bureaucracy and reduce capacity to adapt to changes. The optimal combination between institutional rules and social rules (i.e. value-based) always depends on particular circumstances.

5.4.3.3 Technology

Hofstede argued that cultures with weak uncertainty avoidance are more likely to accept new products, new technology and are more likely to stimulate basic innovations[137] as they maintain a greater tolerance towards different ideas. However, according to GLOBE,[138] technology solutions appeal to rule-oriented people as well, since machines and automatic processes tend to make fewer errors than humans, and that is why they are attractive. In fact, the world's ten most innovative countries are scattered along the spectrum, from high to average and low scores.[139]

Since uncertainty is one of the determinants of market transactions between firms, especially in the international context where there is more ambiguity than domestic business,[140] we need to solve this puzzle. A study on national technological development[141] suggests that developing countries need sophisticated technologies, regardless of their uncertainty avoidance level. Over time, they will converge with developed countries at the point where they may have two completely contrasting values, i.e. strong uncertainty avoidance in practice (probably institutional rules) and weak uncertainty avoidance in value (social rules/values). This corresponds with Maslow's hierarchy of needs, in the sense that rich people already have their lower-order needs met, and are more likely to aim for self-actualization with freedom and excitement.[142]

- *Uncertainty avoidance is universal, but the degree of avoidance is influenced by human migration. Frontier spirit was useful in this context; hence, it has coevolved with genes to biologically prepare humans for adjustment. This is the evolutionary root of low uncertainty avoidance.*
- *We reduce uncertainty with religion, law and technology.*
- *The level of avoidance varies, depending on national, organizational and group cultures, individuals and particular context.*

CASE STUDIES

In the following mini-cases, how can we use the values discussed in this chapter and other factors such as behaviors, environment and particular context to explain these outward expressions? How do change, paradox and the non-binary of values play a role? You may want to read about other values first.

1. Gunpowder weapons originated in China, and were used with expertise by the Japanese, the Ottomans and the Indians. But the Europeans adopted them to wage wars at home. Ironically, the intense military competition between European states gave them an edge, as they were forced to innovate and adopt new technologies. The result was that, by 1800, Europeans had conquered 35 per cent of the globe.[143] Radar, microwave, satellite and internet are all the products of wars.

2. On New Year's Eve 2016, a number of women celebrating in public were surrounded and assaulted by groups of men on the streets of Cologne, Germany. Cologne's mayor received harsh criticism when she advised women to stay at "arm's length" from strangers.[144] A Cologne-based imam also said the reason why women were attacked was because they were "running around half naked."[145]

In Bhutan, the phallus is a symbol of good luck and is painted outside of homes and buildings to ward off bad spirits. The phallus is an integral part of Bon – the early ethnic religion that existed in Bhutan before Buddhism. Seemingly confronting and contrasting, in fact, these religious patterns coexist peacefully and symbolize the tolerant nature of the spiritual life in Bhutan. The mixing of religion is a sign of low uncertainty avoidance with regard to the absolute Truth. Monotheisms, such as Christianity, Judaism and Islam, are more concerned about the ultimate answer.[146] There is one Book, one God, and one set of rules. They have been debating for hundreds of year whose perception of these elements is correct/ "Paintings outside a shop in Thimphu, (Bhutan)," MAI NGUYEN-PHUONG-MAI.

3. Many end-user agreements for services are notoriously written in a small print, with legal and technical languages that are unreadable, extensive, detailed and containing many terms, conditions, and penalties. The French law of contract is based on a principle of morality, stressed by the canonists, who believed it was a sin for a person not to fulfill his promises. For the British, a contract is a bargain.[147] British common law posits that a valid contract must offer, at least theoretically, the opportunity for negotiation. End user license agreements violate that legal principle. Conduct research to find out why Britain does not have a written constitution.

5.5   Time orientation

Time perspective is a universal construct that refers to thoughts and attitudes towards the past, the present and the future.[148] We measure days and nights, calculate the cycles of seasons and stars, predict the coming and going of natural phenomenon, organize our life activities in a way that ensures our survival in the most effective way. We even think about time far beyond what we can possibly prove to be fact, for instance a time machine, life after death, or what the universe looked like at the beginning of time. In essence, time is a crucial dimension in shaping our lives and existence.

5.5.1   The Terms: Time Orientation and Chronemics

In Chapter 4 on non-verbal communication, we discussed the concept of chronemics: polychronic and monochronic. The former refers to how time can be a support system, a *servant* for humans, and a flexible framework in which humans dynamically arrange their activities in a non-rigid manner. The latter refers to how time is a *master*, a rigid framework that governs and control humans' activities.

In this section, we will touch on another aspect of time that focuses on the past, the present and the future. Besides Hall, *Time Orientation* has been discussed in the theoretical frameworks of Kluckhohn and Strodtbeck,[149] Hofstede,[150] Trompenaars and Hampden-Turner[151] and GLOBE.[152] It is defined as the extent to which one emphasizes the past, the present or the future.

5.5.2 Time Orientation in the Inverted Pyramid Model

5.5.2.1 *Time Orientation at the Universal Level*

The sense of time in all three dimensions (past, present and future) is crucial for survival. Culture is essentially the accumulation and selection of knowledge over a spectrum of time – a sea of resources from the past that humans can sample, adopt, change and improve for advancement in the present and future. The universality of time orientation can be encapsulated in the famous saying of the Dagestan poet Abutalib Gafurov: "If you fire at the past from a pistol, the future will shoot back from a cannon."

5.5.2.2 *Time Orientation at the Collective and Individual Level*

Differing in degree of orientation. While all three dimensions of time are essential, Tom Cottle's famous "circle test"[153] of 1967 suggests that different cultures, individuals may vary in how we let their weight influence our life course, depending on particular context. Participants were asked to draw three circles depicting the importance of the past, the present and the future. The size of each circle indicated the dominance of each time dimension, and the degree of overlap among the circles indicated their relationship. 65 per cent of the sample drew bigger future circles, followed by 10 per cent whose present circles were larger, and about 7 per cent who emphasized the past circle. With regards to time relations, about 63 per cent drew past, present and future circles that were not touching, indicating that, for them, these are separate entities; 26 per cent drew touching but not overlapping circles, indicating that time was continuous; and for 11 per cent of the participants, time was integrated, with three circles more or less overlapping.

Philip Zimbardo put it in more details:

A positive past orientation connects us with our roots, heritage, family, religion and national rituals. It gives us a sense of stability, of our self over time; it's where positive self-esteem is nourished. A future orientation gives us wings to soar to new destinations, to seek challenges and opportunities by envisioning scenarios of possible future selves. A present time perspective allows spontaneity, sensation seeking, openness to novelty, being in the moment and fully experiencing and expressing emotions.[154]

Static ranking. Theorists often translate the influence of time into a binary construct of "short term" vs. "long term." The former focuses on the past and the present, the latter focuses on the future.

	Long-term	Average	Short-term
Hofstede[155]	118. China	56. Thailand	23. Canada
	96. Hong Kong	50. Hungary	19. Philippines
	87. Taiwan	48. Singapore	19. Spain
	80. Vietnam	46. Denmark	16. Nigeria
	80. Japan	44. Netherlands	13. Czech Republic
Trompenaars & Hampden-Turner[156]	5.7 Hong Kong	4.5 Norway	3.8 Brazil
	5.6 Portugal	4.5 Indonesia	4.0 Ireland
	5.5 Czech Republic	4.5 Argentina	3.4 Philippines

Paradox and change. The biggest paradox of time orientation can be seen in Eastern Asian cultures. They value tradition, family, religion and heritage (short-term); yet, at the same time, they emphasize thrift, saving, stability, education, secured investment, hard work, stable relationships and future planning (long-term). Scandinavian countries, Ireland and Canada score low but consider long-term policies as trademarks of their national values, putting forward progressive visions and practices with regard to the environment, social welfare, animal rights, diversity and multiculturalism.

Three separate values. A critical review, comparing Hofstede and GLOBE on this dimension suggests that the past, the present and the future are not interchangeable, since they represent different characteristics of societies and individuals.[157] Millennials, for example, increasingly shop for sustainable products and want their employers to put sustainability on the priority list (future-oriented),[158] but they also value the idea of living life to the fullest (present-oriented).

Individual level. One of the most widely accepted tests for individuals on time orientation is the *Stanford Time Perspective Inventory* (STPI).[159] It measures five dimensions of time: past-oriented: (nostalgic, conservative, concerned over maintaining status-quo, work and live under pressure of obligation); present-hedonistic (self-indulgent, process-oriented, intrinsic motivation and emotional); present-fatalistic (believe in luck than hard work, religious, whatever will be, will be); future-oriented: (rational thinking, goal-oriented, controlling and planning).[160] An individual can simultaneously score high or low on all these time orientations.

The driving factors of diversity in time orientation. The diversity in time perception is strongly influenced by how a society is structured. Bands and tribes lived a primarily first-person existence in the present, with a lack of vocabulary that implies the passage of time. They hunted animals and gathered fruits without worrying much about the future. For them, the past was also not important, because it had gone. The sense of past and future probably developed with the formation of chiefdoms and agricultural states, when humans drew on sophisticated observation of the nature to calculate the best time for crops and harvests. Tradition played a crucial role because it was the knowledge accumulated throughout generations. This explains the pan-orientation (across the past, the present and the future) of many Asian and Middle Eastern cultures – fittingly, as they were also the world's cradles of agricultures. The emphasis on the present and future without a strong regard for the past may stem from the previously mentioned frontier theory. In a new territory, where humans were unable to rely on existing knowledge and tradition, the "can-do spirit," if-then reasoning and long-term planning were essential.

In the modern era, various social and environmental factors can influence time orientation. For example, the urge to achieve economic growth has forced many countries to turn a blind eye to permanent destruction of natural resources and ecological balance. Globalization goes hand in hand with perceived external threats against cultural identities and economic stability – a reason for some communities to roll back and take refuge in the past's glory or heritage.

Religion certainly has an impact as well. Buddhist teaching focuses on the present (fully aware of living in each moment). Confucian teaching focuses both on the past (tradition) and the future (education) with a strong sense of pragmatism in the present (what works is more important than what is right). Many Asian beliefs emphasize the cyclical and pan-orientation of time, as in the concept of reincarnation. While being religious can be interpreted as past-oriented, the appeal of monotheist religions such as Islam, Christianity and Judaism are more future-oriented, since life on earth is only temporary, and the purpose is to please the Almighty so one's eternal life will be in God's Kingdom.

Many Pacific islands are disappearing due to rising seas and erosion, forcing entire villages to relocate. The impact of global warming is most destructive in the Maldives, Tuvalu, Kiribati, Fiji, Marshall Island, and the Solomon Islands. In 2012, the Maldivian government stated that they intended to purchase islands in Australia, Sri Lanka or India to relocate their people when the inevitable happens/ "A woman walking in the sea in Maldives," MAI NGUYEN-PHUONG-MAI.

5.5.3 Outward Expressions of Time Orientation

5.5.3.1 *Past-orientation*

In contexts where past-orientation prevails, people are more concerned with *experience* and *values* than degree and competence. Paying respect to their history, highlighting common views or events in the past, reciting classic literature, praising the origin of the family/company/nation, visiting historical sites, proposing change as a way of *recreating* great glory of the past, etc. are some of the strategies that can quickly establish positive and warm relationships.

For past-orientation, the past is never gone, and people may constantly look to the past – real or imaginary – for inspiration, motivation, sustenance, hope, guidance and direction. Some literal branches of monotheism such as Salafism can be extremely past-oriented, in the sense that every modern day practice should be based on religious books. Some practitioners adhere to the smallest detail, from how to grow a beard,[161] how to dress,[162] how to clean the teeth,[163] etc., exactly the way the prophet Muhammad used to do in the 7th century. For many Muslims, Islam and its glorious past plays a central role and is a motivation to stride ahead. For example, Malaysian students were encouraged to excel in astronomy by following the footsteps of great Muslim scientists.[164] Knowing that this view of life in the context of tradition can be critical. The author of this book was able to convince a conservative family to allow their daughter to pursue her PhD by citing proper verses from the Quran and *hadith* (words and deeds of Muhammad) in which education for girls is said to be an obligation.

Veneration of the dead, including one's ancestors, is to show love and respect for the deceased. It is an act of looking after ancestors in their afterlives as well as seeking their guidance. The past, the present and the future are intertwined in this practice. The tradition is prevalent in Madagascar and Asia. In Europe, there are dedicated days and festival to honor the dead (e.g. All Saints' Day, All Souls' Day, Kalan Gwav, Samhain, etc.). In many Asian cultures, major decisions in life and business are made after a consultation ritual with the ancestors/ "Worshipping the Holy Death in Mexico," THELMADATTER.[165]

Leaders are known for using bygone glory to inspire followers. In 2006, the Dutch Prime Minister Jan P. Balkenende called for a return to the trading spirit of the VOC (Dutch East India Company). The tactic backfired, as many people of Surinamese descent identified the success of the VOC with slavery. Support for the party among citizens with a non-Western background fell by 25 per cent.[166] Even in a fairly young country like the US, "Make America great again" has been repeatedly used as a powerful campaign slogan by presidential candidates: Ronald Reagan in 1980, Bill Clinton in 1992 and Donald Trump in 2016.

5.5.3.2   Present-orientation

The American cartoonist Bil Keane famously said: "Yesterday is history, tomorrow is a mystery, today is a gift of God, which is why we call it the present." Following this spirit, we'd better focus on today. This mentality consequently leads to *short-term benefits* and *quick rewards, immediate results*, more *spending* than saving, with either *enjoyment of life* or a *fatalistic view of life*. Management is a matter of going with the flow, letting things happen naturally in a laissez-faire system.

5.5.3.3   Future-orientation

In contexts where future-orientation prevails, people plan their activities around goals they want to achieve in the future. These long-term goals shape their actions, as they are willing to sacrifice, to work hard, to save every penny and to persistently keep their eye on the prize. The reward and the effect are in the future. Management is a matter of planning, taking action and controlling.

- *Time orientation is critical for our survival because it allows us to deal with the increased complexity of social structure.*
- *The degree of importance we put on the past, the present and the future varies, depending on national, organizational and group cultures, individuals and particular context.*
- *The past-orientation emphasizes values, tradition, history and memories. The present orientation emphasizes short-term benefit, quick reward, immediate result, action and enjoyment. The future-orientation emphasizes goals, saving, planning, controlling and persistence.*

Angus Deaton – Nobel Prize winner in economics – has a very provocative idea about foreign aid. He argues that by trying to help poor people in developing countries, the rich world may actually be corrupting those nations' governments.[167] *One of the problems is the short-term mentality of "helping" and not "empowering," not letting the poor take charge. Foreign experts and volunteers come and go, and so does the knowledge/* "A volunteer in South Africa," MAI NGUYEN-PHUONG-MAI.

CASE STUDIES

In the following mini-cases, how can we use the values discussed in this chapter and other factors such as behaviors, environment and particular context to explain these outward expressions? How do change, paradox and the non-binary of values play a role? You may want to read about other values first.

1. In 1990, the Japanese Matsushita Electric Industrial company acquired MCA Inc., one of the US's largest entertainment companies. Cultural difference surfaced from the outset, when Matsushita proposed a 250-year business plan. In response, the American chairman jokingly said that he had his own 500-year business plan.[168]
2. In 2016, US President Obama visited Vietnam – 41 years after the war ended. In his speech, he quoted many poems and lyrics by Vietnamese scholars and artists, from great music composers and writers in the past to rock and pop stars of the modern day. He won the love of many Vietnamese people for his respect and understanding of the local culture.[169]

3. Snapchat – an image messaging app – allows users to send pictures that will only be available for a short time before they automatically disappear. Conduct research and find out why, from the value point of view, this app has been so successful. Explain why Snapchat has recently introduced a "memories" function that allows certain stories and images to be stored.
4. Go to the following site and take the time orientation test: http://www.the-timeparadox.com/surveys/

In this chapter, we have touched on the five most widely cited concerns and their associated values. While many of the examples discussed seem to fit the assumption of the static paradigm, other cases and phenomenon make us reconsider. We should be aware of the tendency to look for cases and examples that confirm our worldview, to disregard paradoxes as non-typical incidents, and to be selective of what we want to see. It is hard to overemphasize that the description here should be seen as *sophisticated stereotypes* that will only give us the first best guess. Change is dynamic, paradoxes are a natural part of culture, and we are not only the products, but also the producers of our cultures.

We are reminded here that the dynamic view of culture is a "tool box"[170] or a "card game"[171] in which we can respond to each particular situation in life by "playing" a different value. With the brain's plasticity, we can develop a multicultural mind that will enable us to make the best of culture as a survival strategy in an international context. Third-culture kids, or second-generation immigrants offer a good example of how they flexibly and effectively adjust to home vs. school culture, or home vs. work culture, showing the incredible causal link between brain's plasticity and behaviors (see again the Diagram of Diversity, Chapter 1, figure 1.4). You are not an absolutely masculine or feminine person, but in contexts where masculinity or femininity prevails, you are able to act accordingly. To be an expert in intercultural communication is to aim for a multicultural mind. If the world is a kaleidoscope, we'd better be a chameleon.

Summary

1. *Group attachment* is the extent to which one gives her/his ingroup priority over oneself. *Hierarchy acceptance* is the extent to which subordinates accept a hierarchical (unequal) distribution of prestige, status, influential power and resources between them and their superiors. *Gender association* is the extent to which people are associated with either masculine or feminine traits. *Uncertainty avoidance* is the extent to which members of collectives seek orderliness, consistency, structure, formalized procedures and laws to cover

situations in their daily lives. *Time orientation* is defined as the extent to which one emphasizes the past, the present or the future.

2. At the universal level of the Inverted Pyramid model:
    · Group attachment, hierarchy acceptance, gender association, uncertainty avoidance and time orientation are *fundamental concerns* in all societies, because they are the building blocks of our culture (the trunk and the roots of the metaphorical tree). This is the evolutionary root of culture as a survival strategy.
    · All societies and individuals agree on a *baseline value* (i.e. a minimum level) of how one should prioritize one's own ingroup, how subordinates should accept a hierarchical distribution of resources, how masculine and feminine one should at least be, how much orderliness and structure a society should have, and how all three time dimensions should be taken into account (the branches of the tree).
    · There are certain universal *outward expressions* of these concerns and baseline values that we can all agree upon (the leaves of the tree).

3. At the collective level of the Inverted Pyramid model:
    · While these concerns persist (the trunk and roots of the tree),
    · ... each culture differs from the universal baseline values by placing differing degrees of importance on these concerns, projecting "low," "average" or "high" values for the concerns (the branches of the tree),
    · ... which are manifested in different outward expressions (the leaves of the tree).

4. This degree of importance depends on national, organizational and group cultures, individuals and particular context.

5. Descriptions of national cultural values should be seen as sophisticated stereotypes. They are neither rules, nor the indicators, but the first best guess.

6. Change is constant, paradoxes are often the norm and not the exception. Seemingly contrasting values such as strong and weak group attachment coexist in the same culture and individual. Context is the only sure way to understand this dynamic.

7. To be competent in intercultural communication is to develop a multicultural mind.

6. Intercultural Competence – Creating Yourself

Objective
At the end of this chapter, you should be able to:
- Explain why the most cultured individuals are more likely to be the most successful individuals.
- Describe different stages of acculturation according to the Developmental Model of Intercultural Sensitivity (DMIS).
- Describe the requirements of Cultural Intelligence (CQ).
- Given a specific case, recognize stages or components of DMIS and CQ.
- Describe Cultural Shock and its consequences.
- Describe the potential of developing CQ based on the notion of a malleable, evolving, cultivated self.

Chapter outline

Let us first recap our understanding of the evolutionary role of culture. In essence, it has replaced genes to guide humans in the survival game. In order to be successful, we do not need to evolve sharper teeth or bigger wings. Instead of waiting for our genes to evolve – which may take forever – we put the best *ideas* together, creating weapons and aircrafts, destroying enemies a million times more effectively than the sharpest teeth, and flying a million times further than any birds ever existed on earth. From an evolutionary point of view, each culture is an immense archive of ideas – what it is best to do to survive. For every decision we make, we rely on ideas from our immediate culture to give us a hint about the right course of action. We may want to embrace a certain value, dress in a certain way, go to a certain school, or make a certain career choice, depending on the demands and expectations of the specific culture that hosts us at that moment.

Note that genes do not stand idly by, but actively evolve, change and adapt to support our process of adjustment (gene-culture coevolution theory). For example, if you are a taxi driver in a big city, it is likely that your brain is quite different from others, since your job (i.e. co-culture) requires part of your hippocampus to grow bigger to help you store a detailed mental map of your metropolis.[1] In other words, genes change, so you can acquire the necessary culture.

In sum, without culture and its guidance, an individual would be clueless about what to do. Put an abandoned fox in the jungle, it will be led by it genes and start to live like a fox. Put an abandoned baby in the jungle, it will forget that it is a human. It will adopt the culture of whoever saves its life, be it a gorilla or a wolf. This is what makes Tarzan and Mowgli interesting characters. Throughout human history, the most likely survivors are those who can best attune to a culture.

In most cases, that process of attuning happens quite naturally. However, globalization has made cultural borders much more visible. The need to cross those borders has also become *a new survival skill* that humans of the modern era must acquire. A capacity for cultural adaption has never been so vital. Facing this challenge, we have started doing what we are equipped to do best: putting *ideas* together and learning how to adapt quicker and better in the survival game. In this chapter, we will touch on those ideas and discuss some possible routes that can help us to become competent in intercultural communication.

6.1   Seeking similarity

In Chapters 1 and 2, we discussed how cultural diversity plays a critical role in helping us recognize ingroups and outgroups. The former are people we can trust and share resources with; the latter are those we may want to think carefully about, gauging the possibility of cooperation without being exploited. For this reason, the first natural action human beings conduct when communicating with others is seeking similarity.

6.1.1   A Signal of Trust

In Chapter 3, we learned that genes evolved a stereotyping mechanism to help our ancestors quickly recognize who belonged to their ingroup, through simple and visual stimuli such as similar faces and skin color. This bias starts so early that two-day-old infants prefer their mother's face to that of a female stranger.[2] Brain images tell us our amygdala becomes active when we see outgroup members,[3] that even within the *same* race, we also tend to judge faces that resemble our own face more trustworthy.[4]

In multicultural societies, there is a tension between the tendency to integrate and the threat of loss of identity. An effective policy that ensures trust and equality will make diversity an advantage. The lack thereof will create sectarianism as people seek refuge with those who think alike/ "Muslims and Hindus on a day out in Mumbai, (India)," MAI NGUYEN-PHUONG-MAI.

Think about the moment you meet a stranger. It is a very natural inclination that you and this person will talk about something you are both interested in, or something that you are both more likely to agree on. It is not for nothing that people tend to break the ice with comments about the weather. From that moment, the more shared points of contact one can establish, the more likely a relationship is to start forming,[5] leading to the "Similar to me" bias in hiring.[6] We are drawn to people who are like-minded. Social clubs and other forms of community groups based on religion, immigration or professional background, etc. play important roles in helping people getting to know each other and supporting newcomers, allowing them to quickly build up their own network and settle down more easily.

Globalization, with its mind-blowing speed of change and interconnectedness, presents us with an increasingly complex reality. If you live in an environment where change is fast, uncertainty is high, and life is overwhelmed by a constant stream of new events, it is only natural that you seek havens of certainty and security among those who share similar backgrounds in politics, ethnicity, hobbies, faith or economic interests.

6.1.2   Ethnocentrism

Since ingroup trust is crucial to our survival, we have evolved to love our culture and those who look and think in a similar way to us.[7-8] Our brain is conditioned to favor those from our ingroup, to the extent that we feel the pain of our ingroup[9] and we even want to share that pain at the expense of our own safety.[10] We can love our ingroup so much that we may end up *hating others*. This bias is caused by a hormone called oxytocin. An injection of this hormone would increase trust and cooperation among ingroup members,[11] increase the overall liking for social stimuli[12] and, consequently, result in outgroup derogation.[13]

In 1906, sociologist William Graham introduced the concept of *ethnocentrism* to describe the way we see our own culture as central to reality, by interpreting the world from our own viewpoint.[14] For example, those who use chopsticks may judge those who eat with their hands as abnormal; or those whose living context favors femininity may judge masculinity as inappropriate.

Ethnocentrism is universal and rooted in evolution as a mechanism of survival. It helps us to understand why most cultures in the world have their own folklore that wraps up the origins of their people in a myth of supernatural or superior traits. For example, according to Polynesian mythology, natives of New Zealand come from one primal pair, the Sky Father and the Earth Mother. Vietnamese tales depict their people as descendants of a love story between a dragon and fairy. Ethnocentrism is embedded in how the Chinese named their nation the central kingdom on earth (*Zhung Guo*), and how the Japanese emperor is seen as a descendent of the sun goddess, who still proudly emblazons the national flag. The concept of "chosen people" highlights diverse groups who believe that they have a special status for a purpose. Jews consider themselves the chosen ones and to be in a covenant with God; the Nation of Islam teaches that blacks were God's chosen people; the Unification Church posits that Korea is the chosen nation; Rastafarians believe that King Solomon of Israel conceived a child with Ethiopian Queen of Sheba and thus render Ethiopians as the true children of Israel and God's chosen people.

There is nothing wrong with ethnocentrism when your culture is simply preferred over others; indeed, it may result in great pride, from which you draw your psychological support and personal self-worth. However, the natural tendency to use our own culture as a starting point when evaluating the behaviors of others can escalate and result in stereotypes, prejudices and racism, as discussed in Chapter 3. This is the reason why strong uncertainty avoidance with regard to social rules can play a role in xenophobia. "The more ethnocentric we are, the more anxious we are about interacting with other cultures; when we are fearful, we are less likely to expect a positive outcome from such interaction."[15]

ACTIVITY

The "golden rule" is a principle for interacting with others. It appears in many religions:

- Hinduism: "This is the sum of duty: do naught unto others which would cause you pain if done to you." – Brihaspati, Mahabharata, 5:1517.
- Jainism: "In happiness and suffering, in joy and grief, we should regard all creatures as we regard our own self." – Lord Mahavira, 24th Tirthankara.
- Buddhism: "Hurt not others in ways that you yourself would find hurtful." – Udanavara, 5:18.
- Confucianism: "Do not do unto others what you would not have them do unto you." – Analect, 15:23.
- Judaism: "What is hateful to you, do not do to your fellow." – Shabbath folio: 31a, Babylonian Talmud.

- Christianity: "Do unto others as you would have them do unto you." – Matthew, 7:12.
- Islam: "O you who believe! Spend of the good things that you have earned... and do not even think of spending [in alms] worthless things that you yourselves would be reluctant to accept." – Quran, surah 2, verses 267.
- Bahaism: "And if thine eyes be turned towards justice, choose thou for thy neighbor that which thou choosest for thyself." – Bahaullah.
- Scientology: "Try to treat others as you would want them to treat you." – The Way to Happiness, Precept 20.
  1. In what way is the "golden rule" good for intercultural competence?
  2. In what way is it ethnocentric?
  3. Have you ever heard of the "platinum rule"?

6.1.3   Dealing with Differences

Naturally, it is critical to keep the best ideas secret, sharing them only with those we can trust, lest they be stolen. However, we can't possibly confine ourselves to those who are alike and limit the world to our own viewpoint forever, because that would be the end of culture – the very mechanism that advances humans as a species. Hiding the best innovations, seeking comfort in look-alike and think-alike folks would have brought this cumulative cultural adaptation to a halt and caused our species great damage, because of the constant suspicion and rancor.[16] Ethnocentrism as a safeguard instrument to protect the ingroup can be part of evolution, but has never been the ultimate solution to advancing the human species. At the end of the day, the power of culture as a survival mechanism is the power of learning continuously from others, accumulating knowledge throughout time from all available sources, including from those who are different from us.

Balancing between the comfort of familiarity and the need to deal with diversity is not an easy task. But humans are the only species who can extend cooperation beyond kinship and form larger communities of unrelated individuals. Moving from bands to tribes, from chiefdoms to city states, from nations to united nations, history has shown how fences were taken down and boundaries crossed. The tension between "cooperation within ingroup" and "aggression towards outgroups" has tended to give more weight to cooperation and softened group boundaries, resulting in the globalization we see today (see Chapter 1). We are able to step out of our comfort zone to work with strangers, developing social rules that enable us to share goods and ideas, making the cooperation more profitable than unbridled self-interest. In the next section, we will delve deeper into this process and see how we can continue to benefit from it in the era of globalization.

- *Similarity is a signal of ingroup – those we can trust and share resources with. It is natural to seek companions among those with similar traits and backgrounds.*
- *The bias towards our ingroup results in ethnocentrism. We are ethnocentric when we see our own culture as central to reality and interpret the world from our own viewpoint.*
- *However, humans are able to move beyond ethnocentrism and ingroup bias in order to manage resources effectively in the course of survival.*

6.2   Acculturation

The process of interacting with different (co-)cultures is called *acculturation*. The terminology has been used widely to focus on how minority groups adapt to a dominant culture, but by definition, any of us will be involved in this process of change whenever we find ourselves at the meeting points of different cultures.

6.2.1   The Developmental Model of Intercultural Sensitivity (DMIS)

There are many models that can help us to understand acculturation, including DMIS. After years of observing and conducting cultural workshops, Milton Bennett developed a framework for illustrating the stages that his trainees have gone through when dealing with intercultural situations. The first three stages belong to ethnocentrism, which indicates one's culture is the central reality, and the last three belong to *ethnorelativism* – a concept coined by Bennett to describe the opposite of ethnocentrism, i.e. when one's culture is just one of many viable ways of viewing the world.

6.2.1.1   *Denial*
Denial signals a withdrawal from interacting with outgroup people. When seeking similarities fails, people may withdraw at this stage and confine themselves to their own enclave. We can observe this phenomenon among expatriates, who carry on their assignment abroad within a cocoon of their

own comfort, or immigrants who fail or refuse to interact with the culture of their new home. Armed with a certain ideological and political allegiance, even a nation (e.g. North Korea) can be in the denial stage and refuse to engage with the outside world.

People at the denial stage can also be those who simply are not interested in or are ignorant of other cultures. Muslims count for 23 per cent of the world's population, but many of us had never heard of the religion until the horrendous event of September 11. The denial worldview can be the consequence of pillarization – a type of segregation in which the society is divided into pillars, each with their own social institutions, such as newspapers, schools, banks and hospitals. The Netherlands, Belgium, Austria, Northern Ireland and Scotland are famous examples for this social structure. For those in denial, or, in this case, more precisely the "ignorant," the lack of personal contact means they have no framework of reference, and hence they are unable to see cultural patterns.

During the apartheid era, black people were evicted from "white-only" areas and forced to live in segregated townships. However, less well known is that a small but increasing number of white people have become so poor that they now live in "white squatter camps." In the documentary The White Slums,[17] *Reggie Yates asked a group of black partygoers whether they realized that, for eight years, poor white people had been living in make-shift tents across the water in Coronation Park. The answer (at 39:35) was a denial: "No! I don't believe it. You are lying."/ "A family in a white squatter camp in Pretoria, (South Africa)," DEON STEYN.*

The biggest problem with being ethnocentric at this stage of denial is that we may judge others based on our own cultural standards (ethnocentric) without knowing it (denial/ignorant), despite our good intentions. Consider this comment: "Oh, those poor new colleagues from abroad. They should stand up against their boss. It's democracy at work." Does the commentator know enough the culture of these new colleagues? Probably not. Does the commentator mean well? Probably yes.

6.2.1.2   Defense

At this stage of cultural interaction, people have come into contact frequently enough that similarities and differences can be identified in more complex ways, and diversity is obvious for comparison and judgment. The general tendency is for polarization – us against them – in which one's culture is perceived to be different, and these differences are seen as *superior*. Ethnocentrism at the defense stage manifests in forms of negative stereotypes, prejudices and discrimination towards other cultures. The purpose is to make fun of them, to play them down, to blame them for all sorts of problems, to prove their inferiority and, in some extreme cases, to attack them outright in acts of violence or genocide. The need to defend our culture is at its peak here, since losing our culture means losing our source of guidance and advancement.

People at the defense stage belong either to a dominant culture or a co-culture and are experiencing that their values are under attack. Examples are immigrants who feel the pressure to assimilate; natives who perceive foreigners as threats to their identity; religious followers who are told their faith practices have flaws; previously gender-exclusive groups such as all-male military units now confronted with the inclusion of female, homosexual, or non-gender conforming recruits; expatriates who struggle with criticism from their host; or new colleagues faced with the challenge of abandoning their way of interpreting ethics, vision, effectiveness at work, etc.

When embracing a defensive worldview, people may genuinely think they are superior when they joke at or judge different cultural norms and habits. Have you ever said that a certain way of dressing is funny, a certain method of working is ridiculous, or a certain custom is barbarian? In its benign form, those with a defensive worldview even want to "help" people they consider inferior to modernize, humanize or they want to civilize them. Colonialism is the ultimate example of ethnocentrism at this stage, but one can also see a subtle patronization and post-colonial mentality in various training, mentoring and educational programs, where major theories and practices emanate from white authors, with Western viewpoints and a Christian influence. A simple check of your textbooks will give you an idea about how this bias can subconsciously manifest itself.

A variation of the defense stage is *reversal*, often expressed in a loathing of one's own culture and the total adoption of another culture (going native/passing). Such a person may initially come across as someone with an excellent sense of cultural balance and competence, since (s)he can criticize her/his culture of origin while having a positive experience of the new culture. However, such a person is still at the defense stage when (s)he holds an unsophisticated binary worldview of seeing different cultures as good vs. bad or superior vs. inferior. Also because of this reversed judgment, people at this stage risk being criticized as a "sell-out," – someone who compromises her/his authenticity in exchange for personal gain.

CASE STUDY

In June 2015, Rachel Dolezal, president of the National Association for the Advancement of Colored People (NAACP) in Washington was accused of having lied about her racial identity. Born to white parents, she started to identify more as a black woman around 2007. While being an influential activist, she also claimed to face discrimination because of her skin color.

Her self-identification as black caused controversy. Some of her colleagues explained that Dolezal perceived herself as black internally, and that she was only trying to match how she felt on the inside with her outside. The attachment with black culture and fascination with racial justice led her to regard herself as transracial. In her case, Dolezal was said to be psychologically/culturally black, while biologically white. Sociologist Ann Morning and psychologist Halford Fairchild also backed her up, saying that identity is a social construct, and hence, it can change. According to journalist Krissah Thompson, her behavior is "white guilt played to its end."

What is your opinion? Can we compare the case of Dolezal with people who are transgender – those who identify as female but are born in male bodies, and vice versa?

6.2.1.3   *Minimization*

At this last stage of ethnocentrism, people regard their worldview neither as the only one (i.e. denial/ignorant), nor as superior or under attack (i.e. defense), but rather as universal. When we fail to acknowledge, comprehend or deal with differences, we may choose to focus on the 'easy bit', i.e. similarity and make it an overall yardstick for *all cultures*. That is why people at this stage tend to look at the bottom layer of the Inverted Pyramid model with universal elements of culture such as "at the end of the day, we all need good education" (concerns), "we all honor family, integrity and equality" (values), "and despite different skin colors, we are all God's children" (outward expression). Highlighting sameness and similarity is also a good starting point, but getting stuck at this stage can be a disadvantage. This simplified way of looking at cultures succeeds in pointing out that "we are not different in kind," but fails to acknowledge that "we are different at certain levels." That is to say, we probably all see the need for a good educational system, but what we perceive as "good" may differ from others' views; and while we may all appreciate family, integrity or equality, depending on particular context, we may attach differing degrees of importance to each of them.

In society at large, this worldview can be dangerous if it is used to mask institutional privilege and discrimination. Imagine a race where runner No. 1 starts with the full strength of physical and mental power. For example, he was born into a white and affluent family with good connections, he enjoyed good education at a private school, he grew up in safe neighborhoods, and through the connections of his parents, he now works as an intern for a famous company. In comparison, runner No. 2 starts at the same time, but is confronted by a number of obstacles on the track. She was raised by a single parent, who has to work two jobs to support the family. She grew up in a troublesome neighborhood and attended poorly funded public schools. She was constantly bullied for her religious practice, subjected to racial profiling, micro-aggressions and subconscious bias. It has taken tremendous effort for her to find an internship in an ordinary company. Who do you think would make it first to the finishing line when applying for a job?

A minimization worldview would disregard all the historical data regarding runner No. 2 and close the deadline at the same time for all candidates: "We treat everyone the same." But "the same" is not "equal." Applying universal standards to all groups of cultures, males and females, majority and minority, may indicate a failure to acknowledge societal issues and blame the victims instead (e.g. they are lazy). Hence, it is important that we look at demographic information that shows group differences in terms of intelligence, skills, employment success, or crime, etc. with a critical eye and ask ourselves the following question: "Is this the *consequence* of social influence and injustice, or the state of nature?"

6.2.1.4   *Acceptance*

This stage marks the departure of ethnocentrism and signals the ability to recognize that, although we are the same in kind, we may be at different levels, and that differences are equally valid. One's own culture is just one of many equally complex worldviews.

However, this acceptance does not necessarily mean agreement or liking.[18] For instance, you are relocated to work in Finland and you soon find out that, in a country of five million people, there are three million saunas, on average one sauna per household.[19] Many companies have a sauna in the workplace and often invite business partners to enjoy long hours sitting in the hot steam. While you dislike the awkward situation of being half-naked among colleagues and partners you hardly know, you understand their tradition. You know the sauna provides a mechanism of social leverage that fits the Finns egalitarian mentality, that when you dress down in the sauna, you also reduce the level of hierarchy acceptance as everyone becomes more equal. Being high context dependent, neutral, reserved, low-key, quiet and rather formal, saunas also give the Finns a natural setting in which to relax, to open up and strengthen their relationships. This is quite different from what you perceive as an effective way to build camaraderie, but you accept and understand that it is an *equally valid* way for many Finns and other non-Finns, who can see benefits of it.

Different worldviews can be seen as equally valid. What do you see in this image, a young or an old woman?/ "My wife and my mother-in-law," WILLIAM ELY HILL, 1915 (adapted from a German postcard in the 19th century).

The sauna is an important context in which to socialize in many cultures/ "Therme Erding, (Germany)," STUDIE85.[20]

6.2.1.5 *Adaptation*

People at this stage of acculturation have the ability to shift their frame of reference in terms of thinking and action. It does not mean assimilation, i.e. giving up their own norms and values, but rather the extension of their existing repertoire of identities and worldviews.[21] You can consider yourself at this stage if, for example, you can adjust your participating leadership style to a more paternalistic style of high hierarchy acceptance when the context requires such a change. You are capable of maintaining very intense eye contact, but also of lowering your gaze when talking to those who are not accustomed to such body language. You know how to read between the lines and decipher the real message in a subtle conversation (high context dependent), but you don't mind expressing your opinion in a straightforward manner (low context dependence) and fully participating in a heated discussion.

Adaptation aims at extending the capacity to not just *knowing* (cognitive), but *feeling* (affective) and *acting* (behavioral) appropriately according to the respective culture and the particular context. These three elements should go hand in hand with one another, since an act of adaptation needs to be done because it "feels right," not because you "have to." In other words, you naturally want to do it without the pressure to fake it. It takes time to reach this level, and there is an important caveat, which is that adaptation without sincerity can come across as contrived and patronizing to others.[22] Here is an example of what adaptation may look like. The author of this book often organized visits to a Turkish mosque in Amsterdam for her students. The mosque did not explicitly require female visitors to cover their heads, but there were always some students who brought scarves with them. Some even checked with the instructor to make sure their outfits would be deemed modest enough by other mosque goers. Reflecting in their essays, these students reported that they felt comfortable blending in with the Muslims at prayer, and the headdress was naturally part of the experience.

6.2.1.6 Integration

The final stage of acculturation is not necessarily better than adaptation. Rather, it is often related to those who are not attached to any primal cultural identity, and who constantly move in and out several cultural worldviews. A small but growing number of people can recognize themselves at this stage, especially long term expatriates and "global nomads." In a way, their identities become "marginal," since they are loosely attached to all and central to none.[23] In Bennett's word:

> [Constructive marginal] people are able to experience themselves as multicultural beings who are constantly choosing the most appropriate cultural context for their behavior. This living on the edge of cultures may occasionally be stressful and alienating, but it is more often exhilarating and fulfilling. Because they so easily shift cultural perspectives, constructive marginals are likely to take the role of cultural bridge-builders in intercultural situations. They can do this without 'losing themselves' because they self-reflexively define their identities in terms of perspective-shifting and bridge-building.[24]

Being at this stage of integration can be risky too, since one can fall for encapsulated marginality, being stuck between cultures in a dysfunctional way.[25] They may be unable to select appropriate cultural contexts, become self-absorbed, alienated from their broad experience, or become entangled in an identity crisis.

If C = Culture, the Developmental Model of Intercultural Sensitivity (DMIS) has 6 stages:

Denial: C only	*Acceptance: $C_1 \neq C_2$*
Defense: $C_1 > C_2$	*Adaptation: C_1 or C_2*
Minimization: $C_1 = C_2$	*Integration: $C_1 + C_2$*

6.2.2   Where Are You at DMIS?

Acculturation does not happen smoothly and, in many cases, it may not happen in the stages that the DMIS model describes. Consequently, the unidirectional logic of DMIS has been questioned, since it seems to assume that we cannot regress to an earlier stage.[26] Firstly, globalization and a vast array of access to different cultures through media and technology mean that we can be at the "adaptation" stage with one culture and then find ourselves at the stage of "defense" with another. Secondly, culture is dynamic and not a fixed entity, especially when we talk about multicultural societies, which some parts of the world have rapidly become. This means the culture(s) we are dealing with is in a constant state of flux and our process of acculturation may not be linear. Any of us can be in denial, ignorant, or ethnocentric at some point, without even knowing it, since it is impossible for us to be aware of every culture that we happen to come across, all the dynamic changes within and across its borders, and it is quite unlikely that we are able to completely shed our own cultural baggage. Lastly, everything is context dependent. Research on priming suggests that we may "adapt" in one situation, and get caught up with "denial" in another.[27] It has been an additional strength of DMIS that a measure, the Intercultural Development Inventory (IDI)[28] was developed, aiming to assess which stage of acculturation one is at.

ACTIVITY

For each of the following (co-)cultures, evaluate your current stage of DMIS.

- Start with three words that automatically come to your mind when this culture is mentioned. These words often reflect your stereotypes.
- Think critically about your viewpoint with regard to that culture. Be honest with yourself, and ask yourself the following question: "Which stage of DMIS am I at when it comes to the overall perception of this culture?" "Which stage of DMIS am I at when it comes to the people, their values, their habits, their appearance, their religion, or their politics, etc.?"

1. A neighboring country
2. A co- or dominant culture of your choice, (e.g. the Muslim or Christian community, the immigrants, the exchange students at your college, etc.)
3. The LGBTQ community
4. A profession of your choice (e.g. the bankers)
5. Right-wing politicians and their supporters
6. A company or organization with a well-known organizational culture

CASE STUDY

Pope Benedict XV once said: "We are building a dictatorship of relativism that does not recognize anything as definitive."[29] His remark has been linked to criticism of *cultural relativism* – a notion that there are no absolute criteria for judging other cultures as "low" or "noble."[30] After the Second World War, cultural relativism is often understood as "moral relativism," that all cultures and value systems are equal with no absolute or universal moral standards. This is erroneous. Cultural relativism means one's moral standard makes sense in terms of her/his own culture. But it does not mean the moral standard of one culture can be applied to another.

The idea of cultural relativism clashes head-on with the Universal Declaration of Human Rights (UDHR). Its statements are meant to be of world-wide applicability, setting up *baseline values* and *baseline outward expressions* for all individuals and cultures at the universal level of the Inverted Pyramid model. However, a number of countries criticized UDHR, claiming that it was written from a Western point of view and hence, does not reflect the universal baseline values and practices for all.

This is an important and on-going debate for many of the issues we are seeing today: Where the baseline should be? What should be considered universal and hence be *enforced*? What can be regarded as cultural values and outward expressions, and hence be *respected*?[31]

Consider this example: Female genital mutilation is a wide spread practice in North Africa, and to a lesser extent in Indonesia and the Middle East. It is practiced by Muslims, Christians and Jews alike, despite the lack of religious theoretical support.[32] At the age of five or older, part of the genitalia such as the clitoral hood, clitoral glans, or the labia is removed. In the most extreme form known as infibulation, a small hole is left for the passage of urine and menstrual fluid, and the vagina is opened for intercourse and opened further for childbirth.[33]

The practice is rooted in a patriarchal attempt to control women's sexuality and traditional ideas about purity. However, it is considered by those who practice it as a source of honor, and failing to do so may risk social exclusion. Genital mutilation can result in severe health problems and tremendous pressure.

1. The practice violates UDHR, but should we accept UDHR or should we regard this practice as part a cultural right? Where does a cultural right stop and the universal ethic start?
2. With regard to DMIS, if we consider a cultural value or outward expression as a violation of the universal baseline, our "defense" stage does not reflect ethnocentrism but a *righteous fight* for universal values. Go back to the previ-

ous activity and think about any issues that you don't agree with any of the cultures listed. Analyze your discontent to see if it comes from your lack of understanding (hence, ethnocentrism), or if it comes from your view that the issue violates the universal baseline in values and outward expressions.

6.2.3   Cultural Shock

Acculturation can be complex. The ineffectiveness of matching the old and the new patterns of culture can lead to *cultural shock* – a term coined by anthropologist Kalervo Oberg. Cultural shock is a normal part of the acculturation. Getting to know a culture without experiencing cultural shock "is like practicing swimming without water."[34]

6.2.3.1   What Does Cultural Shock Look Like?

Imagine you are assigned to work in Lebanon – a crucial business and cultural hub in the Middle East. Since culture is a survival mechanism, you need to learn how the Lebanese go about life, so that you, too, can survive in this new environment and fulfil your mission. However, cultural shock hits you. And this mental state makes everything seem wrong, despite the fact that you consciously prepared and learned about Lebanon before your departure.

You are irritated that the Lebanese food is different from the restaurant you enjoyed back at home. There is too much flavor, and you are terrible at eating with your hands. You feel like you are walking on a minefield with the invisible lines that separate different religious communities, and it can be so easy to unintentionally disrespect someone. You are bombarded with information and tasks that need to be done. At the same time, you are angry that nobody regards deadline as a firm commitment, worse, many see a deadline imposed on them as an insult. You are annoyed at the loud and animated way people speak. You are intimidated by their widespread network of connections that you don't have. And most of all, you feel helpless when you realize that your proficiency in Arabic cannot compensate for the fact that most of your colleagues prefer French. Moreover, your spouse is depressed as he couldn't find a job as quickly as he hoped, and your children are demotivated due to the many problems they are facing at their new school.

The population of Lebanon is very diverse, and religious contrast is both striking and hidden, causing excite-ment but also confusion for expatriates and immigrants. The main groups are Shia Muslim (27%), Sunni Muslim (26%), Christian Maronite (21%), Greek Orthodox (8%), Druze (7%), Melkites (4%), and Protestants (1%). There are more Lebanese living outside of Lebanon (8-14 million) than within (4 million). Some 450,000 Palestine refugees are registered in Lebanon. The war in Syria also forced more than a million refugees across the border into Lebanon. The main sectarian groups have agreed on a pact along religious lines: The President has to be a Maronite Christian, the Speaker of the Parliament has to be a Shia Muslim, and the Prime Minister has to be a Sunni Muslim/ "Beirut center, (Lebanon)," MAI NGUYEN-PHUONG-MAI.

6.2.3.2   The Consequences of Cultural Shock

The consequences of this trauma differ widely among individuals. It can be a sense of disorientation, a feeling of rejection, spiritual drift, depression, homesickness and even physical ailments. Cultural shock contributes significantly to premature return. Among American expatriates (i.e. those who plan to return home after foreign assignments), 68 per cent return from Saudi Arabia, 36 per cent from Japan, 27 per cent from Belgium, and 18 per cent from the UK.[35] Considering that it costs a firm between three and five times an employee's base salary to keep an employee and her/his family in a foreign assignment,[36] the financial loss of a premature return is staggering. On average, repatriation of a family creates a direct cost of between US $250,000 and 1,250,000,[37] including training, relocation and compensation for a replacement. Indirect cost is hard to measure,[38] since it is related to the loss of customers, market share, staff morale, partnership, relationship with the host, and at the same time the human resource department will need to invest in looking for new candidates, and the emotional as well physical damage of both the returned expatriates and her/his family.[39]

6.2.3.3   Stages of Cultural Shock

The U-shape model explains how sojourners may experience cultural shock, although in reality, the transition from one stage to another is not always clear-cut.

Initially, sojourners are often in the *honeymoon* phase, which is at the top left of the "U." The starting of a new adventure can be exciting and brings a sense of euphoria. You are full of anticipation for successful cooperation, achievement and fruitful relationships. In the end, reaching beyond kinship has been the trademark of humans' advantage as a species.

But as with marriages, honeymoons do not last forever. The second stage kicks in when the excitement has turned to disappointment as you fail to see sufficient similarity, and encounter more differences instead. *Disenchantment* is marked at the bottom of the "U," a shock that comes with irritation, impatience, anger and depression. Some people cope with this situation by using "denial" strategies (DMIS), withdrawing physically and psychologically into a "ghetto" of their own world. They may develop coping behaviors of excessive drinking or drug use. Others might adopt "defense" strategies, often referred to as the "fight-back" technique, by making disparaging remarks about the new culture: "How can they be so paranoid?," "Why are they so obsessed with work, don't they have a life?," "So greedy?" Finally, if you keep following DMIS, "minimization" is also a coping strategy, as sojourners try to sideline the differences. However, this can be superficial since differences and all the related problems remain unsolved.

The third stage of *adjustment* slowly pulls you up the right side of the "U" as you gain some cultural insight and start to "adapt" accordingly. The chaos slowly shows its patterns, which enables a certain level of predictability. You may have picked up the language, and your circle of friends and colleagues has widened. A good sign of this stage is the ability to see humor and to laugh at yourself or the situation.

In the last stage of cultural shock, *effective functioning*, sojourners are able to comfortably live in the new culture. You have adopted many customs and habits, and your mind may automatically think in the same cultural patterns as the locals.

Similar to DMIS, cultural shock according to this U-shaped model has been questioned in relation to its assumed unidirectional structure. Sojourners do not always experience their acculturation in a linear fashion, and cultural shocks can still happen unexpectedly after an extended period of time living in a different culture. Newer and more sophisticated models suggest that the adaptation process is cyclic, with intermittent periods of adaptation and disenchantment.[40]

6.2.3.4   Reversed, Re-entry Cultural Shock

Reverse or re-entry cultural shock happens when sojourners return home and encounter the (old) life that is now so different from what they have adjusted to. The consequence is that they may go through another U-shaped experience, and hence a W-shaped model is used to describe this whole cycle.

The problem starts with a gap of expectation. In general, repatriates assume that with their experience abroad, they will be offered better job opportunities, an increased level of authority, more autonomy, and respect as well as admiration from co-workers. However, repatriates face countless challenges at home. Not all companies recognize the high cost of posting and strategically seek a return on this investment. Frequently, repatriates' previous positions have been filled with no job guarantee upon return, and the policy is unclear.[41] There is a loss of status, a lack of autonomy, promotion opportunities and sufficient support.[42] The home organizations are often ignorant of the *newly gained skills* that expatriates have acquired.[43-44] While repatriates are proud of their newly acquired competence and experience, their organization devalue it, resulting in disillusion and disappointment. Their colleagues do not appreciate it either. In an article that defines this phenomenon as "cultural shock boomerangs in the office,"[45] returnees were advised to prepare a three-sentence answer to the question: "Oh, you lived in [fill in the blank]. What was that like?" The answer to this question should take no more than three minutes because most people lose interest after that.

Coming home take times too. Expatriates are given time to settle in and adjust to a new culture, but it is often taken for granted that returnees will automatically fit back into their home culture, which is not always the case. For this reason, reversed cultural shock when coming home becomes even more difficult than going abroad.

While there are always proactive returnees who can incorporate the best experience from both the foreign and the home culture, many fail to combine the best of the two worlds. Some returnees choose to re-socialize, i.e. forgetting the overseas experience and fitting back into the home situation. On the opposite side, other returnees become alienated, speaking in glowing terms of the overseas experience and criticizing the home customs. The consequence is that turnover intention is frequently observed after repatriation, with 20 per cent to 50 per cent[46] and even up to 60 per cent [47] of returnees seriously consider leaving their home organization. One of the main reasons is that returnees with international experience believe more in a "boundary-less career," and when their career advancement is not clear within their company, they are more likely to seek it elsewhere.[48]

To conclude, acculturation is a complex process of adaptation (or the lack thereof) when people venture in and out different cultures. It can happen at the individual and collective level of the Inverted Pyramid model. The dynamic interaction between and within these two levels creates a myriad of issues, both beneficial and challenging.

- *Cultural shock is part of acculturation, referring to the mismatch of old and new cultural patterns. Cultural shock contributes to early return and it is costly.*
- *Stages of cultural shock are: honeymoon, disenchantment, adjustment and reversed cultural shock.*

6.3   Intercultural competence

The world is increasingly characterized by interrelated, interdependent communities. In 2015, international migrants – people living in a country other than where they were born – reached 244 million, split equally between men and women and with a median age of 39.[49] The largest diasporas come from India, Mexico and Russia. International tourist arrivals reached 1.2 billion in 2015.[50] In fact, we don't even need to go abroad to encounter different cultural patterns since they are ubiquitous: a purchase at the local store, a neighbor next door, an email exchange, a foreign commercial product, a new team mate, etc. We may not travel the world, but the world has come to us. Even if we lock ourselves away constant streams of cultural interactions through the TV screen still bring the globe's immense diversity right into our living room. With technology, the world has gone from connected to hyper-connected.[51] In cyberspace, the like-minded find each other and form communities online where specific cultures have evolved without actual physical connection. While social mobility and technology play crucial roles in bringing the world together, political dynamics and global challenges such as conflicts and climate change have showed us that we have no choice but to work together. If the survival of an individual depends on how (s)he can learn a culture at birth (enculturation), or adapts to a new culture on demand (acculturation), then "the survival of mankind [...] depends to a large extent on the ability of people who think differently to act together."[52]

Evolutionarily speaking, we are endowed with the ability to acquire a culture. Nevertheless, since it is not the survival of the fittest, but the survival of the most cultured, how can we make this ability to learn a new culture even more effective? In this section, we will discuss *cultural intelligence* and the *evolving self*. The former is a construct that helps you identify components of cultural competence, the latter is a viewpoint that will help you to see yourself as a dynamic and active agent in the process of developing a multicultural mind.

6.3.1   Cultural Intelligence

Intercultural competence is the ability to think, feel and act appropriately and effectively in a given context. You are interculturally competent when you: (1) have a repertoire of knowledge to draw upon; (2) are motivated; and (3) possess requisite communication skills.[53] Many models and frameworks have been developed to help us measure this competence, such as the Cross-Cultural Adaptability Inventory, Cross-Cultural World Mindedness, Cultural Shock Inventory, Cultural-General Assimilator, Global Awareness Profile Test, Multicultural Awareness-Knowledge-Skills Survey, Overseas Assignment Inventory, Sociocultural Adaptation Scale and Intercultural Adjustment Potential Scale. In this book, we will introduce to you one of the most popular concepts and instruments: *Cultural Intelligence* or CQ, a term coined by Christopher Earley and Soon Ang.[54]

So what are the differences between IQ (Intelligence Quotient), EQ (Emotional Intelligence) and CQ (Cultural Intelligence)? To make it simple, IQ is based on how your mind works in solving individual problems with logics; EQ is based on how you identify and manage the emotion of yourself and others. To have high EQ does not mean you will have high CQ. For example, you have a strong empathy, knowing how to read between lines and handle the communication well with your cultural fellows in a situation of high context dependence. However, you may find out that this very capacity to pick up hidden messages can backfire in situations where low context dependence prevails. You may select totally wrong and unintended information. That explains why a good team player from a multinational in Serbia is not necessarily someone pleasant to work with in an urban mid-size family-owned company in Kyrgyzstan. While EQ is culture-bound (applicable in one culture only), CQ is culture-free (applicable in all cultures). It is fundamentally about knowing different cultural contexts, having the knowledge to understand and adapt to it accordingly.

Let's take a look at the three main components of CQ. The symbolic keywords of *Head-Heart-Hand* should only be seen as reminders, since they do not thoroughly reflect the nature of each CQ component.

6.3.1.1   CQ Head – Metacognitive/ Cognitive

Metacognitive CQ refers to the level of conscious cultural awareness during intercultural interaction.[55] To help you understand the concept, let us meet a woman who we will call Orla. She is an engineer from a tech giant in the Silicon Docks of Dublin – a famous digital hub in Europe due to its progressive number of technology firms. Her company has a participating corporate culture of low hierarchy acceptance and femininity, with a rigorous policy in diversity and sustainability.

Being a person with high *metacognitive CQ*, she is aware, vigilant and mindful when approaching a counterpart coming from an IT start-up in Arfa Software Technology Park, Pakistan. Not knowing her business partner very well, Orla mindfully observes the situation, and pays attention to every detail. She does not take things for granted, and she constantly asks herself questions such as: "Why is this person silent?" "Is there a hidden message behind this silence?" "Should I just smile when there is silence?" She thinks carefully about what she wants to say and do to be appropriate in each specific situation. In short, the strong ability to resist stereotypes and impulsive reaction, to *stop, watch, and think* signals a high level of metacognitive CQ.

However, metacognitive should be supported by *cognitive* CQ. Orla may be very good at actively thinking about the people and situation, but what if she does not have a *large repertoire of knowledge* to help her understand and decode the incidents? The cognitive factor of CQ therefore reflects a person's level of cultural knowledge. How much does Orla know about the Pakistani IT industry and the corporate culture of the Arfa Software Technology Park? What are the similarities and differences between an established organization where Orla works, and the start-ups that have been springing up in this newly emerging silicon valley of Pakistan? What are the values and typical outward expressions of Pakistani culture? What are the values and habits of her Pakistani colleagues? How do the political and religious system influence the way people live, work, communicate, negotiate and approach outsiders?

Orla may find out that her company did not prepare her well on this part of CQ. In contrast, the Pakistani company organized intensive training for those who are sent abroad to work with Orla and her team. Business culture training has become an essential part of international mobility. However, short-term thinking companies often hesitate with the cost – a mistake that will seriously influence business outcomes.

CQ cognitive or CQ-head is a repertoire of knowledge that you can develop in many different ways. Besides training, you can learn languages, expose yourself to as many cultures as possible, reach out to different political ideas, religious practices, working styles and living philosophies. Studying the world's diversity and cultivating your empathy can be done through reading, making friends, joining different communities and travelling as much as possible. Ask yourself these questions: "When is the last time I communicated in a foreign language?" "How many books on international politics, economics and religion have I read this month?" "What did I do in my last travel to get a deep understanding of that foreign culture?" etc. Of course, this world's diversity is endless, and hardly anyone can say (s)he is a Know-It-All person. It is possible to have the feeling that the more you know, the more ignorant you feel, since there is so much to learn. That is actually a good attitude, because it truly reflects how infinite knowledge is. As Socrates once said: "To know, is to know that you know nothing. That is the meaning of true knowledge."

6.3.1.2 CQ Heart – Motivational

Motivational CQ reflects the capability to invest attention and energy in learning about intercultural diversity. It is a drive that makes a person show interest and confidence in *wanting to know, wanting to try, and wanting to challenge* her/himself in different cultural interactions. You show motivational CQ if you repeatedly choose a different local dish when everyone else dreams of some familiar food back home, if you are enthusiastic in talking with strangers when everyone else has retreated to their comfortable ingroups, if you insist on trying a new working method when everyone else is still held up in speculation. In short, it is an innate passion for all thing diverse.

Motivational CQ is often overlooked, since it is not expressed in tangible elements such as cognitive or behavioral CQ (the third component). In the end, it is a "feeling" that someone is motivated, and feelings can be objective. Many organizations undermine this component by not assessing or cultivating the motivation level among personnel. It is not effective and even counterproductive when people receive training or execute diversity policy without believing in it. This lack of motivation contributes to the bigger problem of employee disengagement. The statistics are alarming: 70 per cent of the American workforce negatively influence their colleagues, miss workdays and drive customers away. This costs the US 550 billion US dollars each year in lost productivity,[56] the UK 340 billion pounds,[57] and Australia 54.8 billion Australian dollars.[58]

6.3.1.3 CQ Hand – Behavioral

Behavioral CQ reflects the capability to exhibit appropriate verbal and non-verbal outward expressions when interacting in intercultural situations.

This component is the most salient, the most visible feature when you translate your understanding and your motivation into action. It is where the rubber meets the road, and the goal is to figure out which behaviors need to remain or to change in order to accomplish your objectives.

Behavioral CQ manifests itself in all aspects of communication and beyond, such as the decisions to make, the policies to take and the strategies to follow. As such, it is not only the capability to switch from energetically animated body language (affective) to a more neutral style of talking, or from corporate jargons to more academic vocabulary. It is also about the switch from low to high hierarchy acceptance in leadership, or from a masculine competitive mentality to a more feminine way of negotiating the contract.

At this point, it is only fair if one begins to wonder: "Does this adaptation mean I lose my authentic self?" which is an excellent question. How can you be yourself and still behave in all these alternative ways? We will discuss this further in the next section.

- *Emotional Intelligence (EQ) is culture-bound while Cultural Intelligence (CQ) is culture-free.*
- *CQ is the ability to think (Metacognitive CQ-Head), to know a large repertoire of knowledge (Cognitive CQ),*
- *… to be intrinsically engaged (Motivational CQ-Heart), and*
- *… to bring everything in action and strategies in a culturally appropriate way (Behavioral CQ-Hand).*

ACTIVITY

Set up a plan to improve your CQ. Examples of your plans can be:
- CQ Head: Before the end of the course, publish one article in a newspaper or magazine (no blog) on the subconscious bias and sexism at my workplace.
- CQ Head: Before the end of the course, publish on Kindle Direct a complete booklet, a minimum of 50 pages, on "How to survive a Nepalese boss, a Philippine team, in an Australian company – A cultural guide for expats in multicultural Asia."
- CQ Hand/ Heart: Learn about the Sikh culture and religion. Wear their traditional *dastar* (turban) to do the grocery. The measurement will be a video, and two A4 pages reflecting on my experience and connecting it with theories.

- CQ Head/Hand/Heart: Volunteer to work in a local shop of non-dominant cultural background for a week and learn about their family business model, as well as the impact that their culture has on running the business. The measurement will be a report of at least eight pages analyzing the work experience and connecting it with theories.

Politicians are often mindful of adjusting their outward expressions to show respect to local cultures/ "Secretary of State Hillary Clinton recounts a story outside the Sultan Hassan Mosque in Cairo, (Egypt)," PETE SOUZA.[59]

6.3.2   The Self, or the Lack Thereof

We are often driven, especially when we embrace the value of weak group attachment or individualism, by a need, an expectation that the most important purpose in our life is to find our true self. We look inward to seek the inner truth, "to thine own self be true" (Shakespeare). The goal of self-actualization is to find the true self and live it authentically, so you can be you, be free, be happy.[60] This profound authenticity guides us to study the major that is meant to be, follow a career that is meant to be, and pair with a partner who is meant to be. This true self already exists. We just need to be brave and dedicated to the adventure of finding it, as it is the key to living happily ever after.

This notion of self and good life is rooted in religion, the very idea of predestination that God has laid out a plan for each individual to fulfil.

Even when we are no longer religious, much of our current thinking is a legacy of these religious views.[61]

6.3.2.1   The Self-fulfilling Prophecy of the Self

In 2013, the third most popular course at Harvard promised students that "it will change your life." Professor Puett used ancient Chinese philosophies to tell students to "stop trying to find yourself" simply because the self doesn't exist.

What does Puett mean?

More often than not, what we discover about the true self is only a *snapshot* of who we are at a particular time and place in life.[62] One day, we sit down and start thinking seriously about who we really are. The analysis ends up with labels such as "hot tempered but honest," "good at art, bad at science," "low hierarchy acceptance and a team player," "easily get provoked" or "my life is shaped by the traumatic experience working as the intern in an office full of bullies." We are then told to embrace this true self, lovingly accept this genuine version of our authenticity, and let it define us forever. The fact is that when *snapshots become labels*, they will drive our behavior and guide our decisions, creating our life's patterns, slowly transforming incidents into habits, temporary emotional dispositions into more permanent characteristic, and constructing the so-called personality. In other words, the "true" self is nothing other than the result of self-fulfilling prophecy, and of patterns that have been built up over time. You have *become* an "easily provoked" person because that is how you have behaved and who you believe you are, but it is not who you are, or all that you can be.

So who are you?

6.3.2.2   The Malleable Evolving Self

A contemporary view of the self – the post-modern perspective – has been popular in humanities and other interpretive disciplines. By this, sociologists such as Michael Wood and Louis Zurcher refer to a self that emphasizes impulse, process and change.[63] You are not a single, unified being. You are complex, multifaceted and changing constantly. Buddhism has been exerting a similar notion for a long time, stating that nothing is constant and the stable selfhood is just an illusion.

Neuroscience concludes this independently, that the brain and body is constantly in flux and there's nothing that corresponds to the sense that there's an unchanging self.[64] In Chapter 1, we learned that the brain's plasticity enables us to represent multiple cultures. A simple difference between plural pronouns (e.g. "we" and "our") or singular pronouns (e.g. "I" and "me") can activate relevant cultural mindsets and their associate networks. Our brain is so flexible that we are capable of representing *multiple cultures* in our mind and switching between values simultaneously, depending on the given priming culture.[65-66-67] We are capable of having *both* strong and weak group attachment. We will think about selfhood in a way that is consistent with the cultural schema provided. As much as the plasticity of the brain, the self is malleable rather than static. In the same vein, William James – a famous philosopher and the father of American psychology – once concluded: "A man has a many social selves as there are individuals who recognize him."

In the DMIS model, Bennett refers the self in the "adaptation" stage to an "expanded" self. Let's return to Orla. In addition to her primary "Irish," "affective," "feminine," "low context" self, her brain plasticity allows her to respond to diverse contexts and become a more complex version of the Orla at this moment. Upon working with her Pakistani counterparts, she can react to the high context cues and think, feel or behave in a more subtle and implicit manner. Insofar as this behavior emerged from her feeling for the cultural patterns in Pakistan, it would be considered part of her selfhood.[68] Bennett's argument is compatible with the wholesomeness of CQ. Orla would not be a person with high CQ if her adapted behavior does not go hand in hand with heartfelt interest and intrinsic CQ motivation for the Pakistan's high context dependent culture. In another word, she can fake it, but the expanded self and CQ are achieved only when the faking gives way and evolves to genuine feeling from the heart.

6.3.2.3   *The Cultivated Self*
At this point, there is good news and bad news. The good news is that we can *acquire more than one culture*, internalizing even seemingly conflicting values, and becoming multifaceted, multicultural and complex individuals. The bad news is that we tend to *fall into patterned, habitual responses*. If we were to stay true to ourselves and behave accordingly, we would be stuck in this perpetual pattern, old thinking and behaviors, and limiting our potential to a self-perception, a snapshot, a frozen moment, a very narrow sense of who we actually are, or who we actually can be.

Breaking the pattern. In their book *The Path*, Puett and Gross-Loh[69] address the possibility of becoming different versions of a better self, and the challenge of being pulled down to a spiral of habitual responses that would eventually become one's personal traits. The question they posed to readers is "Will you act according to where you are stuck in the moment, or will you act in a way that opens up a constellation of possibilities?"

Their advice, which makes Puett's course one of the most popular at Harvard, is to intentionally break the pattern, even if that goes against your emotion at that moment. For example, you are in a long-simmering resentment with your colleague. The first step is to acknowledge that the problem is *not* because you two are incompatible, but that your communication has fallen into a pattern. Both you and him have responded to the genuine emotion of anger, irritation and apathy. To break this pattern, you need to see him as a complex, multifaceted person with a pleasant side. And so do you. There is a more tolerant side in you that would not mind talking to the pleasant side of him at all. Ask yourself "Can I act *as if* this side of me is talking to that positive side of him?" If the answer is "yes," you are off to a good start. You may begin with a friendly greeting, even though that would be the last word you want to utter. You may want to force a deliberate moment of silence the next time you want to snarl. The chance is big that your colleague will react differently to that "as if" behavior, and that means both of you stand a chance to break away from the dangerous pattern. Puett argues that by actively working to shift ourselves "as if" we were different people in that moment, we may open up infinite possibilities that we did not know existed.

Your body postures influence your mind. This ancient wisdom of how rituals inculcate personality has been lost in the modern age, but starts to revive with modern studies of neurosciences and psychology. It is based on the notion that if the body leads, the mind will follow. In the 19th century, William James referred to this wisdom and emphasized that our emotions are both the result and the cause of our physical expression. In Chapter 4, where we discussed the impact of non-verbal communication, a study of Amy Cuddy was mentioned to illustrate how body language influenced our state of mind. In what has become the second most-watched TED talk in history – "Your body shapes who you are"[70] – she showed the powerful connection between the body and the mind. The high-power posers (hands on hips or clasped behind the head, chin tilted upwards, feet planted wide apart) showed a 19 per cent increase in testosterone, and a 25 per cent decrease in cortisol. The low-power posers (hands rested closer to the body, legs closed together, heads held downward) showed the opposite pattern, a 10 per cent decrease in testosterone, and a 17 per cent increase in cortisol.[71] In sum, if you expand your body when you feel powerful, then you also naturally feel powerful when you expand your body.[72] Based on this result, Cuddy advises us to take up a confident body posture to boost our hormones before an important event, and definitely stop crouching over small devices such as the mobile phones.

A power pose makes you feel powerful and can influence your performance outcome/ "Jenifer Patel's power pose," JUHAN SONLN.[73]

Fake it until you become it. Arnold Schwarzenegger, the world's biggest bodybuilding icon, once had breakfast with his rival, Lou Ferrigno, prior to facing off for their big competition. Ferrigno's parents were also at the breakfast table. When Arnold was asked about how he felt going into the competition, he said he had already called his mom and told her he had won![74]

Since the Soviets started using it back in the 1970s to compete in sports, such mental training has become popular among professional athletes. They would act as if they had already won the competition, by using their dominant body language, even pounding their chests like gorillas, or announcing "I'm the greatest," as legendary boxer Muhammad Ali did. Brain research shows that the same patterns activated when a weightlifter lifts hundreds of pounds are also activated when they only *imagine* lifting the weight. Mental training has proved to increase athletes' strength by 35 per cent with only mental exercises, without even budging a finger, compared to 53 per cent with physical training.[75] It may sound too good to be true, but it is fact: Your muscles will get stronger just by imagining exercise (i.e. sitting still for 11 minutes, 5 days a week, for 4 weeks, as conducted in a neurophysiology research).[76] For Matthew Nagle, whose whole body is paralyzed, a silicon chip implanted in his brain helps him to use his thoughts to move a computer cursor, open emails and control robotic arms.[77]

The powerful connection between the body and the mind tells us that when we adopt a certain body language and ritual, or when we imagine a certain vision, our mind will react accordingly, and we will eventually *feel* accordingly. Note that thought is not fact (e.g. you only *imagine* you have won a major contract), and the action may not be originated from genuine feeling (you deliberately gave a friendly greeting to the colleague you often have quarrels with). But by doing exactly that you are able to tap into your personal power and unleash the braver, nicer, better version of who you really are; or, better put, who you are meant to become. Little by little, you can develop parts of yourself you never knew existed.

Aristotle said "we are what we repeatedly do." By deliberately changing what we repeatedly do, i.e. breaking the pattern and adopting an "as-if" action, we can expand the perspectives to the hidden and the unknown. As you cultivate yourself in a certain direction, it slowly becomes second nature and radiates outward. This applies to all aspects of your life, in Puett's and Gross-Loh's words:

> "[...] intentionally seek out things you don't love, or aren't good at; pay attention to interests you think you have no time for; choose experiences precisely because they are so not you. The point is not to [...] develop expertise in a new area. The point is to get in the habit of expanding your perspective and expanding your life. It's to practice constantly engaging in anything that that forces you away from the constraints that come from living as a singular, authentic self. You're opening yourself up to living life as a series of breaks: breaks from your true feelings, your true interests, your true strengths."[78]

Knowing that you have just as much potential to be gentle as you do to be angry, to experience empathy as well as apathy, be masculine as well as feminine means giving yourself a world of infinite possibilities in which to grow and to be competent. Cultivating yourself by conducting a small action repeatedly every day, by breaking the pattern repeatedly every day, by telling yourself you are not necessarily who you think you are at this moment. Don't try to discover who you are, try cultivate who you can become. "Don't embrace yourself, overcome yourself."[79]

For our Irish engineer Orla and her Pakistani colleagues, this means they can develop their CQ to the point that both sides become bicultural, that they can genuinely communicate in both high and low context dependent ways, or execute their project with both a masculine-competitive spirit and a feminine corporate policy of work-life balance. For Orla, her source of inspiration is closer to home. It is her iconic country fellowman, playwright Bernard Shaw, who famously said: "Life isn't about finding yourself. Life is about *creating* yourself."

- *There is no such thing as a stable self. What we perceive as selfhood is often a snapshot of who we are at a particular time in our life.*
- *Regardless of cultural affiliation, we are capable of representing multiple cultures in our mind and switching between values to fit different contexts.*
- *The "as-if" ritual is meant to break the pattern, using the action to influence the mind and create your extended, new self.*

Summary

1. The most culturally attuned individuals are likely to be the most successful.
2. Similarity is a signal of ingroup – those we can trust and share resources with. It is natural that we seek companions among those with similar traits and backgrounds.
3. The bias towards ingroup results in *ethnocentrism*. We are ethnocentric when we see our own culture as central to reality and interpret the world from our own viewpoint.
4. However, humans are able to move beyond ethnocentrism and ingroup bias in order to accumulate knowledge from outgroup people, fusing different cultures, continuing to make culture an effective mechanism to survive and advance.
5. *Acculturation* is a process of interacting with different (co-)cultures.
6. DMIS is a framework of acculturation. If "C" represents "culture," then it goes from *denial* (C only) to *defense* ($C_1 > C_2$), *minimization* ($C_1 = C_2$), *acceptance* ($C_1 \neq C_2$), *adaptation* (C_1 or C_2), and *integration* ($C_1 + C_2$).
7. *Cultural shock* is part of acculturation, referring to the mismatch of old and new cultural patterns. Cultural shock contributes to early return and it is costly.
8. Stages of cultural shock may follow the U and W-shape: *honeymoon, disenchantment, adjustment, effective functioning* and *reversed cultural shock.*
9. Emotional Intelligence (EQ) is culture-bound while *Cultural Intelligence* (CQ) is culture-free. CQ is to know, to be motivated and to act in a culturally appropriate way.
10. Regardless of cultural affiliation, we are capable of representing *multiple cultures* in our mind and switching between values to fit different contexts. This indicates that we can develop CQ to become bicultural/multicultural individuals and not be held back by self-perceived personal traits.

7. Diversity management and inclusion

Objective
At the end of this chapter, you should be able to:
- Identify the major categories of diversity in organizations.
- Explain the nature of creativity and the connection with diversity.
- Describe the advantages and challenges of a diverse workforce.
- Describe the pros and cons of various diversity strategies

Chapter outline

In Chapter 2, we discussed how the "difference and problem-focused view" of culture has guided much of the theory development in the literature of intercultural communication. Under the influence of the Cold War, the underlying assumption of the mainstream theories is that differences are a source of problem, cost, risk, danger, and difficulties. Cultural gaps are a source of conflict than of synergy and often a disaster. This approach is not always helpful. It fails to look at the bright side of diversity. Focusing on the potential mismatches when cultures collides may do our brain a disservice, by preparing us to be reactive rather than proactive, defensive rather than cooperative, viewing differences as problems rather than opportunities

This chapter describes the historical context behind the need for diversity. It also identifies various dimensions of diversity and discusses the benefits as well as challenges of fostering a diverse workforce. Finally, it addresses a range of strategies and how organizations can employ them to optimize their positive impact.

7.1 The drivers and dimensions of workforce diversity

We are living in an era of international networking and mobility. The contrast of everything around us has become increasingly obvious, and diversity management has emerged as a critical discipline of theories and practices. Good diversity policies can turn cultural differences into strengths and benefits. Hence, diversity management has moved to the top of the organizational development agenda. What began as *token initiatives* to meet legal requirements have now become *strategic programs* aimed at achieving organizational outcomes. This strategy mindset captures the essence of diversity management, which has been defined as a "management philosophy of recognizing and valuing heterogeneity in organizations with a view to improve organizational performance."[1] In short, it is not diversity for the sake of diversity, but an acknowledgement that it should be seen as a performance driver and a business imperative.

7.1.1 The Drivers of Workforce Diversity

Managing a diverse population and workforce is not new. Indeed, great empires throughout history have conquered lands comprised of fragmented peoples and nations, yet learned to rule them effectively for centuries.[2]

However, the kind of diversity management we are witnessing today is driven by historical factors that characterize the fast-changing pace of the modern era.

7.1.1.1   Social Movements

Although the term "diversity management" came into use in the 1980s, the overall movement was a response to the social protests, civil rights and affirmative legislation that emerged after the Second World War.[3] Historical court rulings and women's liberation movements shaped the way organizations addressed the racio-ethnic diversity of the workforce. In 1954, the US Supreme Court overturned the 1896 separate-but-equal doctrine and ordered desegregation of public schools soon after. Whereas first-wave feminism focused on voting rights, the second wave spread through Europe in the 1960s and 1970s and broadened to include equal opportunities at work, reproduction rights and the freedom of choice in sexuality. Against this background, political events in the wider world significantly influenced young and educated people in the West. Movements such as decolonization in Africa, the Vietnam War, the rise of Marxism, the reemergence of neo-Nazi white supremacy groups, and the Quebec sovereignty movement fighting for its distinct cultural right, etc. became focal points of rallies and protests. In sum, the views of government and mainstream culture were challenged in the context of social justice, equality, rights and the system of industrial capitalism.

In this context, organizations began to address diversity out of the concern that social unrest would spill over into the workplace. Human resources were also under the obligation to act in compliance with affirmative actions that outlawed discrimination against women and other minorities. For many organizations, addressing diversity was seen as an ethical issue, to right the wrong, and to embrace socially progressive values. These three reasons (workplace harmony, law, and ethics) underpinned the first practices in diversity management initiatives.[4]

7.1.1.2   Economic and Demographic Changes

Since the social movements that diversified the workplace for more women and minorities, the demographic change in labor force has become even more dramatic. While baby boomers are retiring en masse, Gen Xers are taking leading positions, and the millennials (born between the 1980s and 2000s) will account for half the workforce by 2020, and will soon begin to hold leadership positions. The available pool of talent has changed in both size and composition. In the first ten years of the 21st century, migrants accounted for 47 per cent of the increase in the workforce in the US and 70 per cent in Europe.[5] In the Gulf, non-national workers account for 48 per cent of the total workforce, with 88.5 per cent in the UAE and 85.7 per cent in Qatar.[6] For many developed countries, a large number of immigrants is constantly needed to maintain their working-age population levels.

Asia hosts three of the world's top economies, measured by purchasing power parity. Western immigrants are now being replaced by Asian-born, internationally educated and multilingual immigrants within the region.[7] Intra-regional moves have created many foreign communities in each country. For example, the Korean population in Ho Chi Minh city comprises up to 100,000 people, making it the fourth largest Korean diaspora in the world[8] / "Night view of Ho Chi Minh city, Vietnam," DIEGO DELSO.[9]

Together with the demographic change, the economic development that transformed the business landscape in the 1980s and 1990s profoundly influenced how organizational efforts in diversity shifted from previous concerns about "workplace harmony," "laws" or "ethics" to "profit" and "innovation." During this time, high-growth economy and a boom in the technology industry required organizations to compete for a large number of skilled workers and to open a hiring process not only for more women and people of color, but also other unconventional recruits such as foreign guest workers.[10] Globalization started to show its powerful impact and organizations were challenged by increasingly international markets. Domestic competitive pressure pushed them beyond borders. This means serving clients from new demographic groups and hiring new employees who can best understand and serve these groups. Business impetus began to demand that organizations see diversity as an economic value, rather than from the "workplace harmony," "laws" or "ethics" perspectives that prevailed before the 1980s.[11]

7.1.2   The Dimensions of Workforce Diversity

Diversity management of the modern era also consists of a wide variety of dimensions that typify the complex intersectionality of the modern organization. In a heterogeneous workforce, within the same organization, co-cultures and distinctions such as gender, ethnicity, language, age, religion, disability, social class and work experience, etc. co-exist and interact rigorously with one another. These dimensions are the surface level of diversity and are the most frequently used categories in diversity management.

However, organizations have recently started to pay attention to a new frontier of diversity: the deep-level diversity or the *diversity of thought*, which refers to different cognitive abilities such as thinking styles. Some people are analyst thinkers, some are pragmatic and meticulous planners, while others are idealists. This variable is not readily apparent and hence can be difficult to measure, but it allows organizations to address diversity with a more powerful and nuanced approach. Each individual is a unique blend of identities, cultures and experiences that shape the way this person thinks and brings her/his thoughts to the table. Harnessing the diversity of thought therefore can stimulate out-of-the-box thinking, spur insight and increase efficiency.

Diversity management is driven by:
- *Concern for workplace harmony*
- *Compliance with law*
- *Ethics: it is the right thing to do*
- *Business imperatives*

7.2   The benefits of a diverse workforce

The business case for diversity has never been more central than it is now. Having a diverse workforce can benefit organizations in a variety of ways. In general, five arguments have been used to advocate diversity: creativity, cost, marketing, resource acquisition and public reputation.

7.2.1   The Creativity Argument

In its 2013 report,[12] Deloitte made a bold statement that it was time to rethink diversity. Advances in neurological research show that diversity of thought is the future of the workforce, which enables us to blend the "cacophony of ideas" in the workplace to "spark innovation and creativity."

7.2.1.1   *Creativity is a Process*

In his famous book *A Technique for Producing Ideas,* the advertising icon James Webb Young wrote that "an idea is nothing more nor less than a new combination of old elements," and creativity is basically a capacity to see that combination.[13] In simple terms, creativity requires (1) a large amount of information, and (2) the ability to see relationship of the information. Creativity can be measured by testing a person's level of *divergent thinking,* an ability to come up with a large number of responses to an open-ended probe.

According to neuroscience, creativity is created by flashes of insight that arise from unconscious information reservoirs of the mind and brain. Every day, we expose ourselves to a vast amount of information that leaves marks on our subconscious, which we may not even be aware of. This is the above-mentioned point (1). Even when we are relaxing, our brain never rests. It keeps combining information and neural patterns connecting unrelated thoughts and experiences until stable relationships emerge, subconsciously,[14] which is point (2). Day in, day out, a person nurtures her/his creativity process by gathering materials and letting the subconscious process the data and find connections. The "Aha!" moment will hit her/him when (s)he is least expecting it. It sounds like a sudden insight, disconnected from the immediately preceding thought, but it is the culmination of a series of brain states and activities across a long period of time.[15] Creativity is not the result of some magic inspiration, but rather is achieved through "systematic daily effort."[16] Archimedes's "Eureka!" didn't happen because he got into a bathtub, and Newton didn't accidently figure out the force of gravity when an apple hit his head. Their brilliant ideas had been "concocted" subconsciously as a result of endless brain activities connecting and making sense of endless information.

The lesson is that we need to keep gathering data so our brain has abundant resources to form new connections, and the "Aha!" moment will emerge when the time is right. The plasticity of the brain also means that training in divergent thinking can result in a bigger volume of gray matter a higher level of creativity.[17]

7.2.1.2 *Diversity of Thought and Creativity*

Knowing that the creativity process relies on (1) the amount of information available, and (2) how our brain can make sense of the connection, having different perspectives around the table will act as a "collective brain," in which everyone can give input data, and the communication between them can mirror the neural connection in creating a great variety of data relationships. Research shows that diverse thinking fosters an environment of creativity. A one standard deviation in diversity from the mean will result in a boost in innovation, reflected by 26 per cent increase in the number of patents and a 31 per cent increase in the number of patent citations.[18] Neuroscience tells us that it is not the IQ of individual members, but actually the *average social intelligence* of a team that can help them mitigate a number of biases using completely different perspectives.[19] Even if the members of homogeneous teams are more capable, diversity teams still perform better, in other words: "Diversity trumps ability."[20]

Striving for diversity of thought can significantly change the way we view competence. A scenario used in *The Difference*[21] illustrates this point clearly. In the table 7.1 below, you will find the hiring performance test result of three candidates. Naturally, we are inclined to pick top scorers Jeff and Rose. But notice that Spencer also answered all the questions that the other two candidates missed correctly, suggesting that hiring Spencer would bring different thinking to the table.

Table 7.1. Job candidates test results[22]

	Q1	Q2	Q3	Q4	Q5	Q6	Q7	Q8	Q9	Q10
Spencer			X	X	X			X	X	
Jeff	X	X			X	X	X		X	X
Rose	X	X				X	X		X	X

Diversity helps guard against "group think." When we hear disagreement from someone who is different from us, it provokes more thought than when it comes from someone who is similar to us. In a study on the impact of racial diversity, researchers reported that when a black person presents a dissenting argument, the audience values and benefits from it much more than when a white person introduced *that same dissenting perspective*.[23] Similarly, diversity also helps to reduce "overconfidence," which may cloud the picture due to the air of authority inherent in experts' knowledge.

Finally, *physical* diversity triggers *thinking* diversity. In a homogeneous group, people feel more comfortable and *assume* they understand one another. This has to do with a common bias called "fluency heuristic," which means people prefer information that is easy to process, just like we have a positive bias towards familiar songs (e.g. old songs are better). Consequently, a team of similar people feels comfortable. But "comfortable" is not always good for performance, especially in the long term. Why? The moment people start to recognize they are socially or cognitively different from one another, they expect differences and assume they will need to *work harder* to come to a consensus. In a study, self-identified Republican and Democrat participants were told to write a persuasive essay to convince a partner who disagreed. The result was that people prepared better for their discussions when their partners were from the other party. They were less prepared when they knew they were going to argue with people from the same party.[24] Adding an outsider versus an insider actually doubles the chances of arriving at the correct solution, from 29 to 60 per cent.[25] The work feels more challenging, but the outcomes are better. In fact, working in diverse teams produces better outcomes precisely *because* it is more difficult. No pain no gain. Conclusion: diversity prompts us to work harder.[26]

Creativity is simply a new combination of old data. A diverse workforce can act as a "collective brain" in creating a great variety of data combinations:

- *diversity trumps ability*
- *diversity guards against "group think" and "overconfidence in experts"*
- *differences prompt us to work harder*

7.2.2 The Cost Argument

Organizations have realized that recruiting and keeping a diverse workforce should be more than a luxury (i.e. it is ethical to do so) or a necessity (i.e. the law says so). In fact, diversity should be a strategy because it is *beneficial.*

7.2.2.1 *Gender Diversity and Financial Profit*

When hunter-gatherer societies shifted to agrarian ones, in many areas women became the first agriculturalists as they made the transition from "gathering" fruits and seeds to "cultivating" plants.[27] In Africa, women are the backbone of the continent's rural economy, growing at least 70 per cent of its food and they are responsible for half of all animal husbandry.[28] Today, we discuss women being the "richer sex" and replacing men as "future breadwinners" within 20 years,[29] but black women are already the lifeblood of their families, especially in communities hard hit by recessions and in countries where black men are challenged by racism and obstacles to employment.[30]

In the West, women started to enter the workforce during the Industrial Revolution because their cheap labor helped factory owners earn more profit.[31] As more and more jobs require brainpower and not physical strength, and with education becoming a women's game (women earn 53.5 per cent of all bachelor's degrees and make up 57.4 per cent of graduate students in 28 European countries),[32] the two sexes are more evenly matched, sometimes, to women's advantage, as in the case of leadership.

Women are the backbone of agriculture and animal husbandry/ "A farmer in Pakistan," MAI NGUYEN-PHUONG-MAI.

Research among 7,280 global leaders in 2011 (64 per cent of the data set was male) shows that women outscore their male counterparts in 15 out of 16 identified leadership competencies.[33] This partly explains why the gender mix of an organization's top management relates positively to its performance. A report examining 2,360 companies globally demonstrates that companies with one or more women on the board delivered higher than average returns on equity, lower gearing and better than average growth.[34] On average, "female representation on top management leads to an increase of $42 million in firm value."[35] In Asian markets, female board directors have a positive effect on performance in more than 800 companies in Malaysia,[36] in the top 30 firms on India's Bombay Stock Exchange,[37] and Vietnamese companies led by women made twice as much profit as others over five years.[38]

The benefit of gender diversity is also profound when women take part *in all others aspects of employment.* In the UK, for every ten per cent increase in gender diversity, EBIT (Earnings Before Interests and Taxes) rose by 3.5 per cent.[39] Another good example is the Sweden-based fast-fashion retailer H&M, which is close to reaching gender equality. Women make up 58 per cent of the board, 41 per cent of its top leadership team, and 80 per cent of the employees. In 2016, H&M ranked at the top of Ledbetter's list, composed of companies culled from the Fortune 100.

If we take a step back and look at the big picture, the benefit of incorporating women into the economy is staggering. According to a report by McKinsey,[40] if all countries match the rate of improvement of the fastest-improving country in their region, we could add 12 trillion dollars to global growth. A "full potential" scenario, in which women play an identical role in labor markets to that of men, could add $28 trillion, or 26 per cent to the global annual GDP by 2025.

CASE STUDY

Europe and the US

During the two World Wars, as men were sent to battle, the labor shortage was filled by women. Women were encouraged to join the workforce firstly for patriotic reasons, pushed by the propaganda of the day.

Bangladesh

The participation of women in the workforce not only makes direct financial sense, but it is also a "cure" for social issues. In Bangladesh, an all-female driving school aims to improve the country's appalling road safety record and "de-testosterone" the traffic.[41] 20,000 people die every year on Bangladesh's roads – one of the highest road fatality rates per capita in the world. It is rare for women to drive, let alone work as drivers.

Japan

Japan's gender equality ranks 105th out of 145 countries, much lower than many emerging economies, including Rwanda (6th) and the Philippines (7th).[42] Approximately 70 per cent of women give up their career after having their first child.[43] Welfare systems also encourage the "male breadwinner model" by allowing husbands to claim a tax deduction if their wife's income is below a certain level, and families can also claim a state pension without paying any premiums. 70 per cent of Japanese companies provide a dependents allowance for wives so their husbands can focus on work.[44]

However, with its recovering economy, the world's lowest birthrate, a shrinking and greying workforce and an acute labor shortage, Japan is being forced to change its view on gender diversity. Closing the gender employment gap could boost Japan's GDP by 13 per cent.[45] The government now aims to see women account for 30 per cent of corporate managers by 2020. This is quite a turnaround for Abe's Conservative Party, which, in 2005, was still warning against the damage of gender equality and referred to women as "baby-making machines."[46]

Saudi Arabia

While Saudi women still cannot drive and need permission from their male guardians to open a bank account or to go abroad, this country is also witnessing an unprecedented rate of women entering the workforce at 48%, more than double the rate for men.[47]

In the face of a changing global energy market and the plunging oil price, Saudi can no longer rely on oil revenue and has approved sweeping economic reforms to ensure the country can live without oil by 2020. A major task in the reform is to increase women in the workforce.[48] Female graduates make up 49.6 per cent, but women only account for 16.4 per cent of the job market.[49]

Vietnam

In Vietnam, a great number of women traditionally took the role of primary or co-breadwinners. The exalted status of women may actually date back millennia to when Vietnam had a matriarchal society. This changed under the influence of Confucianism when the country was invaded by the Chinese. However, compared to other Confucianism-influenced cultures such as China, Japan and Korea, matriarchal values leave a strong legacy. Europeans who arrived in the 1600s observed that women were prominent in trading and commerce. The decades-long Vietnam War witnessed active roles for women, fighting side by side with men, which helped them to approach gender parity more easily than other conservative societies.[50] As of 2012, the number of female Vietnamese entrepreneurs is higher (51.35 per cent) than male entrepreneurs (41.11 per cent).[51]

1. Analyze the causes of women's employment in each case and find similarities among them.
2. What are the dominant cultural values in each culture?
3. Did these values give way to specific context (history, economy, circumstances, etc.)?
4. What conclusion can we draw from these cases: (a) culture is static; (b) culture is dynamic? How can we relate this to the notion of "culture as survival mechanism", i.e. culture evolves to help humans advance and survive?

"We Can Do It," a Second World War propaganda poster, also called "Rosie the Riveter" after the fictional character of a strong female war production worker, designed to attract women into work/ "We Can Do It," HOWARD MILLER.[52]

7.2.2.2   Racial Diversity and Financial Profit

The financial benefit of racial diversity is no less promising than gender diversity. Two studies of 146 Swiss firms[53] and 366 public companies in Canada, Latin America, the UK and the US found that having nationality diverse top management teams is significantly and positively associated with firm performance, with 35 per cent more likelihood of financial returns above their respective national industry medians.[54] The mean revenues and numbers of customers also positively correlate to racial diversity (table 7.2). Combined with gender diversity, these factors account for 16.5 per cent of the variance in sales revenue (every one per cent increase in gender diversity correlates to a three per cent increase in sales revenue, and every one per cent increase in racial diversity correlates to a nine per cent increase in sales revenue).[55]

Table 7.2. Mean revenues and numbers of customers for businesses with high, medium and low levels of racial diversity

Level of racial diversity	Low (<10%)	Medium (10–24%)	High (25%+)
Mean sale revenues (in millions)	**$51.9**	**$383.8**	**$761.3**
Mean numbers of customers (in thousands)	**20.7**	**30.0**	**35.0**

7.2.2.3   Ability Diversity and Financial Profit

The number of people with a disability may surprise us. It is estimated that one in every eight Canadians[56] and one in every five Australians[57] has some form of disability. In the US, a quarter of today's 20-year-olds in the US will become disabled before they retire[58] and one person becomes disabled every 49 minutes as a result of injuries.[59]

Based on that statistic alone, the economic cost of ignoring 20–25 per cent of the population is unsustainable. In fact, employing people with disabilities brings benefits. A 2001 Statistics Canada survey reported that 90 per cent of people with disabilities did as well or better at their jobs than non-disabled co-workers; 86 per cent rated average or better in attendance; and staff retention was 72 per cent higher among persons with disabilities.[60] Employees with disabilities are also loyal, reliable, and hardworking.[61]

The common perception is that people with disabilities cost more and employers are understandably concerned about bottom lines. However, 59 per cent of the respondents in a study[62] acknowledged that the kinds of accommodations they request cost nothing, such as scheduling flexibility, allowances in dress code rules or allowing somebody to sit (or stand) when other positioning is customary. Any costs incurred are, generally, a one-time cost, typically of $500.

Under the premise of diversity, we should rethink the concept of disability and its negative connotation. For example, according to a noted doctor, half of the innovators in Silicon Valley may have Asperger's syndrome, reflected in their ability to program for long hours.[63] In fact, German software firm SAP actively recruits people with autism diagnoses since they can perform complex tasks that require a high level of concentration and exhibit potent ability in relation to finding patterns and making connections.[64] Their "Autism at Work" program aims to have one per cent of its total workforce (approx. 650 people) fall on the spectrum by 2020 – an initiative that Microsoft has since adopted.[65]

7.2.3   The Marketing Argument

Organizations with a diverse workforce are not only more likely to understand different market segments *better*, but they are also more likely to *enter new markets*.

7.2.3.1   Better Customer Satisfaction

In a pro-diversity working environment, positive and pleasant employees are more likely to "spill over" a social contagion process to patrons during service delivery, resulting in greater customer satisfaction.[66] But that is not the only reason. Let's take the words of Brad Jakeman – President Global Beverages at PepsiCo – as a hint: "I am sick and tired as a client of sitting in agency meetings with a whole bunch of white, straight males talking to me about how we are going to sell our brands that are bought 85 per cent by women."[67]

We discussed in a previous chapter that seeking similarity is intuitive, since similarities subconsciously give our brain the signal of "ingroup," i.e. those we can trust. Therefore, customer service can benefit hugely from having a staff that reflects the communities they serve. When one member of a team shares a client's trait, such as ethnicity or gender, the *entire* team is 152 per cent more likely to understand that user better than another team.[68] Hence, diversifying the workforce to truly represent customers is an essential strategy in terms of preventing them from going to competitors. A good example is Westpac Australia's financial service, which over a period of ten years successfully changed the workforce from predominantly under-35-year-olds to an age diversity of between 18 and 70, because it wants to truly reflect its customer base.[69]

7.2.3.2 New Markets

She-Economy. The most impressive emerging market is closer than you think, one that has been coined "womenomics," the "she-economy" or the "female economy." In aggregate, women represent a growth market more than twice as big as China and India combined.[70] Women drive an estimated 70–80 per cent of consumer spending,[71] influence 91 per cent of all home purchase and make 70 per cent of all travel decisions in the US,[72] influence 60 per cent of new car purchases in Japan and make up about 47 per cent of European computer users.[73] The name on the credit card does not tell the whole story as women influence purchases even when their husbands pay. Even with the pay gap factored into the equation, by 2024, the average woman will out-earn the average man in some developed Western countries.[74] In the UK, 53 per cent of millionaires will be women by the year 2020.[75]

However, marketers still need to capture the power of this considerable purchasing force. Nearly half of women surveyed say that marketers don't understand them[76] and 90 per cent say that advertisers don't advertise to them.[77] Sales representatives fail to get women's specific buying patterns and preferences, which is partly due to the high percentage of men acting as creative directors in advertising agencies.[78] To capitalize on the growth of female consumers, businesses should tailor their marketing[79] and change the gender balance of product development teams.[80] Becoming *women literate* is a must if businesses want to tap into the female economy.

CASE STUDY

Olive Bowers is a 13-year-old surfer. Disappointed with how *Tracks* magazine, a publication dubbed "the surfers' bible" portrays women in the sport, she penned a fierce letter to complain:[81]

Dear Tracks Surf Magazine,

I want to bluntly address the way you represent women in your magazine. I am a surfer, my dad surfs and my brother has just started surfing.

Reading a Tracks magazine I found at my friend's holiday house, the only photo of a woman I could find was "Girl of the month". She wasn't surfing or even remotely near a beach.

I clicked on your web page titled "Girls" hoping I might find some women surfers and what they were up to, but it entered into pages and pages of semi-naked, non-surfing girls.

These images create a culture in which boys, men and even girls reading your magazine will think that all girls are valued for is their appearance.

My posse of female surfers and I are going to spread the word and refuse to purchase or promote Tracks *magazine. It's a shame that you can't see the benefits of an inclusive surf culture that, in fact, would add a whole lot of numbers to your subscription list.*

I urge you to give much more coverage to the exciting women surfers out there, not just scantily clad women (who may be great on the waves, but we'll never know).

I would subscribe to your magazine if only I felt that women were valued as athletes instead of dolls. This change would only bring good.

Olive

1. Why is there such a bias? Please find similar examples.
2. What would you do if you were the editor of the magazine?

Consumers with disabilities. With an estimated population of 1.3 billion, i.e. nearly one in five people on the planet, this emerging market is the size of China. Adding their friends and families means another 2.2 billion potential customers. In sum, we are looking at $8 trillion in annual disposable income globally.[82] In the US, this spending power is double that of teens and more than 17 times of tweens (8–12 year-olds), the two most avidly sought after demographic groups.[83] That is why the term "handicapitalism" has been used to describe this increasingly powerful cohort. People with a disability are not charity cases or burdens, but more precisely profitable marketing targets. We may lose sight of them simply because a majority of this market has invisible disabilities such as myopia, chronic pain or a hearing impairment.

People with a disability are tech-savvy and early adopters. This explains why some of the most involved companies are from tech, telecommunication and banking sectors because of their assistive technology products. Many products originally designed for people with disabilities have become popular in the mainstream market: vibrating mobile function, texting, voice activation software, audiobooks and curb cuts for wheelchair users.

Consumers with a disability and their loved ones make purchase decisions based on much more than just personal taste or medical condition.

They are more brand-loyal than other consumers[84] and are well aware of organizations that promote their voice, employ positive advertising messages,[85] and include staff with a disability in the marketing team. 92 per cent of people with disabilities favor companies that employ individuals with disabilities, and 87 per cent would do business with them.[86] It is a simple rule: customers will purchase products that *support their personal identities and causes.*

"Toy like me" is a campaign and art collective that aims at asking global toy industry to better represent 150 million children with disabilities/ "Snowman with a hearing aid," REBECCA ATKINSON.[87]

LGBTQ (Lesbian-Gay-Bisexual-Transgender-Queer or Questioning). For marketers, LGBTQ have been "the next big thing." It is difficult to provide an accurate figure, since most data available reflects only those who are openly LGBTQ, but the baseline assumption is that LGBTQ account for 6.5 per cent of the population. The annual spending power or the "pink pound" of the global LGBTQ community has been estimated at approximately $3.7

trillion, with Asia leading (1.1 trillion), representing half of the LGBTQ on the planet, followed by Europe ($950 billion) and the US ($900 billion).[88]

Much research done to date tells us that LGBTQ consumers often earn more and spend more. They are more likely to move to big cities where incomes are higher, more likely to focus on careers, have more savings, are more likely to pay extra for top-of-the-line or cutting-edge products.[89] In general, they spend seven per cent more than heterosexual consumers.[90] Not only do they earn more and spend more, LGBTQ also significantly influence the market as taste makers and *trend setters*. Many companies in music, sports, apparel and media keep a close look eye on them for inspiration, creativity and role models that can change the content of their products.

The fact that LGBTQ still suffer discrimination in almost every aspect of their lives[91] plays a crucial role in making them extremely loyal customers of a brand. Similar to consumers with a disability, they are highly aware of organizations that appear to be allies and those that are not yet catching up in the equality game.[92] Brands that are ignorant or insensitive of LGBTQ issues are often collectively boycotted, while brands that are progressive and supportive not only attract new customers but win their loyalty. Sympathizing with their pleas, their friends and families advocate LGBTQ policies[93] and 78 per cent of them would make a switch to a more LGBTQ-friendly brands.[94] In order to be really effective in marketing to the LGBTQ community, organizational commitment should start from the inside out. Having a transgender or a lesbian featuring in an advertisement is not enough, and can be easily seen as "tokenism if the organization itself does not have its own house in order."[95] The representation and well-being of LGBTQ employees should be first taken care of: "You want to be known as an inclusive employer *before* trying to market to the larger community."[96]

Global market. Making diversity a market-based policy helps organizations gain access to new international customer bases with more success.[97] The complexity of local markets often challenges established multinationals, and that is why a diverse management and marketing team can better reflect the breadth of the company's new geographical footprint and the changing consumer landscape. A good example is Australia where, by 2020, one in four jobs will be Asia-related and the future of the country's business will be on this continent. The government has been actively shaping an "Australia in the Asian century" with a "National Taskforce for an Asia-Capable Australia."[98] Efforts to be more "Asia-literate" and "Asia-capable" begin with early education, such as teaching Asian languages at primary school.[99] Organizations actively recruit staff who understand Asia's cultures since this has become a must for doing business with this continent.[100] In short, as the head of HR at Royal Bank of Canada – a Tanzanian immigrant herself – said: "To win the market, one needs to *hire the market*."[101]

CASE STUDY

For the first time in the history of the car industry, American women have more driving licenses than men.[102] Dealers of General Motors' Cadillac division reported that women wield influence in anywhere from 85 to 95 per cent of car purchases.[103] In the Philippines, women account for 45 per cent of new vehicle purchases.[104] Among millennials – the young adults that all industries have started fighting for – 53 per cent of car buyers are female.[105] As you are reading, the numbers are increasing, and this trend is being seen in many other markets.

However, companies continue to have outdated marketing narratives that promote female stereotypes. Women are still advised to "bring a man with you to buy a car." Advertisements mainly focus on men with an air of masculinity. In the shops, women complain that macho car salesmen don't treat them fairly, using intimidating or patronizing sales tactics, believing that women don't know much about cars. A CarMax poll shows that 19 per cent of the surveyed women thought they missed a fair trade-in value; 15 per cent didn't have a trustworthy salesperson; 13 per cent missed fair pricing; and the same number thought they didn't get a good finance rate.[106] A study found that women and black customers are consistently quoted *higher prices* than men because car dealers think they are "easy to mislead." [107]

1. Car designs often prioritize speed, not utility, which matters more to women. Conduct research on other automotive features that are more relatable to women, but often ignored by car producers, e.g. child comfort or environmental impact.
2. Expand the previous question to other markets such as millennials, LGBTQ, people with a disability and people of color.
3. Search for successful strategies from the automotive industry that attract the target markets of women, millennials, LGBTQ, people with a disability and people of color.

7.2.4   The Resource Acquisition Argument

Since it was coined by a McKinsey study in 1997, the "War for Talent" has become even more competitive due to a dramatic demographic shift that is seeing more women, millennials, foreigners and other minorities joining the workforce.

Together with this shifting demographic, employees are now more frequently *free agents*. They have greater choices, their bargaining power has increased and the job market is highly transparent, all of which make attracting top-skilled employees fiercely competitive. Talent retention is an important issue for business, second only to the challenge of building global leadership.[108] Employees jump jobs more frequently, only 13 per cent of them are actively engaged at work,[109] two thirds believe they could find a better job in less than 60 days,[110] and more than 70 per cent of millennials expect their employers to focus on societal problems and creativity at work in order for them to stay.[111] If they do not stay, the cost of replacing an employee can be up to 75 per cent of their annual salary.

Talent retention in Asia comes with some important differences. For example, many managers in Asia are young, but their parents often have strong influence over their adult children, to the extent that they can veto job change decisions. Therefore, connecting with employees' families through formal or informal company events is a good strategy. If family members believe in the values of the company, they can be counted upon to support an employees' loyalty to the company/ "Participants in a diversity conference," OREGON DEPARTMENT OF TRANSPORTATION.

Talent retention is challenging also because new generations of employees have very different base competencies (more tech-savvy, consultative and entrepreneurial skills) and hence expect a very different organizational culture, leaning towards feminine and future-oriented values: flexibility, opportunities, sustainability, meaningful jobs, less-structured career paths, and greater work-life balance. In short, the employee-work contract has shifted. Employers are slowly stripped of the power to *fire* people and given the mission to *keep* the talent. This forces business leaders to focus on building an irresistible organization where workers feel that they are at home, that their passion is nurtured and their personal values are matched.

Obviously, hiring from the narrow, conventional pool means losing the war for talent. HR now finds new recruits in what have hitherto been minority groups in the workforce. This gives them a larger pool of candidates that may result in wider selection, higher quality and lower costs.[112] However, these potential employees must be convinced that organizations are genuinely interested in diversity and that their career path will be supported. Tech companies have proven to be forerunners in this race by publishing their diversity data for the world to review.

It goes without saying that an organization with effective diversity management will significantly attract and retain talent. A simple calculation reveals the reason why: when half of all graduates are female and non-white, but the number of new recruits does not mirror this reality, then clearly the talent is going to competitors. The "person-organization fit" theory[113] tells us that individuals make job choices based on the compatibility between their personal identities and that of the organization. Black applicants are more likely to accept jobs in organizations that depict Blacks in managerial positions,[114] and high achievers are more likely to say yes to organizations that commit to diversity policies.[115] A study of Indian IT workers shows that diversity results in greater retention and loyalty, because employees build their sense of belonging and strong group attachment with an organization that values their uniqueness.[116] For example, a practice such as granting religious accommodation also has a significant impact on staff morale (62 per cent), retention (38 per cent) and loyalty (37 per cent).[117] In conclusion, the end goal in this war for talent is to become an "Employer of Choice," a magnet for talent, an irresistible place where workers feel that they are at home, where their passion is nurtured and their personal values are matched.

7.2.5   The Positive Publicity and Reputation Argument

Diversity on boards has been connected with better corporate governance and more ethical behavior. As women have a higher rate of attendance and a tougher monitoring ability, they pull along male directors as well.[118] Research looking at more than 6,500 organizations globally shows that having women on a board is linked to fewer scandals such as bribery, fraud or shareholder conflicts.[119] It is not that women are more ethical than men, more that diversity is a good proxy for better problem solving and cross-checking.

Board diversity has been linked with increased corporate social responsibility (CSR) in France,[120] Indonesia,[121] Vietnam[122] and a number of multinationals.[123] In a study that measures the corporate philanthropic disaster response of privately owned Chinese firms after two devastating earthquakes, researchers concluded that having at least three women on the board was associated with a more significant corporate response to natural disasters.[124]

However, there has been a trend for companies to remove diversity from CSR reports and make it a poster child for quality. An impressive diversity report, one that is not necessarily related to CSR, is at the core of a brutal competition[125] among businesses. Customers now demand it, often supported by the media, who scrutinize the numbers, investigate evidence of policies and initiatives, compare with other competitors, analyze practices, and call on customers to make a responsible choice. A good report may result in a media marketing blitz and a profit windfall. In fact, winning a diversity award can make a company's share price increase within ten days; by contrast, a diversity complaint going public will slash the share price within 24 hours.[126-127]

Having a good reputation on diversity also helps to minimize legal exposure and risk. Regardless of the outcome, once a case is filed, the legal fees are often incredibly expensive (approx. $55,000 per case). This goes hand in hand with negative publicity, a damage payment that could reach millions of dollars, the risk of losing contracts with critical clients[128] and the loss of trust among customers. In Asia, where white supremacy leads to "reverse discrimination,"[129] organizations were sued by employees for favoring white men over local Asians during downsizing.[130] That is why the proactive and effective management of diversity can prevent costly and embarrassing litigation.

The benefits of diversity are manifold:
- *a boost in creativity, productivity and reduction of group-think*
- *increased financial gain*
- *improved customer satisfaction*
- *access to new markets*
- *winning the "War for Talent"*
- *showcasing of positive publicity and good reputation*
- *reduction in number of legal cases*

ACTIVITY

Conduct a quick research to find out why the organizations were confronted with costly lawsuits:

1. Coca Cola in 1999 with a record of $192.5 million settlement
2. Sumitomo Electric in 2004 with 10 million yen ($94,000) in compensation.
3. Eddie Jordan, the district attorney of New Orleans in 2007, with a $3.7 million lawsuit and a resignation

7.3   The challenges of diversity

Despite the arguments, the data supporting the positive effects of diversity is not as clear and consistent as one might believe. For a number of reasons, diversity can also become a major source of conflict, and the consequence of poor diversity management can be harmful.

7.3.1   Diversity and Conflict

Diversity is primarily challenged by our biological tendency to prefer similar attributes,[131] such as the "similar to me" bias in hiring.[132] It also creates the perception of easiness and comfort when we work with think-alike look-alike people. By contrast, diversity and differences *initially* activate our threat-detective system amygdala. According to neuroscience, differences can overwhelm the cerebral cortex – part the brain that mediates cognitive logical processing – and hence, prevent us from a sophisticated exploration of the environment.[133]

Diversity has been a factor in organizational conflicts for various reasons: the feeling that someone is chosen not on the basis of merit, or the mismatch between values and practices. Fear, distrust, prejudices and discrimination can arise as different ways of working conflict with one another, or if members of the dominant culture see newcomers as a threat. However, while the bad news is that "differences can increase conflict," the good news is that "there is not as much conflict as we may think."

In one study, researchers found that when reading exactly *the same* team discussion transcript, observers perceived *more* conflict when teams were described as racially diverse rather than racially homogeneous. Not only do we tend to *assume* that diverse teams have more problems, we are also less likely to provide them with financial support[134] due to our overblown fear of potential failure. This unconscious bias for similarity can negatively impact recruitment, team management and team evaluation.

Diversity teams may go through stages of the Developmental Model of Intercultural Sensitivity (DMIS – as discussed in the previous chapter) and all the challenges that come with each step of "denial," "defense," and "minimization" before team members can "accept" the differences, "adapt" to one another and see the "integrated" benefit of a heterogeneous make-up. If an inclusive and safe environment is absent, people do not feel able to voice their opinions. The "defense" mode can be triggered especially when team members do not bring different ideas but different values to the table; there is a psychological tendency to compare and *judge* those values from their own ethnocentric perspectives. Fear, distrust, prejudices and discrimination can arise when different ways of working clash, or if members of the dominant culture see newcomers as a threat.

In dealing with diversity, people often seek to gloss over the differences and see harmony as the condition to move forward as a team. Interestingly, the "minimization" stage may happen much earlier, even when a diverse team is being formed. However, this intuitive reaction is counterproductive. The bottom line on diversity is that differences should be *highlighted* so that teams can benefit from diverse viewpoints. People are more productive when each member is explicitly assigned a distinct role,[135] when their unique identities are intentionally celebrated[136] and when the message endorsing multiculturalism is made clear.[137]

It can be disheartening and confusing when efforts invested in diversity do not result in expected benefits, or worse, lead to corrosive conflicts. In fact, as diversity increases, the likelihood of problems also increases together with the potential gain. However, when an organization becomes truly diverse, the concepts of "minority," "underrepresented" or "marginalized group" slowly disappear together with most of the related problems. This is when an organization can benefit immensely from diversity. Hence, despite the rising number of issues associated with a diverse workforce, in order to reap the rewards, an organization should not back down, but move forward in making itself even more diverse, to the point that it becomes a truly multicultural organization.

ACTIVITY

In the second layer of the Inverted Pyramid Model, cultures can be analyzed at four levels: global, national, organizational and group. Conduct research and discuss the following questions:

1. How strongly does national culture influence an organizational culture?
2. How strongly does group culture influence an organizational culture?
3. How easy or difficult is it to change an organizational culture?
4. Which set of values will be more likely to enhance the likelihood of success-ful diversity management (i.e. the degree of hierarchy acceptance/ group attachment/ masculinity or femininity/ uncertainty avoidance/ time orienta-tion)?

7.3.2   Diversity without Inclusion

Poor diversity management can lead to the perception that benefits received by underrepresented people come at the cost of the others. In the graphic, this means that the boxes on which the tall person stood should not be removed and given to the shorter person, technically *taking away the resource* and *reducing her/his status* and potentially causing resentment. In fact, this is backed up by research. In a study where half of the job seekers were informed about the company's diversity policies and the other half not, white candidates in the informed group expressed concerns about being treated unfairly. In comparison with those who were not informed about the company's pro-diversity policies, they also made a poorer impression during the interview and their cardiovascular responses indicated they endured more stress.[138] This suggests that diversity messages can be very sensitive for high-status individuals because they trigger identity threats and resentment.

Diversity without inclusion is worse than useless. Organizations should find ways to make all employees feel included and engaged, unless they want to face the burden of "reverse discrimination," polarization in the work place, reduced morale and bitterness among those who perceive themselves as being excluded or even victims of the policies. PR "window dressing" diversity programs will not bring in the expected benefit and can be counterproductive for workplace morale. That is to say, effective diversity management goes hand in hand with *significant changes* in the organizational philosophy and vision with regard to the role of diversity.

This is the ultimate test of an organization's commitment. It requires the (re)construction of a comprehensive framework for leadership and management, one that can systematically bring down the deep-seated institutional barriers and drive the changes from inside.

In the graphic, the existence of the fence creates categories such as "the marginalized" and "the privileged." It represents the inherent discrimination that is deeply embedded in the institutional structure and the mindset of the people, such as subconscious bias, subtle and micro prejudices, or privileges that have long been taken for granted. Giving support (the boxes) is not the answer; rather, *dismantling the fence*, which is the root of the problem, is the ultimate solution. When the fence is down, the boundary that defines dominant and marginalized groups is also dismantled. Being tall is valued as much as being short, since "tall" and "short" are no longer limitations, but uniqueness that can contribute to the organization. Each individual can stand on his own, supporting costs are no longer needed, and the view as well as the fun (read benefits) are much greater. In other words, true diversity and inclusion effort is about identifying the root causes instead of fixing the symptoms; changing the structure and mindset instead of fixing the people.

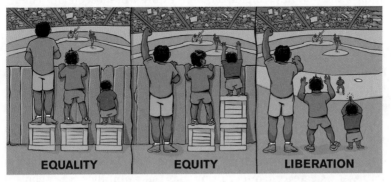

"Equality – Equity – and Liberation"/ CENTER FOR STORY-BASED STRATEGY [139]

- *The challenges of a diverse workforce include: potential conflicts, distrust, prejudices, and misunderstanding, experienced by both dominant and co-cultures within an organization.*
- *Organizations should not back down, but push forward the level of diversity and employ effective strategies. Optimal reward comes from a truly multicultural strategy.*

7.4   Strategies for diversity

Diversity is a double-edged sword that can unlock tremendous potential but can also have consequences. The original famous phrase of Gestalt psychologist Kurt Koffka "The whole is *other* than the sum of the parts" is often incorrectly translated as "The whole is *greater* than the sum of its parts." Differences do not automatically bring benefits. For this reason, employing effective strategies is essential in making diversity work. In this section, we will discuss the pros and cons of some of the most frequently applied practices in diversity management.

7.4.1   Diversity Enlargement

The assumption of this strategy is that by changing the demographic composition of the workforce, organizational culture will subsequently change. The mere presence of new hires from diverse backgrounds will slowly but surely exert an impact on the working mentality and environment, without further management intervention.

7.4.1.1   *Affirmative Action*
The main criticism of affirmative action has been built around the idea that it contradicts the premise of "all people are equal under the laws," which makes affirmation action technically *reverse discrimination*. It can also undermine meritocracy by using demographic categories instead of ability. This categorical recruiting may put not-fully-ready people in positions and unwittingly perpetuate the stereotypes that they are *by nature* not qualified for the job: "We hired two foreign-born and they both lag far behind. Typical!" In sum, affirmative action should only be at the *initial stage* of diversity management with the purpose to create a level playing field.

7.4.1.2   *Fault Lines*

The enlargement approach risks fault lines,[140-141] a situation in which sub-groups exist with little or no common ground. For example, figure 7.1 shows that there is a strong fault line (age, race, gender) in the first group, while in the second group, the fault line is weaker since members can relate more to one another. The art of group composition is then to add or mix certain categories as bridging factors to bring divided subgroups together.

Millennial Arab female	GenX Asian male
Millennial Arab female	GenX Asian male
Millennial Arab female	GenX Asian male

GenX Arab female	GenX Asian female
Millennial Arab female	GenX Asian male
Millennial Arab female	GenX Asian male

Figure 7.1. Potential fault lines in diversity enlargement

7.4.1.3   *Surface Diversity*

However, the major issue of diversity management through increasing demographic variety is that simply putting people of different backgrounds together can only trigger innovation if there is a thoughtful structure and comprehensive system to support it in the long run. In his classic book *Building a House for Diversity,* Roosevelt Thomas Jr used the fable about a giraffe and an elephant to illustrate strategies in diversity management. The giraffe had a wonderful shop and wanted to invite the elephant to work with her. But the door was too small, and as the elephants walked around, things started to crack and collapse. Very soon they both understood that the shop had been built specifically for the giraffe, and the elephant would not be able to work there unless there were *major changes in the structure* of the shop.

The lesson is that simply raising the number of multicultural talents alone runs the risk of resembling the giraffe's workshop after inviting the elephant to come in. New hires can't fit in and may bear the brunt of any disorder and system failures. Surface diversity or any catch-all strategies that treat diversity as a checkbox can damage organizational structure and lead to decreased productivity. This is also the challenge of diversity without inclusion that we mentioned in the previous section.

7.4.2   Diversity Training

Diversity training aims at sensitizing employees to subconscious bias, stereotypes and value conflicts. It is often seen as the cornerstone of diversity initiatives.[142] However, several forms of training may have mixed results. Here, we will discuss the forms of training that have been debated in terms of their effectiveness.

7.4.2.1   Mandatory Training to Avoid Legal Actions

By nature, this goal is worthy, but the method used in diversity training of this kind strongly focuses on a *preventive* approach by listing "what not to do" and "what not to say." This is to avoid the situation that members of minority or underprivileged groups are offended and sue the organization. Preventive training of this sort can instill a reactive atmosphere where employees are trained to constantly keep their guard up. Ironically, this situation actually triggers them to see co-workers as a potential threat, which breeds both resentment and ridicule. Further, a "Do's and Don'ts" method can give people a *false sense of understanding and confidence*, since it only scratches the surface and can't possibly cover the immense dynamic of reality.

Far from reaping reward, mandatory training that emphasizes the threat of lawsuits actually has a negative effect.[143] To reassert their autonomy, force-feeding training participants may psychologically challenge the whole system by doing exactly the opposite, hence perpetuating the bias and stereotypes rather than confronting them. Mandatory training triggers extrinsic motivation, i.e. the reason to have training comes from outside (e.g. to avoid legal cases). Since it is not intrinsic (e.g. I truly want it myself), mandatory training may actually elicit rebellion on the part of managers.[144]

By contrast, voluntary training is more promising. When reading a brochure that encouraged people to *make a choice* against prejudice, white subjects tended to agree and reduce their bias. But when they read a brochure that *urged them to comply* with social norms of non-prejudices, they felt pressure to agree and actually strengthened their bias.[145] This study helps us to understand why strategies aimed at prejudice reduction can be counterproductive, despite billions of dollars spent annually on diversity programs.[146]

7.4.2.2   Categorical Training

Diversity training is often conducted on the basis of group cultures such as gender, age, race, religious background or thinking styles. However, if conducted solely based on this level, diversity training can reinforce borderlines and solidify the group bias. We should be reminded here that the top layer of the Inverted Pyramid model is *individuals,* and each person can have a very complex identity. In 1989, Kimberlé Crenshaw coined the term "intersectionality" and it brilliantly reflects the relationship between identity and power, or the lack thereof. A gay person has to deal with homophobia, a person of color has to deal with racism and a woman has to deal with sexism. But a non-white lesbian has to deal with all these forms of discrimination *at the same time*. Adding ableism, ageism or Islamophobia to that list, one can start to imagine why categories unfairly simplify the complexity of a human being: "Being a person with an intersectional identity is like standing in the middle of the road being hit by cars from many sides."[147]

Having multiple subordinate identities, none of which belong to the dominant culture with decision making power, will also render people "invisible" because they do not fit the common prototypes.[148] Think LGBTQ, then the common prototype is white gay men; think racial minority, then the common prototype is black people. The consequence is that a lesbian Middle Eastern woman is less likely to fit any prototype and so experiences what is called *intersectional invisibility*.

It is hard to overemphasize that at the end of each international exchange, we do not work with a culture, but individuals. For example, when we send an email to our colleague in Iran, we do not work with "the Iranian," but a unique person. Let's say her name is Shirin, and she has many different identities: as an Iranian, a millennial, an entrepreneur, a practicing Zoroastrian (an ancient Persian religion), a trans woman who is waiting for state-sponsored gender reassignment surgery,[149] and a social activist who greatly values low hierarchy acceptance and femininity. Since we cannot compartmentalize these components, it makes much more sense to perceive her as a unique person. Seeing her without labels will help us put aside stereotypical traits and assumptions about what an "Iranian" or a "woman" aspires to, and think instead about what Shirin herself aspires to, since she is so much more complex than the these two labels. To quote the CEO of a consultancy: "If you want diversity, think about an individual, then another, then another."[150]

7.4.3   Affinity Network

Affinity or employee resource networks are voluntary groups organized around shared interests within or across organizations. They help recruitment and retention,[151] provide built-in comfort zones for diverse new hires, create a learning environment for employees to develop and seek advice,[152] offer insights for management,[153] help companies to explore new markets,[154] and empowering employees.[155] Affinity networks perform best when they support one another in the promotion of diversity and do not compete for funds, managerial priorities, or create social tensions among groups.

Participating in women's networks is associated with higher levels of career-related social support, a greater sense of well-being, and more positive attitudes towards the organizations for whom the woman works[156]/ "New Delhi Dell Women's entrepreneur network, India," DELL'S OFFICIAL FLICKR PAGE.[157]

However, organizations with affinity networks are still in the minority, and those with such networks may not realize their full potential and optimize their capacity. In many cases, immature networks serve as little more than safe gathering places to exchange experiences among like-minded people, and the network itself has limited influence on the decision making process.

7.4.4   Managerial Discretion Control

To prevent managers from bias and discrimination, a range of tools have been designed to preempt lawsuits, such as hiring tests and performance ratings based on merit, or grievance systems where employees can submit discrimination complaints. While these tools certainly have impact, there are also setbacks.

Hiring tests assess the skills of job candidates and makes sure that only the top candidates will be hired, and performance ratings are quantitative scorecards that show objective measures of each employee's achievement in terms of production, efficiency, leadership and teamwork.[158] However, both methods do not stop managers (who are still mainly white men) from interpreting the scores subjectively,[159] cherry picking who fits best in their own notion of talent,[160] or circumventing the system to justify their unjust decisions[161] due to subconscious bias.

A grievance procedure is a channel where employees can challenge their managers and submit their complaints of discrimination. While this tool is effective in combating discrimination, its procedures run the risk of making managers feel they are the *source of the problems*, being policed and put in the spotlight,[162] which consequently triggers them to rebel and resist the system. For example, of all the 89,385 complaints submitted to the US Equal Employment Opportunity Commission in 2015, 44.4 per cent included a charge of retaliation,[163] which suggests that managers punish those who complain. Retaliation then restrains employees from stepping up, giving the management the illusion that their organization has no more problems.

7.4.5   Engaging the Managers

The previous strategy of managerial discretion control suggests that it is crucial to give ownership to managers and let them become the advocates of diversity instead of being policed by different tools. If managers themselves do not believe in diversity and are being held accountable for what they do, other strategies can only have limited impact. A statistical analysis of 829 firms in the US over 31 years shows us that the three strategies that have brought the most significant impact on diversity are "diversity manager," "mentor program" and "task force."[164]

7.4.5.1   *Diversity Managers*
A Chief Diversity Officer (CDO) is not hired to maintain the status quo, so the function can be best defined as "change management specialist."[165] An invaluable lesson from the world's ten most diverse companies in 2015 is that CEOs should also act as CDO by heading the executive diversity council themselves.[166]

Some critical responsibilities of a CDO include: conduct diversity audits to identify strengths, challenges, and progress; identify quantifiable and measurable diversity Key Performance Indicators (e.g. equalize the pay among different ethnicities within two years); nurture and cultivate diversity as an institutional resource; and demonstrate the Return On Investment of diversity by linking diversity data to business outcomes (e.g. gender equality in payment has attracted an increase of female talents as new hires).

Accounting Inclusion Maturity Model is a tool used by accounting firms to assess their diversity policies and practices.[167] Here are some examples of the survey items:

Workplace
1. In our organization, executive leaders' annual bonus and/or pay are tied to the performance of diversity and inclusion indicators.
2. In our organization, diversity and inclusion measures are a part of the organization's overall scorecard, linked to the organizational strategy.
3. In our organization, leaders receive coaching in diversity and inclusion at least once a year, and provide coaching to others.

Workforce
1. Hiring managers are not permitted to recruit or interview until they have been educated in understanding cultural differences, biases, and their impact in hiring.
2. Our organization tracks the advancement and promotion of our employees, at a minimum by: gender, generation, ethnicity/national origin, and/or race/color.
3. In our organization, attempts are made to accommodate religious practices and to schedule around religious and cultural holidays even if they are not the holidays of the majority.
4. In our organization, leaders are not permitted to execute performance evaluations until they have been educated in understanding cultural differences, biases, and their impact on evaluating performance.

Marketplace
1. Advertising and marketing are tested to ensure they are not offensive or perpetuate negative stereotypes towards any religious group or demographic.
2. Our professionals/staff/associates/client service professionals receive training that ensures they know how to respectfully address specific customer needs and interest.

Community and Supplier
1. Our organization provides financial resources as well as employee time and labor in a variety of community projects that impact underserved populations.

7.4.5.2 *Mentoring Program*

Diversity training is often a great starting point for raising awareness, but that is not enough to change the behavior. Where training finishes, mentoring programs should begin, since they take the theories and awareness from the classroom into the reality, giving mentors the opportunities to walk the talk and exercise transformational leadership. For mentees, this exchange creates a safe environment for honest dialogues, helping them develop skills to deal with issues raised in the training, providing them the access to the social connections that the privileged can develop so easily but not the marginalized. This type of professional relationship touches an individual level, dealing with real issues that directly affect a specific person, holding them accountable for the outcomes, and paving the way for internal change within the organization.

So what does a mentoring program look like? Here is an example: The French food service and facility management Sodexo [168] matches mentors and mentees based on their need and abilities. After a full day session, the pairs draw plans on how to achieve their goals and meet monthly for one year. This is supported by a social networking website where mentees and mentors have a profile with clear statements of needs and expertise.

7.4.5.3 *Diversity Task Force*

A task force is an effective way to engage managers and maintain accountability, since they are formed by *existing* managers and employees. Task forces investigate the problems, set goals, come up with solutions, monitor the progress and take responsibility for the outcomes in their own units. Collecting data – a crucial process in managing diversity and combating stereotypes – is also more likely to be prioritized with a task force. A good example comes from Google. When they noticed that women engineers were nominating themselves for promotion at lower rates than men, a senior manager sent an email describing the data and nudging women to apply. Immediately, the application rate for women soared and the rate of women who received promotions rose higher than that for male engineers. This phenomenon kept occurring until, at one point, he forgot to send the email and the number of female applicants dropped sharply.[169] In sum, it is a very powerful case of how effective diversity policies can be when leaders are directly engaged and held accountable for the outcomes.

The most frequently applied practices in diversity management, such as diversity enlargement, diversity training, managerial discretion control and affinity networks have shown mixed results. They are best to combine with direct engagement from managers.

ACTIVITY

Conduct research and discuss the following affirmative actions. What else should be done to ensure that diversity would effectively work in the long term?

1. Brazil's affirmative action requires companies with more than 100 employees to fill two to five per cent of their positions with either social security beneficiaries or skilled disabled employees.

2. After a genocide that saw the deaths of more than 800,000 people, since 1994, Rwanda has worked hard to create a peaceful state, and one strategy was to establish a quota for women in the government. The 2003 Rwanda constitution provides for a minimum 30 per cent quota for women in all decision-making organs. Rwandan has now become the only country where there are more female MPs than male (64 per cent).

Summary

1. Diversity within an organization can be understood in terms of gender, ethnicity, sexual orientation, religious background, disability, etc. Other deeper dimensions of diversity are thinking style, educational background or professional background.

2. A diverse workforce holds tremendous potential for competitive advantage: financial gain, better customer service, winning new markets, retaining talents, increased corporate social responsibility and positive public reputation.

3. At a deeper level, diversity of thought is what best illustrates the advantages of diversity. It boosts creativity and innovation that come from diverse perspectives, regardless of any categories (e.g. race or gender).

4. The challenges of a diverse workforce include: potential conflicts, fear and distrust, prejudices, discrimination and misunderstanding. These challenges can be experienced by both dominant and co-cultures (or minority) within an organization.

5. When confronted with these challenges, in order to benefit from diversity, organizations should not back down but push forward the level of diversity and employ effective strategies to deal with it. An organization will reap optimal reward from diversity when it is truly multicultural.

6. Differences do not automatically bring benefits. Diversity only works if there are effective strategies.

7. The most frequently applied practices in diversity management such as diversity enlargement, diversity training, managerial discretion control and affinity networks have shown mixed results. These strategies work better if there is direct engagement from managers (mentoring program, appointing diversity manager, or task force) who will be held accountable for the outcomes.

8. The chapter utilizes two metaphors: the giraffe's cooperation with the elephant and the people behind a fence. Both metaphors imply that a truly diverse and multicultural organization requires much more than increasing the number of people from non-dominant culture. It is about a critical change in organizational philosophy and the willingness to build a new system that values differences so everyone can eventually maximize reward from a culture of inclusion.

To the readers

The author has set up a Facebook page to communicate with readers about the content of the book. This is a place for fruitful and interactive discussions, where answers to case studies will be analyzed, where lecturers and students can share their experience in carrying out teaching and learning activities. Through this page, the author would like to learn more about examples and cases from non-mainstream cultures. Together, we can shine the spotlight on under-representative communities, reducing the US-centric and Euro-centric view of cultural discourse. Your contribution will be credited in the next edition of the book.

www.facebook.com/culturemove

CultureMove@CultureMove.com

The name Culture Move derives from a taming technique used by elephant trainers in Southeast Asia. Young elephants are loosely chained to a pillar and can only walk within the circle created by the length of the rope. As they get used to the habit, even when untied, they will tend to stay within the invisible border.

Similarly, each of us is metaphorically tied to the first culture seen at birth. But we are capable of unchaining the shackles, crossing the line, and adapting to the new environment. Only by moving can we realize that we are tied.

Legs that move feel the chain.

7 takeaways from this book

- Instead of waiting for a change in genes so humans can evolve wings to fly (which may never happen), as our survival strategy, culture allows us to pull ideas together and build airplanes.
- Think global – Plan local – Act individual.
- Whenever we are surprised, it probably means we have just stereotyped.
- People will forget what you say, but they will never forget how you make them feel.
- To be competent in intercultural communication is to develop a multicultural mind.
- "Life isn't about finding yourself. Life is about creating yourself." – Bernard Shaw.
- "The whole is *different* from the sum of its parts" – Kurt Koffka. Diversity does not necessarily mean benefit. Only good diversity management can turn this into: "The whole is *greater* than the sum of its parts."

Up and coming book from the same author

Cross-Cultural Management (*International Business Series, 2018*) *is a comprehensive read for both international business students and scholars who are interested in the field. The first part of the book gives a critical introduction on cross-cultural communication and business etiquette. The second part is dedicated to management topics such as Corporate Culture, Diversity and Inclusion, Cross-Cultural Leadership Competence, Culturally Responsive Marketing, Negotiation without Borders, and Cultural Finance. This wide range of management topics is meant to provide readers with a big picture of the impact of culture in international business, covering critical aspects that are often neglected in cross-cultural management textbooks.*

Notes

Preface

1. "Geert Hofstede," *The Economist,* accessed November 28, 2008, http://www.economist.com/node/12669307.
2. Geert Hofstede, Gert-Jan Hofstede and Michael Minkov, *Cultures and Organizations: Software of the Mind* (New York: McGraw-Hill, 2005), back cover.

Chapter 1

1. Samuel Levy et al., "The Diploid Genome Sequence of an Individual Human," *PLOS Biology* 5, no. 10 (2007), accessed March 28, 2017, doi: 10.1371/journal.pbio.0050254.
2. David Derbyshire, "Borders Folk May Be Descended from Africans," *The Telegraph,* June 11, 2004, accessed March 28, 2017, http://www.telegraph.co.uk/news/uknews/1464209/Borders-folk-may-be-descended-from-Africans.html.
3. Douglas Harper, "Genus," *Online Etymology Dictionary*, accessed March 28, 2017, http://www.etymonline.com/index.php?allowed_in_frame=0&search=genus.
4. "Declaration on Race and Racial Prejudice, 1978," *UNESCO*, November 27, 1978, accessed March 28, 2017, http://www.unesco.org/webworld/peace_library/UNESCO/HRIGHTS/107-116.HTM.
5. Peter J. Richerson and Robert Boyd, *Not by Genes Alone. How Culture Transformed Human Evolution* (Chicago: University of Chicago Press, 2005).
6. William C. McGrew, review of *Not by Genes Alone: How Culture Transformed Human Evolution,* ed. Peter J. Richerson and Robert Boyd, *Journal of Human Evolution* 50 (2006), 237.
7. Linda Fuoco and Chico Pittsburgh, "Wolf Dogs Killed Owner, Autopsy Determines," *Post-Gazette,* July 19, 2006, accessed March 28, 2017, http://www.post-gazette.com/westmoreland/2006/07/19/Wolf-dogs-killed-owner-autopsy-determines/stories/200607190197#ixzz0jmzOZkCX.
8. Douglas K. Candland, *Feral Children and Clever Animals: Reflections on Human Nature* (Oxford: Oxford University Press, 1995).
9. Peter Richerson, "Custom Built," *Nature* 482 (February 16, 2012): 304-305, accessed March 28, 2017, doi: 10.1038/482304a.
10. Mark Pagel, *Wired for Culture: Origins of the Human Social Mind* (New York: W.W. Norton & Company, 2012).
11. Ibid.

12.   Stuart Oscamp, "Multiple Paths to Reducing Prejudice and Discrimination," in *Reducing Prejudice and Discrimination*, ed. Stuart Oscamp (Mahwah: Lawrence Erlbaum, 2000), 9.

13.   Richard Stockton, "The World's Extreme Climates And The People Who Live There," *All that is interesting*, December 12, 2014, accessed March 28, 2017, http://all-that-is-interesting.com/extreme-climates.

14.   Clarence Glacken, *Traces on the Rhodian Shore: Nature and Culture in Western Thought from Ancient Times to the End of the Eighteenth Century* (Berkeley: Berkeley University Press, 1967).

15.   Charles Darwin, *The Origin of Species* (New York: New American Library, 1958).

16.   Ellen Churchill Semple, *Influences of Geographic Environment: On the Basis of Ratzel's System of Anthropo-Geography* (New York: H. Holt & Co, 1911).

17.   Thomas Jefferson, "Notes on the State of Virginia," in *Call and Response: Key Debates in African American Studies*, ed. Henry Louis Gates and Jennifer Burton (New York: W.W. Norton & Company), 17–24.

18.   "Why We Are Antisemites – Text of Adolf Hitler's 1920 speech at the Hofbräuhaus," Carolyn Yeager, January 29, 2013, accessed march 29, 2017, https://carolynyeager.net/why-we-are-antisemites-text-adolf-hitlers-1920-speech-hofbr%C3%A4uhaus.

19.   Jared Diamond, *Guns, Germs and Steel* (New York: W.W. Norton, 1997).

20.   Workneh Ayalew, "Genetic and Cultural Significance of Indigenous Pigs in Papua New Guinea and Their Phenotypic Characteristics," *Animal Genetic Resources* 48 (2011): 37-46, accessed March 28, 2017, doi: 10.1017/s2078633611000026.

21.   Don Kulick, *Language Shift and Cultural Reproduction: Socialization, Self, and Syncretism in a Papua New Guinean Village* (Cambridge: Cambridge University Press, 1992), 2.

22.   Photo by DVL2. "Naro Bushmen Drinking Water from the Bi Bulb Plant," *Wikipedia,* August 20, 2008, accessed March 29, 2017, https://commons.wiki-media.org/w/index.php?curid=4591704 Link to License https://creativecom-mons.org/licenses/by-sa/3.0/legalcode.

23.   Juliette Jowit, "Humans Driving Extinction Faster than Species Can Evolve, say Experts," *The Guardian*, March 7, 2010, accessed March 28, 2017, https://www.theguardian.com/environment/2010/mar/07/extinction-species-evolve

24.   Peter J. Richerson, Monique Borgerhoff Mulder and Bryan J. Vila, *Principles of Human Ecology* (London: Pearson Custom Publishing, 1996).

25.   Oskar H.K. Spate, "How Determined is Possibilism?" *Geographical Studies* 4, no.1 (1957): 2-12.

26.   Julian H. Steward, *Theory of Culture Change: The Methodology of Multilinear Evolution* (Urbana: University of Illinois Press, 1955).

27.   Peter J. Richerson, Monique Borgerhof Mulder, and Bryan J. Vila, *Principle of Human Ecology* (Pearson Custom Publishing, 1996), accessed Macrh 29, 2017 from http://www.des.ucdavis.edu/faculty/Richerson/BooksOnline/101text.htm

28.   R.C. Sturgis, *The Mammals That Moved Mankind: A History of Beasts of Burden* (Bloomington: Author House, 2015).

29. Mark Pagel, "Mark Pagel: How Language Transformed Humanity," TED Talks, filmed July 2011, accessed March 28, 2017, https://www.ted.com/talks/mark_pagel_how_language_transformed_humanity.

30. Mark Pagel, *Wired for Culture: Origins of the Human Social Mind* (New York: W.W. Norton & Company, 2012).

31. Naoki Masuda and Feng Fu, "Evolutionary Models of In-group Favouritism," *F1000Prime* 7, no. 27 (2015), accessed March 28, 2017, doi: 10.12703/P7-27.

32. Robert Boyd and Peter J. Richerson, *Culture and the Evolutionary Process* (Chicago: University of Chicago Press, 1985).

33. Avshalom Caspi et al., "Influence of Life Stress on Depression: Moderation by a Polymorphism in the 5-HTT Gene," *Science* 301, no. 5631 (2003): 386-389, accessed March 27, 2017, doi: 10.1126/science.1083968.

34. Joan Y. Chiao and Katherine D. Blizinsky, "Culture-Gene Coevolution of Individualism Collectivism and the Serotonin Transporter Gene," *Proceedings of the Royal Society B: Biological Sciences* 277, no. 1681 (2009): 529-537, doi: 10.1098/rspb.2009.1650.

35. *Happy Planet Index, accessed March 29, 2017, http://happyplanetindex.org*

36. Maureen Meyer, "Mexico's Police: Many Reforms, Little Progress," *WOLA*, May 2014, accessed March 28, 2017, https://www.wola.org/sites/default/files/Mexicos%20Police.pdf.

37. Gene E. Robinson, "Brains Work via Their Genes Just as Much as Their Neurons," *The Conversation*, October 14, 2015, accessed March 28, 2017, https://theconversation.com/brains-work-via-their-genes-just-as-much-as-their-neurons-47522.

38. Yiyuan Tang et al., "Arithmetic Processing in the Brain Shaped by Cultures," *Proceedings of the National Academy of Sciences* 103, no. 26 (2006): 10775-10780, accessed March 28, 2017, doi: 10.1073/pnas.0604416103.

39. Li Hai Tan et al., "Reading Depends on Writing, in Chinese," *PNAS* 102, no. 24 (2005): 8781-8785, accessed March 28, 2017, doi: 10.1073/pnas.0503523102.

40. Shihui Han et al., "Neural Substrates of Self-referential Processing in Chinese Buddhists," *Social Cognitive and Affective Neuroscience* 5, nos 2/3 (2010): 332-339, accessed March 28, 2017, doi: 10.1093/scan/nsp027.

41. Angela H. Gutchess et al., "Cross-Cultural Differences in the Neural Correlates of Picture Encoding," *Cognitive, Affective, and Behavioral Neuroscience* 6, no.2 (2006): 102-109.

42. Keiko Iishii, Yuki Kobayashi and Shinobu Kitayama, "Interdependence Modulates the Brain Response to Word-Voice Incongruity," *Social Cognitive and Affective Neuroscience* 5, nos 2/3 (2009), accessed March 28, 2017, doi: 10.1093/scan/nsp044.

43. Jonathan B. Freeman et al., "Culture Shapes a Mesolimbic Response to Signals of Dominance and Subordination that Associates with Behaviour," *NeuroImage* 47, no. 1 (2009): 353-359, accessed March 28, 2017, doi:10.1016/j.neuroimage.2009.04.038.

44. Jie Sui and Shihui Han, "Self-Construal Priming Modulates Neural Substrates of Self-Awareness," *Psychological Science* 18, no. 10 (2007): 861-866, accessed March 28, 2017, doi: 10.1111/j.1467-9280.2007.01992.x.

45. Vani A. Mathur et al., "Neural Basis of Extraordinary Empathy and Altruistic Motivation," *NeuroImage* 51, no.4 (2010): 1468-1475, accessed March 28, 2017, doi:10.1016/j.neuroimage.2010.03.025.

46. Jonathan B. Freeman et al., "Culture Shapes a Mesolimbic Response to Signals of Dominance and Subordination that Associates with Behaviour," *NeuroImage* 47, no.1 (2009): 353-359, accessed March 28, 2017, doi:10.1016/j.neuroimage.2009.04.038.

47. Photo by BruceBlaus, "Anatomy of a Multipolar Neuron," *Wikipedia,* September 2013, accessed March 29, 2017, https://en.wikipedia.org/wiki/Neuron#/media/File:Blausen_0657_MultipolarNeuron.png License link: https://creativecommons.org/licenses/by/3.0/legalcode.

48. Frederic Gougoux et al., "Voice Perception in Blind Persons: A functional Magnetic Resonance Imaging Study," *Neuropsychologia* 47, no.13 (2009): 2967-2974, accessed March 28, 2017, doi: 10.1016/j.neuropsychologia.2009.06.027.

49. Eleanor A. Maguire et al., "Navigation-Related Structural Change in the Hippocampi of Taxi Drivers," *Proc Natl Acad Sci USA* 97, no. 8 (2000): 4398-4403, accessed March 28, 2017, doi: 10.1073/pnas.070039597.

50. Bogdan Draganski et al., "Neuroplasticity: Changes in Grey Matter Induced by Training," *Nature* 427 (2004): 311-312, accessed March 28, 2017, doi: 10.1038/427311a.

51. Yi-Yuan Tang et al., "Mechanisms of White Matter Changes Induced by Meditation," *Proceedings of the National Academy of Sciences* 109, no. 26 (2012): 10570-10574, accessed March 28, 2017, doi: 10.1073/pnas.1207817109.

52. Beatriz Calvo-Merino et al., "Action Observation and Acquired Motor Skills: An fMRI Study with Expert Dancers," *Cereb Cortex* 15, no. 8 (2004): 1243-1249, accessed March 28, 2017, doi: 10.1093/cercor/bhi007.

53. Daphna Oyserman et al., "Accessible Cultural Mind-set Modulates Default Mode Activity: Evidence for the Culturally Situated Brain," *Social Neuroscience* 8, no. 3 (2014): 203-216, accessed March 28, 2017, doi: 10.1080/17470919.2013.775966.

54. Ying-yi Hong et al., "Multicultural Minds: A Dynamic Constructivist Approach to Culture and Cognition," *American Psychologist* 55, no. 7 (2010): 709-720, accessed March 28, 2017, doi: 10.1037//0003-066X.55.7.709.

55. Kaiping P. Peng and Eric D. Knowles, "Culture, Education, and the Attribution of Physical Causality, Personality and Social Psychology," *Bulletin* 29, no. 10 (2002): 1272-1284, accessed March 28, 2017, doi: 10.1177/0146167203254601.

56. Joan Y. Chiao et al., "Dynamic Cultural Influences on Neural Representations of the Self," *Journal of Cognitive Neuroscience* 22, no. 1 (2010): 1-11, accessed March 28, 2017, doi:10.1162/jocn.2009.21192.

57. Arnaud D'Argembeau, "On the Role of the Ventromedial Prefrontal Cortex in Self-Processing: The Valuation Hypothesis," *Frontiers in Human Neuroscience* 7, no. 372 (2013), accessed March 28, 2017, doi: 10.3389/fnhum.2013.00372.

58. Pasi Väliaho, *Biopolitical Screens: Image, Power, and the Neoliberal Brain* (Boston: MIT Press, 2014), 84.

59. Tuija Takala and Tom Buller, "Neural Grafting: Implications for Personal
     Identity and Personality," *Trames* 15(65/60), no. 2 (2011): 168-178, accessed
     March 28, 2017, doi: 10.3176/tr.2011.2.05.

60. Madhura Ingalhalikar et al., "Sex Differences in the Structural Connectome
     of the Human Brain," *PNAS* 111, no. 2 (2014): 823-828, accessed March 28,
     2017, doi: 10.1073/pnas.1316909110.

61. Ruben C. Gur et al., "Age Group and Sex Differences in Performance on a
     Computerized Neurocognitive Battery in Children Age 8-21," *Neuropsychol-
     ogy* 26, no. 2 (2012): 251-265, accessed March 28, 2017, doi: 10.1037/a0026712.

62. Christiana M. Leonard et al., "Size Matters: Cerebral Volume Influences Sex
     Differences in Neuroanatomy," *Cereb. Cortex* 18, no. 12 (2008): 2920-2931, ac-
     cessed March 28, 2017, doi: 10.1093/cercor/bhn052.

63. Kiho Im et al., "Brain Size and Cortical Structure in the Adult Human Brain,"
     Cerebral Cortex 18, no. 9 (2008): 2181-2191, accessed March 28, 2017, doi:
     10.1093/cercor/bhm244.

64. Lise Eliot, *Pink Brain, Blue Brain: How Small Differences Grow Into Trouble-
     some Gaps – And What We Can Do About It* (New York: Mariner Books, 2010).

65. Cordelia Fine, *Delusions of Gender: How Our Minds, Society, and Neurosex-
     ism Create Difference* (New York: W.W. Norton & Company, 2011).

66. Daphna Joel et al., "Sex beyond the Genitalia: The Human Brain Mosaic,"
     PNAS 112, no. 50 (2015): 15468-15473, accessed March 28, 2017, doi: 10.1073/
     pnas.1509654112.

67. Charles Choi, "Strange but True: When Half a Brain Is Better than a Whole
     One," *Scientific American*, May 24, 2007, accessed March 28, 2017, https://
     www.scientificamerican.com/article/strange-but-true-when-half-brain-
     better-than-whole/.

68. Naveen Jain, "If Men are From Mars, Then Women are Too," *Inc.*, August 14,
     2012, accessed March 28, 2017, http://www.inc.com/naveen-jain/study-men-
     and-women-do-think-the-same.html.

69. Rebecca Jordan-Young and Raffaella I. Rumiati, "Hardwired for Sexism?
     Approaches to Sex/Gender in Neuroscience," *Neuroethics* 5, no. 3 (2012):
     305-315, accessed March 28, 2017, doi: 10.1007/s12152-011-9134-4.

70. Anelis Kaiser, "Re-conceptualizing 'Sex' and 'Gender' in the Human Brain,"
     Zeitschrift für Psychologie 220, no. 2 (2012): 130-136, accessed March 28, 2017,
     http://dx.doi.org/10.1027/2151-2604/a000104.

71. Cordelia Fine, "Is There Neurosexism in Functional Neuroimaging Investi-
     gations of Sex Differences?" *Neuroethics* 6, no. 2 (2013): 369-409, accessed
     March 28, 2017, doi: 10.1007/s12152-012-9169-1.

72. Cordelia Fine, "Explaining, or Sustaining, the Status Quo? The Potentially
     Self-Fulfilling Effects of 'Hardwired' Accounts of Sex Differences," *Neuroeth-
     ics* 5, no. 3 (2011): 285-294, accessed March 28, 2017, doi: 10.1007/s12152-011-
     9118-4.

73. Cordelia Fine et al., "Plasticity, Plasticity, Plasticity and the Rigid Problem
     of Sex," *Trends in Cognitive Sciences* 17, no. 11 (2013): 550-551, accessed March
     28, 2017, doi: 10.1016/j.tics.2013.08.010.

74. Michael. I. Posner, "Seeing the Mind," *Science* 262, no. 5134 (1993): 673-674.

75. Nalini Ambady, "The Mind in the World: Culture and the Brain," *Observer*, May/June 2011, accessed March 28, 2017, http://www.psychologicalscience. org/observer/the-mind-in-the-world-culture-and-the-brain#.WEjMYvl97IU.

76. Joan Y. Chiao et al., "Cultural Neuroscience: Understanding Human Diversity," in *Advances in Culture Psychology*, ed. Michele J. Gelfand, Chie-yue Chiu and Ying-yi Hong (Oxford: Oxford University Press), 1–77.

77. Dean Ornish et al., "Changes in Prostate Gene Expression in Men Undergoing an Intensive Nutrition and Lifestyle Intervention," *PNAS* 105, no. 24 (2008): 8369-8374, accessed March 28, 2017, doi: 10.1073/pnas.0803080105.

78. Salim Yusuf et al., "Effect of Potentially Modifiable Risk Factors Associated with Myocardial Infarction in 52 countries (the INTERHEART Study): Case-Control Study," *Lancet* 364, no. 9438 (2004): 937-952, accessed March 28, 2017, doi: 10.1016/S0140-6736(04)17018-9.

79. Elliot M. Tucker-Drob et al., "Emergence of a Gene × Socioeconomic Status Interaction on Infant Mental Ability between 10 Months and 2 Years," *SAGE Journals* 22, no. 1 (2010): 125-133, accessed March 28, 2017, doi: 10.1177/0956797610392926.

80. Dean Ornish et al., "Effect of Comprehensive Lifestyle Changes on Telomerase Activity and Telomere Length in Men with Biopsy-proven Low-risk Prostate Cancer: 5-year Follow-up of a Descriptive Pilot Study," *Lancet Oncol* 9, no. 11 (2008): 1048-1057, accessed March 28, 2017, doi: 10.1016/S1470-2045(08)70234-1.

81. Rustum Roy, "Integrative Medicine to Tackle the Problem of Chronic Diseases," *Journal of Ayurveda and Integrative Medicine* 1, no. 1 (2010): 118-121, accessed March 28, 2017, doi: 10.4103/0975-9476.59822.

82. Ann Swidler, "Culture in Action: Symbols and Strategies," *American Sociological Review* 51, no. 2 (1986): 273-286, accessed March 28, 2017, http://www. jstor.org/stable/2095521.

83. Richard Grunberger, *A social history of the Third Reich* (London: Penguin Books, 1971).

84. Daryl J. Bem, *Beliefs, Attitudes, and Human Affairs* (Belmont: Brooks/Cole, 1970).

85. Elliot Aronson, "The Return of the Repressed: Dissonance Theory Makes a Comeback," *Psychological Inquiry* 3, no. 4 (1992): 303-311, accessed March 28, 2017, doi: 10.1207/s15327965pli0304_1.

86. Nicolas Guéguen et al., "The Combined Effect of the Foot-in-the-door Technique and the 'But You Are Free' Technique: An Evaluation on the Selective Sorting of Household Wastes," *Ecopsychology* 2, no. 4 (2010): 231-237, accessed March 28, 2017, doi: 10.1089/eco.2009.0051.

87. Brad Power, "If You're Going to Change Your Culture, Do It quickly," *Harvard Business Review*, November 18, 2013, accessed March 28, 2017, https://hbr. org/2013/11/if-youre-going-to-change-your-culture-do-it-quickly.

88. Bill Gammage, *The Biggest Estate on Earth How Aborigines made Australia* (St. Leonards: Allen & Unwin, 2011).

89. John E. Kutzbacha et al., "Climate Model Tests of the Anthropogenic Influ-
     ence on Greenhouse-induced Climate Change: The Role of Early Human
     Agriculture, Industrialization, and Vegetation Feedbacks," *Quaternary
     Science Reviews* 27, nos 13/14 (2008): 1410-1425, accessed March 28, 2017, doi:
     10.1016/j.quascirev.2008.04.011.

90. Marshall McLuhan, *Understanding Media* (Berkeley: Gingko Press, 1964,
     2003), 6.

91. Ian F. Collard and Robert A. Foley, "Latitudinal Patterns and Environmental
     Determinants of Recent Human Cultural Diversity: Do Humans Follow
     Biogeographical Rules," *Evolutionary Ecology Research* 4 (2002): 371-383, ac-
     cessed March 28, 2017, http://citeseerx.ist.psu.edu/viewdoc/download?doi=
     10.1.1.451.9624&rep=rep1&type=pdf.

92. Aubrey Silberston, "Economies of Scale in Theory and Practice," *The
     Economic Journal* 82, no. 325 (1972): 369-391, accessed March 28, 2017, doi:
     10.2307/2229943.

93. Kathy A. Svitil, "Discover Dialogue: Evolutionary Biologist Mark Pagel,"
     Discover Magazine, May 01, 2005, accessed March 28, 2017, http://discover-
     magazine.com/2005/may/discover-dialogue.

94. Thomas Henry Huxley, "The Struggle for Existence in Human Society,"
     Huxley's Collected Essays Volume IX (1888), accessed March 28, 2017, http://
     alepho.clarku.edu/huxley/CE9/Str.html.

95. Saint Augustine of Hippo, *The Confessions of St. Augustine* (Greensboro:
     Empire Books, 2011).

96. Thomas Hobbes, "Of the Natural Condition of Mankind as Concerning
     Their Felicity and Misery," *Leviathan* (The University of Adelaide, 2016),
     accessed March 28, 2017, https://ebooks.adelaide.edu.au/h/hobbes/thomas/
     h68l/chapter13.html.

97. Konrad Lorenz, *On Aggression*, 1st ed. (San Diego: Harvest Books, 1974).

98. Oliver E. Williamson, *The Economic Institutions of Capitalism* (New York:
     Free Press, 1985), 47.

99. Judith. M. Burkart et al., "The Evolutionary Origin of Human Hyper-cooper-
     ation," *Nature Communications* 5, no. 4747 (2014), doi: 10.1038/ncomms5747.

100. Robert W. Sussman and Robert C. Cloninger, *Origins of Altruism and Coop-
     eration* (New York: Springer-Verlag, 2011).

101. Christopher Boehm, *Moral Origins: The Evolution of Virtue, Altruism, and
     Shame,* 1st ed. (New York: Basic Books; May 1, 2012).

102. Michael Tomasello, *Why We Cooperate* (Boston: The MIT Press, Boston
     Review Books, August 28, 2009).

103. Ernst Fehrl and Urs Fischbacherl, "The Nature of Human Altruism," *Nature* 425
     (October 23, 2003): 785-791, accessed March 29, 2017, doi: 10.1038/nature02043.

104. Samuel Bowles and Herbert Gintis, *A cooperative species: Human reciproc-
     ity and its evolution* (Princeton: Princeton University Press, 2011), accessed
     March 29, 2017, http://library.uniteddiversity.coop/Money_and_Economics/
     Cooperatives/A_Cooperative_Species-Human_Reciprocity_and_Its_Evolu-
     tion.pdf.

105.   "How the Human Species came to be Both Nasty and Nice," Santa Fe
       Institute, September–October 2011, accessed March 29, 2017, http://samoa.
       santafe.edu/media/update_pdf/SFI_Update_Sept_Oct2011_FNL.pdf.

106.   Lawrence H. Keeley, *War before Civilization: The Myth of the Peaceful Savage*
       (Oxford: Oxford University Press, December 18, 1997).

107.   Felix Warneken and Michael Tomasello, "Altruistic Helping in Human In-
       fants and Young Chimpanzees," *Science* 311, 5765 (2006): 1301-1303, accessed
       March 29, 2017, doi: 10.1126/science.1121448.

108.   David G. Rand, Joshua D. Greene and Martin A. Nowak, "Spontaneous
       Giving and Calculated Greed," *Nature* 489 (September 20, 2012): 427-429,
       accessed March 29, 2017, doi: 10.1038/nature11467.

109.   Ernst Fehr, "The Economics of Fairness, Reciprocity and Altruism – Experi-
       mental Evidence and New Theories," in *Handbook of the Economics of Giv-
       ing, Altruism and Reciprocity,* ed. Serge-Christophe Kolm and Jean Mercier
       Ythier (Amsterdam: Elsevier, 2006), doi: 10.1016/S1574-0714(06)01008-6.

110.   Tania Singer, "How to Build a Caring Economy," *World Economic Forum*,
       January 24, 2015, accessed March 28, 2017, https://www.weforum.org/agen-
       da/2015/01/how-to-build-a-caring-economy/.

111.   Thomas R. Insel and Larry J. Young, "The Neurobiology of Attachment,"
       Nature Reviews Neuroscience 2, no. 2 (2001): 129-136, accessed March 29, 2017,
       doi: 10.1038/35053579.

112.   Riane Eisler, "Building a Caring Economy and Society," *Cadmus* 2, no. 6
       (2013), accessed March 29, 2017, http://rianeeisler.com/building-a-caring-
       economy-and-society/.

113.   Tania Singer, *Caring Economics: Conversations on Altruism and Compassion,
       Between Scientists, Economists, and the Dalai Lama* (New York: Picador, 2015).

114.   Mark Pagel, *Wired for Culture: Origins of the Human Social Mind* (New York:
       W.W. Norton & Company, 2012).

115.   Alvin Toffler, *The Future Shock* (New York: Bantam, 1984).

116.   Virginia H. Garrison et al., "African and Asian Dust: From Desert Soils to
       Coral Reefs," *BioScience* 53, no. 5 (2003): 469-480, accessed March 29, 2017,
       doi: https://doi.org/10.1641/0006-3568(2003)053[0469:AAADFD]2.0.CO;2.

117.   Anil K. Gupta and Vijay Govindarajan, *Global strategy and organization*
       (New York: John Wiley, September 2007).

Chapter 2

1.   Mark Pagel, *Wired for Culture: Origins of the Human Social Mind* (New York:
       W. W. Norton & Company, 2012).

2.   Geert Hofstede and Gert Jan Hofstede, *Culture and Organization: Software of
       the mind,* 2nd ed. (New York: McGraw-Hill, 2005).

3.   Karl E. Weick and Robert E. Quinn, "Organizational Change and Develop-
       ment," *Annual Review of Psychology* 50 (1999): 361-386, accessed March 29,
       2017, doi: 10.1146/annurev.psych.50.1.361.

4. Carrie R. Leana and Bruce Barry, "Stability and Change as Simultaneous Experiences in Organizational Life," *Academy of Management Review* 25, no. 4 (2000): 753-759, accessed March 29, 2017, http://www.jstor.org/stable/259203.

5. Miriam Erez and P. Christopher Earley, *Culture, Self-Identity, and Work* (Oxford: Oxford University Press, 1993).

6. Paul J. Hanges, Robert G. Lord and Robert M. W. Dickson, "An Information Processing Perspective on Leadership and Culture: A Case for Connectionist Architecture," *Applied Psychology: An International Review* 49, no. 1 (2000): 133-161, accessed March 29, 2017, doi: 10.1111/1464-0597.00008.

7. Ying-yi Hong et al., "Multicultural Minds: A Dynamic Constructivist Approach to Culture and Cognition," *American Psychologist* 55, no. 7 (2000): 709-720, accessed March 29, 2017, doi: 10.1037//0003-066X.55.7.70.

8. Kaiping Peng and Eric D. Knowles, "Culture, Education, and the Attribution of Physical Causality," *Personality and Social Psychology Bulletin* 29, no. 10 (2003): 1272-1284, accessed March 29, 2017, doi: 10.1177/0146167203254601.

9. Catherine H. Tinsley and Susan E. Brodt, "Conflict Management in Asia: A Dynamic Framework and Future Directions," in *Handbook of Asian Management*, ed. Kwon Leung and Steven White (New York: Kluwer, 2004), 439–458.

10. Shinobu Kitayama, "Cultural Psychology of the Self: A Renewed Look at Independence and Interdependence," in *Psychology at the Turn of the Millennium, Vol. 2: Social, Developmental, and Clinical Perspectives*, ed. Claes von Hofsten and Lars Backman (Florence: Taylor & Francis/Routledge, 2002), 305–322.

11. John W. Berry et al., *Cross-Cultural Psychology: Research and Application,* 2nd ed. (New York: Cambridge University Press, 2002).

12. Tony Fang, "From 'Onion' to 'Ocean': Paradox and Change in National Cultures," *International Studies of Management & Organization* 35, no. 4 (2005-2006): 71-90, accessed March 29, 2017, http://www.jstor.org/stable/40397646.

13. Nazih N. Ayubi, *Political Islam: Religion and Politics in the Arab World* (Oxford: Routledge, 1991), 113.

14. Lizzie Dearden, "Iranian Women Call on Western Tourists to Violate Hijab Law to Fight Against Oppression," *Independent,* April 22, 2016, accessed March 29, 2017, http://www.independent.co.uk/news/world/middle-east/iranian-women-in-my-stealthy-freedom-campaign-call-on-western-tourists-to-violate-headscarf-law-to-a6996136.html.

15. Kristine Sudbeck, "The Effects of China's One-Child Policy: The Significance for Chinese Women," *Nebraska Anthropologist*, Paper 179 (2012), accessed March 29, 2017, http://digitalcommons.unl.edu/cgi/viewcontent.cgi?article=1178&context=nebanthro.

16. Riadh Ladhari, Nizar Souiden and Yong-Hoon Choi, "Culture Change and Globalization: The Unresolved Debate between Cross-national and Cross-cultural Classifications," *Australian Marketing Journal* 23, no. 3 (2015): 235-245, accessed March 29, 2017, doi: 10.1016/j.ausmj.2015.06.003.

17. Rodney H. Jones, "The Paradox of Culture in a Globalized World," *Language and Intercultural Communication* 13, no. 2 (2013): 237-244, accessed March 29, 2017, doi: 10.1080/14708477.2013.770869.

18. Kim S. Cameron and Robert E. Quinn, "Organizational Paradox and Trans-
     formation," in *Paradox and Transformation: Toward a Theory of Change in
     Organization and Management*, ed. Robert E. Quinn and Kim S. Cameron
     (Cambridge: Ballinger, 1988), 1–18.

19. Riadh Ladhari, Nizar Souiden and Yong-Hoon Choi, "Culture Change and
     Globalization: The Unresolved Debate between Cross-national and Cross-
     cultural Classifications," *Australian Marketing Journal* 23, no. 3 (2015): 235-
     245, accessed March 29, 2017, doi: 10.1016/j.ausmj.2015.06.003.

20. Joyce S. Osland and Allan Bird, "Beyond Sophisticated Stereotyping: Cul-
     tural Sensemaking in Context," *Academy of Management Executive* 14, no. 1
     (2000): 65-79, accessed March 29, 2017, http://www.jstor.org/stable/4165609.

21. Allan Bird and Michael J. Stevens, "Toward an Emergent Global Culture and
     the Effects of Globalization on Obsolescing National Cultures," *Journal of
     International Management* 9, no. 4 (2003): 395-407, accessed March 29, 2017,
     doi:10.1016/j.intman.2003.08.003.

22. Tony Fang, *Chinese Business Negotiating Style* (Thousand Oaks: Sage, 1999).

23. "Fig Fact-sheet Four: Hooliganism," Football Industry Group, University of
     Liverpool, accessed March 29, 2017, https://www.liverpool.ac.uk/manage-
     ment/football/.

24. Clifford Stott and Geoff Pearson, *Football Hooliganism: Policing the War on
     the English Disease* (London: Pennant Books, 2007).

25. Zoe Khor and Peter Marsh, "Britain: A Nation of Emotion?" *Social Issues
     Research Centre* (January 2007), accessed March 30, 2017, http://www.sirc.
     org/publik/emotion.pdf.

26. Tony Fang, "From 'Onion' to 'Ocean': Paradox and Change in National Cul-
     tures," *International Studies of Management & Organization* 35, no. 4 (2005-
     2006): 71-90, accessed March 29, 2017, http://www.jstor.org/stable/40397646.

27. Mai Nguyen-Phuong-Mai, Cees Terlouw and Albert Pilot, "Revisiting Face-
     work with a New Analysis Instrument. Face Strategies and Face Negotiation
     in Intercultural Communication," *Journal of Intercultural Communication*
     36 (2014), accessed March 29, 2017, http://www.immi.se/intercultural/nr36/
     nguyen.html.

28. Graham Priest, "The Martial Arts and Buddhist Philosophy," in *Philosophy
     and the Martial Arts – Engagement*, ed. Graham Priest and Damon Young
     (Oxford: Routledge, 2014).

29. Photo by Kishi Shiotani. "Bishounen Oranges," *Animexx*, April 30,
     2008, accessed March 29, 2017, https://commons.wikimedia.org/wiki/
     File:Bishounen_Oranges.jpeg#filelinks License Link https://creativecom-
     mons.org/licenses/by-sa/3.0/legalcode.

30. Joyce S. Osland and Allan Bird, "Beyond Sophisticated Stereotyping: Cul-
     tural Sensemaking in Context," *Academy of Management Executive* 14, no. 1
     (2000): 65-79, accessed March 29, 2017, http://www.jstor.org/stable/4165609.

31. Ann Swidler, "Culture in Action: Symbols and Strategies," *American Socio-
     logical Review* 51, no. 2 (1986): 273-286, accessed March 29, 2017, http://www.
     jstor.org/stable/2095521.

32. Joyce S. Osland and Allan Bird, "Beyond Sophisticated Stereotyping: Cultural Sensemaking in Context," *Academy of Management Executive* 14, no. 1 (2000): 65-79, accessed March 29, 2017, http://www.jstor.org/stable/2095521.

33. Daphna Oyserman et al., "Integrating Culture-as-Situated-Cognition and Neuroscience Prediction Models," *Culture Brain* 2, no. 1 (2014): 1-26, accessed March 29, 2017, doi: 10.1007/s40167-014-0016-6.

34. Jie Sui and Shihui Han, "Self-Construal Priming Modulates Neural Substrates of Self-Awareness," *Psychological Science* 18, no. 10 (2007): 861-866, accessed March 29, 2017, doi: 10.1111/j.1467-9280.2007.01992.x.

35. Chenbo Wang et al., "Accessible Cultural Mind-set Modulates Default Mode Activity: Evidence for the Culturally Situated Brain," *Social Neuroscience* 8, no. 3 (2013): 203-216, accessed March 29, 2017, http://dx.doi.org/10.1080/1747 0919.2013.775966.

36. Tokiko Harada, Zhang Li and Joan Y. Chiao, "Differential Dorsal and Ventral Medial Prefrontal Representations of the Implicit Self Modulated by Individualism and Collectivism: An fMRI Study," *Social Neuroscience* 5, no. 3 (2010): 257-271, doi: 10.1080/17470910903374895.

37. Zhicheng Lin, Yan Lin and Shihui Han, "Self-Construal Priming Modulates Visual Activity: Underlying Global/Local Perception," *Biological Psychology* 77, no. 1 (2008): 93-97, accessed March 29, 2017, doi: 10.1016/j.biopsycho.2007.08.002.

38. Ulrich Kühnen and Daphna Oyserman, "Thinking about the Self Influences Thinking in General: Cognitive Consequences of Salient Self-concept," *Journal of Experimental Social Psychology* 38 (2002): 492-499, accessed March 29, 2017, https://deepblue.lib.umich.edu/bitstream/handle/2027.42/64245/Thinking%20about%20the%20self%20influences%20thinking%20in%20general.pdf?sequence=1.

39. Daphna Oyserman et al., "Connecting and Separating Mind-sets: Culture as Situated Cognition," *Journal of Personality and Social Psychology* 97, no. 2 (2009): 217-235, accessed March 29, 2017, doi: 10.1037/a0015850.

40. Joan Y. Chiao et al., "Dynamic Cultural Influences on Neural Representations of the Self," *Journal of Cognitive Neuroscience* 22, no. 1 (2010): 1-11, accessed March 29, 2017, doi:10.1162/jocn.2009.21192.

41. Ying-yi Hong et al., "Multicultural Minds: A dynamic Constructivist Approach to Culture and Cognition," *American Psychologist* 55, no. 7 (2010): 709-720, accessed March 29, 2017, doi: 10.1037//0003-066X.55.7.709.

42. Diana Crane, "Introduction: The Challenge of the Sociology of Culture to Sociology as a Discipline," in *The sociology of culture: Emerging Theoretical Perspectives,* ed. Diana Crane, (Oxford: Blackwell, 1994), 1–19.

43. Joseph LeDoux, *The Emotional Brain: The Mysterious Underpinnings of Emotional Life* (New York: Touchstone Books, 1996).

44. Jack Denfeld Wood and Gianpiero Petriglieri, "Transcending Polarization: Beyond Binary Thinking," *Transactional Analysis Journal* 35, no. 1 (2005), accessed March 29, 2017, http://www.imd.org/programs/oep/generalmanagement/bot/upload/Transcending_polarization_article_by_Wood-Petriglieri.pdf.

45. Tony Fang, "From 'Onion' to 'Ocean': Paradox and Change in National Cultures," *International Studies of Management & Organization* 35, no. 4 (2005-2006): 71-90, accessed March 29, 2017, http://www.jstor.org/stable/40397646.

46. Geert Hofstede, Gert-Jan Hofstede and Michael Minkov, *Cultures and Organizations: Software of the Mind* (New York: McGraw-Hill, 2005), 120.

47. Richard A. Shweder and Maria Sullivan, "The Semiotic Subjects of Cultural Psychology," in *Handbook of personality: Theory and research,* ed. Lawrence A. Pervin (New York: Guilford, 1990), 399–416.

48. Erkan Gören, "Economic Effects of Domestic and Neighbouring Countries' Cultural Diversity," *ZenTra Working Paper in Transnational Studies* No. 16/2013 (2013), accessed March 29, 2017, https://papers.ssrn.com/sol3/papers.cfm?abstract_id=2255492.

49. Tony Fang, "From 'Onion' to 'Ocean': Paradox and Change in National Cultures," *International Studies of Management & Organization* 35, no. 4 (2005-2006): 71-90, accessed March 29, 2017, http://www.jstor.org/stable/40397646.

50. Sunil Venaik and Paul Brewer, "Avoiding Uncertainty in Hofstede and GLOBE," *Journal of International Business Studies* 41, no. 8 (2010): 1294-1315, accessed March 29, 2017, doi: 10.1057/jibs.2009.96.

51. Mansour Javidan et al., "Conceptualizing and Measuring Cultures and Their Consequences: A Comparative Review of GLOBE's and Hofstede's Approaches," *Journal of International Business Studies* 37, no. 6 (2006): 897-914, accessed March 29, 2017, doi: 10.1057/palgrave.jibs.8400234.

52. Edward T. Hall, *Beyond Culture* (New York: Doubleday, 1976).

53. Wendell French and Cecil Bell, *Organization development*, 5th ed. (Englewood Cliffs: Prentice-Hall International, 1995).

54. Geert Hofstede and Gert Jan Hofstede, *Culture and Organization: Software of the mind,* 2nd ed. (New York: McGraw-Hill, 2005).

55. Nick Barter and Sally Russell, "Organisational Metaphors and Sustainable Development: Enabling or Inhibiting?" *Sustainability Accounting, Management and Policy Journal* 4, no. 2 (2013): 145-162, accessed March 29, 2017, http://dx.doi.org/10.1108/SAMPJ-Jan-2012-0002.

56. Markus J. Milne, Kate Kearins and Sara Walton, "Creating Adventures in Wonderland: The Journey Metaphor and Environmental Sustainability Organization," *The Critical Journal of Organization, Theory and Society* 13, no. 6 (2006): 801-840.

57. George Lakoff and Mark Johnson, *Metaphors We Live By* (Chicago: University of Chicago Press, 1980).

58. Patrick H. Thibodeau and Lera Boroditsky, "Natural Language Metaphors Covertly Influence Reasoning," *PLoS ONE* 8, no. 1 (2013), accessed March 29, 2017, http://dx.doi.org/10.1371/journal.pone.0052961.

59. Gregory Barnard, *Cross-Cultural Communication: A Practical Guide* (New York: Thomson Learning, 1995), 13.

60. Geert Hofstede, Gert-Jan Hofstede and Michael Minkov, *Cultures and Organizations: Software of the Mind* (New York: McGraw-Hill, 2005).

61. Edward T. Hall, *Beyond Culture* (New York: Doubleday, 1976).

62.   Wendy Leeds-Hurwitz, "Notes in the History of Intercultural Communica-
      tion: The Foreign Service Institute and the Mandate for Intercultural Train-
      ing," *Quarterly Journal of Speech* 76, no. 3 (1990): 262-281, accessed March 29,
      2017, http://dx.doi.org/10.1080/00335639009383919.

63.   Bruce Kogut and Harbir Singh, "The Effect of National Culture on the
      Choice of Entry Mode," *Journal of International Business Studies* 19, no. 3
      (1988): 411-432, accessed March 29, 2017, http://www.jstor.org/stable/155133.

64.   Geert Hofstede, Gert-Jan Hofstede and Michael Minkov, *Cultures and Or-
      ganizations: Software of the Mind* (New York: McGraw-Hill, 2005).

65.   Richard D. Lewis, *When Cultures Collide: Managing Successfully across Cul-
      tures,* 2nd ed. (London: Nicholas Brealey, 2000).

66.   Gunter K. Stahl and Rosalie L. Tung, "Towards a More Balanced Treatment
      of Culture in International Business Studies: The need for Positive Cross-
      Cultural Scholarship," *Journal of International Business Studies* 46, no. 4
      (2015): 391-414, accessed March 29, 2017, doi: 10.1057/jibs.2014.68.

67.   "Geert Hofstede," *The Economist*, November 28, 2008, accessed March 29,
      2017, http://www.economist.com/node/12669307.

68.   Milton J. Bennett, "Culture is Not like an Iceberg," *IDR Institute*, May
      06, 2013, accessed March 29, 2017, http://www.idrinstitute.org/page.
      asp?menu1=14&post=1.

69.   Milton J. Bennett, "The Ravages of Reification: Considering the Iceberg and
      Cultural Intelligence, Towards De-reifying Intercultural Competence," *IDR
      Institute*, September 28, 2013, accessed March 2017, http://www.idrinstitute.
      org/allegati/IDRI_t_Pubblicazioni/77/FILE_Documento_Intercultura_Reifi-
      cation.pdf.

70.   Jesper Edman, "The Paradox of Foreignness: Norm-Breaking MNEs in the
      Japanese Banking Industry," (PhD diss., Stockholm School of Economics,
      2009), accessed March 29, https://www.academia.edu/2870298/The_Para-
      dox_of_foreignness.

71.   Bo Bernhard Nielsen and Sabina Nielsen, "Top Management Team Nationality
      Diversity and Firm Performance: A Multilevel Study," *Strategic Management
      Journal* 34, no. 3 (2013): 373-382, accessed March 29, 2017, doi: 10.1002/smj.2021.

72.   Günter K. Stahl et al., "A Look at the Bright Side of Multicultural Team
      Diversity," *Scandinavian Journal of Management* 26, no. 4 (2010): 439-447,
      accessed March 29, 2017, doi: 10.1016/j.scaman.2010.09.009.

73.   Rosalie L. Tung and Alain Verbeke, "Beyond Hofstede and GLOBE: Improv-
      ing the Quality of Cross-Cultural Research," *Journal of International Business
      Studies* 41, no. 8 (2010): 1259-1274, accessed March 29, 2017, http://www.jstor.
      org/stable/40863977.

74.   Srilata Zaheer, Margaret Spring Schomaker and Lilach Nachum, "Distance
      without Direction: Restoring Credibility to a Much-Loved Construct," *Jour-
      nal of International Business Studies* 43, no. 1 (2012): 18-27, accessed March
      29, 2017, doi: 10.1057/jibs.2011.43.

75.   Gail E. Walton, N. J Bower and T. G Bower, "Recognition of Familiar Faces by
      Newborns," *Infant Behavior & Development* 15, no 2 (1992): 265-269.

76. Naoki Masuda and Feng Fu, "Evolutionary Models of In-group Favoritism," *F1000Prime Reports* 7, no. 27 (2015), doi: 10.12703/P7-27.

77. Irene V. Blair et al., "The role of Afrocentric Features in Person Perception: Judging by Features and Categories," *Journal of Personality and Social Psychology* 83, no. 1 (2002): 5-25, accessed March 29, 2017, http://citeseerx.ist. psu.edu/viewdoc/download?doi=10.1.1.492.3610&rep=rep1&type=pdf.

78. Donn Erwin Byrne, *The Attraction Paradigm* (New York: Academic Press, 1971).

79. Steven J. Heine, Julie-Ann B. Foster and Roy Spina, "Do Birds of a Feather Universally Flock Together? Cultural Variation in the Similarity-Attraction Effect," *Asian Journal of Social Psychology* 12, no. 4 (2009): 247-258, accessed March 29, 2017, doi: 10.1111/j.1467-839X.2009.01289.x.

80. Bruno Laeng, Oddrun Vermeer and Unni Sulutvedt, "Is Beauty in the Face of the Beholder?" *Plos One* 8, no. 7 (2013), accessed March 29, 2017, doi:10.1371/journal.pone.0068395.

81. Angela J. Bahns et al., "Similarity in Relationships as Niche Construction: Choice, Stability, and Influence within Dyads in a Free Choice Environment," *Journal of Personality and Social Psychology* 112, no. 2 (2016): 329-355, doi: 10.1037/pspp0000088.

82. Eva C. Klohnen and Shanhong Luo, "Interpersonal Attraction and Personality: What is Attractive – Self Similarity, Ideal Similarity, Omplementarity, or Attachment Security?" *Journal of Personality and Social Psychology* 85, no. 4 (2003): 709-722, doi: 10.1037/0022-3514.85.4.709.

83. Lauren A. Rivera, "Hiring as Cultural Matching: The Case of Elite Professional Service Firms," *American Sociological Review* 77, no.6 (2012): 999-1022, accessed March 29, 2017, doi: 10.1177/0003122412463213.

84. Joseph LeDoux, *The Emotional Brain: The Mysterious Underpinnings of Emotional Life* (New York: Touchstone Books, 1996).

85. Shalom H. Schwartz, "Universals in the Content and Structure of Values: Theory and Empirical Tests in 20 Countries," in *Advances in Experimental Social Psychology, Vol. 25,* ed. Mark Zanna (New York: Academic Press, 1992), 1–65.

86. Kin K. Leung et al., "Social Axioms: The Search for Universal Dimensions of General Beliefs about How the World Functions," *Journal of Cross-Cultural Psychology* 33, no.3 (2002): 286-302, accessed March 29, 2017, doi: 10.1177/0022022102033003005.

87. Photo by Jérôme. "Café in Baarle-Nassau (Netherlands), on the Border with Belgium. The Border is Marked on the Ground (N119/N260)," *Baarle-Nassau Frontier*, September 2001, accessed March 29, 2017, https://commons.wikimedia.org/w/index.php?curid=1564073 License Link https://creativecommons.org/licenses/by-sa/3.0/legalcode.

88. Pat Caldwell and John Caldwell, "High Fertility in Sub-Saharan Africa," *Scientific American* 13, no. 3 (May 1990): 118-125, accessed March 30, 2017, doi: 10.2307/1973133.

89. Pippa Norris, "Global Governance and Cosmopolitan Citizens," in *Governance in a Globalizing World*, ed. Joseph S. Nye Jr. and John D. Donahue (Washington: Brookings Institution Press, 2000): 155–177.

90.   Laura Oxley and Paul Morris, "Global Citizenship: A Typology for Distin-
      guishing its Multiple Conceptions," *British Journal of Educational Studies* 61,
      no. 3 (2013): 301-325, accessed March 30, 2017, http://dx.doi.org/10.1080/0007
      1005.2013.798393.

91.   Allan Bird and Michael J. Stevens, "Toward an Emergent Global Culture and
      the Effects of Globalization on Obsolescing National Cultures," *Journal of
      International Management* 9, no. 4 (2003): 395-407, accessed March 30, 2017,
      doi:10.1016/j.intman.2003.08.003.

92.   Anil K. Gupta and Vijay Govindarajan, "Knowledge Flows within Multina-
      tional Corporations," *Strategic Management Journal* 21, no. 4 (2000): 473-496,
      accessed March 30, 2017, http://www.jstor.org/stable/258980.

93.   Stephen Reysen and Iva Katzarska-Miller, "A Model of Global Citizenship:
      Antecedents and Outcomes," *International Journal of Psychology* 48, no. 5
      (2013): 858-870, accessed March 30, 2017, doi: 10.1080/00207594.2012.701749.

94.   Ying-yi Hong and Chi-yue Chiu, "Toward a Paradigm Shift: From Cross-
      cultural Differences in Social Cognition to Social-Cognitive Mediation of
      Cultural Differences," *Social Cognition* 19, no. 3 (2001): 181-196, accessed
      March 30, 2017, https://pdfs.semanticscholar.org/9b35/1400b259a5cc1443219
      4ee882712fb88e7bf.pdf.

95.   Richard A. Shweder and Maria Sullivan, "The Semiotic Subjects of Cultural
      Psychology," in *Handbook of Personality: Theory and Research,* ed. Lawrence.
      A. Pervin (New York: Guilford, 1990), 399–416.

96.   Hubert J. M. Hermans and Harry J. G. Kempen, "Moving Culture," *Ameri-
      can Psychologist* 53, no. 10 (1998): 1111-1120, accessed March 30, 2017, doi:
      10.1037/0003-066X.53.10.1111.

97.   Philip L. White, "Globalization and the Mythology of the Nation State," in
      Global History: Interactions between the Universal and the Local, ed. Antony
      Gerald Hopkins (Palgrave: Macmillan, 2006), 257–284.

98.   "Summary of Votes Cast," Scottish Independence Referendum, September
      24, 2014, accessed March 30, 2017, http://scotlandreferendum.info/.

99.   Wei Zheng, Baiyin Yang and Gary McLean, "Linking Organizational Culture,
      Structure, Strategy, and Organizational Effectiveness: Mediating Role of
      Knowledge Management," *Journal of Business Research* 63, no. 7 (2010): 763-
      771, accessed March 30, 2017, doi: 10.1016/j.jbusres.2009.06.005.

100. Madelyn Geldenhuys, Karolina Łaba and Cornelia M. Venter, "Meaningful
      Work, Work Engagement and Organisational Commitment," *SA Journal of
      Industrial Psychology* 40, no. 1 (2014), accessed March 30, 2017, doi: 10.4102/
      sajip.v40i1.1098.

101. Kang Yang Trevor Yu, "Organizational Behavior and Human Decision Pro-
      cesses," *Person–Organization Fit Effects on Organizational Attraction: A Test
      of an Expectations-based Model* 124, no. 1 (2014): 75-94.

102. Mehlika Sarac, Ismail Efil and Mehmet Eryilmaz, "A Study of the Relation-
      ship between Person-Organization Fit and Employee Creativity," *Manage-
      ment Research Review* 37, no. 5 (2014): 479–501, accessed March 30, 2017, doi:
      10.1108/MRR-01-2013-0025.

103. Hemang Jauhari and Shailendra Singh, "Perceived Diversity Climate and Employees' Organizational Loyalty," *Equality, Diversity and Inclusion: An International Journal* 32, no. 3 (2013): 262–276, accessed March 30, 2017, doi: 10.1108/EDI-12-2012-0119.

104. Jennifer A. Chatman and Sandra E. Cha, "Leading by Leveraging Culture," *California Management Review* 45, no. 4 (2003): 20–30, accessed March 30, 2017, http://www.hbs.edu/faculty/Publication%20Files/02-088_5a72f8e4-9c95-4a78-868c-c75c5c522746.pdf.

105. "FPT culture," FPT, accessed March 31, 2017, https://fpt.com.vn/en/about-us/culture.

106. Vy Nguyen, "FPT và vũ khí mang tên Văn hóa doanh nghiệp," [FPT and the weapon of corporate culture], *SAGE Brand and Communications Academy*, August 10, 2015, accessed March 31, 2017, http://sage.edu.vn/blog/fpt-va-vu-khi-mang-ten-van-hoa-doanh-nghiep/.

107. Bao Linh, "Văn hoá độc lạ đến kỳ quái cuả FPT" [The unique culture of FPT], *VTC News,* June 9, 2015, accessed march 31, 2017, http://www.vtc.vn/van-hoa-doc-la-den-ky-quai-cua-fpt-d209597.html.

108. Anthony M. Smith et al., "Sex in Australia: Sexual Identity, Sexual Attraction and Sexual Experience among a Representative Sample of Adults," *Public Health* 27, no. 2 (2003): 138-145, accessed March 30, 2017, doi: 10.1111/j.1467-842X.2003.tb00801.x.

109. Marieke de Mooij, *Consumer Behavior and Culture: Consequences for Global Marketing and Advertising* (Thousand Oaks: SAGE, 2010), 8.

110. Padma Rani, "Privatisation, Convergence and Broadcasting Regulations: A Case Study of the Indian Television Industry," *The Asian Conference on Media and Mass Communication* (2013): 387-396, accessed march 31, 2017, http://eprints.manipal.edu/141096/1/Asia13.pdf.

111. Tom Embury-Dennis, "Ikea bans 'illegal' blind-dating group from store cafeteria in Shanghai," *Independent,* Oct 13, 2015, accessed March 31, 2017, http://www.independent.co.uk/news/world/asia/ikea-bans-illegal-blind-dating-group-store-cafeteria-in-shanghai-china-a7359271.html.

112. John Calvert, *Sayyid Qutb and the Origins of Radical Islamism* (Oxford: Oxford University Press, 2009).

113. Kevin Roberts, "Running on empty," *Media and Marketing in Europe,* January 8, 2002, accessed March 30, 2017, http://www.saatchikevin.com/wp-content/uploads/2014/06/1017_scan_MM-Europe-Jan02-Run-on-Empty.pdf.

114. Hsiu-Ching Ko and Mu-Li Yang, "The Effects of Cross-Cultural Training on Expatriate Assignments," *Intercultural Communication Studies* 20, no. 1 (2011): 158-174, accessed March 30, 2017, http://web.uri.edu/iaics/files/12Hsiu-ChingKoMu-LiYang.pdf.

Chapter 3

1.   William E. Thompson and Joseph V. Hickey, *Society in Focus: Introduction to Sociology*, 10th ed. (New York: Longman, 1999).

2.   Elizabeth A. Phelps and Joseph E. LeDoux, "Contributions of the Amygdala to Emotion Processing: From Animal Models to Human Behavior," *Neuron* 48, no. 2 (2005): 175-187, accessed March 30, 2017, doi: 10.1016/j.neuron.2005.09.025.

3.   Andreas Olsson, Katherine I. Nearing and Elizabeth A. Phelps, "Learning Fears by Observing Others: The Neural Systems of Social Fear Transmission," *Social Cognitive Affective Neuroscience* 2, no. 1 (2007): 3-11, accessed March 30, 2017, doi: 10.1093/scan/nsm005.

4.   Douglas Martin et al., "The Spontaneous Formation of Stereotypes via Cumulative Cultural Evolution," *Psychological Science* 25, no. 9 (2014): 1777-1786, accessed March 30, 2017, doi: 10.1177/0956797614541129.

5.   Manfred Zimmermann, "Neurophysiology of Sensory Systems," in *Fundamentals of Sensory Physiology*, ed. Robert F. Schmidt (Heidelberg: Springer-Verlag, 1986), 68–116.

6.   Anthony G. Greenwald et al., "Measuring Individual Differences in Implicit Cognition: The Implicit Association Test," *Journal of Personality and Social Psychology* 74, no. 6 (1998): 1464-1480, accessed March 30, 2017, doi:10.1037/0022-3514.74.6.1464.

7.   Robin W. Simon and Anne E. Barrett, "Nonmarital Romantic Relationships and Mental Health in Early Adulthood: Does the Association Differ for Women and Men?" *Journal of Health and Social Behavior* 51, no. 2 (2010): 168-182, accessed March 30, 2017, doi: 10.1177/0022146510372343.

8.   Helen Regan, "Male Nurses Worldwide," *RealMansWork*, May 5, 2012, accessed March 30, 2017, https://realmanswork.wordpress.com/2012/05/05/male-nurses-worldwide/.

9.   "St. Camillus de Lellis," *Catholic Online*, accessed March 30, 2017, http://www.catholic.org/saints/saint.php?saint_id=265.

10.   "Alcohol Consumption," World Health Organization, 2014, accessed March 30, 2017, http://www.who.int/substance_abuse/publications/global_alcohol_report/msb_gsr_2014_3.pdf.

11.   Ronan McGreevy, "Have an Alcohol Problem? Neither Does 97 Per Cent of Irish People," *The Irish Times*, October 19, 2016, accessed March 30, 2017, http://www.irishtimes.com/news/health/have-an-alcohol-problem-neither-does-97-of-irish-people-1.2835485.

12.   Edward W. Said, *Orientalism* (New York: Vintage Books, 1979).

13.   Ulrich Kühnen and Daphna Oyserman, "Thinking about the Self Influences Thinking in General: Cognitive Consequences of Salient Self-concept," *Journal of Experimental Social Psychology* 38, no. 5 (2002): 492-499, accessed March 30, 2017, doi: 10.1016/S0022-1031(02)00011-2.

14.   Daphna Oyserman et al., "Connecting and Separating Mind-sets: Culture as Situated Cognition," *Journal of Personality and Social Psychology* 97, no. 2 (2009): 217-235, accessed March 30, 2017, doi: 10.1037/a0015850.

15. Joan Y. Chiao et al., "Dynamic Cultural Influences on Neural Representa-
     tions of the Self," *Journal of Cognitive Neuroscience* 22, no. 1 (2010): 1-11,
     accessed March 30, 2017, doi:10.1162/jocn.2009.21192.

16. Jie Sui and Shihui Han, "Self-Construal Priming Modulates Neural Sub-
     strates of Self-Awareness," *Psychological Science* 18, no. 10 (2007): 861-866,
     accessed March 30, 2017, doi: 10.1111/j.1467-9280.2007.01992.x.

17. Daphna Oyserman et al., "Accessible Cultural Mind-set Modulates
     Default Mode Activity: Evidence for the Culturally Situated Brain," *So-
     cial Neuroscience* 8, no. 3 (2014): 203-216, accessed March 30, 2017, doi:
     10.1080/17470919.2013.775966.

18. Tokiko Harada, Zhang Li and Joan Y. Chiao, "Differential Dorsal and Ventral
     Medial Prefrontal Representations of the Implicit Self Modulated by
     Individualism and Collectivism: An fMRI study," *Social Neuroscience* 5, no. 3
     (2010): 257-271, accessed March 30, 2017, doi: 10.1080/17470910903374895.

19. Zhicheng Lin, Yan Lin and Shihui Han, "Self-construal Priming Modulates
     Visual Activity: Underlying Global/Local Perception," *Biological Psychol-
     ogy* 77, no. 1 (2008): 93-97, accessed March 30, 2017, doi: 10.1016/j.biopsy-
     cho.2007.08.002.

20. Ying-yi Hong et al., "Multicultural Minds: A Dynamic Constructivist Ap-
     proach to Culture and Cognition," *American Psychologist* 55, no. 7 (2010):
     709-720, accessed March 30, 2017, doi: 10.1037//0003-066X.55.7.709.

21. Jeffrey E. Brand, Pascaline Lorentz and Trishita Mathew, "Digital Australia
     DA14," *Interactive Games & Entertainment Association*, 2014, accessed March
     30, 2017, http://www.igea.net/wp-content/uploads/2013/11/Digital-Australia-
     2014-DA14.pdf.

22. Ibid.

23. Dirk Bosmans and Paul Maskell, "Videogames in Europe: Consumer Study,"
     Interactive Software Federation of Europe, November 2012, 36–51, accessed
     March 30, 2017, http://www.isfe.eu/sites/isfe.eu/files/attachments/euro_
     summary_-_isfe_consumer_study.pdf.

24. Charles Custer, "Which Country Has the Most Gamer Girls," *Tech Asia*, June
     27, 2013, accessed March 30, 2017, https://www.techinasia.com/what-coun-
     try-has-the-most-gamer-girls.

25. Marc Graser, "Videogame Biz: Women Still Very Much in the Minority," *Vari-
     ety*, October 1, 2013, accessed March 30, 2017, http://variety.com/2013/digital/
     features/womengamers1200683299-1200683299/.

26. Photo by Gamesinger. "Only Boys Playing Video Games Exemplifies a
     Common Stereotype that Video Games are Predominantly Made for and
     Played by Boys," *Wikipedia*, March 27, 2012, accessed March 30, 2017, https://
     en.wikipedia.org/wiki/Stereotype#/media/File:Children_playing_video_
     games.jpg License Link https://creativecommons.org/licenses/by-sa/3.0/.

27. Photo by Julia Kishkaruk. "Modern fashion standards," *Wikipedia,* December
     16, 2016, accessed March 31, 2017, https://commons.wikimedia.org/wiki/
     File:Modern_fashion_standards.jpg License link https://creativecommons.
     org/licenses/by-sa/4.0/legalcode.

28. Jeffrey W. Sherman, Frederica R. Conrey and Carla J. Groom, "Encoding Flexibility Revisited: Evidence for Enhanced Encoding of Stereotype-inconsistent Information under Cognitive Load," *Social Cognition* 22, no. 2 (2004): 214-232, accessed March 30, 2017, doi: 10.1521/soco.22.2.214.35464.

29. Ryan M. Stolier and Jonathan B. Freeman, "Neural Pattern Similarity Reveals the Inherent Intersection of Social Categories," *Nature Neuroscience* 19, no. 6 (2016): 795-797, accessed March 30, 2017, doi:10.1038/nn.4296.

30. Carol Tavris and Elliot Aronson, *Mistakes Were Made (But Not by Me): Why We Justify Foolish Beliefs, Bad Decisions, and Hurtful Acts* (New York: Houghton Mifflin Harcourt, 2007).

31. Ullrich K. Ecker et al., "Correcting False Information in Memory: Manipulating the Strength of Misinformation Encoding and its Retraction," *PubMed* 18, no. 3 (2011): 570-578, accessed March 30, 2017, doi: 10.3758/s13423-011-0065-1.

32. Brendan Nyhan and Jason Reifler, "When Corrections Fail: The Persistence of Political Misperceptions," *Political Behavior* 32, no. 2 (2010): 303-330, accessed March 30, 2017, doi: 10.1007/s11109-010-9112-2.

33. James H. Kuklinski et al., "Misinformation and the Currency of Democratic Citizenship," *The Journal of Politics* 62, no. 3 (2000): 790-816, accessed March 30, 2017, http://www.jstor.org/stable/2647960.

34. Sam Killermann, "3 Reasons Positive Stereotypes Aren't That Positive," *It's Pronounced Metrosexual*, 2012, accessed March 30, 2017, http://itspronouncedmetrosexual.com/2012/04/reasons-positive-stereotypes-are-not-positive/#sthash.P7VFB8Fn.dpbs.

35. Nancy J. Adler, *International Dimensions of Organizational Behavior*, 2nd ed. (Boston: PWS-KENT, 1991), 74.

36. Claude M. Steele and Joshua Aronson, "Stereotype Threat and the Intellectual Test Performance of African Americans," *Journal of Personality and Social Psychology* 69, no. 5 (1995): 797-811, accessed March 30, 2017, http://dx.doi.org/10.1037/0022-3514.69.5.797.

37. Jeff Stone et al., "Stereotype Threat Effects on Black and White Athletic Performance," *Journal of personality and social psychology* 77, no. 6 (1999): 1213-1227, accessed March 30, 2017, doi: 10.1037/0022-3514.77.6.1213.

38. Steven J. Spencer, Claude M. Steele and Diane M. Quinn, "Stereotype Threat and Women's Math Performance," *Journal of Experimental Social Psychology* 35, no. 1 (1999): 4-28, accessed March 30, 2017, http://dx.doi.org/10.1006/jesp.1998.1373.

39. Margarete Delazer et al., "Learning Complex Arithmetic – an fMRI Study," *Cognitive Brain Research* 18, no. 1 (2003): 76-88, doi:10.1016/j.neuroimage.2004.12.009.

40. Stanislas Dehaene et al., "Sources of Mathematical Thinking: Behavioral and Brain-imaging Evidence," *Science* 284 (1999): 970-974.

41. Joe M. Moran et al., "Neuroanatomical Evidence for Distinct Cognitive and Affective Components of Self," *Journal of Cognitive Neuroscience* 18, no. 9 (2006): 1586-1594, accessed March 30, 2017, doi: 10.1162/jocn.2006.18.9.1586.

42. Leah H. Somerville, Todd F. Heatherton and William M. Kelley, "Anterior Cingulate Cortex Responds Differentially to Expectancy Violation and

Social Rejection," *Nature Neuroscience* 9, no. 8 (2006): 1007-1008, accessed March 30, 2017, doi: 10.1038/nn1728.

43. Natsu Taylor Saito, "Model Minority, Yellow Peril: Functions of Foreignness in the Construction of Asian American Legal Identity," *Asian American Law Journal* 4, no. 6 (1997): 71, accessed March 30, 2017, https://doi.org/10.15779/Z38FZ9V.

44. Jay Mathews, "Learning to Stand out among the Standouts: Some Asian Americans Say Colleges Expect More from Them," *Washington Post*, March 22, 2005, accessed March 30, 2017, http://www.washingtonpost.com/wp-dyn/articles/A55160-2005Mar21.html.

45. "Asian American Student Suicide Rate at MT is Quadruple the National Average," *Reappropriate,* May 20, 2015, accessed March 31, 2017, http://reap-propriate.co/2015/05/asian-american-student-suicide-rate-at-mit-is-quadru-ple-the-national-average/.

46. Cynthia Lee, *Murder and the Reasonable man: Passion and Fear in the Criminal Courtroom* (New York: NYU Press, 2003), 162.

47. Anne Soon Choi, *Korean Americans* (New York: Infobase Publishing, 2009), 75.

48. "African Immigrants in the United States are the Nation's Most Highly Educated Group," *The Journal of Blacks in Higher Education*, no. 13 (Autumn, 1996): 33-34, accessed March 30, 2017, http://www.aracorporation.org/files/14._africans_most_educated.pdf.

49. "High School Students Conducting Experiments," *National Cancer Institute*, September 1989, accessed March 30, 2017, https://commons.wikimedia.org/wiki/File:High_school_students_conducting_experiments.jpg Public Domain.

50. Neha Mahajan et al., "The Evolution of Intergroup Bias: Perceptions and Attitudes in Rhesus Macaques," *Journal of Personality and Social Psychology* 100, no. 3 (2011): 387, accessed March 30, 2017, doi: 10.1037/a0022459.

51. David D. Franks and Jonathan H. Turner, *Handbook of Neurosociology* (New York: Springer, 2013), 351.

52. Henri Tajfel and John C. Turner, "An Integrative Theory of Intergroup Conflict," in *The Social Psychology of Intergroup Relations,* ed. William G. Austin and Stephen Worchel (Monterey: Brooks/Cole, 1979): 33–47.

53. Marilynn B. Brewer, "The Psychology of Prejudice: Ingroup Love or Outgroup Hate," *Journal of Social Issues* 55, no. 3 (1999): 429-444, accessed March 30, 2017, doi: 10.1111/0022-4537.00126.

54. Jennifer T. Kubota, Mahzarin R. Banaji and Elizabeth A. Phelps, "The Neuroscience of Race," *Nature Neuroscience* 15, no. 7 (2012): 940-948, accessed March 30, 2017, doi:10.1038/nn.3136.

55. Allen J. Hart et al., "Differential Response in the Human Amygdala to Racial Outgroup vs Ingroup Face Stimuli," *Neuroreport* 11, no. 11 (2000): 2351-2355, accessed March 30, 2017, https://pdfs.semanticscholar.org/0ee6/4e6fe4c286e5b87e13058b6c2cc25f67bf1c.pdf.

56. Meghan L. Meyer et al., "Empathy for the Social Suffering of Friends and Strangers Recruits Distinct Patterns of Brain Activation," *Social Cognitive*

and Affective Neuroscience 8, no. 4 (2012): 1-9, accessed March 30, 2017, doi: 10.1093/scan/nss019.

57.   Grit Hein et al., "Neural Responses to Ingroup and Outgroup Members Suffering Predict Individual Differences in Costly Helping," *Neuron* 68, no. 1 (2010): 149-160, accessed March 30, 2017, http://dx.doi.org/10.1016/j.neuron.2010.09.003.

58.   Michael W. Brough, "Dehumanization of the Enemy and the Moral Equality of Soldiers," in *Rethinking the Just War Tradition,* ed. Michael W. Brough, John W. Lango and Harry van der Linden (Albany: State University of New York Press, 2007): 149–167.

59.   David M. Amodio, "The Neuroscience of Prejudice and Stereotyping," *Nature Reviews Neuroscience* 15, no. 10 (2014): 670-682, accessed March 30, 2017, doi: 10.1038/nrn3800.

60.   Donald T. Campbell, "Ethnocentric and Other Altruistic Motives," in *Nebraska Symposium on Motivation 13*, ed. David Levine (Lincoln: University of Nebraska Press, 1965): 283–311.

61.   Carol Tavris and Elliot Aronson, *Mistakes were made (but not by me): Why we justify foolish beliefs, bad decisions, and hurtful acts* (New York: Houghton Mifflin Harcourt, 2008), 64.

62.   Robert M. Baird and Stuart E. Rosenbaum, *Hatred, bigotry, and prejudice: Definitions, causes, and solutions* (New York: Prometheus Books, 1999), 130.

63.   Lincoln Quillian, "Prejudice as a Response to Perceived Group Threat: Population Composition and Anti-immigrant and Racial Prejudice in Europe," *American Sociological Review* 60, no. 4 (1995): 586-611, accessed March 30, 2017, doi: 10.2307/2096296.

64.   David H. Clark, Benjamin O. Fordham and Timothy Nordstrom, "Preying on the Misfortune of Others: When Do States Exploit their Opponents' Domestic Troubles," *The Journal of Politics* 73, no. 1 (2011): 248-264, accessed March 30, 2017, doi: 10.1017/s002238161000099x.

65.   Painting by Muhammad Qasim, "Shah Abbas ad Wine Boy," *Wikipedia,* September 1, 2010, accessed March 31, 2017, https://commons.wikimedia.org/wiki/File:Modern_fashion_standards.jpg Public Domain.

66.   Andrea Müller et al., "Public sector labour relations in four European countries compared: Long-term convergence and short-term divergences," in *Industrial Relations in Europe Conference (IREC) 2014/Research Network on Work, Employment and Industrial Relations (RN nr. 17) of the European Sociological Association (ESA) conference 10-12/09/2014, Dublin, Ireland,* 2014, accessed March 31, 2017, http://www.fatk.uni-tuebingen.de/files/mueller_et_al_2014.pdf.

67.   Stuart Oskamp, "Multiple Paths to Reducing Prejudice and Discrimination," in *Reducing prejudice and discrimination*, ed. Stuart Oskamp (New York, Psychology Press, 2000), 3.

68.   Colin Simpson, "Good Salary, Depending on Where You're Coming From," *The National,* April 27, 2012, accessed March 30, 2017, http://www.thenational.ae/news/uae-news/good-salary-depending-on-where-youre-coming-from.

69. Eric Luis Uhlmann and Geoffrey L. Cohen, "Constructed Criteria Redefining Merit to Justify Discrimination," *American Psychological Science* 16, no. 6 (2005): 474-480, accessed March 30, 2017, doi: 10.1111/j.0956-7976.2005.01559.x.

70. "Shadow Report on Racism & Discrimination in Employment," *ENAR*, March 17, 2014, accessed March 30, 2017, http://www.enar-eu.org/ENAR-Shadow-Report-on-racism.

71. Ibid.

72. Marianne Bertrand and Sendhil Mullainathan, "Are Emily and Greg More Employable Than Lakisha and Jamal? A Field Experiment on Labor Market Discrimination," *American Economic Review* 94, no. 4 (2004): 991-1013, accessed March 30, 2017, doi: 10.1257/0002828042002561.

73. Janene Pieters, "Dutch PM Rutte calls anonymous job applications "terrible"." *NL Times*. March 02, 2017. Accessed March 20, 2017. http://nltimes.nl/2017/03/02/dutch-pm-rutte-calls-anonymous-job-applications-terrible.

74. Babson-College, "Current State of Businesses Owned by Women of Color," *PRN*, May 9, 2008, accessed March 30, 2017, http://www.prnewswire.com/news-releases/current-state-of-businesses-owned-by-women-of-color-57226042.html.

75. Alicia Robb and San Rafael, "Access to Capital among Young Firms, Minority-owned Firms, Women-owned Firms, and High-tech Firms," *Report to the Small Business Administration Office of Advocacy* 403, April 2013, accessed March 30, 2017, https://www.sba.gov/sites/default/files/files/rs403tot(2).pdf.

76. Patrick Clark, "Bank Discrimination and Its 'Debilitating' Effect on Minority Entrepreneurs," *Bloomberg Business*, May 30, 2014, accessed March 30, 2017, https://www.bloomberg.com/news/articles/2014-05-30/bank-discrimination-and-its-debilitating-effect-on-minority-entrepreneurs.

77. Ashley Nellis, "The Color of Justice: Racial and Ethnic Disparity in State Prisons," *The Sentencing Project,* June 14, 2016, accessed March 30, 2017, http://www.sentencingproject.org/wp-content/uploads/2016/06/The-Color-of-Justice-Racial-and-Ethnic-Disparity-in-State-Prisons.pdf.

78. "Data Collection: Police-Public Contact Survey (PPCS)," *Bureau of Justice Statistics*, last updated 2011, accessed March 30, 2017, https://www.bjs.gov/index.cfm?ty=dcdetail&iid=251.

79. Shanti Fernando, *Race and the City: Chinese Canadian and Chinese American Political Mobilization* (Vancouver: UBC press, 2011), 32.

80. Nicholas D. Kristof, "Racism without Racists," *The New York Times*, October 4, 2008, March 30, 2017, http://www.nytimes.com/2008/10/05/opinion/05kristof.html.

81. Richard F. Martell, David M. Lane and Cynthia Emrich, "Male-Female Differences: A Computer Simulation," *American Psychologist* 51, no. 2 (1996): 157-158, accessed March 30, 2017, http://dx.doi.org/10.1037/0003-066X.51.2.157.

82. Maria Armoudian, "Constructing "the Others" During Conflict: How Journalism's Norms and Structures Temper Extreme Portrayals," *The Interna-*

tional Journal of Press/Politics 20, no. 3 (2015), accessed March 30, 2017, doi: 10.1177/1940161215577450.

83. Sally Kohn, "Muslim shooter = entire religion guilty; Black shooter = entire race guilty; White shooter = mentally troubled lone wolf," *Twitter*, December 21, 2014, accessed March 30, 2017, https://twitter.com/sallykohn/status/546701181310218240.

84. Marvin Perry and Frederick M. Schweitzer, *Anti-Semitism: Myth and hate from antiquity to the present* (New York: Palgrave Macmillan, 2002), 125–126.

85. Jerry Z. Muller, *Capitalism and the Jews* (Princeton: Princeton University Press, 2010), 161.

86. Allan Hall, "Confiscated Jewish Wealth 'Helped Fund the German War Effort'," *The Telegraph*, November 9, 2010, accessed March 30, 2017, http://www.telegraph.co.uk/news/worldnews/europe/germany/8119805/Confiscated-Jewish-wealth-helped-fund-the-German-war-effort.html.

87. Loriann Roberson et al., "Stereotype Threat and Feedback Seeking in the Workplace," *Journal of Vocational Behavior* 62, no. 1 (2003): 176-188, accessed March 30, 2017, doi: 10.1016/S0001-8791(02)00056-8.

88. Rosabeth Moss Kanter, *Men and Women of the Corporation* (New York: Basic Book, 1977).

89. Arnold Ahlert, "The Gruesome Reality of Racist South Africa," *FrontPage Mag*, March 10, 2013, accessed March 30, 2017, http://www.frontpagemag.com/fpm/180781/gruesome-reality-racist-south-africa-arnold-ahlert.

90. Justice Malala, "Does Race Still Matter in South Africa," *BBC*, August 29, 2012, accessed March 30, 2017, http://www.bbc.com/news/world-africa-19402353.

91. Michael I. Norton and Samuel R. Sommers, "Whites See Racism as a Zero-sum Game that They Are Now Losing," *Perspectives on Psychological Science* 6, no. 3 (2011): 215-218, accessed March 30, 2017, doi: 10.1177/1745691611406922.

92. Gareth Stokes, "The Problem with Affirmative Action," *FANews*, March 19, 2010, accessed March 30, 2017, https://www.fanews.co.za/article/talked-about-features/25/the-stage/1145/the-problem-with-affirmative-action/7618.

93. Wim De Neys, Oshin Vartanian and Vinod Goel, "Smarter than We Think When Our Brains Detect That We Are Biased," *Psychological Science* 19, no. 5 (2008): 484-489, accessed March 30, 2017, doi: 10.1111/j.1467-9280.2008.02113.x.

94. Vincent van Veen and Cameron S. Carter, "Conflict and Cognitive Control in the Brain," *Current Directions in Psychological Science* 15, no. 5 (2006): 237-240, accessed March 30, 2017, http://www.jstor.org/stable/20183122.

95. David M. Amodio et al, "Neurocognitive Correlates of Liberalism and Conservatism," *Nature Neuroscience* 10, no. 10 (2007): 1246-1247, accessed March 30, 2017, doi:10.1038/nn1979.

96. Ryota Kanai et al, "Political Orientations Are Correlated with Brain Structure in Young Adults," *Current Biology* 21, no. 8 (2011): 1-4, accessed March 30, 2017, doi: 10.1016/j.cub.2011.03.017.

97. Mary E. Wheeler and Susan T. Fiske, "Controlling Racial Prejudice. Social-Cognitive Goals Affect Amygdala and Stereotype Activation," *Psychological*

Science 16, no. 1 (2005): 56-63, accessed March 19, 2017, doi: 10.1111/j.0956-7976.2005.00780.x.

98. Margo J. Monteith, Aimee Y. Mark and Leslie Ashburn-Nardo, "The Self-regulation of Prejudice: Toward Understanding its Lived Character," *Group Processes & Intergroup Relations* 13 (2010): 183-200, accessed March 30, 2017, doi: 10.1177/1368430209353633.

99. Kerry Kawakami, John F. Dovidio and Simone van Kamp, "The Impact of Counterstereotypic Training and Related Correction Processes on the Application of Stereotypes," *Group Processes & Intergroup Relations* 10, no. 2 (2007): 139-156, accessed March 10, 2017, doi: http://dx.doi.org/10.1177/1368430207074725.

100. Andrew R. Todd et al., "Perspective Taking Combats Automatic Expressions of Racial Bias," *Journal of Personality and Social Psychology* 100, no. 6 (2011): 1027-1042, accessed March 30, 2017, doi: 10.1037/a0022308.

101. Derald Wing Sue et al., "Racial Microaggressions in Everyday Life – Implications for Clinical Practice," *American Psychological Association* 62, no. 4 (2007): 271-286, accessed March 30, 2017, doi: 10.1037/0003-066X.62.4.271.

102. "Dental Health among Children," OECD, 2009, accessed March 30, 2017, http://www.oecd-ilibrary.org/sites/health_glance-2009-en/01/10/index.html?itemId=/content/chapter/health_glance-2009-12-en&_csp_=73419db2d8639c2c6d43934472010be1.

103. "Plastic Makes Perfect," *The Economist*, January 30, 2013, accessed March 30, 2017, http://www.economist.com/blogs/graphicdetail/2013/01/daily-chart-22?fsrc=scn/fb/dc/plasticsurgery.

104. Geert H. Hofstede, *Culture's Consequences: Comparing Values, Behaviors, Institutions and Organizations across Nations* (Thousand Oaks: Sage Publications, Inc., 2001), 14.

105. Annika Feige et al., "Impact of Sustainable Office Buildings on Occupant's Comfort and Productivity," *Journal of Corporate Real Estate* 15, no. 1 (2013): 7-34, accessed March 30, 2017, http://dx.doi.org/10.1108/JCRE-01-2013-0004.

106. Yousef Al Horr et al., "Occupant Productivity and Office Indoor Environment Quality: A Review of the Literature," *Building and Environment* 105 (2016): 369-389, accessed March 30, 2017, http://dx.doi.org/10.1016/j.buildenv.2016.06.001.

107. Sapna Cheryan et al., "Ambient Belonging: How Stereotypical Cues Impact Gender Participation in Computer Science," *Journal of Personality and Social Psychology* 97, no. 6 (2009): 1045-1060, accessed March 30, 2017, doi: 10.1037/a0016239.

108. Derald Wing Sue et al., "Racial Microaggressions in Everyday Life – Implications for Clinical Practice," *American Psychological Association* 62, no. 4 (2007): 271-286, accessed March 19, 2017, doi: 10.1037/0003-066X.62.4.271.

109. "Donald Trump rails against judge's 'Mexican heritage'," *CNN Politics*, accessed March 30, 2017, http://edition.cnn.com/videos/politics/2016/06/03/donald-trump-judge-mexican-trump-university-case-lead-sot.cnn.

110. Adam Grant and Sheryl Sandberg, "Madam C.E.O., Get Me a Coffee," *The New York Times*, February 6, 2015, accessed March 30, 2017, https://www.

nytimes.com/2015/02/08/opinion/sunday/sheryl-sandberg-and-adam-grant-on-women-doing-office-housework.html?_r=0.

111. German Lopez, "Why You Should Stop Saying 'All Lives Matter,' explained in 9 different ways," *VOX*, July 11, 2016, accessed March 30, 2017, http://www.vox.com/2016/7/11/12136140/black-all-lives-matter.

112. Jane G. Stout et al., "STEMing the Tide: Using Ingroup Experts to Inoculate Women's Self-concept in Science, Technology, Engineering, and Mathematics (STEM)," *Journal of Personality and Social Psychology* 100, no. 2 (2011): 255-270, accessed March 30, 2017, doi: 10.1037/a0021385.

113. Nilanjana Dasguptaa, Melissa McManus Scircle and Matthew Hunsinger, "Female Peers in Small Work Groups Enhance Women's Motivation, Verbal Participation, and Career Aspirations in Engineering," *Psychological and Cognitive Sciences* 112, no. 16 (2015): 4988-4993, accessed March 30, 2017, doi: 10.1073/pnas.1422822112.

114. Eimear Finnegan, Jane Oakhill and Alan Garnham, "Counter-Stereotypical Pictures as a Strategy for Overcoming Spontaneous Gender Stereotypes," *Frontiers in Psychology* 6, no. 1291 (2015), accessed March 30, 2017, doi: 10.3389/fpsyg.2015.01291.

115. Irene V. Blair, Jennifer E. Ma and Alison P. Lenton, "Imagining Stereotypes Away: The Moderation of Implicit Stereotypes through Mental Imagery," *Journal of Personality and Social Psychology* 81, no. 5 (2001): 828-841, accessed March 30, 2017, doi: I0.1037//0022-3514.81.5.828.

116. Brian Welle, "Watch Unconscious Bias @ Work," *Google People Analytics*, accessed March 30, 2017, https://rework.withgoogle.com/guides/unbiasing-raise-awareness/steps/watch-unconscious-bias-at-work/.

117. Madeline E. Heilman and Michelle C. Haynes, "No Credit Where Credit Is Due: Attributional Rationalization of Women's Success in Male-Female Teams," *Journal of Applied Psychology* 90, no. 5 (2005): 905-916, accessed March 30, 2017, http://dx.doi.org/10.1037/0021-9010.90.5.905.

118. Farhad Manjoo, "Exposing Hidden Bias at Google," *The New York Times*, September 24, 2014, accessed March 30, 2017, https://www.nytimes.com/2014/09/25/technology/exposing-hidden-biases-at-google-to-improve-diversity.html.

119. Jay J. Van Bavel, Dominic J. Packer and William A. Cunningham, "The Neural Substrates of In-Group Bias. A Functional Magnetic Resonance Imaging Investigation," *Psychological Science* 19, no. 11 (2008): 1131-1139, accessed March 30, 2017, doi: 10.1111/j.1467-9280.2008.02214.x.

Chapter 4

1. Janine Willis and Alexander Todorov, "First Impressions: Making up Your Mind after a 100-Ms Exposure to a Face," *Psychological Science* 17, no. 7 (2006): 592-598, accessed March 31, 2017, doi: 10.1111/j.1467-9280.2006.01750.x.

2.   Barbara Pease and Allan Pease, *The Definitive Book of Body Language* (New York: Bantam Books, 2004).

3.   Paul Ekman, E. Richard Sorenson and Wallace V. Friesen, "Pan-cultural Elements in Facial Displays of Emotion," *Science* 164, no. 3875 (1969): 86-88, accessed March 31, 2017, http://www.jstor.org/stable/1726987.

4.   Charles Darwin, *The Expression of the Emotions in Man and Animals* (Oxford: Oxford University Press, 1998).

5.   Laura K. Guerrero and Kory Floyd, *Nonverbal Communication in Close Relationships* (Mahwah: Laurence Erlbaum Associates, Publisher, 2006), 2.

6.   Marcel Danesi, *Messages, Signs, and Meanings: A Basic Textbook in Semiotics and Communication*, 3ʳᵈ ed. (Toronto: Canadian Scholars' Press, 2004), 57.

7.   Albert Mehrabian, *Silent Messages* (Belmont: Wadsworth, 1971).

8.   Judee K. Burgoon, David B. Buller and W.G. Woodall, *Nonverbal Communication: The Unspoken Dialogue* (New York: Harper and Row, 1989), 9–10.

9.   Janine Willis and Alexander Todorov, "First Impressions: Making up Your Mind after a 100-Ms Exposure to a Face," *Psychological Science* 17, no. 7 (2006): 592-598, accessed March 31, 2017, doi: 10.1111/j.1467-9280.2006.01750.x.

10. Peter Harris, "Four Things Employers Decide About You in Four Seconds," *Workopolis*, October 16, 2015, accessed March 31, 2017, http://careers.workopolis.com/advice/first-impressions-four-things-employers-decide-about-you-in-four-seconds/.

11. Nalini Ambady and Robert Rosenthal, "Half a Minute: Predicting Teacher Evaluations from Thin Slices of Nonverbal Behavior and Physical Attractiveness," *Journal of Personality and Social Psychology* 64, no. 3 (1993): 431-441, accessed March 31, 2017, http://dx.doi.org/10.1037/0022-3514.64.3.431.

12. Misty Annette Gotcher, "Nonverbal Communication in the Job Interview: First Impressions and Nonverbal Immediacy," (Bachelor diss., Texas Tech University, 1990), accessed March 31, 2017, https://ttu-ir.tdl.org/ttu-ir/bitstream/handle/2346/23067/31295005954705.pdf?sequence=1.

13. Telge D. McShane, "Effects of Non-verbal Cues and Verbal First Impressions in Unstructured and Situational Interview Settings," *Applied HRM Research* 4, no. 2 (1993): 137-150, accessed March 31, 2017, http://www.xavier.edu/appliedhrmresearch/1993-Winter/Effects per cent20of per cent20Nonverbal per cent20Cues per cent20and per cent20Verbal per cent20First per cent20Impressions per cent20in per cent20Un.pdf.

14. Robert L. Dipboye, "Structured and Unstructured Selection Interviews: Beyond the Job-Fit Model," *Research in Personnel and Human Resources Management* 12, no. 79 (1994): 79-123, accessed March 31, 2017, https://www.researchgate.net/profile/Robert_Dipboye/publication/234095559_Structured_and_unstructured_selection_interviews_beyond_the_job-fit_model/links/0fcfd50f07cc277c11000000/Structured-and-unstructured-selection-interviews-beyond-the-job-fit-model.pdf.

15. Albert Mehrabian, *Silent Messages*, 1ˢᵗ ed. (Belmont: Wadsworth, 1971).

16. "New CareerBuilder Survey Reveals Top Body Language Mistakes Candidates Make in Job Interviews," *CareerBuilder*, July 28, 2010, accessed March

31, 2017, http://www.careerbuilder.com/share/aboutus/pressreleasesdetail.
aspx?sd=7 per cent2F29 per cent2F2010&id=pr581&ed=12 per cent2F31 per
cent2F2010.

17. "What You Wish You'd Known before Your Job Interview," *Classes and Careers*, accessed March 31, 2017, http://blog.classesandcareers.com/advisor/
what-you-wish-youd-known-before-your-job-interview/#comment-5632.

18. "New CareerBuilder Survey Reveals Top Body Language Mistakes Candidates Make in Job Interviews," *CareerBuilder*, July 28, 2010, accessed March
31, 2017, http://www.careerbuilder.com/share/aboutus/pressreleasesdetail.
aspx?sd=7 per cent2F29 per cent2F2010&id=pr581&ed=12 per cent2F31 per
cent2F2010.

19. R. J. Forbes and P. R. Jackson, "Non-verbal Behaviour and the Outcome of
Selection Interviews," *Journal of Occupational Psychology* 53, no.1 (1980):
65-72.

20. Edward C. Webster and Clifford Wilfred Anderson, *Decision Making in the
Employment Interview* (Montreal: Industrial Relations Centre, McGill University, 1964).

21. John M. Darley and Russel H. Fazio, "Expectancy Confirmation Processes
Arising in the Social Interaction Sequence," *American Psychologist* 35, no. 10
(1980): 867-881, accessed March 31, 2017, doi: 10.1037/0003-066X.35.10.867.

22. Photo by Albin Olsson. "Conchita Wurst at the Winners Press Conference,
Right After Winning the Eurovision Song Contest 2014 in Copenhagen,"
ESC2014 winner's press conference 11, May 11, 2014, accessed March 31, 2017,
https://commons.wikimedia.org/w/index.php?curid=32741075. License link
https://creativecommons.org/licenses/by-sa/3.0/.

23. Andy Bennett, *Culture and Everyday Life* (London: Sage, 2005), 96.

24. "French Veil Law: Muslim Woman's Challenge in Strasbourg," *BBC*, November 27, 2013, accessed March 31, 2017, http://www.bbc.com/news/world-
europe-25118160.

25. Heather Saul, "Men in Iran Are Wearing Hijabs in Solidarity with Their
Wives Who Are Forced to Cover Their Hair," *Independent*, July 28, 2016,
accessed March 31, 2017, http://www.independent.co.uk/news/people/men-
in-iran-are-wearing-hijabs-in-solidarity-with-their-wives-a7160146.html.

26. Foo Jie Ying, "Ho Ching's White House Purse Designed by Autistic Youth,"
The Newpaper, August 4, 2016, accessed March 31, 2017, http://www.tnp.sg/
news/singapore/ho-chings-white-house-purse-designed-autistic-youth.

27. Chris Barker, "Youth, Style and Resistance," in *Cultural Studies: Theory and
Practice*, ed. Chris Barker (London: Sage, 2000).

28. Maria A. Arapova, "A Cross-Cultural Study of the Smile in the Russian- and
English-Speaking World," *Journal of Language and Cultural Education*
4, no. 2 (2016), accessed March 31, 2017, doi: https://doi.org/10.1515/jol-
ace-2016-0016.

29. Tatiana G. Stefanenko, "Ulybka i vysokokontextnost' tradicionnoi russkoi
kultury [The Smile and the high context of traditional Russian culture],"
Nacional'nyj Psychologicheskij Zhurnal 2 (2014): 13-18.

30. Katherine Frith, Ping Shaw and Hong Cheng, "The Construction of Beauty: A Cross-Cultural Analysis of Women's Magazine Advertising," *Journal of Communication* 55, no. 1 (2005): 56-70, accessed March 31, 2017, doi: 10.1111/j.1460-2466.2005.tb02658.x.

31. Edward T. Hall, *Beyond Culture* (Garden City with Anchor Books, 1976), 91.

32. Ibid.

33. Hannah Faye Chua, Julie E. Boland and Richard E. Nisbett, "Cultural Variation in Eye Movements during Scene Perception," *PNAS* 102, no. 35 (2005): 12629-12633, accessed March 31, 2017, doi: 10.1073/pnas.0506162102.

34. Takahiko Masuda and Richard E. Nisbett, "Attending Holistically vs. Analytically: Comparing the Context Sensitivity of Japanese and Americans," *J. Pers. Soc. Psychol.* 81, no. 5 (2001): 922-934, accessed March 31, 2017, http://dx.doi.org/10.1037/0022-3514.81.5.922.

35. Alison Gopnik. and Soonja Choi, "Names, relational words, and cognitive development in English and Korean speakers: Nouns are not always learned before verbs," in *Beyond Names for Things: Young Children's Acquisition of Verbs,* ed. M. Tomasello et al. (Hillsdale: Lawrence Erlbaum Associates Inc, 1995): 63–80.

36. Li-Jun Ji et al., "Is It Culture or is It Language? Examination of Language Effects in Cross-Cultural Research on Categorization," *J. Pers. Soc. Psychology* 87, no. 1 (2005): 57-65, accessed March 31, 2017, doi: 10.1037/0022-3514.87.1.57.

37. Michael W. Morris and Kaiping Peng, "Culture and Cause: American and Chinese Attributions For Social and Physical Events," *Journal of Personality and Social Psychology* 67, no. 6 (1994): 949-971, accessed March 31, 2017, doi: 10.1037//0022-3514.67.6.949.

38. Heejung S. Kim, "We Talk, Therefore We Think? A Cultural Analysis of the Effect of Talking on Thinking," *Journal of Personality and Social Psychology* 83, no. 4 (2002): 828-842, accessed March 31, 2017, doi: 10.1037//0022-3514.83.4.828.

39. Ibid.

40. Tarun Khanna, Krishna G. Palepu and Jayant Sinha, "Strategies. That Fit Emerging Markets," *Harvard Business Review*, June 2005, accessed March 31, 2017, http://csbweb01.uncw.edu/people/keatingb/classes/INB300/Strategies per cent20That per cent20Fit per cent20Emerging per cent20Markets.pdf.

41. "2016 Asian Trailblazers Study-Masters of Multitasking and Transformation," *Willis Towers Watson,* April 26, 2016, accessed March 31, 2017, https://www.willistowerswatson.com/en/insights/2016/04/Willis-Towers-Watson-2016-Asian-Trailblazers-Study.

42. Edward T. Hall and Mildred Reed Hall, *Understanding Cultural Differences* (Yarmouth: Intercultural Press Inc., 1990).

43. Colin White and Laurie Boucke, *The UnDutchables: An Observation of the Netherlands, Its Culture and Its Inhabitants*, 3rd ed. (Glendale: White-Boucke Publishing, 2013).

44. "Global Retail Expansion at a Crossroad," *ATKearney*, 2016, accessed March 31, 2017, https://www.atkearney.com/documents/10192/8226719/

Global+Retail+Expansion+at+a+Crossroads per centE2 per cent80 per cent932016+GRDI.pdf/dc845ffc-fe28-4623-bdd4-b36f3a443787.

45. V. Emre Ozdemir and Kelly Hewett, "The Effect of Collectivism on the Importance of Relationship Quality and Service Quality for Behavioral Intentions: A Cross-National and Cross-Contextual Analysis," *Journal of International Marketing* 18, no. 1 (2010): 41-62, accessed March 31, 2017, doi: 10.1509/jimk.18.1.41.

46. Raymond R. Liu and Peter McClure, "Recognizing Cross-Cultural Differences in Consumer Complaint Behavior and Intentions: An Empirical examination," *Journal of Consumer Marketing* 18, no. 1 (2001): 54-75, accessed March 31, 2017, doi: 10.1108/07363760110365813.

47. Robert East, "Complaining as Planned Behavior," *Psychology & Marketing* 17, no. 12 (2000): 1077-1098, accessed March 31, 2017, doi: 10.1002/1520-6793(200012)17:12<1077::AID-MAR4>3.0.CO;2-W.

48. Jainaba Jagne et al., "Cross-cultural interface Design Strategy," *Interaction Design Centre* (2004), accessed March 31, 2017, http://citeseerx.ist.psu.edu/viewdoc/download?doi=10.1.1.99.4635&rep=rep1&type=pdf.

49. Elizabeth Würtz, "Intercultural Communication on Web Sites: A Cross-Cultural Analysis of Web Sites from High-Context Cultures and Low-Context Cultures," *Journal of Computer-Mediated Communication* 11, no. 1 (2005), accessed March 31, 2017, doi: 10.1111/j.1083-6101.2006.tb00313.x.

50. Thomas J. Bruneau, "Chronemics and the Verbal-Nonverbal Interface," in *The Relationship of Verbal and Nonverbal Communication*, ed. Mary Ritchie Key (The Hague: Mouton Press, 1980): 101–119.

51. Benjamin Franklin, "Advice to a Young Tradesman, Written by an Old one," in *The Writings of Benjamin Franklin* (Philadelphia: Yale University Library, 2007): 1726–1757.

52. Peter B. Smith and Michael Harris Bond, *Social Psychology across Culture: Analysis and Perspective* (Boston: Allyn and Bacon, 1994), 149.

53. Ibid.: 147.

54. Peter B. Smith and Michael Harris Bond, *Social Psychology across Culture: Analysis and Perspective* (Boston: Allyn and Bacon, 1994), 149.

55. Edward T. Hall and Mildred Reed Hall, *Understanding Cultural Differences* (Yarmouth: Intercultural Press Inc., 1990).

56. Edward T. Hall, "The Silent Language in Overseas Business," *Harvard Business Review* 38, no. 3 (1960): 89, accessed March 31, 2017, https://hbr.org/1960/05/the-silent-language-in-overseas-business.

57. David Stanley, *Fiji* (Emeryville: Avalon Travel Publishing, 2001), 105.

58. Susan Roraff and Laura Camacho, *Culture Shock: Chile* (Portland: Graphic Arts Center Publishing, 1998), 131.

59. Mark A. Ashwill, *Vietnam Today: A Guide to a Nation at a Crossroads* (Yarmouth: Nicholas Brealey, 2004).

60. "Is Informal Normal? Toward More and Better Jobs," OECD Observer, March 2009, accessed March 31, 2017, http://e-regulations.org/media/website/OECD_is_informal_normal.pdf.

61. Robert Neuwirth, "The Shadow Superpower," *Foreign Policy,* October 28, 2011, accessed March 31, 2017, http://foreignpolicy.com/2011/10/28/the-shadow-superpower/.

62. Kristina Flodman Becker, "The Informal Economy: Fact Finding Study," Sida, 2004, accessed March 31, 2017, http://www.rrojasdatabank.info/sida.pdf.

63. "Shadow Economy Defies Crisis – Year-End Note with a Wry Pitch," Deutsche Bank Research, December 21, 2009, accessed March 31, 2017, http://www.dbresearch.de/PROD/DBR_INTERNET_EN-PROD/PROD0000000000252019.pdf.

64. Friedrich Schneider, Andreas Buehn and Claudio E. Montenegro, "Shadow Economies All over the World. New Estimates for 162 Countries from 1999 to 2007," *Policy Research Working Paper* 5356 (2010), accessed March 31, 2017, http://www.gfintegrity.org/storage/gfip/documents/reports/world_bank_shadow_economies_all_over_the_world.pdf.

65. Vanessa Ratten, "Female Entrepreneurship and the Role of Customer Knowledge Development, Innovation Outcome Expectations and Culture on Intentions to Start Informal Business Ventures," *Journal of Entrepreneurship and Small Business* 27, nos 2/3 (2016): 262, accessed March 31, 2017, doi: http://dx.doi.org/10.1504/IJESB.2016.073977.

66. Jane Engle, "Punctuality: Some Cultures Are Wound Tighter than Others," *Los Angeles Times,* December 11, 2005, accessed March 31, 2017, http://articles.latimes.com/2005/dec/11/travel/tr-insider11.

67. Edward T. Hall, *The Dance of Life* (Garden City: Anchor Press, 1983), 53–54.

68. Edward T. Hall, *The Silent Language* (New York: Fawcett, 1959).

69. Daniel P. Kennedy et al., "Personal Space Regulation by the Human Amygdala," *Nat Neurosci.* 12, no. 10 (2009): 1226-1227, accessed March 31, 2017, doi: 10.1038/nn.2381.

70. Mike B. Beauchamp, "Don't Invade My Personal Space: Facebook's Advertising Dilemma," *Journal of Applied Business Research* 29, no. 1 (2013): 91, accessed March 31, 2017, doi: 10.19030/jabr.v29i1.7558.

71. David Cohen, "Brands, Maintain a Facebook Page, But Bon't Bother Me," *AdWeek,* February 23, 2012, accessed March 31, 2017, http://www.adweek.com/digital/facebook-page-consumers/.

72. Figure by WebHamster. "Diagram Representation of Personal Space Limits," *Personal Space,* March 8, 2009, accessed March 31, 2017, https://commons.wikimedia.org/w/index.php?curid=6147809. License Link: https://creativecommons.org/licenses/by-sa/3.0/.

73. Peter Clayton, *Body Language at Work,* (Barnes & Noble, 2003), location 1818.

74. Alexandra Marx, Urs Fuhrer and Terry Hartig, "Effects of Classroom Seating Arrangements on Children's Question-Asking," *Learning Environment Research* 2, no. 3 (2006): 249-263, accessed March 31, 2017, doi: 10.1023/A:1009901922191.

75. Victor Alberto Tagliacollo, Gilson Luiz Volpato and Alfredo Pereira Jr., "Association of Student Position in Classroom and School Performance," *Educational Research* 1, no. 6 (2010): 198-201, accessed March 31, 2017, http://

www2.ufersa.edu.br/portal/view/uploads/setores/190/0artigo%20Gil-son%20Volpato%20escola.pdf.

76. Moses Waithanji Ngware et al., "The Influence of Classroom Seating Posi-tion on Student Learning Gains in Primary Schools in Kenya," *SciRes* 4, no. 11 (2013): 705-712, accessed March 31, 2017, http://dx.doi.org/10.4236/ce.2013.411100.

77. Annika Feige et al., "Impact of Sustainable Office Buildings on Occupant's Comfort and Productivity," *Journal of Corporate Real Estate* 15, no. 1 (2013): 7-34, accessed March 31, 2017, doi: 10.1108/JCRE-01-2013-0004.

78. Yousef Al Horr et al., "Occupant Productivity and Office Indoor Environ-ment Quality: A Review of the Literature," *Building and Environment* 105 (2016): 369-389, accessed March 31, 2017, http://dx.doi.org/10.1016/j.build-env.2016.06.001.

79. Sapna Cheryan, "Ambient Belonging: How Stereotypical Cues Impact Gender Participation in Computer Science," *Journal of Personality and Social Psychology* 97, no. 6 (2009): 1045-1060, accessed March 31, 2017, doi: 10.1037/a0016239.

80. "The Privacy Crisis," *360 Magazine*, November 12, 2014, accessed March 31, 2017, https://www.steelcase.com/insights/articles/privacy-crisis/.

81. Stephen E. Palmer and Karen B. Schloss, "An Ecological Valence Theory of Human Color Preference," *Proceedings of the National Academy of Sci-ences* 107, no. 19 (2010): 8877-8882, accessed March 31, 2017, doi: 10.1073/pnas.0906172107.

82. Nancy Kwallek, Kokyung Soon and Carol M. Lewis, "Work Week Productiv-ity, Visual Complexity, and Individual Environmental Sensitivity in Three Offices of Different Color Interiors," *Color Research & Application* 32, no. 2 (2007): 130-143, accessed March 31, 2017, doi: 10.1002/col.20298.

83. Nancy J. Stone, "Environmental View and Color for a Simulated Telemar-keting Task," *Journal of Environmental Psychology* 23, no. 1 (2003): 63-78, accessed March 31, 2017, doi: 10.1016/S0272-4944(02)00107-X.

84. Mami Kido, "Bio-Psychological Effects of Color," *Journal of International Society of Life Information Science* 18, no. 1 (2000): 254-262.

85. Nancy Kwallek et al., "Effects of Nine Monochromatic Office Interior Colors on Clerical Tasks and Worker Mood," *Color Research & Application* 21, no. 6 (1996): 448-458, accessed March 31, 2017, doi: 10.1002/(SICI)1520-6378(199612)21:6<448::AID-COL7>3.0.CO;2-W.

86. Jamie Livingstone, "The Value of Art in the Workplace," *New Hampshire Business Committee for the Arts and the International Association for Profes-sional Art Advisors*, 2003, accessed March 31, 2017, http://artiq.co/art/the-power-of-art-in-the-workplace/.

87. Joseph G. Allen et al., "Associations of Cognitive Function Scores with Carbon Dioxide, Ventilation, and Volatile Organic Compound Exposures in Office Workers: A Controlled Exposure Study of Green and Conventional Office Environments," *Environmental Health Perspectives*, 26 October 2015,

accessed March 31, 2017, https://ehp.niehs.nih.gov/wp-content/uploads/
advpub/2015/10/ehp.1510037.acco.pdf.

88.   Deepak Malhotra, "Control the Negotiation Before It Begins," *Harvard Business Review*, December 2015, accessed March 31, 2017, https://hbr.org/2015/12/control-the-negotiation-before-it-begins.

89.   Emory A. Griffin, "Proxemics," in *A First Look at Communication Theory* (Boston: McGraw Hill, 2012), 60.

90.   Charles Francis, *Wisdom Well Said* (El Prado: Levine Mesa Press, 2009), 144.

91.   Edward T. Hall, *The Silent Language* (New York: Anchors Books, 1973), 185.

92.   Edward T. Hall, "The Anthropology of Manners," *Scientific American* 192, no. 4 (1955): 85-89, accessed March 31, 2017, doi: 10.1038/scientificamerican0455-84.

93.   Peter Clayton, *Body Language at Work: Read the Signs and Make the Right Moves* (New York: Barnes & Noble, 2003).

94.   Rob Crilly, "Sofa Provokes Diplomatic Row between Israel and Turkey," *The Telegraph*, January 13, 2010, accessed March 31, 2017, http://www.telegraph.co.uk/news/worldnews/europe/turkey/6982023/Sofa-provokes-diplomatic-row-between-Israel-and-Turkey.html.

95.   Larry A. Samovar, Richard Porter, and Edwin McDaniel, *Communication between Cultures,* 6th ed. Belmont: (Wadsworth Publishing, 2006), 218.

96.   Chuong Tuong, "Nguon Goc, Y Nghia Tuc Tho Than Tai va Than Tho Dia," [The origin and Significance of the Tradition of Worshipping the God of Earth], *Doi Song Phap Luat, Doi Song Phap Luat,* February, 27, 2015, accessed March 331, 2017, http://www.doisongphapluat.com/gia-dinh/nguon-goc-y-nghia-tuc-tho-than-tai-va-than-tho-dia-a84964.html.

97.   Tsai-Yun Mou, Tay-Sheng Jeng and Chun-Heng Ho, "Sociable Kitchen: Interactive Recipe System in Kitchen Island," *International Journal of Smart Home* 3, no. 2 (2009): 641-650, accessed March 31, 2017, doi: 10.1007/978-3-642-02580-8_70.

98.   Edward T Hall, "The Silent Language of Overseas Business," *Harvard Business Review,* May-June 1960, accessed March 31, 2017, https://hbr.org/1960/05/the-silent-language-in-overseas-business.

99.   Edwin R. McDaniel, "Nonverbal Communication: A Reflection of Cultural Themes" in *Intercultural Communication: A Reader,* 9th ed., ed. Larry A. Samovar and Richard E. Porter (Belmont: Wadsworth, 2000).

100.   Lee W. Bass and Jerome H. Wolfson, *The Style and Management of a Pediatric Practice* (Washington: Beard Books, 2003), 31.

101.   Peter Clayton, *Body language at work: read the signs and make the right moves* (Barnes & Noble, 2003), location 1913.

102.   Mubeen M. Aslam, "Are You Selling the Right Colour? A Cross-Cultural Review of Colour as a Marketing Cue," *Journal of Marketing Communications* 12, no. 1 (2005): 1-14, accessed March 31, 2017, http://ro.uow.edu.au/cgi/viewcontent.cgi?article=2092&context=commpapers.

103.   Quran, Sura 18, The Cave (Al-Kahf).

104. Vanessa LoBue and Judy S. DeLoache, "Pretty in Pink: The Early Develop-
      ment of Gender-Stereotyped Colour Preferences," *British Journal of Develop-
      mental Psychology* 29, no. 3 (2011): 656-667, accessed March 31, 2017, http://
      onlinelibrary.wiley.com/doi/10.1111/j.2044-835X.2011.02027.x/abstract.

105. Caroline Smith and Barbara Lloyd, "Maternal Behavior and Perceived Sex of
      Infant: Revisited," *Society for Research in Child Development* 49, no. 4 (1978):
      1263-1265, accessed March 31, 2017, doi: 10.2307/1128775.

106. "Is the White Feminine," Android Forums, accessed March 31, 2017, http://
      androidforums.com/threads/is-the-white-feminine.566244/.

107. Brynn Holland, "Woman in White: Hillary Clinton's Suffragette Tribute," *His-
      tory in the Headlines*, October 21, 2016, accessed March 31, 2017, http://www.
      history.com/news/woman-in-white-hillary-clintons-suffragette-tribute.

108. Phillip Tang, "Different Disneylands around the World," *BBC*, December 18,
      2012, accessed March 31, 2017, http://www.bbc.com/travel/story/20121213-
      different-disneylands-around-the-world.

109. Fons Trompenaars and Charles Hampden-Turner, *Riding the Waves of
      Culture: Understanding Diversity in Global Business*, 3rd ed. (New York: The
      McGraw Hill Companies, 2012).

110. Peter B. Smith and Michael Harris Bond, *Social Psychology across Cultures:
      Analysis and Perspective* (Boston: Allyn and Bacon, 1994), 141.

111. Yuka Shigemitsu, "Different interpretations of pauses, Japanese, Chinese,
      and Americans," *The Academic Reports*, Tokyo Polytechnic University 28,
      no.2 (2005): 8-14, accessed March 31, 2017, https://www.t-kougei.ac.jp/re-
      search/pdf/vol2-28-02.pdf.

112. Michael Lynn, "Seven Ways to Increase Servers' Tips," *Cornell Hospi-
      tality Quarterly* 37, no. 3 (1996): 24-29, accessed March 31, 2017, doi:
      10.1177/001088049603700315.

113. Peter Clayton, *Body language at work: read the signs and make the right
      moves* (Barnes & Noble, 2003), location 716.

114. Barbara Pease and Allan Pease, *The definitive book of body language* (New
      York: Random House LLC, 2008), 167.

115. Peter Clayton, *Body language at work: read the signs and make the right
      moves* (Barnes & Noble, 2003), location 815.

116. Photo by Auguel. "Princess Diana Opens The Paisley Centre and Pays a Visit
      to the Accord Hospice. Colorized," *Ain Wirk*, February 15, 2017, accessed
      March 31, 2017, https://sco.wikipedia.org/wiki/File:Princess_Diana_at_Ac-
      cord_Hospice_colorized.png License Link: https://creativecommons.org/
      licenses/by-sa/4.0/deed.en.

117. Greg Nees, *Germany: Unraveling an Enigma* (Boston: Intercultural Press,
      2000), 93.

118. Ailsa Chang, "What Eye Contact and Dogs Can Teach Us about Civility in
      Politics," *NPR*, May 8, 2015, accessed March 31, 2017, http://www.npr.org/
      sections/itsallpolitics/2015/05/08/404991505/what-eye-contact-and-dogs-
      can-teach-us-about-civility-in-politics.

119. Madison Fantozzi, "UM Researcher Pioneered Massaging Premature Infants to Stimulate Growth," *The Miami Herald*, November 4, 2014, accessed March 31, 2017, http://www.miamiherald.com/living/health-fitness/article3556835.html.

120. Michael Lynn, "Seven ways to increase servers' tips," *Cornell Hotel and Restaurant Administration Quarterly* 37, no.3 (1996): 24-29, accessed March 31, 2017, http://scholarship.sha.cornell.edu/cgi/viewcontent.cgi?article=1112&context=articles.

121. Carol Kinsey Goman, "10 Simple and Powerful Body Language Tips for 2012," *Forbes*, January 3, 2012, accessed March 31, 2017, https://www.forbes.com/sites/carolkinseygoman/2012/01/03/10-simple-and-powerful-body-language-tips-for-2012/#55005d307e99.

122. AFP, "Bill Gates 'Disrespects' South Korean President with Casual Handshake," *The Telegraph*, April 23, 2013, accessed March 31, 2017, http://www.telegraph.co.uk/technology/bill-gates/10011847/Bill-Gates-disrespects-South-Korean-president-with-casual-handshake.html.

123. Helena Horton, "Donald Trump Mocked for 'Awkward' Handshake with Japanese Prime Minister Shinzo Abe," *The Telegraph*, February 11, 2017, accessed March 31, 2017, http://www.telegraph.co.uk/news/2017/02/11/donald-trump-mocked-awkward-handshake-japanese-prime-minister/.

124. Peter Collett, Peter Marsh and Marie O'Shaughnessy, *Gestures: Their Origins and Distribution* (London: Cape, 1979).

125. Christian Keysers and Valeria Gazzola, "Social Neuroscience: Mirror Neurons Recorded in Humans," *Current Biology* 20, no. 8 (2010): 353-354, doi: 10.1016/j.cub.2010.03.013.

126. Jaime A. Pineda, *Mirror Neuron Systems: The Role of Mirroring Processes in Social Cognition* (Atlanta: Emory University, 2007), 191–212.

127. Christian Keysers, *The Empathic Brain* (Social Brain Press, 2011).

128. Marco Iacoboni, *Mirroring People: The New Science of How We Connect With Others* (New York: Picador, 2008).

129. Carl O. Word, Mark P. Zanna and Joel Cooper, "The Nonverbal Mediation of Self-fulfilling Prophecies in Interracial Interaction," *Journal of Experimental Social Psychology* 10, no. 2 (1974): 109-120, accessed March 31, 2017, http://dx.doi.org/10.1016/0022-1031(74)90059-6.

130. Lora E. Park et al., "Stand Tall, But Don't Put Your Feet up: Universal and Culturally-Specific Effects of Expansive Postures on Power," *Journal of Experimental Social Psychology* 49, no. 6 (2013): 965-971, accessed March 31, 2017, doi: 10.1016/j.jesp.2013.06.001.

131. Jo Adetunji, "Pakistan President Targeted by Shoe-Throwing Protester in Birmingham," *The Guardian, August* 9, 2010, accessed March 31, 2017, https://www.theguardian.com/global/2010/aug/09/pakistan-president-shoe-throwing-birmingham.

132. "Sudan Shoe-Thrower Targets President Omar al-Bashir," *BBC*, January 26, 2010, accessed March 31, 2017, http://news.bbc.co.uk/2/hi/africa/8479185.stm.

133. "Defiant Mubarak Refuses to Resign," *Al Jazeera*, February 11, 2011, ac-
      cessed March 31, 2017, http://www.aljazeera.com/news/middleea
      st/2011/02/2011210172519776830.html.

134. Shirzad Bozorghmehr, "Iranian President Targeted by Shoe Thrower," *CNN*,
      December 13, 2011, accessed March 31, 2017, http://edition.cnn.com/2011/12/12/
      world/meast/iran-shoes-ahmadinejad/index.html?hpt=hp_t2.

135. "Mongolian Economic Forum 2016 Concluded," *Montsame Daily News*, April
      1, 2016, accessed March 31, 2017, http://www.sanfrancisco.consul.mn/eng/
      index.php?moduls=101&id=324.

136. Per Nyberg et al., "Protester Throws Shoe at China's Premier," *CNN*, Febru-
      ary 3, 2009, accessed March 31, 2017, http://edition.cnn.com/2009/WORLD/
      europe/02/02/china.uk.shoe.protest/.

137. "Student Throws Shoe at Former Australian PM John Howard," *The Tel-
      egraph*, November 04, 2009, accessed March 31, 2017, http://www.telegraph.
      co.uk/news/worldnews/australiaandthepacific/australia/6498119/Student-
      throws-shoe-at-former-Australian-PM-John-Howard.html.

138. Martin Asser, "Bush Shoe-ing Worst Arab Insult," *BBC*, December 15, 2008, ac-
      cessed March 31, 2017, http://news.bbc.co.uk/2/hi/middle_east/7783325.stm.

139. Photo by 美國之音黃耀毅拍攝. "Taiwanese People Donate Shoes to Sup-
      port Protest and Shoe-throwing against KMT Ma Ying-jeou.png," *VOAcan-
      tonese,* October 1, 2013, accessed March 31, 2017, http://www.voacantonese.
      com/content/taiwan-protest-20131001/1760440.html. Public Domain.

140. Fons Trompenaars and Charles Hampden-Turner, *Riding the Waves of
      Culture: Understanding Diversity in Global Business,* 3rd ed. (New York: The
      McGraw Hill Companies, 2012).

141. Maarten W. Bos and Amy J.C. Cuddy, "iPosture: The Size of Electronic
      Consumer Devices Affects Our Behavior," *Harvard Business School*, no.
      13-097 (2013), accessed March 31, 2017, http://www.hbs.edu/faculty/Publica-
      tion%20Files/13-097_4c473e46-e91b-4c9a-9070-ff61c7f70d3a.pdf.

142. Amy J.C. Cuddy, Caroline A. Wilmuth and Dana R. Carney, "The Benefit of
      Power Posing Before a High-Stakes Social Evaluation," *Harvard Business
      School Working Paper*, no. 13-027 (2012), accessed March 31, 2017, https://
      dash.harvard.edu/bitstream/handle/1/9547823/13-027.pdf?sequence=1.

143. Suzanne Osborn and Michael T. Motley, *Improving Communication* (Boston:
      Houghton Mifflin College Div., 1999), 50.

144. Joyce S. Osland et al., "Beyond Sophisticated Stereotyping: Cultural Sense-
      making in Context [and Executive Commentaries]," *Academy of Manage-
      ment* 14, no. 1 (2000): 65-79, accessed March 31, 2017, https://www.jstor.org/
      stable/4165609?seq=1#page_scan_tab_contents.

145. Richard D. Lewis, *Finland, Cultural Lone Wolf* (Yarmouth: Intercultural Press,
      2005).

146. Shoji Nishimura, Anne Nevgi and Seppo Tella, "Communication Style and
      Cultural Features in High/Low Context Communication Cultures: A Case
      Study of Finland, Japan and India," *University of Helsinki*, accessed March 31,
      2017, http://www.helsinki.fi/~tella/nishimuranevgitella299.pdf.

147. James Kynge, "EU Trade Deal Clears China's Way into WTO," *Financial Times,* 20/21 May 2000, 1.

148. Carolyn Blackman, "An Inside Guide to Negotiating," *The China Business Review,* May-June 2000, 44-46.

149. Kenneth Tan, "China Introduces Surprisingly Progressive Sex Education Curriculum for Kids, Some Parents Freak Out," *Shanghaiist*, March 6, 2017, accessed March 31, 2017, http://shanghaiist.com/2017/03/06/comprehensive-sexuality-education.php.

150. Tony Fang, "From 'Onion' to 'Ocean': Paradox and Change in National Cultures," *International Studies of Management & Organization* 35, no. 4 (2005–2006): 71-90, accessed March 31, 2017, http://www.jstor.org/stable/40397646.

Chapter 5

1. Florence Rockwood Kluckhohn and Fred L. Strodtbeck, *Variations in Value Orientations* (Evanston: Row, Peterson, 1961).

2. Ibid.

3. Harry Triandis, *Analysis of Subjective Culture* (New York: Wiley, 1972).

4. Shalom H. Schwartz, "Beyond Individualism/Collectivism: New Cultural Dimensions of Values," in *Individualism and Collectivism: Theory, Method, and Applications*, ed. Uichol Kim et al., (Thousand Oaks: Sage Publications, 1994), 85–119.

5. Geert Hofstede, *Culture's Consequences: International Differences in Work-Related Values*, 2nd ed. (Beverly Hills: SAGE Publications, 1984).

6. Charles Hampden-Turner and Fons Trompenaars, *Riding The Waves of Culture: Understanding Diversity in Global Business,* 3rd ed. (London: Nicholas Brealey Publishing, 2012).

7. Robert J. House et al., *Culture, Leadership, and Organizations: The GLOBE Study of 62 Societies* (Thousand Oaks: Sage Publications, 2004).

8. Paul J. Watson and Ronald J. Morris, "Individualist and Collectivist Values: Hypotheses Suggested by Alexis de Tocqueville," *The Journal of Psychology* 136, no. 3 (2010): 263-271, accessed March 31, 2017, doi: 10.1080/00223980209604154.

9. Owenites is also considered to be the author of this term. See Gregory Claeys, "'Individualism,' 'Socialism,' and 'Social Science': Further Notes on a Process of Conceptual Formation, 1800–1850," *Journal of the History of Ideas* 47, no. 1 (1986): 81–93. doi: 10.2307/2709596. JSTOR 2709596.

10. Alexis de Tocqueville, *Democracy in America* (Project Gutenberg, 1840), accessed April 1, 2017, https://www.marxists.org/reference/archive/de-tocqueville/democracy-america/.

11. Koenraad W. Swart, "Individualism in the Mid-Nineteenth Century (1826–1860)," *Journal of the History of Ideas* 23, no. 1 (1962): 77-90, accessed March 31, 2017, doi: 10.2307/2708058.

12. Jennifer T. Kubota, Mahzarin R. Banaji and Elizabeth A. Phelps, "The Neuroscience of Race," *Nature Neuroscience* 15, no. 7 (2012): 940-948, accessed March 31, 2017, doi: 10.1038/nn.3136.

13. Allen J. Hart et al., "Differential Response in the Human Amygdala to Racial Outgroup vs Ingroup Face Stimuli," *Neuroreport* 11, no. 11 (2000): 2351-2355, accessed March 31, 2017, https://pdfs.semanticscholar.org/0ee6/4e6fe4c286e 5b87e13058b6c2cc25f67bf1c.pdf.

14. Meghan L. Meyer, "Empathy for the Social Suffering of Friends and Strangers Recruits Distinct Patterns of Brain Activation," *Social Cognitive and Affective Neuroscience* 8, no. 4 (2012): 1-9, accessed March 31, 2017, doi: 10.1093/ scan/nss019.

15. Grit Hein et al., "Neural Responses to Ingroup and Outgroup Members Suffering Predict Individual Differences in Costly Helping," *Neuron* 68, no. 1 (2010): 149-160, accessed March 31, 2017, doi: 10.1016/j.neuron.2010.09.003.

16. Geert Hofstede, Gert-Jan Hofstede and Michael Minkov, *Cultures and Organizations: Software of the Mind* (New York: McGraw-Hill, 2005), 78–79.

17. Fons Trompenaars and Charles Hampden-Turner, *Riding The Waves of Culture: Understanding Diversity in Global Business,* 3rd ed. (New York: Nicholas Brealey, 1997), 51.

18. Riadh Ladhari, Nizar Souiden and Yong-Hoon Choi, "Culture Change and Globalization: The Unresolved Debate between Cross-National and Cross-Cultural Classifications," *Australian Marketing Journal* 23, no. 3 (2015): 235-245, accessed March 31, 2017, doi: 10.1016/j.ausmj.2015.06.003.

19. David A. Ralston, Nguyen Van Thang and Nancy K. Napier, "A Comparative Study of the Work Values of North and South Vietnamese Managers," *Journal of International Business Studies* 30, no. 4 (1999): 655-672, accessed March 31, 2017, doi: 10.1057/palgrave.jibs.8490889.

20. Robert J. House et al., *Culture, Leadership, and Organizations: The GLOBE Study of 62 Societies* (Thousand Oaks: Sage Publications, 2004).

21. Theodore M. Singelis et al., "Horizontal and Vertical Dimensions of Individualism and Collectivism: A Theoretical and Measurement Refinement," *Cross-Cultural Research* 29, no. 3 (1995): 240-275, accessed March 31, 2017, doi: 10.1177/106939719502900302.

22. Peter Walker, "Japanese Men and Women 'Giving up Dating and Marrying Friends'," *The Independent*, December 6, 2016, accessed March 31, 2017, http://www.independent.co.uk/life-style/japanese-sex-problem-so-bad-people-giving-up-dating-a7458461.html.

23. Chris Weller, "Japanese People Who Can't Afford Elder Care Are Reviving a Practice Known as 'Granny Dumping'," *Business Insider*, January 30, 2017, accessed March 31, 2017, http://www.businessinsider.com/japanese-people-reviving-granny-dumping-practice-2017-1?international=true&r=US&IR=T.

24. Shibley Telhami, *The World through Arab Eyes* (New York: Basic Books, 2013).

25. Chenbo Wang et al., "Accessible Cultural Mind-set Modulates Default Mode Activity: Evidence for the Culturally Situated Brain," *Social Neuroscience* 8,

no. 3 (2013): 203-216, accessed March 31, 2017, http://dx.doi.org/10.1080/17470 919.2013.775966.

26. Ying-yi Hong et al., "Multicultural Minds: A Dynamic Constructivist Approach to Culture and Cognition," *American Psychologist* 55, no. 7 (2010): 709-720, accessed March 31, 2017, doi: 10.1037//0003-066X.55.7.709.

27. Richard Ball, "Individualism, Collectivism, and Economic Development," *Sage Publications* 573, no. 1 (2001): 57-84, accessed March 31, 2017, https:// www.jstor.org/stable/pdf/1049015.pdf.

28. Phuong-Mai Nguyen et al., "Cooperative Learning that Features a Culturally Appropriate Pedagogy," *British Educational Research Journal* 35, no. 6 (2010): 857-875, accessed March 31, 2017, doi: 10.1080/01411920802688762.

29. Zhen Wang et al., "Cooperative Goals and Team Agreeableness Composition for Constructive Controversy in China," *Asia Pacific Journal Management* 27, no. 1 (2010): 139-153, doi: 10.1007/s10490-009-9175-y.

30. Nancy Chen Yi-Feng and Dean Tjosvold, "Guanxi and Leader Member Relationships between American Managers and Chinese Employees: Open-minded Dialogue as Mediator," *Asia Pacific Journal of Management* 24, no. 2 (2007): 171-189, accessed March 31, 2017, doi: 10.1007/s10490-006-9029-9.

31. Michelle Jamrisko and Wei Lu, "These Are the World's Most Innovative Economies," *Bloomberg*, January 20, 2016, accessed March 31, 2017, https:// www.bloomberg.com/news/articles/2016-01-19/these-are-the-world-s-most-innovative-economies.

32. Stella Ting-Toomey, "The Matrix of Face: An Updated Face-Negotiation Theory," in *Theorizing About Intercultural Communication*, ed. William B. Gudykunst (Thousand Oaks: Sage Publications, 2005), 73.

33. Mai Nguyen-Phuong-Mai, Cees Terlouw and Albert Pilot, "Revisiting Face-work with a New Analysis Instrument: Face Strategies and Face Negotiation in Intercultural Communication," *Journal of Intercultural Communication* 36 (2014), accessed April 1, 2017, https://www.immi.se/intercultural/nr36/ nguyen.html.

34. Wei-Lin Melody Chang and Michael Haugh, "Strategic Embarrassment and Face Threatening in Business Interactions," *Journal of Pragmatics* 43, no. 12 (2011): 2948-2963, accessed March 31, 2017, http://ro.uow.edu.au/cgi/view-content.cgi?article=3094&context=lhapapers.

35. Stella Ting-Toomey and Atsuko Kurogi, "Facework Competence in Intercultural Conflict: An Updated Face-Negotiation Theory," *International Journal of Intercultural Relations* 22, no. 2 (1998): 202, accessed March 31, 2017, doi: 10.1016/S0147-1767(98)00004-2.

36. Meiling Wong, "Guanxi Management as Complex Adaptive Systems: A Case Study of Taiwanese ODI in China," *Journal of Business Ethics* 91, no. 3 (2010): 419-432, accessed March 31, 2017, doi: 10.1007/s10551-009-0093-1.

37. David E. Hawkins, "The Importance of Relationships," accessed March 31, 2017, http://kmhassociates.ca/resources/4/The%20importance%20of%20 relationships%20in%20business.pdf.

38. Andy H. Barnett, Bruce Yandle and George Naufal, "Regulation, Trust, and Cronyism in Middle Eastern Societies: The Simple Economics of 'Wasta," *Discussion Paper* 7201, February 2013, accessed March 31, 2017, http://ftp.iza. org/dp7201.pdf.

39. "Don't Worry, I Have Ksharim (Connections)," *TLV 1*, May 7, 2014, accessed March 31, 2017, http://tlv1.fm/streetwise-hebrew/2014/05/07/ksharim-con-nections-streetwise-hebrew/.

40. Svetla Ivanova Stoyanova-Bozhkova, "Tourism Development in Transition Economies: An Evaluation of the Development of Tourism at a Black Sea Coastal Destination during Political and Socio-Economic Transition," *Bournemouth University*, March 2011, accessed March 31, 2017, http://eprints. bournemouth.ac.uk/18828/1/Bozhkova,_Stoyanova_Ph.D_2011_THESIS.pdf.

41. Graham Faiella, *Spain: A Primary Source Cultural Guide* (New York: The Rosen Publishing Group, 2004), 110.

42. "Ave Madrid. Spain Plans the Most Extensive High-Speed Rail Network in Europe," *The Economist*, February 5, 2009, accessed March 31, 2017, http:// www.economist.com/node/13061961.

43. Mairi Maclean, Charles Harvey and Robert Chia, "Dominant Corporate Agents and the Power Elite in France and Britain," *Organization Studies* 31, no. 3 (2010): 327-348, accessed March 31, 2017, doi: 10.1177/0170840609357377.

44. Stefania Vitali, James B. Glattfelder and Stefano Battiston, "The Network of Global Corporate Control," *PLOS* 6, no. 10 (2011), accessed March 31, 2017, doi: 10.1371/journal.pone.0025995.

45. Daniel McAllister, "Affect and Cognition-Based Trust as Foundations for Interpersonal Cooperation in Organizations," *Academic of Management Journal* 38, no. 1 (1995): 24-59, accessed March 31, 2017, doi: 10.2307/256727.

46. Choe Sang-Hun, "Despair Overwhelmed Former South Korean Leader Embroiled in Scandal," *The New York Times*, May 23, 2009, accessed March 31, 2017, http://www.nytimes.com/2009/05/24/world/asia/24roh.html.

47. Malcolm Moore, "Captain Abandoned Ship – And Then Dried out His Banknotes," *Telegraph,* Apr 18, 2014, accessed March 31, 2017, http://www. telegraph.co.uk/news/worldnews/asia/southkorea/10775498/Captain-aban-doned-ship-and-then-dried-out-his-banknotes.html.

48. "Princess Maxima," *Hello Magazine*, accessed March 31, 2017, http://www. hellomagazine.com/profiles/crown-princess-maxima-of-the-netherlands/.

49. Alan P. Fiske, "The Four Elementary Forms of Sociality: Framework for a Unified Theory of Social Relations," *Psychological Review* 99, no. 4 (1992): 689-723, doi: 10.1037/0033-295X.99.4.689.

50. Alex Inkeles and Daniel J. Levinson, "National Characters: The Study of Modal Personality and Sociocultural Systems," In *The handbook of Social Psychology,* ed. G. Lindzey and E. Aronson, 2nd ed., vol.4 (Reading: Addison-Wesley, 1969).

51. Florence Kluckhohn and Fred Strodtbeck, *Variations in Value Orientations* (Evanston: Row, Peterson, 1961).

52.   Geert Hofstede, Gert-Jan Hofstede and Michael Minkov, *Cultures and Organizations: Software of the Mind* (New York: McGraw-Hill, 2005).

53.   Fons Trompenaars and Charles Hampden-Turner, *Riding The Waves of Culture: Understanding Diversity in Global Business,* 3rd ed. (London: Nicholas Brealey, 1997).

54.   Mark van Vugt and Anjana Ahuja, *Why Some People Lead, Why Others Follow, And Why It Matters* (London: Profile Books Ltd, 2010).

55.   Michael E. Price and Mark van Vugt, "The Service for Prestige Theory of Leadership," in *Handbook of the Biology of Organizational Behavior,* ed. Stephen M. Colarelli and Richard D. Arvey (Chicago: Chicago University Press, 2014).

56.   Mark van Vugt and Joshua M. Tybur, "The Evolutionary Foundations of Status Hierarchy," *The Handbook of Evolutionary Psychology* 6, no. 32 (2015): 1-22, accessed March 31, 2017, doi: 10.1002/9781119125563.evpsych232.

57.   Henok Mengistu et al., "The Evolutionary Origins of Hierarchy," *PLOS* 12, no. 6 (2016), accessed March 31, 2017, doi: 10.1371/journal.pcbi.1004829.

58.   Felicia Pratto, Jim Sidanius and Shana Levin, "Social Dominance Theory and the Dynamics of Intergroup Relations: Taking Stock and Looking Forward," *European Review of Social Psychology* 17, no. 1 (2006): 271-320, accessed March 31, 2017, doi: 10.1080/10463280601055772.

59.   Richard Sosis, "Religion and Intragroup Cooperation: Preliminary Results of a Comparative Analysis of Utopian Communities," *Cross-Cultural Research* 34, no. 1 (2000): 70-87, accessed March 31, doi: 10.1177/106939710003400105.

60.   Fons Trompenaars and Charles Hampden-Turner, *Riding The Waves of Culture: Understanding Diversity in Global Business,* 3rd ed. (London: Nicholas Brealey, 1997).

61.   Sook-Lei Liew et al., "Who's Afraid of the Boss: Cultural Differences in Social Hierarchies Modulate Self-Face Recognition in Chinese and Americans," *PLOS* 6, no. 2 (2011), accessed March 31, 2017, doi: 10.1371/journal.pone.0016901.

62.   Geert Hofstede, Gert-Jan Hofstede and Michael Minkov, *Cultures and Organizations: Software of the Mind* (New York: McGraw-Hill, 2005), 43–44.

63.   Fons Trompenaars and Charles Hampden-Turner, *Riding The Waves of Culture: Understanding Diversity in Global Business,* 3rd ed. (London: Nicholas Brealey, 1997), 106.

64.   Ben Kiernan, *The Pol Pot Regime: Politics, Race, and Genocide in Cambodia under the Khmer Rouge, 1975-1979* (New Haven: Yale University Press, 1996).

65.   Harry Harding, *China's Second Revolution: Reform after Mao* (Washington: Brookings Institution Press, 1987).

66.   Edward E. Moise, *Land Reform in China and North Vietnam* (Chapel Hill: University of North Carolina Press, 1983).

67.   Daphna Oyserman, "High Power, Low Power, and Equality: Culture beyond Individualism and Collectivism," *Journal of Consumer Psychology* 16, no. 4 (2006): 352-356.

68.   Robert J. House et al., *Culture, Leadership and Organizations: The GLOBE Study of 62 Societies* (Thousand Oaks: Sage, 2004).

69.   "Semco – Insanity That Works," *Freibergs*, accessed March 31, 2017, http://www. freibergs.com/resources/articles/leadership/semco-insanity-that-works/.

70.   Mary Petersson and Anna Spängs, "Semco & Freys: A multiple-case Study of Workplace Democracy," (Master Diss., Sodertorns Bogskola, 2005), accessed March 31, 2017, http://www.diva-portal.org/smash/get/diva2:16517/FULL-TEXT01.pdf.

71.   Jae Min Jung, Kawpong Polyorat and James Kellaris, "A Cultural Paradox in Authority-Based Advertising," *International Marketing Review* 26, no. 6 (2009): 601-632, accessed March 31, 2017, doi: 10.1108/02651330911001314.

72.   Ronald Fischer, "Gene-Environment Interactions are associated with Endorsement of Social Hierarchy Values and Beliefs across Cultures," *Journal of Cross-Cultural Psychology* 44, no. 7 (2013): 1107-1121, accessed March 31, 2017, doi: 10.1177/0022022112471896.

73.   Helene Hofman, "Girl, 14, Drowns Saving Kim Jong II Portrait in North Korea," *PRI*, June 27, 2012, accessed March 31, 2017, https://www.pri.org/stories/2012-06-27/girl-14-drowns-saving-kim-jong-il-portrait-north-korea.

74.   Photo by J.A. de Roo. "The Statues of Kim Il Sung (left) and Kim Jong Il on Mansu Hill in Pyongyang", *Wikipedia*, April 17, 2012, accessed March 31, 2017, https://commons.wikimedia.org/w/index.php?curid=21244159. License Link: https://creativecommons.org/licenses/by-sa/3.0/legalcode.

75.   Haru Yamada, *Different Games, Different Rules. Why Americans and Japanese Misunderstand Each Other* (Oxford: Oxford University Press, 1997).

76.   Lauren Mackenzie and Megan Wallace, "The Communication of Respect as a Significant Dimension of Cross-Cultural Communication Competence," *Cross Cultural Communication* 7, no. 3 (2011): 10-18, accessed March 31, 2017, doi: 10.3968/j.ccc.1923670020110703.175.

77.   Yousuf Griefat and Tamar Katriel, "Life Demands Musayara: Communication and Culture among Arabs in Israel," in *Language, Communication, and Culture: Current Directions*, ed. Stella Ting-Toomey and Atsuko Kurogi (Thousand Oaks: Sage, 1989).

78.   Ike Nnia Mba Sr., "Conflicts Encountered by Multinational Corporations in Cross-Cultural Communication and its Solutions," *Journal of International Business and Economics* 3, no. 1 (2015): 86-92, accessed March 31, 2017, doi: 10.15640/jibe.v3n1a10.

79.   "Japan Government: On the Fall of the Employment System," *Global Voices*, March 28, 2010, accessed March 31, 2017, https://globalvoices. org/2010/03/28/japan-government-on-the-fall-of-the-employment-system/.

80.   Anick Tolbize, "Generational Differences in the Workplace," *University of Minnesota*, August 16, 2008, accessed March 31, 2017, http://rtc.umn.edu/docs/2_18_Gen_diff_workplace.pdf.

81.   Simone de Beauvoir, *The Second Sex* (New York: Knopf, 2010).

82.   Adam Salandra, "Her Father Wouldn't Walk Her Down The Aisle, So This Lesbian Banker's Boss Did The Honors," *New Now Next*, March 8, 2017,

accessed March 31, 2017, http://www.newnownext.com/lesbian-wedding-bank-ceo/03/2017/.

83.   Sir David Frost, "I Have Impeached Myself," *The Guardian*, September 7, 2007, accessed March 31, 2017, https://www.theguardian.com/theguardian/2007/sep/07/greatinterviews1.

84.   Raymond Fisman and Edward Miguel, "Corruption, Norms, and Legal Enforcement: Evidence from Diplomatic Parking Tickets," *Journal of Political Economy* 115, no. 6 (2007), accessed March 31, 2017, doi: 10.1086/527495.

85.   Stanley Milgram "Behavioral Study of Obedience," *Journal of Abnormal and Social Psychology* 67, no. 4 (1963): 371-378, accessed March 31, 2016, doi: 10.1037/h0040525.

86.   Amanda B. Diekman and Alice H. Eagly, "Stereotypes as Dynamic Constructs: Women and Men of the Past, Present, and Future," *Personality and Social Psychology Bulletin* 26, no. 10 (2000): 1171-1188, accessed March 31, 2017, doi: 10.1177/0146167200262001.

87.   Lise Eliot, *Pink Brain, Blue Brain: How Small Differences Grow Into Troublesome Gaps – And What We Can Do About It* (New York: Mariner Books, 2010).

88.   Cordelia Fine, *Delusions of Gender: How Our Minds, Society, and Neurosexism Create Difference* (New York: W. W. Norton & Company, 2011).

89.   Judith Butler, "Sex and Gender in Simone de Beauvoir's Second Sex," *Yale French Studies*, no. 72 (1986): 35-49, accessed March 31, 2017, doi: 10.2307/2930225.

90.   Daphna Joel et al., "Sex beyond the Genitalia: The Human Brain Mosaic," *PNAS* 112, no. 50 (2015): 15468-15473, accessed March 31, 2017, doi: 10.1073/pnas.1509654112.

91.   Andrew Marshall, *The Trouser People: A Story of Burma in the Shadow of the Empire* (London: Penguin Books Ltd., 2002), 213.

92.   Laura Fortunato, "The Evolution of Matrilineal Kinship Organization," *Proceedings of the Royal Society of London B: Biological Sciences* 279, no. 1749 (2012): 4939-4945, accessed March 31, 2017, doi: 10.1098/rspb.2012.1926.

93.   Tran Ngoc Them, *Tim ve Ban Sac Van Hoa Viet Nam* [*Discovering The Identity of Vietnamese Culture: Typological-systematic Views*], (Ho Chi Minh: HCM city Publisher, 1996).

94.   Carole Wade and Carol Tavris, "The Longest War: Gender and Culture," in *Psychology and Culture*, ed. Walter J. Lonner and Roy Malpass (Boston: Allyn and Bacon, 1994).

95.   Alice Schlegel, "Hopi Gender Ideology of Female Superiority," *Quarterly Journal of Ideology: A Critique of the Conventional Wisdom* 8, no. 4 (1984): 44-52.

96.   Hannah Booth, "The Kingdom of Women: The Tibetan Tribe Where a Man is Never the Boss," *The Guardian,* April 1, 2017, accessed April 2, 2017, https://www.theguardian.com/lifeandstyle/2017/apr/01/the-kingdom-of-women-the-tibetan-tribe-where-a-man-is-never-the-boss.

97.   Geert Hofstede, Gert-Jan Hofstede and Michael Minkov, *Cultures and Organizations: Software of the Mind* (New York: McGraw-Hill, 2005), 120–121.

98.   Irena D. Ebert, Melanie C. Steffens and Alexandra Kroth, "Warm, but Maybe Not So Competent? – Contemporary Implicit Stereotypes of Women and Men in Germany," *Sex Roles* 70, no. 9 (2014): 359-375, accessed March 31, 2017, doi: 10.1007/s11199-014-0369-5.

99.   Tony Fang, "Yin Yang: A New Perspective on Culture," *Management and Organization Review* 8, no. 1 (2012): 25-50, accessed March 31, 2017, doi: 10.1111/j.1740-8784.2011.00221.x.

100. "Northern Theatre: Sisu," *Time*, January 8, 1940, accessed March 31, 2017, http://content.time.com/time/magazine/article/0,9171,763161,00.html.

101. Jill G. Morawski, "The Measurement of Masculinity and Femininity: Engendering Categorical Realities," in *Gender and Personality: Current Perspectives on Theory and Research*, ed. Abigail J. Stewart and M. Brinton Lykes (Durham: Duke University Press, 1985).

102. Sandra L. Bem, "The Measurement of Psychological Androgyny," *Journal of Consulting and Clinical Psychology* 42, no. 2 (1974): 155-162, accessed March 31, 2017, doi: 10.1037/h0036215.

103. Janet T. Spence and Robert L. Helmreich, *Masculinity and Femininity: Their Psychological Dimensions, Correlates, and Antecedents* (Austin: University of Texas Press, 1978).

104. Jean M. Twenge, "Changes in Masculine and Feminine Traits over Time: A Meta-Analysis," *Sex Roles* 36, no. 5 (1997): 305-325, accessed March 31, 2017, doi: 10.1007/BF02766650.

105. David M. Buss, "Psychological Sex Differences: Origins through Sexual Selection," *American Psychologist* 50, no. 3 (1995): 164-168, accessed March 31, 2017, doi: 10.1037//0003-066X.50.3.164.

106. Sondra A. Zeidenstein, "Review: Woman's Role in Economic Development," review of *Women's Role in Economie Development,* by Ester Boserup, *The Bangladesh Economic Review* 2, no. 1 (1970): 507-510, accessed March 31, 2017, http://www.jstor.org/stable/40795751.

107. Alberto Alesina, Paola Giuliano and Nathan Nunn, "On the Origins of Gender Roles: Women and the Plough," *The Quarterly Journal of Economics* 128, no. 2 (2013): 469-530, accessed March 31, 2017, doi: 10.3386/w17098.

108. Painting by Frederick Forbes. "Seh-Dong-Hong-Beh, Leader of the Dahomey Amazons," *Dahomey Amazon*, 1851, accessed March 31, 2017, https://commons.wikimedia.org/w/index.php?curid=3259041. Public Domain.

109. Wendy Wood and Alice H. Eagly, "A Cross-Cultural Analysis of the Behavior of Women and Men: Implications for the Origins of Sex Differences," *Psychological Bulletin* 128, no. 5 (2002): 699-727, accessed March 31, 2017, doi: 10.1037//0033-2909.128.5.699.

110. Emma Teitel, "Sweden Takes Gender Neutrality Seriously," *Macleans,* April 25, 2012, accessed March 31, 2017, http://www.macleans.ca/news/world/neither-he-nor-she/.

111. Maurice Punch, Bob Hoogenboom and Kees Van Der Vijver, "Community Policing in The Netherlands: Four Generations of Redefinition," in *The*

Handbook of Knowledge Based Policing: Current Conceptions and Future, ed. Tom Williamson (Hoboken: John Wiley and Sons Ltd, 2008), 65.

112. Marieke de Mooij, Consumer Behavior and Culture: Consequences for Global Marketing and Advertising (Thousand Oaks: SAGE, 2010).

113. "How History, Philosophy, and Culture Shape Education," The Middlebury Institute Site Network, February 26, 2013, accessed March 31, 2017, http://sites.miis.edu/costarica/2013/02/26/how-history-philosophy-and-culture-shape-education/.

114. "Case Study: Karoshi: Death from Overwork," International Labour Organization, April 23, 2013, accessed March 31, 2017, http://www.ilo.org/safework/info/publications/WCMS_211571/lang--en/index.htm.

115. Grace Huang and Stephen Stapczynski, "Suicide of Overworked Woman, 24, Prompts Ad Giant Dentsu to Trim Overtime Hours," Bloomberg, October 19, 2016, accessed March 31, 2017, http://www.japantimes.co.jp/news/2016/10/19/business/suicide-overworked-woman-24-prompts-ad-giant-dentsu-trim-overtime-hours/#.WMbxuFMrLIU.

116. Arthur C. Brooks, Gross National Happiness: Why Happiness Matters for America and how We Can Get More of It (New York: Basic Books, 2008).

117. Gretchen Livingston, "Among 38 Nations, U.S. is the Outlier When it Comes to Paid Parental Leave," PewResearchCenter, December 12, 2013, accessed March 31, 2017, http://www.pewresearch.org/fact-tank/2013/12/12/among-38-nations-u-s-is-the-holdout-when-it-comes-to-offering-paid-parental-leave/.

118. James G. March and J.P. Olsen, Ambiguity and Choice in Organization (Bergen: Universitetsforlaget, 1976).

119. Geert Hofstede, Gert-Jan Hofstede and Michael Minkov, Cultures and Organizations: Software of the Mind (New York: McGraw-Hill, 2005), 165.

120. Marry Sully de Luque and Mansour Javidan, "Uncertainty Avoidance," in Culture, Leadership, and Organizations: The GLOBE Study of 62 Societies, ed. Robert J. House et al. (Thousand Oaks: SAGE Publication, 2004), 603.

121. Mark Pagel, Wired for Culture: Origins of the Human Social Mind (New York: W. W. Norton & Company, 2012), 83.

122. Carolyn Evan, "The Double-Edged Sword: Religious Influences on International Humanitarian Law," Melbourne Journal of International Law 6, accessed March 31, 2017, http://law.unimelb.edu.au/__data/assets/pdf_file/0003/1681140/Evans.pdf.

123. "UK Chooses 'Most Ludicrous Laws'", BBC, November 7, 2007, accessed March 31, 2017, http://news.bbc.co.uk/2/hi/7081038.stm.

124. Geert Hofstede, Gert-Jan Hofstede, and Michael Minkov, Cultures and Organizations: Software of the Mind (New York: McGraw-Hill, 2005), 168–169.

125. Noah Plaue, "If You Think the Soda Ban is Bad, Check Out All the Things That Are Illegal in Singapore", Business Insider, June 19, 2012, accessed March 31, 2017, http://www.businessinsider.com.au/absurd-laws-of-singapore-2012-6.

126. Sunil Venaik and Paul Brewer, "Avoiding Uncertainty in Hofstede and GLOBE," Journal of International Business Studies 41, no. 8 (2010): 1294-1315, accessed March 31, 2017, doi: 10.1057/jibs.2009.96.

127. Anna Dreber et al., "The Dopamine Receptor D4 Gene (DRD4) and
      Self-Reported Risk Taking in the Economic Domain," *Harvard University*,
      2011, accessed March 31, 2017, https://dash.harvard.edu/bitstream/han-
      dle/1/5347066/RWP11-042_Zeckhauser_alia.pdf?sequence=1.

128. Marcus R. Munafò et al., "Association of the Dopamine D4 Receptor (DRD4)
      Gene and Approach-Related Personality Traits: Meta-Analysis and New
      Data," *Biological Psychiatry* 63, no. 2 (2008): 197-206, accessed March 31, 2017,
      doi: 10.1016/j.biopsych.2007.04.006.

129. Perez de Castro et al., "Genetic Association Study between Pathological
      Gambling and a Functional DNA Polymorphism at the D4 Receptor Gene,"
      Pharmacogenetics and Genomics 7, no. 5 (1997): 445, accessed March 31,
      2017, doi: 10.1097/00008571-199710000-00001.

130. Eric Wang et al., "The Genetic Architecture of Selection at the Hu-
      man Dopamine Receptor D4 (DRD4) Gene Locus," *American Journal of
      Human Genetics* 74, no. 5 (2004): 931-944, accessed March 31, 2017, doi:
      10.1086/420854.

131. Chuansheng Chen et al., "Population Migration and the Variation of Dopa-
      mine (DRD4) Allele Frequencies around the Globe," *Evolution and Human
      Behavior* 20, no. 5 (1999): 309-324, accessed March 31, 2017, doi: http://dx.doi.
      org/10.1016/S1090-5138(99)00015-X.

132. Michael W. Kidd, "The Frontier in American History," *University of Vir-
      ginia*, September 30, 1997, accessed March 31, 2017, http://xroads.virginia.
      edu/~HYPER/TURNER/.

133. David Robson, "How East and West Think in Profoundly Different Ways,"
      BBC, January 19, 2017, accessed March 31, 2017, http://www.bbc.com/future/
      story/20170118-how-east-and-west-think-in-profoundly-different-ways.

134. Melvin J. Lerner, *The Belief in a Just World: A Fundamental Delusion* (New
      York: Plenum Press, 1980).

135. "Religiously Unaffiliated," *PewResearchCenter*, December 18, 2012, accessed
      April 1, 2017, http://www.pewforum.org/2012/12/18/global-religious-land-
      scape-unaffiliated/.

136. Mike J. Jones and Steve Sanghi, *Driving Excellence: How The Aggregate Sys-
      tem Turned Microchip Technology from a Failing Company to a Market Leader*
      (Hoboken: John Wiley & Sons, 2006).

137. Geert Hofstede, Gert-Jan Hofstede and Michael Minkov, *Cultures and Or-
      ganizations: Software of the Mind* (New York: McGraw-Hill, 2005), 181.

138. Marry Sully de Luque and Mansour Javidan, "Uncertainty Avoidance," in
      Culture, Leadership, and Organizations: The GLOBE Study of 62 Societies, ed.
      Robert J. House et al. (Thousand Oaks: SAGE Publication, 2004), 633.

139. Michelle Jamrisko and Wei Lu, "These Are the World's Most Innovative
      Economies," *Bloomberg*, January 20, 2016, accessed April 1, 2017, https://
      www.bloomberg.com/news/articles/2016-01-19/these-are-the-world-s-most-
      innovative-economies.

140. Oded Shenkar, "Cultural Distance Revisited: Towards a More Rigorous
      Conceptualization and Measurement of Cultural Differences," *Journal of*

International Business Studies 23, no. 3 (2001): 519-535, accessed April 1, 2017, doi: 10.1057/jibs.2011.40.

141.   Marry Sully de Luque and Mansour Javidan, "Uncertainty Avoidance," in *Culture, Leadership, and Organizations: The GLOBE Study of 62 Societies,* ed. Robert J. House et al. (Thousand Oaks: SAGE Publication, 2004), 602–653.

142.   Sunil Venaik and Paul Brewer, "Avoiding Uncertainty in Hofstede and GLOBE," *Journal of International Business Studies* 41, no. 8 (2010): 1294-1315, accessed April 1, 2017, doi: 10.1057/jibs.2009.96.

143.   Philip T. Hoffman, "Why Was It Europeans Who Conquered the World?" *Global Prices and Incomes Project,* March 21, 2012, accessed April 1, 2017, http://economics.yale.edu/sites/default/files/files/Workshops-Seminars/Economic-History/hoffman-120409.pdf.

144.   "Twitter Storm as Cologne Mayor Suggests Women Stay at 'Arm's Length' from Strangers," *DW,* January 5, 2016, accessed April 1, 2017, http://www.dw.com/en/twitter-storm-as-cologne-mayor-suggests-women-stay-at-arms-length-from-strangers/a-18962430.

145.   "Nach Umstrittenem Kommentar: Beck Stellt Strafanzeige Gegen Kölner Imam," *Leipziger Volkszeitung,* January 22, 2016, accessed April 1, 2017, http://www.lvz.de/Nachrichten/Politik/Nach-umstrittenem-Kommentar-Beck-stellt-Strafanzeige-gegen-Koelner-Imam.

146.   Geert Hofstede, Gert-Jan Hofstede and Michael Minkov, *Cultures and Organizations: Software of the Mind* (New York: McGraw-Hill, 2005), 198.

147.   René David, *English Law and French Law : A comparison in Substance* (London: Stevens, 1980), 223, accessed April 1, 2017, http://14.139.60.114:8080/jspui/bitstream/123456789/16729/1/045_English%20Law%20and%20French%20Law%20-%20A%20Comparison%20in%20Substance%20(638-642).pdf.

148.   Zena R. Mello and Frank C. Worrell, "The Past, the Present, and the Future: A Conceptual Model of Time Perspective in Adolescence," in *Time perspective: Theory, Research and Application: Essays in Honor of Philip G. Zimbardo,* ed. Maciej Stolarski et al. (Cham: Springer, 2015), 115–129.

149.   Florence Rockwood Kluckhohn and Fred L. Strodtbeck, *Variations in Value Orientations* (Evanston: Row, Peterson, 1961).

150.   Geert Hofstede, *Culture's Consequences: International Differences in Work-Related Values,* 2nd ed. (Beverly Hills: SAGE Publications, 1984).

151.   Fons Trompenaars and Charles Hampden-Turner, *Riding the Waves of Culture: Understanding Diversity in Global Business,* 3rd ed. (London: Nicholas Brealey, 1997).

152.   Robert J. House et al., *Culture, Leadership, and Organizations: The GLOBE Study of 62 Societies* (Thousand Oaks: Sage Publications, 2004).

153.   Thomas J. Cottle, "The Circles Test: An Investigation of Perceptions of Temporal Relatedness and Dominance," *Journal of Projective Techniques and Personality Assessment* 31, no. 5 (2010): 58-71, accessed April 1, 2017, doi: 10.1080/0091651X.1967.10120417.

154. Jacek T. Walinski, "Reflection of Temporal Horizon in Linguistic Performance," in *Conceptualizations of Time,* ed. Barbara Lewandowska-Tomaszczyk (Amsterdam: John Benjamins Publishing, 2016), 278.

155. Geert Hofstede, Gert-Jan Hofstede and Michael Minkov, *Cultures and Organizations: Software of the Mind* (New York: McGraw-Hill, 2005), 211.

156. Fons Trompenaars and Charles Hampden-Turner, *Riding The Waves of Culture: Understanding Diversity in Global Business,* 3rd ed. (London: Nicholas Brealey, 1997), 128.

157. Sunil Venaik, Yunxia Zhu and Paul Brewer, "Looking into the Future: Hofstede Long Term Orientation Versus GLOBE Future Orientation," *Cross Cultural Management: An International Journal* 20, no. 3 (2013): 361-385, accessed April 1, 2017, doi: 10.1108/CCM-02-2012-0014.

158. "The Nielsen Global Survey of Corporate Social Responsibility and Sustainability," *Credit Suisse,* 2015, accessed April 1, 2017, https://www.nielsen.com/content/dam/nielsenglobal/dk/docs/global-sustainability-report-oct-2015.pdf.

159. Philip G. Zimbardo, *Draft manual, Stanford time perspective inventory* (Stanford: Stanford University, 1992).

160. John Boyd, "An Overview of Time Perspective Types," *The Time Paradox,* August 3, 2008, accessed April 1, 2017, http://www.thetimeparadox.com/2008/08/03/an-overview-of-time-perspective-types/.

161. Shaykh Muhammad Saalih al-Munajjid, "Jurisprudence and Islam Rulings," *Islam Question and Answer,* accessed April 1, 2017, https://islamqa.info/en/75525.

162. Shaykh Muhammad Saalih al-Munajjid, "Rulings on Dress," *Islam Question and Answer,* accessed April 1, 2017, https://islamqa.info/en/cat/451.

163. Shaykh Muhammad Saalih al-Munajjid, "Manners," *Islam Question and Answer,* accessed April 1, 2017, https://islamqa.info/en/2577.

164. "Strive to Revive Islam's Past Glory in Astronomy, Muslim Students Told," *The Borneo Post,* October 20, 2015, accessed April 1, 2017, http://www.pressreader.com/malaysia/the-borneo-post/20151020/281938836761992.

165. Photo by Thelmadatter. "Raising of Santa Muerte Images During a Service for the Deity on Alfareria Street Tepito Mexico City," *Wikipedia,* December 1, 2009, accessed April 1, 2017, https://commons.wikimedia.org/w/index.php?curid=8700627. License Link: https://creativecommons.org/licenses/by-sa/3.0/legalcode.

166. "CDA Support Down among Minorities," *Dutch News,* November 3, 2006, accessed April 1, 2017, http://www.dutchnews.nl/news/archives/2006/11/cda_support_down_among_minorit/.

167. Ana Swanson, "Why Trying to Help Poor Countries Might Actually Hurt Them," *The Washington Post,* October 13, 2015, accessed April 1, 2017, https://www.washingtonpost.com/news/wonk/wp/2015/10/13/why-trying-to-help-poor-countries-might-actually-hurt-them/?utm_term=.bad86odd1587.

168. Geraldine Fabrikant, "The Deal for MCA," *The New York Times,* November 27, 1990, accessed April 1, 2017, http://www.nytimes.com/1990/11/27/business/the-deal-for-mca.html?pagewanted=all.

169. Thanh Van, "Vietnamese Literature, Music Mentioned in Obama's Speech," *Vietnam Net*, May 26, 2016, accessed April 1, 2017, http://english.vietnamnet.vn/fms/art-entertainment/157073/vietnamese-literature--music-mentioned-in-obama-s-speech.html.

170. Ann Swidler, "Culture in Action: Symbols and Strategies," *American Sociological Review* 51, no. 2 (1986): 273-286, accessed April 1, 2017, http://www.jstor.org/stable/2095521.

171. Joyce S. Osland and Allan Bird, "Beyond Sophisticated Stereotyping: Cultural Sensemaking in Context," *Academy of Management Executive* 14, no. 1 (2000): 65-79, accessed April 1, 2017, doi: 10.5465/AME.2000.2909840.

Chapter 6

1.   Eleanor A. Maguire et al., "Navigation-Related Structural Change in the Hippocampi of Taxi Drivers," *Proc Natl Acad Sci USA* 97, no. 8 (2000): 4398-4403, accessed March 25, 2017, doi: 10.1073/pnas.070039597.

2.   Gail E. Walton, N. J Bower and T. G Bower, "Recognition of familiar faces by newborns," *Infant Behavior & Development* 15, no. 2 (1992): 265–269.

3.   Jennifer T. Kubota, Mahzarin R. Banaji and Elizabeth A. Phelps, "The Neuroscience of Race," *Nature Neuroscience* 15, no. 7 (2012): 940-948, accessed March 25, 2017, doi:10.1038/nn.3136.

4.   Irene V. Blair et al., "The Role of Afrocentric Features in Person Perception: Judging by Features and Categories," *Journal of Personality and Social Psychology* 83, no. 1 (2002): 5-25, accessed March 25, 2017, http://psycnet.apa.org/index.cfm?fa=buy.optionToBuy&id=2002-01515-001 .

5.   Emory A. Griffin, *A First Look at Communication Theory,* 2nd ed. (New York: McGraw-Hill, 1994), 173.

6.   Lauren A. Rivera, "Hiring as Cultural Matching: The Case of Elite Professional Service Firms," *American Sociological Review* 77, no.6 (2012): 999-1022, accessed March 25, 2017, doi: 10.1177/0003122412463213.

7.   Naoki Masuda and Feng Fu, "Evolutionary Models of In-Group Favoritism," *F1000Prime Reports* 7, no. 27 (2015), accessed March 25, 2017, doi:10.12703/P7-27.

8.   Irene V. Blair et al., "The Role of Afrocentric Features in Person Perception: Judging by Features and Categories," *Journal of Personality and Social Psychology* 83, no. 1 (2002): 5-25, accessed March 25, 2017, http://psycnet.apa.org/index.cfm?fa=buy.optionToBuy&id=2002-01515-001.

9.   Meghan L. Meyer et al., "Empathy for the Social Suffering of Friends and Strangers Recruits Distinct Patterns of Brain Activation," *Social Cognitive and Affective Neuroscience* 8, no. 4 (2013): 1-9, accessed March 25, 2017, doi: 10.1093/scan/nss019.

10.   Grit Hein et al., "Neural Responses to Ingroup and Outgroup Members' Suffering Predict Individual Differences in Costly Helping," *Neuron* 68, no. 1 (2010):149-160, accessed March 25, 2017, doi: 10.1016/j.neuron.2010.09.003.

11. Carsten K.W. De Dreu et al., "The Neuropeptide Oxytocin Regulates Parochial Altruism in Intergroup Conflict Among Humans," *Science* 328, no. 5984 (2010): 1408-1411, accessed March 25, 2017, doi: 10.1126/science.1189047.

12. Xiaole Ma et al., "Oxytocin Increases Liking for a Country's People and National Flag But Not For Other Cultural Symbols or Consumer Products," *Frontiers in Behavioral Neuroscience* 8 (2014): 266, accessed March 25, 2017, doi: 10.3389/fnbeh.2014.00266.

13. Marilynn B. Brewer, "The Psychology of Prejudice: Ingroup Love or Outgroup Hate?" *Journal of Social Issues* 55, no. 3 (1999): 429-444, accessed March 25, 2017, doi: 10.1111/0022-4537.00126.

14. William Graham Summer, *Folkways* (Boston: Ginnand, 1940), 13.

15. Teri Kwal Gamble and Michael W. Gamble, *Contacts: Interpersonal Communication in Theory, Practice, and Context* (Boston: Houghton Mifflin Company, 2005), 281.

16. Mark Pagel, "Adapted to Culture," *Nature* 482 (February 16, 2012): 297-299.

17. Reggie Yates, "White Slums," BBC, 39:35, broadcasted Feb 2014, posted June 30, 2015, https://www.dailymotion.com/video/x2vzujs.

18. Janet M. Bennett and Milton J. Bennett, "Developing Intercultural Sensitivity," in *Handbook of Intercultural Training,* ed. Daniel Landis, Janet M. Bennett and Milton J. Bennett (Thousand Oaks: Sage, 2004), 147–165.

19. "Housing," Statistics Finland, accessed August 16, 2016, http://www.stat.fi/tup/suoluk/suoluk_asuminen_en.html.

20. Photo by Therme Erding. *Therme Erding*, April 20, 2010, accessed March 29, 2017. Original uploader was Studi85, https://commons.wikimedia.org/w/index.php?curid=11633346 License link https://creativecommons.org/licenses/by-sa/3.0/de/legalcode.

21. Milton J. Bennett, "Becoming Intercultural Competent," in *Toward Multiculturalism: A Reader in Multicultural Education,* ed. Jaime S. Wurzel (Newton: Intercultural Recourse Corporation, 2004), 62–77.

22. Janet M. Bennett and Milton J. Bennett, "Developing Intercultural Sensitivity," in *Handbook of Intercultural Training,* ed. Daniel Landis, Janet M. Bennett and Milton J. Bennett (Thousand Oaks: Sage, 2004), 156.

23. Milton J. Bennett, "Towards Ethnorelativism: A Developmental Model of Intercultural Sensitivity," in *Education for the Intercultural Experience,* ed. R. Michael Paige (Yarmouth: Intercultural Press, 1993), 21–71.

24. Milton J. Bennett, "Becoming Intercultural Competent," in *Toward Multiculturalism: A Reader in Multicultural Education,* ed. Jaime S. Wurzel (Newton: Intercultural Recourse Corporation, 2004), 62–77.

25. Janet M. Bennett and Milton J. Bennett, "Developing Intercultural Sensitivity," in *Handbook of Intercultural Training,* ed. Daniel Landis, Janet M. Bennett and Milton J. Bennett (Thousand Oaks: Sage, 2004), 157.

26. Jason E. Warnick and Dan Landis, "Introduction and Rationale for This Book," in *Neuroscience in Intercultural Contexts,* ed. Jason E. Warnick and Dan Landis (New York: Springer, 2015), 9–30.

27. Sharon Glazer et al., "Implications of Behavioral and Neuroscience Research for Cross-Cultural Training," in *Neuroscience in Intercultural Contexts,* ed. Jason E. Warnick and Dan Landis (New York: Springer, 2015), 171–202.

28. Mitchell R. Hammer and Milton J. Bennett, *The Intercultural Development Inventory (IDI) manual* (Portland: Intercultural Communication Institute, 1998).

29. "Mass Pro Eligendo Romano Pontifice: Homily of Card. Joseph Ratzinger," Vatican, accessed March 20, 2017. http://www.vatican.va/gpII/documents/homily-pro-eligendo-pontifice_20050418_en.html.

30. Claude Lévi-Strauss and Didier Eribon, *De Près et De Loin* (Paris: Edisons Odile Jacob, 1988), 229.

31. Roger Lloret Blackburn, "Cultural Relativism in the Universal Periodic Review of the Human Rights Council," *SSRN*, working paper no. 2011/3 (September 1, 2011), accessed March 26, 2017, http://dx.doi.org/10.2139/ssrn.2033134.

32. I. El-Damanhoury, "The Jewish and Christian View on Female Genital Mutilation," *African Journal of Urology* 19, no. 3 (2013): 127-129, accessed March 26, 2017, doi:10.1016/j.afju.2013.01.004.

33. Jasmine Abdulcadir et al., "Care of Women with Female Genital Mutilation/Cutting," *Swiss Medical Weekly* 6, no. 14 (2011), accessed March 26, 2017, doi:10.4414/smw.2011.

34. Geert Hofstede, Gert-Jan Hofstede, and Michael Minkov, *Cultures and Organizations: Software of the Mind,* (New York: McGraw-Hill, 2005), xi.

35. Shari Caudron, "Training Ensures Success Overseas," *Personnel Journal* 70, no. 12 (1991): 27-30.

36. Samuel Greengard, "Technology is Changing Expatriate Training," *Workforce* 78, no. 12 (1999): 106-107, accessed March 26, 2017, http://www.workforce.com/1999/12/01/technology-is-changing-expatriate-training/.

37. Nina D. Cole, "Managing Global Talent: Solving the Spousal Adjustment Problem," *International Journal of Human Resources Management* 22, no. 7 (2011): 1504-1530, accessed March 26, 2017, http://dx.doi.org/10.1080/0958519 2.2011.561963.

38. Hung Wen Lee, "Factors that Influence Expatriate Failure. An Interview Study," *International Journal of Management* 24, no. 3 (2007): 403-413.

39. Nick Forster, "Expatriates and the Impact of Cross Cultural Training," *Human Resource Management Journal* 10, no. 3 (2000): 63-78, accessed March 26, 2017, doi: 10.1111/j.1748-8583.2000.tb00027.x.

40. Nancy J. Adler, *International Dimensions of Organizational Behavior* (Mason: Thompson South-Western, 2008), 278.

41. Annette B. Bossard and Richard B. Peterson, "The Repatriate Experience as Seen by American Expatriates," *Journal of World Business* 40, no. 1 (2005): 9-28, accessed March 26, 2017, doi: 10.1016/j.jwb.2004.10.002.

42. Jobert E. Abueva, "Many Repatriation Fail at Huge Cost to Companies," *New York Times,* May 17, 2000, accessed March 26, 2017, http://www.nytimes.com/2000/05/17/business/management-return-native-executive-many-repatriations-fail-huge-cost-companies.html.

43. Catherine M. Daily, S. Trevis Certo and Dan R. Dalton, "International Experience in the Executive Suite: The Path to Prosperity?" *Strategic Management Journal* 21, no. 4 (2000): 515-523, accessed March 26, 2017, doi: 10.1002/(SICI)1097-0266(200004)21:4<515::AID-SMJ92>3.0.CO;2-1.

44. Günter K. Stahl, Edwin L. Miller and Rosalie L. Tung, "Toward the Boundaryless Career: A Closer Look at the Expatriate Career Concept and the Perceived Implication of an International Assignment," *Journal of World Business* 37, no.3 (2002): 216-227, accessed March 26, 2017, doi: 10.1016/S1090-9516(02)00080-9.

45. Elizabeth Garone, "Expat Culture Shock Boomerangs in the Office," *BBC*, November 3, 2014, accessed March 26, 2017, http://www.bbc.com/capital/story/20130611-returning-expat-culture-shock.

46. Yehuda Baruch, D.J. Steele and G. A. Quantrill, "Management of Expatriation and Repatriation for Novice Global Player," *International Journal of Manpower* 23, no. 7 (2002): 659-671, accessed March 26, 2017, http://dx.doi.org/10.1108/01437720210450824.

47. Vesa Suutari and Chris Brewster, "Repatriation: Empirical Evidence from a Longitudinal Study of Careers and Expectations among Finnish Expatriates," *International Journal of Human Resource Management* 14, no. 7 (2003): 1132-1151, accessed March 27, 2017, doi: 10.1080/0958519032000114200.

48. Annette B. Bossard and Richard B. Peterson, "The Repatriate Experience as Seen by American Expatriates," *Journal of World Business* 40, no. 1 (2005): 9-28, accessed March 27, 2017, doi: 10.1016/j.jwb.2004.10.002.

49. "International Migrant Stock 2015," UN, accessed August 16, 2016, http://www.un.org/en/development/desa/population/migration/data/estimates2/estimates15.shtml.

50. "International tourist arrivals up 4 per cent reach a record 1.2 billion in 2015," World Tourism Organization UNWTO, accessed August 16, 2016, http://media.unwto.org/press-release/2016-01-18/international-tourist-arrivals-4-reach-record-12-billion-2015.

51. Thomas L. Friedman, "A Theory of Everything (Sort Of)," *New York Times,* August 13, 2011, accessed March 27, 2017, http://www.nytimes.com/2011/08/14/opinion/sunday/Friedman-a-theory-of-everyting-sort-of.html?partner=rssnyt&emc=rss.

52. Geert Hofstede, *Culture's Consequences: Comparing Values, Behaviors, Institutions, and Organizations across Nations*, 2nd ed. (Thousand Oaks: Sage, 2001), 15.

53. Brian H. Spitzberg and William R. Cupach, *Interpersonal Communication Competence* (Beverly Hills: Sage, 1984).

54. Christopher Earley and Soon Ang, *Cultural Intelligence: Individual Interactions across Cultures* (Stanford: Business Books, 2003).

55. Soon Ang and Linn Van Dyne, "Conceptualization of Cultural Intelligence," in *Handbook of Cultural Intelligence, Theory, Measurement and Applications,* ed. Soon Ang and Linn Van Dyne (New York: Sharpe, Inc, 2008), 3-15.

56. Susan Sorenson and Keri Garman, "How to Tackle U.S. Employees' Stagnating Engagement," *Business Journal,* June 11, 2013, accessed August 16, 2016,

http://www.gallup.com/businessjournal/162953/tackle-employees-stagnat-ing-engagement.aspx.

57.   "Employee Disengagement Costs UK £340bn Every Year," Haygroup, accessed August 16, 2016, http://www.haygroup.com/uk/press/details. aspx?id=7184.

58.   "Australians disengaged at work," *AAP*, October 9, 2013, accessed August 16, 2016, http://www.theaustralian.com.au/national-affairs/australians-disen-gaged-at-work-report/story-fn59niix-1226735435897.

59.   Photo by Pete Souza. "Secretary of State Hillary Clinton recounts a story outside the Sultan Hassan Mosque in Cairo," *Obama White House,* on Flickr, June 4, 2009, accessed March 29, 2017, https://www.flickr.com/photos/oba-mawhitehouse/3611567664/ License link https://www.usa.gov/government-works Pubic Domain.

60.   Sherrie Dillard, *Discover Your Authentic Self: Be You, Be Free, Be Happy* (Woodbury: Llewellyn Worldwide, 2016).

61.   Michael Puett and Christine Gross-Loh, *The path: What Chinese Philoso-phers Can Teach Us About the Good Life* (New York: Simon & Schuster, 2016), location 193.

62.   Ibid.: location 512.

63.   Judith Howard, "Introduction: The self-society dynamic," in *The Self-Society Dynamic: Cognition, Emotion and Action*, ed. Judith A. Howard and Peter L. Callero (Cambridge: Cambridge University Press, 2006).

64.   Cortland J. Dahl, Antoine Lutz and Richard J. Davidson, "Reconstructing and Deconstructing the Self: Cognitive Mechanisms in Meditation Practice," *Trends in Cognitive Sciences September* 19, no. 9 (2015): 515-523, accessed March 27, 2017, doi: 10.1016/j.tics.2015.07.001.

65.   Ying-yi Hong et al., "Multicultural minds: A Dynamic Constructivist Ap-proach to Culture and Cognition," *American Psychologist* 55, no. 7 (July 2010): 709-720, accessed March 27, 2017, doi: 10.1037//0003-066X.55.7.709.

66.   Kaiping P. Peng and Eric D. Knowles, "Culture, Education, and the Attribu-tion of Physical Causality, Personality and Social Psychology," *Bulletin* 29, no. 10 (2002): 1272-1284, accessed March 27, 2017, doi: 10.1177/0146167203254601.

67.   Joan Y. Chiao et al., "Dynamic Cultural Influences on Neural Representa-tions of the Self," *Journal of Cognitive Neuroscience* 22, no. 1 (2010): 1-11, ac-cessed March 27, 2017, doi:10.1162/jocn.2009.21192.

68.   Milton J. Bennett and Ida Castiglioni, "Embodied Ethnocentrism and the Feeling of Culture: A Key to Training for Intercultural Competence," in *Handbook of Intercultural Training,* ed. Daniel Landis, Janet M. Bennett and Milton J. Bennett (Thousand Oaks: Sage, 2004): 249–265.

69.   Michael Puett and Christine Gross-Loh, *The path: What Chinese Philoso-phers Can Teach Us about the Good Life* (New York: Simon & Schuster, 2016).

70.   Amy Cuddy, "Amy Cuddy: Your Body Language Shapes Who You Are," TED video, filmed June 2012, accessed March 27, 2017, http://www.ted.com/talks/ amy_cuddy_your_body_language_shapes_who_you_are?language=en.

71.   Amy J.C. Cuddy, Caroline A. Wilmuth and Dana R. Carney, "The Benefit of Power Posing Before a High-Stakes Social Evaluation," *Harvard Business School Working Paper*, no. 13-027 (September 2012), accessed March 27, 2017, https://dash.harvard.edu/bitstream/handle/1/9547823/13-027.pdf?sequence=1.

72.   Amy Cuddy, *Presence: Bringing your boldest self to your biggest challenges* (New York: Little, Brown and Company, 2015).

73.   Photo by Juhan Sonln. "Jennifer Patel's Power Pose," *Flickr*, Sept 17, 2014, accessed Macrh 29, 2017, https://www.flickr.com/photos/juhan-sonin/15270359572 License link https://creativecommons.org/licenses/by/2.0/legalcode.

74.   Amy Cuddy, *Presence: Bringing your boldest self to your biggest challenges* (New York: Little, Brown and Company, 2015).

75.   Vinoth K. Ranganathan et al., "From Mental Power to Muscle Power--Gaining Strength by Using the Mind," *Neuropsychologia* 42, no. 7 (2004): 944-956, accessed March 27, 2017, doi: 10.1016/j.neuropsychologia.2003.11.018.

76.   Brian C. Clark et al., "The Power of the Mind: The Cortex as a Critical Determinant of Muscle Strength/Weakness," *Journal of Neurophysiology* 112, no. 12 (2014): 3219-3226, accessed March 27, 2017, doi: 10.1152/jn.00386.2014.

77.   Richard Martin, "Mind Control," *Wired,* January 1, 2005, accessed March 27, 2017, http://www.wired.com/2005/03/brain-3/.

78.   Michael Puett and Christine Gross-Loh, "The Importance of Breaking Free of ... Yourself," *Best The News,* May 14, 2016, accessed March 27, 2017, http://bestthenews.com/article/importance-breaking-free-yourself-sat-05142016-2255.html.

79.   Ibid.

Chapter 7

1.   Mustafa Ozbilgin and Ahu Tatli, "Mapping out the Field of Equality and Diversity: Rise of Individualism and Voluntarism," *Human Relations* 64, no.9 (2011): 1229-1253, accessed April 1, 2017, doi: 10.1177/0018726711413620.

2.   Alev Katrinli, Gulem Atabay and Gonca Gunay, "A Historical View of Diversity Management: The Ottoman Empire Case," *International Journal of Business Research* 8, no. 2 (2008): 137-155.

3.   Stella Nkomo and Jenny M. Hoobler, "A historical Perspective on Diversity Ideologies in the United States: Reflections on Human Resource Management Research and Practice," *Human Resource Management Review* 24, no. 3 (2014): 245-257, accessed April 1, 2017, doi: 10.1016/j.hrmr.2014.03.006.

4.   Michael Brazzel, "Historical and Theoretical Roots of Diversity Management," in *Handbook of Diversity Management: Beyond Awareness to Competency Based Learning,* ed. Deborah L. Plummer (Lanham: University Press of America, 2003), 51–93.

5.   "Migration Outlook, Renewing the Skills of Ageing Workforces: The Role of Migration," OECD, 2012, accessed April 1, 2017, doi: 10.1787/migr_outlook-2012-7-en.

6.   "GCC: Total Population and Percentage of Nationals and Non-nationals in GCC Countries (latest national statistics, 2010-2015)," Gulf Research Center, accessed April 1, 2017, http://gulfmigration.eu/total-population-and-percentage-of-nationals-and-non-nationals-in-gcc-countries-latest-national-statistics-2010-2015/.

7.   "Expats' Asian Home – The New Breed of Expatriates in Asia," *Spire*, accessed April 1, 2017, https://www.spireresearch.com/spire-journal/2007-2/q1/expats-asian-home-the-new-breed-of-expatriates-in-asia/.

8.   Quynh Trung, "Koreans living in Saigon – P1: Little Korea," *Tuoi Tre News*, August 20, 2014, accessed April 1, 2017, http://tuoitrenews.vn/business/21789/koreans-living-in-saigon-p1-little-korea.

9.   Photo by Diego Delso. "View of Ho Chi Minh City from Bitexco Financial Tower, Vietnam," *Wikipedia*, August 14, 2013, accessed April 1, 2017, https://commons.wikimedia.org/w/index.php?curid=30144370. License Link: https://creativecommons.org/licenses/by-sa/3.0/.

10.   Michalle E. Mor Barak, *Managing Diversity: Towards a Globally Inclusive Workplace,* 2nd ed. (Thousand Oaks: Sage, 2011), 4–5.

11.   Anshuman Prasad, "Understanding Workplace Empowerment as Inclusion: A Historical Investigation of the Discourse of Difference in the United States," *Journal of Applied Behavioral Science* 37, no. 1 (2001): 51-69, accessed April 1, 2017, doi: 10.1177/0021886301371004.

12.   Anesa "Nes" Diaz-Uda, Carmen Medina and Beth Schill, *Diversity's New Frontier: Diversity of Thought and the Future of the Workforce* (Toronto: Deloitte University Press, 2013).

13.   James Webb Young, *A Technique for Producing Ideas,* (London: Thinking Ink Media, 2011).

14.   Nancy C. Andreasen, "A Journey into Chaos: Creativity and the Unconscious," *Mens Sana Monographs* 9, no. 1 (2011): 42-53, accessed April 1, 2017, doi: 10.4103/0973-1229.77424.

15.   John Kounios and Mark Beeman, "The Aha! Moment: The Cognitive Neuroscience of Insight," *Current Directions in Psychological Science August* 18, no. 4 (2009): 210-216, accessed April 1, 2017, doi: 10.1111/j.1467-8721.2009.01638.x.

16.   Edith Wharton, *The Writing of Fiction* (New York: Charles Scribner's Sons, 1997).

17.   Jiangzhou Sun et al., "Training Your Brain to Be More Creative: Brain Functional and Structural Changes Induced by Divergent Thinking Training," *Human Brain Mapping* 37, no. 10 (2016): 3375-3387, accessed April 1, 2017, doi: 10.1002/hbm.23246.

18.   Huasheng Gao and Wei Zhang, "Does Workforce Diversity Pay Evidence from Corporate Innovation," *SSRN Electronic Journal,* July 2014, accessed April 1, 2017, http://images.transcontinentalmedia.com/LAF/lacom/workforce_diversity.pdf.

19.   Karli Petrovic, "Neuroscience Helps Foster Diversity in the Workplace," *IQ,*
      March 15, 2016, accessed April 1, 2017, https://iq.intel.com/neuroscience-
      helps-foster-diversity-in-the-workplace/.

20.   Scott Page, *The Difference: How the Power of Diversity Creates Better Groups,
      Firms, Schools and Societies* (Princeton: Princeton University Press, 2007).

21.   Ibid.

22.   Anesa "Nes" Diaz-Uda, Carmen Medina and Beth Schill, *Diversity's New
      Frontier: Diversity of Thought and the Future of the Workforce* (Toronto: De-
      loitte University Press, 2013).

23.   Mitchell J. Chang et al., "Effects of Racial Diversity on Complex Thinking in
      College Students," *Psychological Science* 15, no. 8 (2004): 507-510, accessed
      April 1, 2017, doi: 10.1111/j.0956-7976.2004.00710.x.

24.   Katherine W. Phillips, "How Diversity Makes Us Smarter," *Scientific Ameri-
      can,* October 1, 2014, accessed April 1, 2017, http://www.scientificamerican.
      com/article/how-diversity-makes-us-smarter/.

25.   David Rock, Heidi Grant Halvorson and Jacqui Grey, "Diverse Teams
      Feel Less Comfortable and That is Why They Perform Better," *Harvard
      Business Review,* September 22, 2016, accessed April 1, 2017, https://hbr.
      org/2016/09/diverse-teams-feel-less-comfortable-and-thats-why-they-
      perform-better?utm_content=bufferc285e&utm_medium=social&utm_
      source=facebook.com&utm_campaign=buffer.

26.   Denise Lewin Loyd et al., "Social Category Diversity Promotes Premeet-
      ing Elaboration: The Role of Relationship Focus," *Organization Science*
      24, no. 3 (2013): 757-772, accessed April 1, 2017, http://dx.doi.org/10.1287/
      orsc.1120.0761.

27.   Bonnie G. Smith, *The Oxford Encyclopedia of Women in World History* (Ox-
      ford: Oxford University Press, 2008), 83.

28.   Paul Valley, "From Dawn to Dusk, The Daily Struggle of Africa's Women,"
      Independent, September 21, 2006, accessed April 1, 2017, http://www.inde-
      pendent.co.uk/news/world/africa/from-dawn-to-dusk-the-daily-struggle-of-
      africas-women-416877.html.

29.   Liza Mundy, *The Richer Sex* (Florence: Free Press, 2013).

30.   Cecilia Conrad, "Black Women: The Unfinished Agenda," *Prospect,* Septem-
      ber 20, 2008, accessed April 1, 2017, http://prospect.org/article/black-wom-
      en-unfinished-agenda.

31.   Alexander Hamilton, *Report on Manufactures,* presented to Congress,
      December 5, 1791, accessed April 1, 2017, http://www.constitution.org/ah/
      rpt_manufactures.pdf.

32.   "Tertiary Education Statistics," Eurostat, last modified November 2016, ac-
      cessed April 1, 2017, http://ec.europa.eu/eurostat/statistics-explained/index.
      php/Tertiary_education_statistics.

33.   Zenger Folkman, "A Study in Leadership: Women Do it Better than Men,"
      in *Real Women, Real Leaders: Surviving and Succeeding in the Business
      World,* ed. Kathleen Hurley and Priscilla Shumway (Hoboken: Wiley, 2015),
      165–169.

34. "Gender Diversity and Corporate Performance," *Credit Suisse*, August 2012, accessed April 3, 2017, http://www.calstrs.com/sites/main/files/file-attachments/csri_gender_diversity_and_corporate_performance.pdf.

35. Cristian L. Dezsö and David Gaddis Ross, "Does Female Representation in Top Management Improve Firm Performance? A Panel Data Investigation," *Strategic Management Journal* 33, no. 9 (2012): 1072-1089, accessed April 1, 2017, doi: 10.2307/23261318.

36. Shamsul Abdullah, Ku Nor Izah Ku Ismail and Lilach Nachum, "Women on Boards of Malaysian Firms: Impact on Market and Accounting Performance," *Social Science Research Network* (2012), accessed April 1, 2017, doi: 10.1002/smj.2352.

37. Anand Rawani, "Women Promoters Beat Big Daddies," *Economic Times,* March 8, 2009, accessed April 1, 2017, http://articles.economictimes.indiatimes.com/2009-03-08/news/28488646_1_growth-rate-biocon-promoters.

38. Bryce Covert, "Vietnamese Companies Led by Women Gained Twice As Much As Others over 5 Years," *Think Progress,* Mar 31, 2014, accessed April 1, 2017, https://thinkprogress.org/vietnamese-companies-led-by-women-gained-twice-as-much-as-others-over-5-years-83168956de9#.ukqu33glm.

39. Vivian Hunt, Dennis Layton and Sara Prince, "Diversity Matters," *McKinsey & Company*, January 2015, accessed April 1, 2017, http://www.mckinsey.com/business-functions/organization/our-insights/why-diversity-matters.

40. Jonathan Woetzel et al., "The Power of Parity: How Advancing Women's Equality Can Add $12 Trillion to Global Growth," *McKinsey & Company*, September 2015, accessed April 1, 2017, http://www.mckinsey.com/global-themes/employment-and-growth/how-advancing-womens-equality-can-add-12-trillion-to-global-growth.

41. Annie Kelly, "Bangladesh Looks to Women Drivers to Quell Testosterone-fueled Fatalities," *The Guardian,* November 14, 2012, accessed April 1, 2017, https://www.theguardian.com/global-development/2012/nov/14/bangladesh-women-drivers-quell-fatalities.

42. "The Global Gender Gap Report," *World Economic Forum*, 2015, accessed April 1, 2017, http://reports.weforum.org/global-gender-gap-report-2015/.

43. Yanfei Zhou, "Career Interruption of Japanese Women: Why Is It So Hard to Balance Work and Childcare," *Japan Labor Review* 12, no. 2 (2015): 106-123, accessed April 1, 2017, http://www.jil.go.jp/english/JLR/documents/2015/JLR46_zhou.pdf.

44. Sophia Yan, "Why Japan is Failing its Women," *CNN*, October 12, 2016, accessed April 1, 2017, http://money.cnn.com/2016/09/15/news/economy/japan-working-women-report-card/.

45. Yoshiaki Nohara, "Closing Japan Gender Gap May Boost GDP 13%," *Bloomberg,* May 7, 2014, accessed April 1, 2017, http://www.bloomberg.com/news/articles/2014-05-07/closing-japan-gender-gap-may-boost-gdp-13-goldman-says.

46. "Holding Back Half the Nation," *Economist,* March 29, 2014, accessed April 1, 2017, http://www.economist.com/news/briefing/21599763-womens-lowly-status-japanese-workplace-has-barely-improved-decades-and-country.

47. Shahd Alhamdam, "With More and More Women Joining Workforce, Demand up for Childcare," *Saudi Gazette,* February 21, 2016, accessed April 1, 2017, http://saudigazette.com.sa/saudi-arabia/with-more-and-more-women-joining-workforce-demand-up-for-childcare/.

48. "Saudi Arabia Agrees Plans to Move Away from Oil Profits," *BBC,* April 25, 2016, accessed April 1, 2017, http://www.bbc.com/news/world-middle-east-36131391.

49. Deema Almashabi and Donna Abu-Nasr, "Saudi Women Get More of a Voice as Economy Needs Boost," *Bloomberg,* August 12, 2015, accessed April 1, 2017, http://www.bloomberg.com/news/articles/2015-08-11/saudi-women-get-more-of-a-voice-as-economy-needs-boost.

50. Laura Santini, "Why in Vietnam Women Are at Top of Corporate Heap," *The Wall Street Journal,* July 19, 2007, accessed April 1, 2017, http://www.wsj.com/articles/SB118480617336071052.

51. Nguyen Hoang Anh et al., "Entrepreneurship in Vietnam Taking into Account Socio-Cultural Norms and the Institutional Ecosystem," *World Trade Institute,* no. 11/2016 (2016), accessed April 1, 2017, http://dx.doi.org/10.2139/ssrn.2905163.

52. Photo by J. Howard Miller. "'We Can Do It!' Poster for Westinghouse, Closely Associated with Rosie the Riveter, Although Not a Depiction of the Cultural Icon Itself," *Smithsonian Institution,* 1942, accessed April 1, 2017, https://commons.wikimedia.org/w/index.php?curid=5249733. Pubic Domain.

53. Bo Bernhard Nielsen and Sabina Nielsen, "Top Management Team Nationality Diversity and Firm Performance: A Multilevel Study," *Strategic Management Journal* 34, no. 3 (2013): 373-382, accessed April 1, 2017, doi: 10.1002/smj.2021.

54. Ibid.

55. Cedric Herring, "Does Diversity Pay?" *American Sociological Review* 74, no. 2 (2009): 208-224, accessed April 1, 2017, http://www.jstor.org/stable/27736058.

56. "Services for People with Disabilities," *Government of Canada,* 2006, accessed Oct 29, 2016, http://www.faslink.org/Disability_Guide_ENG.pdf.

57. "Disability Statistics," *Australian Network on Disability,* accessed April 1, 2017, http://www.and.org.au/pages/disability-statistics.html.

58. Social Security Administration, *Fact Sheet,* accessed Oct 29, 2016, https://www.ssa.gov/news/press/factsheets/basicfact-alt.pdf.

59. "The Council for Disability Awareness," *Disability Statistics Awareness Council,* accessed April 1, 2017, http://www.jbg-inc.com/downloads/Disability%20Statistics%20Awareness%20Council.pdf.

60. "The Road to Inclusion," *Deloitte,* July 2010, accessed April 3, 1017, http://www.employmentaction.org/employers/links-and-resources/diversity,-inclusion-and-employment-equity/The%20Road%20to%20Inclusion.pdf

61. "Exploring the Bottom Line: A Study of the Costs and Benefits of Workers with Disabilities," *De Paul University* and *Illinois Department of Commerce and Economic Opportunity,* October 2007, accessed April 3, 2017, http://bbi.syr.edu/_assets/staff_bio_publications/McDonald_Exploring_the_Bottom_Line_2007.pdf.

62. Beth Loy, "Workplace Accommodation: Low Costs, High Impacts," *Job Accommodation Network*, 2016, accessed April 1, 2017, https://askjan.org/media/downloads/LowCostHighImpact.pdf.

63. Zack Smith, "'Half of Silicon Valley has something You'd call Asperger's:' Interview with Temple Grandin," *Indy Week*, June 13, 2011, accessed April 1, 2017, http://www.indyweek.com/artery/archives/2011/02/21/half-of-silicon-valley-has-something-youd-call-aspergers-interview-with-temple-grandin.

64. "Diversity and Inclusion," *SAP*, accessed April 1, 2017, https://www.sap.com/corporate/en/company/diversity.html.

65. "Microsoft Announces Pilot Programs to Hire People with Autism," *Microsoft Blog*, April 3, 2015, accessed April 1, 2017, http://blogs.microsoft.com/on-the-issues/2015/04/03/microsoft-announces-pilot-program-to-hire-people-with-autism/#sm.00003fsdce10axdt1sq6uyyiwp77p.

66. Patrick F. McKay et al., "Does Diversity Climate Lead to Customer Satisfaction? It Depends on the Service Climate and Business Unit Demography," *Organization Science* 22, no. 3 (2011): 788-803, accessed April 1, 2017, http://www.jstor.org/stable/20868893.

67. E.J. Schultz, "PepsiCo Exec Has Tough Words for Agencies," *AdvertisingAge*, October 15, 2015, accessed April 3, 2017, http://adage.com/article/special-report-ana-annual-meeting-2015/agencies-fire-ana-convention/300942/

68. Sylvia Ann Hewlett, Melinda Marshall and Laura Sherbin, "How Diversity Can Drive Innovation," *Harvard Business Review*, December 2013.

69. "The Balance Act Creating a Diverse Workforce," *Hays*, 2014, accessed April 1, 2017, https://www.hays.com.au/cs/groups/hays_common/@au/@content/documents/digitalasset/hays_154080.pdf.

70. Michael J Silverstein and Kate Sayre, "The Female Economy," *Harvard Business Review*, September 2009, accessed April 2, 2017, https://hbr.org/2009/09/the-female-economy.

71. Bridget Brennan, *Why She Buys: The New Strategy for Reaching the World's Most Powerful Consumers* (New York: Crown Business, 2011).

72. Ibid.

73. "Women Matter," *McKinsey & Company*, 2007, accessed April 1, 2017, http://www.mckinsey.com/global-themes/women-matter.

74. Jessica Bennett and Jesse Ellison, "Women Will Rule the World," *Newsweek, July 5, 2010*, accessed April 1, 2017, http://www.newsweek.com/women-will-rule-world-74603.

75. "Boom Time for Millionaires," *Standard,* January 14, 2006, accessed April 1, 2017, http://www.standard.co.uk/news/boom-time-for-millionaires-7192864.html.

76. "The State of the American Mom," *Marketing to Moms Coalition,* 2011, accessed April 3, 2017, http://www.marketingtomomscoalition.org/docs/2011-SOAM-Highlights.pdf.

77. Marissa Miley and Ann Mack, "The New Female Consumer: The Rise of Real Moms," *Advertising Age*, November 16, 2009, accessed April 1, 2017, http://adage.com/images/random/1109/aa-newfemale-whitepaper.pdf.

78. Bridget Brennan, *Why She Buy: The New Strategy for Reaching the World's Most Powerful Consumers* (New York: Crown Business, 2011).

79. Jane Cunningham, *Inside Her Pretty Little Head: A New Theory of Female Motivation and What It Means for Marketing* (London: Marshall Cavendish International, 2012).

80. "The Gender Dividend," *Deloitte*, 2011, accessed April 1, 2017, https://www2.deloitte.com/global/en/pages/public-sector/articles/the-gender-dividend.html.

81. "Olive Bowers, 13, Writes Fierce Letter to Tracks Magazine over Its Portrayal of Women," *NewsComAu*, March 30, 2014, accessed April 1, 2017, http://www.news.com.au/lifestyle/fitness/olive-bowers-13-writes-fierce-letter-to-tracks-magazine-over-its-portrayal-of-women/news-story/9852ebdd161f512daa9dc9c824a7193d.

82. "Sustainable Value Creation through Disability," *The Global Economics of Disability Annual Report,* April 3, 2013, accessed April 3, 2017, http://returnondisability.com/wp-content/uploads/2012/09/The%20Global%20Economics%20of%20Disability%20-%202013%20Annual%20Report.pdf

83. Charles A. Riley II, "Handshakes, Not Handouts: Building the Business case for Inclusion," *Opportunities for Community Development Finance in the Disability market,* (2010): 51-56, accessed April 1, 2017, https://www.realeconomicimpact.org/data/files/reports/outside%20reports/draft%201-21-10.pdf

84. Jane B. Quinn, "Able to buy," *Incentive* 169, no. 9 (1995), 80.

85. Beth Haller and Sue Ralph, "Profitability, Diversity, and Disability Images in Advertising in the United States and Great Britain," *Disability Studies Quarterly* 21, no. 2 (2001), accessed April 1, 2017, http://dsq-sds.org/article/view/276/301.

86. Gary N. Siperstein et al., "A National Survey of Consumer Attitudes Towards Companies that Hire People with Disabilities," *Journal of Vocational Rehabilitation* 24, no. 1 (2006): 3-9, accessed April 1, 2017, https://pdfs.semanticscholar.org/of1d/169e890fda093a335ba57a534188f76d573f.pdf.

87. *Toy Like Me*, accessed April 3, 2017, http://www.toylikeme.org/

88. "Estimated LGBT Purchasing Power: LGBT-GDP," *LGBT Capital*, August 2015, accessed April 1, 2017, http://www.lgbt-capital.com/docs/Estimated_LGBT-GDP_%28table%29_-_July_2015.pdf.

89. Blake Ellis, "Gay People Earn More, Owe Less," *CNN*, December 6, 2012, accessed April 1, 2017, http://money.cnn.com/2012/12/06/pf/gay-money/.

90. "Proudly Setting Trends," *Nielsen*, 2015, accessed April 1, 2017, http://www.gayadnetwork.com/files/nielsen2015.pdf.

91. Ian Johnson, "Out Now Global LGBT 2030," *LGBT Diversity Show Me the Business Case*, 2015, accessed April 1, 2017, http://www.outnowconsulting.com/media/24545/Report-SMTBC-2015-V30sm.pdf.

92. "LGBT Adults Strongly Prefer Brands That Support Causes Important to Them and That Also Offer Equal Workplace Benefits," *PR Newswire*, July 18, 2011, accessed April 2, 2017, http://www.prnewswire.com/news-releases/lgbt-adults-strongly-prefer-brands-that-support-causes-important-to-them-and-that-also-offer-equal-workplace-benefits-125742178.html.

93. "Out Now Global LGBT 2030," *LGBT Allies – The Power of Friends*, 2016, accessed April 2, 2017, http://www.outnowconsulting.com/media/25562/Report-Allies-2016-V14.pdf.

94. Paul Morrissette, "Market to LGBT community," *American Agent & Broker* 82, no.7 (2010): 50–52.

95. Chris Daniels, "Transgender Consumers in LGBT Marketing," *PR Week,* February 24, 2016, accessed April 2, 2017, http://www.prweek.com/article/1384780/marketing-t-brands-inclusive-transgender-consumers-lgbt-marketing.

96. Ibid.

97. John Wrench, *Diversity management and discrimination: Immigrants and ethnic minorities in the EU* (Hampshire: Ashgate Publishing Company, 2007).

98. "Australia in The Asian Century," *Australian Government*, 2013, accessed April 2, 2017, http://www.defence.gov.au/whitepaper/2013/docs/australia_in_the_asian_century_white_paper.pdf.

99. "Asia Education Foundation," *Asia Literacy Teacher Education Roundtable*, 2013, accessed April 2, 2017, http://www.asiaeducation.*edu*.au/docs/defaultsource/Researchreports/asia_literacy_teacher_education_roundtable.pdf?sfvrsn=2.

100. "Australia's Jobs Future," *ANZ PWC Asialink Business Service Report*, 2015, accessed April 2, 2017, https://www.pwc.com.au/asia-practice/assets/anz-pwc-asialink-apr15.pdf.

101. Jonathan Stoller, "Workplace Diversity: 'To Win in Your Market, You Need to Hire the Market'," *The Globe and Mail,* October 24, 2013, accessed April 2, 2017, http://www.theglobeandmail.com/reportonbusiness/careers/business-education/workplace-diversity-to-win-in-your-market-you-need-to-hire-the-market/article15039793/.

102. Sarwat Singh, "Women in Cars: Overtaking Men on The Fast Lane," *Forbes,* May 23, 2014, accessed April 2, 2017, http://www.forbes.com/sites/sarwantsingh/2014/05/23/women-in-cars-overtaking-men-on-the-fast-lane/#4a1f3c977b1e.

103. A.J. Baime, "Car Sellers retire Pitch to Women," *The Wall Street Journal,* August 20, 2014, accessed October 29, 2016, http://www.wsj.com/articles/car-sellers-refine-pitch-to-women-1408575175.

104. Irma Isip, "More Women Buy Cars, get More Upset with Service," *Malaya*, September 2, 2016, accessed April 2, 2017, http://www.malaya.com.ph/business-news/business/more-women-buy-cars-get-more-upset-service.

105. A.J. Baime, "Car Sellers retire Pitch to Women," *The Wall Street Journal,* August 20, 2014, accessed October 29, 2016, http://www.wsj.com/articles/car-sellers-refine-pitch-to-women-1408575175.

106. Carmax, "Buying A Car Is a Hassle for Women," *Investor*, September 28, 2009, accessed April 2, 2017, http://investors.carmax.com/news-releases/news-releases-details/2009/Buying-a-Car-is-a-Hassle-for-Women/default.aspx.

107. Ian Ayres and Peter Siegelman, "Race and Gender Discrimination in Bargaining for a New Car," *The American Economic Review* 85, no. 3 (1995): 305-321, accessed April 2, 2017, http://www.jstor.org/stable/2118176.

108. Jeff Schwartz, Josh Bersin and Bill Pelster, "Introduction, Global Human Capital Trends," *Deloitte University Press,* March 7, 2014, accessed April 3, 2017, https://dupress.deloitte.com/dup-us-en/focus/human-capital-trends/2014/hc-trends-2014-introduction.html.

109. Steve Crabtree, "Worldwide, 13% of Employees are Engaged at Work," *Gallup,* October 8, 2013, accessed April 2, 2017, http://www.gallup.com/poll/165269/worldwide-employees-engaged-work.aspx#.

110. "Dice Tech Salary Survey Results – 2014," *Dice,* accessed April 2, 2017, http://insights.dice.com/report/dice-tech-salary-survey-results-2014/.

111. "The Millennial Survey 2016: Big Demands and High Expectations," *Deloitte,* 2016, accessed October 29, 2016, https://www2.deloitte.com/us/en/pages/finance/articles/cfo-insights-employee-engagement.html.

112. Muriel Niederle, Carmit Segal and Lise Vesterlund, "How Costly is Diversity? Affirmative Action in Light of Gender Differences in Competitiveness," *Management Science* 59, no. 1 (2013): 1-16, accessed April 2, 2017, http://www.pitt.edu/~vester/msforthcoming.pdf.

113. Jennifer A. Chatman, "Improving Interactional Organizational Research: A Model of Person– Organization Fit," *Academy of Management Review* 14, no. 3 (1989): 333-349, accessed April 2, 2017, doi: 10.2307/258171.

114. Derek R. Avery, "Reactions to Diversity Recruiting Advertising: Are Differences Black and White?" *Journal of Applied Psychology* 88, no. 4 (2003): 672-679, accessed April 2, 2017, doi: 10.1037/0021-9010.88.4.672.

115. Eddy S. W. Ng and Ronald J. Burke, "Person–Organization Fit and the War for Talent: Does Diversity Management Make a Difference?" *International Journal of Human Resource Management* 16, no. 7 (2005): 1195-1210, accessed April 2, 2017, http://dx.doi.org/10.1080/09585190500144038.

116. Hemang Jauhari and Shailendra Singh, "Perceived Diversity Climate and Employees' Organizational Loyalty," *Equality, Diversity and Inclusion: An International Journal* 32, no. 3 (2013): 262-276, accessed April 2, 2017, doi: 10.1108/EDI-12-2012-0119.

117. "Religion and Corporate Culture," *Society for Human Resource Management,* 2008, accessed April 2, 2017, http://diversityinc.com/medialib/uploads/2011/12/08-0625ReligionSR_Final_LowRez.pdf.

118. René B. Adams and Daniel Ferreira, "Women in the Boardroom and Their Impact on Governance and Performance," *Journal of Financial Economics* 94, no. 2 (2009): 291-309, accessed April 2, 2017, http://personal.lse.ac.uk/ferreird/gender.pdf.

119. Sophia Gene and Chris Newlands, "Boards without Women Breed Scandal," *Financial Times,* March 8, 2015, accessed April 2, 2017, https://www.ft.com/content/cdb790f8-c33d-11e4-ac3d-00144feab7de.

120. Hazar Ben Barka and Ali Dardour, "Investigating the Relationship between Director's Profile, Board Interlocks and Corporate Social Responsibility," *Management Decision* 53, no. 3 (2015): 553-570, accessed April 2, 2017, doi: 10.1108/MD-12-2013-0655.

121. Farah Margaretha and Ratna Isnaini, "Board Diversity and Gender Composition on Corporate Social Responsibility and Firm Reputation in Indonesia," *Journal of Management and Entrepreneurship* 16, no. 1 (2014): 1-8, accessed April 2, 2017, doi: 10.9744/jmk.16.1.1-8.

122. Trang Cam Hoang, Indra Abeysekera and Shiguang Ma, "Board Diversity and Corporate Social Disclosure: Evidence from Vietnam," *Journal of Business Ethics* (2016): 1-20, accessed April 2, 2017, doi: 10.1007/s10551-016-3260-1.

123. Taïeb Hafsi and Gokhan Turgut, "Boardroom Diversity and its Effect on Social Performance: Conceptualization and Empirical Evidence," *Journal of Business Ethics* 112, no. 3 (2013): 463-479, accessed April 2, 2017, doi: 10.1007/s10551-012-1272-z.

124. Ming Jia and Zhe Zhang, "Critical Mass of Women on BODs, Multiple Identities, and Corporate Philanthropic Disaster Response: Evidence from Privately Owned Chinese Firms," *Journal of Business Ethics* 118, no. 2 (2012): 303-317, accessed April 2, 2017, doi: 10.1007/s10551-012-1589-7.

125. Stacy Jones and Jaclyn Trop, "See How the Big Tech Companies Compare on Employee Diversity," *Fortune,* July 30, 2015, accessed April 2, 2017, http://fortune.com/2015/07/30/tech-companies-diveristy/.

126. Peter Wright et al., "Competitiveness through Management of Diversity: Effects on Stock Price Valuation," *Academy of Management Journal 30*, no. 1 (1995): 272-287, accessed April 2, 2017, doi: 10.2307/256736.

127. Alison Cook and Christy Glass, "Do Diversity Reputation Signals Increase Share Value?" *Human Resource Development Quarterly* 25, no. 4 (2014): 471-491, accessed April 2, 2017, doi: 10.1002/hrdq.21183.

128. Marisa Kendall, "Department of Labor Accuses Palantir of Discriminating against Asian Job Applicants," *Mercury News,* September 16, 2016, accessed April 2, 2017, http://www.mercurynews.com/2016/09/26/regulators-accuse-palantir-of-discriminating-against-asian-applicants/.

129. Crystal Chen, "I went Back to China and Felt More American than Ever," *Foreign Policy,* October 21, 2016, accessed April 2, 2017, http://foreignpolicy.com/2016/10/21/i-went-back-to-china-and-felt-more-american-than-ever-hong-kong-race-relations/.

130. Dong, N. T., & Kleiner, B. H, "Asian Discrimination In the Workplace," *Equal opportunities International* 18, (1999): 11–15.

131. Jennifer T. Kubota, Mahzarin R. Banaji and Elizabeth A. Phelps, "The Neuroscience of Race," *Nature Neuroscience* 15, no. 7 (2012): 940-948, accessed April 2, 2017, doi: 10.1038/nn.3136.

132. Lauren A. Rivera, "Hiring as Cultural Matching: The Case of Elite Professional Service Firms," *American Sociological Review* 77, no. 6 (2012): 999-1022, accessed April 2, 2017, doi: 10.1177/0003122412463213.

133. Jack D. Wood and Gianpiero Petriglieri, "Transcending Polarization: Beyond Binary Thinking," *Transactional Analysis Journal* 35, no. 1 (2005): 31-39, accessed April 2, 2017, http://www.imd.org/programs/oep/generalmanagement/bot/upload/Transcending_polarization_article_by_Wood-Petriglieri.pdf.

134. Robert B. Lount Jr. et al., "How Much Relationship Conflict Really Exists? Biased Perceptions of Racially Diverse Teams," *SSRN Electronic Journal* (2011), accessed April 2, 2017, doi: 10.2139/ssrn.2120006.

135. Inga J. Hoever et al., "Fostering Team Creativity: Perspective Taking as Key to Unlocking Diversity's Potential," *Journal of Applied Psychology* 97, no. 5 (2012): 982-996, accessed April 2, 2017, doi: 10.1037/a0029159.

136. Victoria C. Plaut, Keeia M. Thomas and Matt J. Goren, "Is Multiculturalism or Color Blindness Better for Minorities?" *Psychological Science* 20, no. 4 (2009): 444-446, accessed April 2, 2017, doi: 10.1111/j.1467-9280.2009.02318.x.

137. Jacquie D. Vorauer, Annette Gagnon and Stacey J. Sasaki, "Salient Intergroup Ideology and Intergroup Interaction," *Psychological Science* 20, no. 7 (2009): 838-845, accessed April 2, 2017, doi: 10.1111/j.1467-9280.2009.02369.x.

138. Tessa L. Dover, Brenda Major and Cheryl Kaiser, "Members of High-Status Groups are Threatened by Pro-diversity Organizational Messages," *Journal of Experimental Social Psychology* 62 (2016): 58-67, accessed April 2, 2017, doi: 10.1016/j.jesp.2015.10.006.

139. Cartoon by Center for Story-Based Strategy. "Equality. Equity. Liberation," *Twitter*, 2016, https://www.storybasedstrategy.org/ accessed Oct 29, 2016, https://twitter.com/kristopherwells/status/721158763881730048.

140. Matthew J. Pearsall, Aleksander P. J. Ellis and Joel M. Evans, "Unlocking the Effects of Gender Faultlines on Team Creativity: Is Activation the Key?" *Journal of Applied Psychology* 93, no. 1 (2008): 225-234, accessed April 2, 2017, doi: 10.1037/0021-9010.93.1.225.

141. John E. Sawyer, Melissa A. Houlette and Erin L. Yeagley, "Decision Performance and Diversity Structure: Comparing Faultlines in Convergent, Crosscut, and Racially Homogeneous Groups," *Organizational Behavior and Human Decision Processes* 99, no. 1 (2006): 1-15, accessed April 2, 2017, doi: 10.1016/j.obhdp.2005.08.006.

142. Evren Esen, *Workplace Diversity Practices Survey Report* (Alexandria: Society for Human Resource Management, 2005).

143. Frank Dobbin, Alexandra Kalev and Erin Kelly, "Diversity Management in Corporate America," *Contexts* 6, no. 4 (2007): 21-27, accessed April 2, 2017, doi: 10.1525/ctx.2007.6.4.21.

144. Alexandra Kalev and Frank Dobbin, "Try and Make Me: Why Corporate Training Fails," *Harvard Business Review*, July-August 2016, accessed April 2, 2017, https://hbr.org/2016/07/why-diversity-programs-fail.

145. Lisa Legault, Jennifer N. Gutsell and Michael Inzlicht, "Ironic Effects of Anti-prejudice Messages: How Motivational Interventions Can Reduce (but Also Increase) Prejudice," *Psychological Science* 22, no. 12 (2011): 1472-1477, accessed April 2, 2017, doi: 10.1177/0956797611427918.

146. Fay Hansen, "Diversity's Business Case: Doesn't Add Up," *Workforce*, April 2, 2003, accessed April 2, 2017, http://www.workforce.com/2003/04/02/diversitys-business-case-doesnt-add-up/.

147. "How to be Better: On Intersectionality, Privilege and Silencing," *Stavvers*, October 22, 2012, accessed April 2, 2017, https://stavvers.wordpress.

com/2012/10/22/how-to-be-better-on-intersectionality-privilege-and-silenc-ing/.

148.   Valerie Purdie-Vaughns and Richard P. Eibach, "Intersectional Invisibility: The Distinctive Advantages and Disadvantages of Multiple Subordinate-Group Identities," *Sex Roles* 59, no. 5 (2008): 377-391, accessed April 2, 2017, doi: 10.1007/s11199-008-9424-4.

149.   Sasha von Oldershausen, "Iran's Sex-Change Operations Provided Nearly Free-Of-Cost," *Huffington Post,* January 23, 2014, accessed April 2, 2017, http://www.huffingtonpost.com/2012/06/04/iran-sex-change-operation_n_1568604.html.

150.   Peter Bregman, "Diversity Training Doesn't Work," *Harvard Business Review,* March 12, 2012, accessed April 2, 2017, https://hbr.org/2012/03/diversity-training-doesnt-work.

151.   Raymond A. Friedman and Brooks Holtom, "The Effects of Network Groups on Minority Employee Turnover Intentions," *Human Resource Management* 41, no. 4 (2002): 405-421, accessed April 2, 2017, doi: 10.1002/hrm.10051.

152.   Maureen A. Scully, "A Rainbow Coalition or Separate Wavelengths? Negotia-tions among Employee Network Groups", *Negotiation and Conflict Manage-ment Research* 2, no. 1 (2009): 74-91, accessed April 2, 2017, doi: 10.1111/j.1750-4716.2008.00029.x.

153.   Priscilla H. Douglas, "Affinity Groups: Catalyst for Inclusive Organizations," *Employment Relations Today* 34, no. 4 (2008): 11-18, accessed April 2, 2017, doi: 10.1002/ert.20171.

154.   Carole Joseph, "Leveraging a Women's Network to Attract, Develop and Retain High Potential Female Talent," *Strategic HR Review* 12, no. 3 (2013): 132-137, accessed April 2, 2017, doi: 10.1108/14754391311324480.

155.   Employees Resource Groups That Drive Business, *Cisco,* 2010, accessed April 2, 2017, http://www.cisco.com/c/dam/en_us/about/ac49/ac55/docs/ERGre-portEXTERNAL.pdf.

156.   Elizabeth Anne Roling, "Women's Network Participation and Workplace Coping Resources," (PhD diss., University of Georgia, 2010), accessed April 2, 2017, https://getd.libs.uga.edu/pdfs/roling_elizabeth_a_201012_phd.pdf.

157.   Photo by Dell's Official Flickr Page. "DWEN Conference 2012 – New Delhi Dell Women's Entrepreneur Network," *Flickr,* May 19, 2013, accessed April 2, 2017, https://commons.wikimedia.org/wiki/File:Deli_womens_entre_net-work.jpg License Link: https://creativecommons.org/licenses/by/2.0/legal-code.

158.   Dean B. Peskin, "Building Groundwork for Affirmative Action EEO Pro-gram," *Personnel Journal* (pre-1986) *ABI/INFORM Global 48*, no. 2 (1969): 130-149.

159.   Uri Shwed and Alexandra Kalev, "Are Referrals More Productive or More Likeable? Social Networks and the Evaluation of Merit," *American Behavio-ral Scientist* 58, no. 2 (2014): 288-308.

160.   Lauren A. Rivera, *Pedigree: How Elite Students Get Elite Jobs* (Princeton: Princeton University Press, 2016).

161. Vincent J. Roscigno, *The Face of Discrimination: How Race and Gender Impact Work and Home Lives* (New York: Rowman and Littlefield, 2007).

162. Frank Dobbin, Daniel Schrage and Alexandra Kalev, "Rage against the Iron Cage: The Varied Effects of Bureaucratic Personnel Reforms on Diversity," *American Sociological Review* 80, no. 5 (2015): 1014-1044, accessed April 2, 2017, doi: 10.1177/0003122415596416.

163. "Charge Statistics," EEOC, accessed April 2, 2017, https://www.eeoc.gov/eeoc/statistics/enforcement/charges.cfm.

164. Frank Dobbin, Alexandra Kalev and Erin Kelly, "Diversity Management in Corporate America," *Contexts* 6, no. 4 (2007): 21-27, accessed April 2, 2017, http://scholar.harvard.edu/dobbin/files/2007_contexts_dobbin_kalev_kelly.pdf.

165. Damon A. Williams and Katrina C. Wade-Golden, "What is a Chief Diversity Officer?" accessed April 2, 2017, https://www.uc.edu/content/dam/uc/diversity/docs/What_is_a_Chief_Diversity_Officer.pdf.

166. Eric Rosenbaum, "The 10 Global Companies Trying to Lead on Diversity: Study," *CNBC,* April 24, 2015, accessed April 2, 2017, http://www.cnbc.com/2015/04/24/the-10-global-companies-trying-to-lead-on-diversity:-study.html.

167. "Diversity and Inclusion," *American Institute of CPAs,* accessed April 3, 2017, http://www.aicpa.org/Career/DiversityInitiatives/Pages/default.aspx

168. Lisa Jennings, "Sodexo Mentor Program Focuses on Diversity," *Nation's Restaurant News* 43, no. 43 (2009): 18.

169. Cecilia Kang, "Google Data-mines Its Approach to Promoting Women," *Washington Post,* April 2, 2014, accessed April 2, 2017, https://www.washingtonpost.com/news/the-switch/wp/2014/04/02/google-data-mines-its-women-problem/.

Index of Names

Index of Subjects

Index of Geography, Culture and Religion